THE BATTLE
OF LEYTE GULF
AT 75

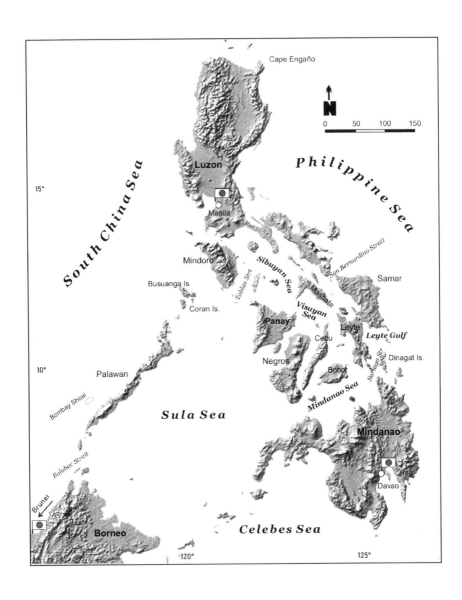

THE BATTLE OF LEYTE GULF

AT 75

A RETROSPECTIVE

Thomas J. Cutler

Naval Institute Press
Annapolis, Maryland

Naval Institute Press
291 Wood Road
Annapolis, MD 21402

© 2019 by Thomas J. Cutler
All rights reserved. No part of this book may be reproduced or utilized in any form or by any means, electronic or mechanical, including photocopying and recording, or by any information storage and retrieval system, without permission in writing from the publisher.

Library of Congress Cataloging-in-Publication Data

Names: Cutler, Thomas J., date, author.
Title: The Battle of Leyte Gulf at 75 : A Retrospective / edited by Thomas J. Cutler.
Other titles: Battle of Leyte Gulf at seventy five, a retrospective
Description: Annapolis, Maryland : Naval Institute Press, [2019] | Includes bibliographical references and index.
Identifiers: LCCN 2019020107 | ISBN 9781682474617 (hardcover : alk. paper)
Subjects: LCSH: Leyte Gulf, Battle of, Philippines, 1944. | Leyte Gulf, Battle of, Philippines, 1944—Anniversaries, etc.
Classification: LCC D774.P5 C873 2019 | DDC 940.54/2599—dc23 LC record available at https://lccn.loc.gov/2019020107

♾ Print editions meet the requirements of ANSI/NISO z39.48–1992 (Permanence of Paper).
Printed in the United States of America.

27 26 25 24 23 22 21 20   9 8 7 6 5 4 3 2

Frontispiece provided by Vincent O'Hara. All photos are official U.S. Navy.

Contents

List of Maps   vii

Introduction
Thomas J. Cutler   1

PART I. ORIGINAL ESSAYS   15

1. Leyte Gulf Reminiscences
   A. Denis Clift   17
2. Planning the Penultimate Stages of the Pacific War
   Lisle Rose   30
3. Allied Plans and Operational Art
   Milan Vego   47
4. The Principle of the Objective at Leyte Gulf
   Norman Friedman   69
5. Halsey's Decision
   Trent Hone   81
6. "Where Is Task Force 34?": The Frustration of Admiral Lee
   Paul Stillwell   101
7. Sibuyan Sea: The Price of Daring
   Karl Zingheim   117
8. Syracuse in the Pacific?
   Kevin J. Delamer   136
9. After the Battle: Sea Power and the Ormoc Campaign
   Vincent P. O'Hara   156
10. Jack & Jim
    David F. Winkler   172
11. The Tin Can Sailors Are Gone: What Naval History Loses with the Passing of the World War II Generation
    James D. Hornfischer   185

PART II. THE ARCHIVES 197

12. Flawed Victory at Sea
    Alan Rems — 201

13. Greatest of All Sea Battles
    Lt. Cdr. Thomas J. Cutler, U.S. Navy (Ret.) — 210

14. The Battle for Leyte Gulf
    Fleet Admiral William F. Halsey Jr., U.S. Navy — 225

15. Admiral Oldendorf Comments on the Battle of Surigao Strait
    Vice Adm. Jesse B. Oldendorf, USN (Ret.) — 237

16. Leyte Gulf: The First Uncensored Japanese Account
    James A. Field Jr. — 243

17. With Kurita in the Battle of Leyte Gulf
    Rear Admiral Tomiji Koyanagi, former Imperial Japanese Navy — 259

18. MacArthur, FDR, and the Politics of Leyte Gulf
    Lt. Cdr. Thomas J. Cutler, U.S. Navy (Ret.) — 278

19. Jeeps versus Giants
    Capt. Walter Karig, USNR, Lt. Cdr. Russell L. Harris, USNR, and Lt. Cdr. Frank A. Manson, U.S. Navy — 289

20. Seven Decades of Debate
    Alan Rems — 304

21. "Where is Task Force Thirty-Four?"
    Capt. Andrew Hamilton, USNR — 313

22. Second Salvo at Surigao Strait
    Adm. James L. Holloway III, U.S. Navy (Ret.) — 319

23. *Iowa* vs. *Yamato*: The Ultimate Gunnery Duel [Professional Notes]
    Thomas Hone and Norman Friedman — 329

24. "*Iowa* vs. *Yamato*: The Ultimate Gunnery Duel" [Comment and Discussion]
    Vice Adm. Lloyd M. Mustin, U.S. Navy (Ret.) — 334

Epitaph 337

Maps

Regional Map	Frontispiece
Halsey's Dispositions	86
Halsey's Concentration	88
Situation 22–24 October 1944	129
Kurita's Passage through the Sibuyan Sea	130
Leyte	157
Battle of Ormoc Bay	165

INTRODUCTION
Thomas J. Cutler

TWENTY-FIVE YEARS AFTER THE PUBLICATION of my book on the Battle of Leyte Gulf, and seventy-five years after the battle itself, I have decided that it is time for another look at the battle that captured my attention at a very young age and continues to be a point of great interest to me—and, I think it is fair to say, to many others—after all these years.

I read—with intense fascination—about Leyte Gulf as a young boy, first in Hanson Baldwin's *Sea Fights and Shipwrecks* and later in C. Vann Woodward's *The Battle for Leyte Gulf*. In college, I convinced (no small task) my English literature professor to allow me to focus on the battle for my major term paper; the result bore little resemblance to literature, but it served to stoke the embers of a long-burning fire. I continued to read about the battle over the intervening years as I expanded my understanding of the Pacific War—probably my choice of "favorite subject" if I were forced to choose. Then one day in 1991, as much attention was being paid to the fiftieth anniversary of the attack on Pearl Harbor, I said to my son, "You know, if someone were smart, he would be thinking ahead right now and start writing about the end of the war; Hiroshima or something." Then the light came on! How about if that someone were me, and I chose to write about Leyte!

My agent at the time, Jim Charlton, was able to land us a generous contract from HarperCollins, and I went to "work" (actually pure pleasure) writing the book that subsequently debuted in time for the fiftieth anniversary. Once New York was finished with putting the book through the normal paces (Book of the Month Club main selection, Military Book

Club, mass-market paperback with Pocket Books, etc.), it was time for the book to be put out to pasture. I am forever grateful that the Naval Institute Press saved it from oblivion by producing a trade paperback that remains in print today.

I normally am pretty good at genuine humility (I honestly, almost skeptically, marvel at the successes I have been fortunate enough to enjoy), but I will stray a bit from my normal practice and say that I am proud of that book. I have received enough feedback over the years to convince me that my biased view of the book is probably not far off. When I reread passages, I am not chagrined but am often amazed that I was able to write those words. Of course, telling one of the best stories in naval history gives anyone a leg up, but I am most gratified when I feel no embarrassment at what I have written and would change little were I to do it over again. That is not to say that my book should be considered the best or the final word on the subject. Far from it! There have been at least twenty-five focused works on the subject, all with their own merits, and collectively still not exhausting the possibilities for telling and retelling. The subject is so vast and so rich that no one author could ever encompass it all, and each attempt is only able to contribute without ever finalizing.

Although there are many enlightening, challenging, and inspiring aspects of this momentous historical convergence, to me five basic elements of the battle stand out: the size of the battle; the possibility that it was the last great fleet engagement; the controversy surrounding Adm. William Halsey's taking his fleet north in pursuit of Ozawa's decoy force; Japanese Admiral Takeo Kurita's retreat at a crucial moment; and, most of all, the incredible courage exhibited by surface sailors and aviators at the Battle off Samar.

Size

In critiquing my Naval War College students' papers, I often warn against superlatives because they often leave the writer open to easy criticism. Yet, in the preface to my book, I describe the Battle of Leyte Gulf as "the biggest and most multifaceted naval battle in all of history." I am not alone in that kind of description. *Time* magazine called it "the greatest battle in the history of naval warfare," and Ron Spector, in his classic history of the Pacific War, *Eagle Against the Sun*, claims it was "the largest naval battle in history." The subtitle of C. Vann Woodward's book describes it as "World

War II's largest naval battle," a description mirrored by David Sears' subtitle ("Biggest Sea Battle of World War II") and Edwin Hoyt's ("Bloodiest Sea Battle of World War II"). And so it goes; many others likewise do not shrink from superlatives when describing this unique engagement.

This repeated assessment is supported by the statistics. The number of American, Japanese, and Australian ships that participated was 282 (contrasted with the famous Battle of Jutland, another enormous engagement that saw 250 British and German ships engaged). Nearly 200,000 men participated in a geographic expanse of more than 100,000 square miles. Dozens of ships were sunk, and thousands of men perished. In addition to the numbers, the battle involved air, surface, submarine, and amphibious operations, and the weapons used included bombs of every type, guns of every caliber, torpedoes, mines, and rockets, as well as introduced the forerunner of the guided missile in the form of the kamikaze (which would later sink more ships and kill more American sailors than any other weapon used in the war). Such numbers leave little room for doubting the superlative nature of this gargantuan naval battle.

Last Major Fleet Engagement

Only time can definitively decide this assertion, but it is one that is often made. H. P. Willmott's book is subtitled *The Last Fleet Action*, Evan Thomas' subtitle includes the words "the Last Great Naval Campaign," David Sears' book is titled *The Last Epic Naval Battle*, and Howard Sauer's book on the Battle of Surigao Strait is titled *The Last Big-Gun Naval Battle*.

Technological and geopolitical trends seem to support this contention, yet some more recent prognosticators are raising the specter of a clash of fleets in the South China Sea as China continues to build an ever-growing fleet and stubbornly persists in its claims to waters and islands that contrast with those of other nations—including the United States. We can safely assume that any future engagements will not include battleships—attempts to resurrect those behemoths and restore them to a relevance they only barely ever had seem to have subsided—but few other assertions about the future can be so firmly established. We will not likely see a major fleet engagement of the type that occurred in October 1944, but by adjusting certain variables (such as types of vessels and technological capabilities), it is possible that the U.S. Seventh Fleet might go toe-to-toe with major elements of the Chinese navy in the future. Or somewhere else with some other foe ... never say never. (And the perpetual advocate for sea power in me compels me to add that we *must* make sure our fleet is ready for that possibility.)

"Bull's Run"

In November 1947, *Life* magazine ran a detailed article with that title followed by the subtitle "Was Halsey Right at Leyte Gulf?" That article pitted Fleet Adm. William F. Halsey and Adm. Thomas C. Kinkaid against one another in a controversy the likes of which had not been seen since the Sampson-Schley dispute following the Battle of Santiago during the Spanish-American War. The article questioned Halsey's decision to take his entire force northward, away from the landing area, to pursue Admiral Jisaburo Ozawa's carrier force. The article is not a polemic against Halsey; it gives him credit for his contributions elsewhere in the war ("no one can deny the brilliance of Halsey's leadership") and recognizes mitigating factors—summed up well by the statement, "Every commander in the battle was immersed in the fog of war." But the article ultimately concludes that "in the matter of Bull's run, [Halsey's] judgement seems so questionable that even one of his most loyal former subordinates, after vigorously defending him, admitted 'Still, it's a damn shame it turned out the way it did, with all those battleships getting away.'"

Most assessments over the years have agreed with the *Life* article, judging that Halsey being lured aware by the decoy force was forgivable—even understandable—but that his taking the entire Third Fleet with him, rather than leaving behind one of his four carrier task groups or at least the battleship-centric Task Force 34 to guard the landing area, was a mistake—a costly one that could have been a great deal more so. The controversy that has lingered all these years generally does not completely exonerate nor condemn Halsey, but instead primarily centers on a sharing of the blame, with emphasis on the command structure that made the errors possible, the nature of the guidance that was provided in the form of orders and commander's intent, and the assumptions made by various commanders. Arguments emerge that fault Adm. Chester W. Nimitz for giving Halsey too much leeway, criticize Kinkaid for relying on the chimera of Task Force 34, make various subordinates culpable for not questioning Halsey's decisions more, and so on. Even FDR is sometimes cited for, early in the war, supporting—for political reasons rather than strategic ones—the dual command structure that initially functioned well but led to the problems experienced at Leyte Gulf once Nimitz's and MacArthur's commands merged their forces and objectives in the Philippines.

The nature of the debate determines its usefulness. When the focus is on personalities (Halsey's aggressive nature as a prime example), the discussion is not without relevance, but loses much of its potency because such things can be factored but not changed. When the focus is on such things as the functionality of command structures, the effectiveness of directives, and the appropriate employment of forces, the debate enters the realm of "case study" and potentially yields relevant food for thought and, hopefully, lessons learned.

When I first embarked on writing about the battle, I had a moment of self-doubt in which I wondered, "Who in the hell am I—a retired O4—to pass judgment on fleet admirals and men whose medals represent so much more than my own?" Yet, after some reflection, I realized that I owed it to my readers to not only relay facts but to also take advantage of the immersion my research had afforded me and provide some insight and a degree of assessment to my account of this momentous historical event. So, I put my lieutenant-commander oak leaves in my desk drawer and picked up the proverbial quill that had armed the likes of Thucydides and Samuel Eliot Morison, and I made my best effort to live up to the exceptional privilege that authorship offers. I passed my own judgements, confident that I did my best to be fair but ever mindful—actually grateful—that those conclusions will never serve as the last judgement and will only contribute to the ongoing debate.

Having said that, I will offer one last caveat by quoting myself from the preface to my book, a passage I stand by today just as I did when I wrote it:

> The criticisms of others found within this work are offered humbly. My purpose in questioning the access and decisions taken a half-century ago is not to defame the men who originated them but rather to let their actions and the criticisms contained herein serve as lessons for future naval officers. Never would I claim to have been able to do better than the men I write about. I have known the awesome responsibility of handling a single ship in moments of challenge; my mind boggles at the thought of handling whole *fleets*. I have experienced the confusion that can reign on the bridge of a

ship in the dark of night when all is not going according to plan; I can only begin to imagine how that would be magnified if my ship were sinking beneath me. And I have known the mind-numbing terror of combat—though never to the degree experienced by most of the men I now write about; I sincerely believe that only those who have never been shot at would disparage the actions of men under fire. I make my judgments from the comfort of a desk chair. I am surrounded by books and documents with a hundred times the information available to those on-site commanders, and I may peruse them at my leisure, pressured only by a publisher's deadline. I write on a machine that dutifully erases my errors, and I sip coffee as I write. Most of all, no one must live or die by what I do here.

So it is with the ultimate humility that I hope that my criticisms and judgments will serve as food for thought, as stimulus for further debate, but never as a substitute for what brave men did under the pressures of command and combat.

Kurita's Retreat

Admiral Takeo Kurita's decision to turn away and head back to San Bernardino Strait, when he clearly had elements of the Seventh Fleet "on the ropes," is one of the great mysteries of World War II. Because of Halsey's aforementioned run to the north, and a combination of other factors, Kurita was able to achieve complete surprise as he found the three "Taffies" (Task Units 77.4.1, 77.4.2, and 77.4.3—which discerning readers will note I mislabeled as "Task *Groups*" in my book) unaware of his approach and very vulnerable to attack.

Kurita survived the war, but never gave a satisfactory explanation for his decision. The few times he did "open up" were marred by vagueness and contradiction, requiring historians to speculate (a nice word for "guess") what caused him to make this nearly inexplicable decision. Over the years, some authors have cited fatigue, pointing out that leading up to this crucial moment, Kurita had taken a wee-hours swim after his flagship was torpedoed in the Palawan Passage, had endured a horrific bombardment by Halsey's air wings prior to the latter's departure, and had navigated through a narrow strait in the dark of night, to mention a few of the tribulations he had faced prior to his encountering the Taffies off Samar.

Another explanation sometimes offered centers on the uncertainty Kurita likely faced as to whose ships he had in his crosshairs as he approached the American ships off Leyte. This contention is supported by the fact that he was unaware that Halsey had taken the bait and ordered his fleet northward and by the realization that the Americans and Japanese had rarely encountered one another at such close range in broad daylight. The latter seems to have contributed to the inflated reports of Kurita's lookouts, calling destroyers cruisers and even battleships and seeing the CVEs as CVs. One intriguing speculation that cannot be verified but is certainly plausible is that the aggressive courage exhibited by the Americans may have caused Kurita to wonder, "What do they know that I do not?"

Whatever the reason(s), Kurita did turn away at a critical moment, thereby sparing his enemy more damage than what he had already inflicted. Undoubtedly, his decision significantly reduced—but did not completely erase—the amount of after-action criticism that would otherwise have followed. It also left open the door to many "what ifs" that can never be fully resolved. What if he had continued to pursue the Taffies and inflicted even more damage? What if he had turned his attention to the vulnerable landing area with all of its mission-essential logistical components? What if his staying would have allowed enough time for Halsey's forces to return and join the fray? Could he have done enough damage to cause the battle to be labeled a defeat rather than a victory? Could such an evaluation have influenced the national elections back home that were occurring on the heels of the battle? These and many other questions remain open and serve as stimulus to ongoing debate.

Given the circumstances at the time—the relative strengths and weaknesses of the two navies involved, the strategy of the Japanese navy at that point in the war, the nature and objectives of Kurita's mission as part of Operation Sho-Go—there seems little room for justification of Kurita's decision. Indeed, the *Life* article cited earlier referred to "Kurita's enormous mistake," and even Kurita's insufficient explanations do not offer much that can be interpreted as justification, certainly not exoneration. One effect of Kurita's decision that does not offer much in cold strategic calculus, but is of significant value to sailors on both sides (and their loved ones), is that by turning away, Kurita granted a virtual "pardon" to those many Japanese and Americans who were condemned to death had he pressed on.

"The Last Stand of the Tin Can Sailors"

Jim Hornfischer's book of that title is a classic in its own right and is regarded by many (including me) as the best account of what his subtitle describes as "The Extraordinary World War II Story of the U.S. Navy's Finest Hour." It is difficult to argue with that description. What those men did in that moment of extreme challenge, when their very existence was on the line, has been equaled—but never exceeded—in the long history of the U.S. Navy.

That long history has had many inspirational moments, including the battle off Flamborough Head where John Paul Jones and his crew captured HMS *Serapis*, the incredible heroism exhibited by Stephen Decatur's men when they burned the *Philadelphia* in Tripoli Harbor, William B. Cushing's sinking of the Confederate ironclad *Albemarle*, and the jaw-dropping courage of James Elliot Williams as he repeatedly took his fiberglass boats into a hornet's nest of enemy soldiers deep in the Mekong Delta. Each of these instances and many others are iconic moments that stand out from the mundane but essential work carried out by sailors every hour of every day. Recognizing this invites one to reflect upon the spectrum of courage required for a Navy—especially a superpower Navy—to complete the missions that are so essential to the nation's survival and well-being. It takes a measure of courage to simply join the armed forces and take an oath to defend the nation. It takes a measure more to go in harm's way when danger is present but not necessarily seen. The ultimate toll is levied when confronted with possible or even certain death. The men who fought off Samar summoned the requisite courage to meet all of those challenges, and they did so in a way that not only brought credit to themselves as individuals and as members of their service, but actually turned the tide of battle in the face of incredibly daunting odds.

Think for a moment what it must have been like to join the Navy during a world war, when ships were sinking in the heat of battle in far-off places most Americans had never heard of, when thousands of their predecessors had perished at Pearl Harbor and in the bloody slugfests in the Solomons. Imagine standing on the pier as part of the crew of USS *Johnston* during her commissioning ceremony in the Tacoma-Seattle Shipyard on 27 October 1943, when her newly appointed captain, Cdr. Ernest E. Evans, tells you, "This is going to be a fighting ship. I intend to go in harm's way, and anyone who doesn't want to go along had better get off right now." And then in a moment that was both ominous and prescient, he said with deep conviction, "I will never retreat from an enemy force."

This brings up a revealing point when considering the realm of courage and all its dimensions. *Not to take anything away from the courageous Marines who sacrificed so much*, a little-appreciated fact is that in the Pacific War nearly twice as many sailors were killed in action than Marines (34,607 sailors compared to 17,373 Marines). But the tally of wounded and invalided shows the reverse, with the Marine total double that of sailors (11,745 to 5,619). This dichotomy in KIA vs. WIA figures is at least partially explained by the fact that when ships are sunk, they often take significant numbers of their crew with them. Wounded Marines are often retrieved from the battlefield and treatment of their injuries prevents many of them from dying.

Related to this observation is that a soldier or Marine in ground combat initially has more choices than the hapless sailor: to move forward or retreat, to raise his or her head during a firefight or stay hunkered down, and so on. In contrast, if the captain of a ship decides to take his or her ship into battle, the sailors on board have no choice but to go along. This includes the mess cook in the scullery along with the gunner's mate in Mount 51. Once in the thick of the action, however, individuals in both situations often have hard choices to make. The Marine may have to risk being cut down in order to advance on and silence an enemy machine-gun emplacement; a sailor may have to enter a compartment that is filling with water or subject to raging flames and thick smoke to retrieve an injured shipmate. In either case, and in so many more like them, these human beings may have to choose the unthinkable rather than the logical, to find in themselves a reserve of courage they never knew they had, to face consequences that most of us cannot even imagine.

During the Battle off Samar, PO Paul Henry Carr continued loading projectiles into the breech of his still-functioning gun after a powder charge cooked off in his 5-inch gun mount and ripped him open from the neck down, exposing his internal organs. S2C Jackson McCaskill, one of only two survivors in the forward fireroom of his destroyer escort after a direct hit by an 8-inch shell, managed to shut down the boilers while all of the flesh was seared from the bottoms of his feet. And, with the help of sailors manually moving the massive rudder from after-steering, Captain Evans continued to conn his ship from the fantail of his mangled destroyer despite multiple wounds and the continuing barrage of enemy fire.

Such instances prompt one to recall the words of Admiral Tarrant in the James Michener novel *The Bridges at Toko-Ri*: "Where do we find such men?" I learned the answer as I was privileged to interview the survivors of the Battle off Samar. As I am sure Jim Hornfischer, Evan Thomas, and the others who likewise interviewed these veterans will agree, the answer is that we find such individuals from among the citizens of this democracy we have inherited through the sacrifices of so many before us. The men who so valiantly fought in the face of terrible odds at Samar were so "ordinary" in many ways—coming from all walks of life, most of them from humble origins—and yet they were so *extraordinary* when faced with incredible adversity.

To say that I was humbled in the presence of these men is a vast understatement. To say that our nation owes them—living and dead—more than we can ever hope to pay goes without saying. We must trust—and I do—that other sailors will perform similarly when faced with their own challenges. We have seen that legacy of courage played out in Korea, Vietnam, and the Middle East, and we shall see it again as the world continues to be a dangerous place and the Navy continues to sail at the proverbial tip of the sword. We can count on it, but we must never take it for granted.

What's Left?

After seventy-five years, a natural question to ask is: What can possibly be said about the Battle of Leyte Gulf that has not been said before? The answer to that question resides within these pages in several forms.

The idea of a seventy-fifth anniversary retrospective was one that made sense to me, and many of my colleagues agreed. While I have learned much since the writing of my 1994 book, I did not feel qualified to do the "retrospecting" alone. In the intervening years, other historians, both popular and academic, many with far greater bona fides and wider readerships than mine, had weighed in on the battle. Trying to synthesize their contributions was a task beyond my capabilities and available time.

Original Essays

With so much already on paper, it seemed to me that a sound approach would be to invite accomplished historians whom I was privileged to know to write about the battle, giving them carte blanche to focus on whatever aspect they felt was important or perhaps still unrecorded.

I was gratified that most of them readily agreed to participate, and I am pleased with the result, as I am confident others will be as well. I am honored that these colleagues and friends have taken time from the many other worthwhile and important things they do to contribute original essays specifically for this volume. We are all the richer for it.

Among the results is a very valuable essay by my fellow United States Naval Institute (USNI) staff member and good friend Denis Clift, who has tapped into his *vast* knowledge of the Institute's oral history program to highlight some of the many edifying and ultimately fascinating memories and insights that reside there. Among his many other achievements, Denis is an unquestioned expert on those oral histories and has done us all a great service by providing an authoritative and enlightening glimpse into this rich collection that many historians have tapped into for their benefit and ours.

Among the other essays in this book, several deal with strategic thinking and operational planning. Lisle Rose provides a detailed and revealing look at the discussions/arguments surrounding Pacific War strategy that led to the decision to accommodate Gen. Douglas MacArthur's promised return to the Philippines, and Milan Vego offers a detailed account of the operational planning that led to that return in a way that makes one appreciate the complexity and degree of planning and organization required for such a gargantuan operation. Kevin Delamer compares the battle and its ramifications, both actual and potential, to the Athenian expedition to Sicily during the Peloponnesian War—an approach that will have great resonance among Naval War College faculty, graduates, and students, as well as reinforcing one of the existential tenets for historians—the value of history to current and future thinking. Vince O'Hara takes a critical look at the aftermath of the Leyte sea battles, contending that "a 'decisive naval battle' in and of itself does not establish sea control" and illustrating the consequences of that contention by an analysis of the operations that followed the initial seizure of Leyte. Norman Friedman brings his unique analytical ability to the fore by examining Halsey's actions during the battle, including a compelling argument as to why Halsey decided to take the battleships with him when he went north after Ozawa.

Not surprisingly, Norman is not the only author to take on Bull's Run as a major component of his essay. Karl Zingheim contends that the actions and ramifications of the Battle of the Sibuyan Sea had much to do with Halsey's controversial decision; Paul Stillwell focuses on Adm. Willis Lee's perspective as the man who "had been preparing for the Battle of Leyte Gulf his entire professional life"; and Trent Hone contends (among other things) that part of Halsey's failure to win a more decisive victory over the Imperial Japanese Navy was his insistence on functioning as a task force commander rather than a fleet commander.

Trent also addresses another factor that has relevance in the aftermath of the tragic collisions of two Seventh Fleet warships that claimed the lives of seventeen American sailors in 2017. Among the conclusions drawn by media and official investigators was the possible contribution of the "fatigue factor," a recognition that sailors—despite the expectations represented by the "can-do" culture that sometimes approaches mythological proportions—are human beings who must sometimes sleep. As mentioned earlier, Kurita's controversial decision to turn away at the crucial moment off Samar is attributed to this fatigue factor by a number of authors (including me). Trent takes that consideration a step further by applying it to Halsey and his staff as one of three major factors, pointing out that they "had been at sea almost two months" and that at the time of his critical decision making, Halsey had been "without sleep for nearly two days."

Dave Winkler offers an unusual portrait of two of the battle's veterans "from totally different backgrounds" whose wartime experiences led them in very different postwar directions yet "gave the two successful men a common bond that would foster a strong friendship in later years."

Jim Hornfischer provides an appropriate and moving retrospective on the valor of those veterans of the Battle off Samar and others of the "greatest generation," asking and partially answering what we get from having such men present at those critical moments in history and in the years that follow. Jim observes that "active duty naval personnel, hearing about the battle, tend to listen closely, often wondering, I sense, whether they have the same mettle as the tin can sailors and pilots of Taffy 3," and he reassures us by his observation that those veterans—who took part in such a cataclysmic moment in history—often deny "any claim to special qualities of heroism" and genuinely see themselves as "ordinary people, doing what ordinary people do."

The combined effect of these eleven essays is an eclectic and worthwhile look back—after three-quarters of a century—at a pivotal moment in history that has never lost its dramatic appeal nor its importance as a case study rich in potential lessons learned.

The Archive

Although not new, a great deal of enlightening information about the battle has appeared in the pages of *Proceedings* and *Naval History* magazines since the smoke of battle has cleared from Leyte Gulf. Collected here in one place is a selection of some of those articles. Readers who are not familiar with the value of the Naval Institute and its treasured open forum will likely be astounded at the breadth and depth of this treasure trove of history and wisdom that has accumulated over the years. Included are articles written by such key players as Admirals Halsey and Jesse Oldendorf, as well as Vice Admiral Tomiji Koyanagi, Kurita's chief of staff during the battle. Some of these articles provide excellent narratives of the events, while others fan the flames of controversy. All contribute to a wider understanding of this rich and complex subject.

The Payoff

Readers—whether veteran students of this momentous event or neophytes engaging for the first time—will find much within these pages to edify and to stimulate further thought. Strategy, tactics, logistics, communications, leadership, operational planning, weaponry, and human nature all abound within these pages. Awash with inspiration and introspection, controversy and reckoning, it is hoped that this unique volume will continue the quest for a better understanding of what happened at Leyte Gulf, drawing from it some hard-earned lessons that the sacrifice of so many brave men has made available, so that others will be spared that necessity in the future. We can pay no greater tribute.

Note

Readers of this volume will likely have no problem seeing an obvious bias toward the Naval Institute. Because I have been employed there for the last twenty-two years (and have been closely associated on the periphery going back to the early 1980s), one might surmise that my bias is derived from a paycheck and an employee's desire to promote the source of that money. That assumption would, of course, be correct; but I feel compelled to add that this bias would be every bit as pronounced were I not privileged to "work" at USNI. I sincerely believe that the sea services—indeed the nation!—are uniquely blessed to have had the Naval Institute for nearly a century and a half, providing a priceless open forum and professional guidance to those who are charged with the awesome responsibility of this nation's defense. I am grateful for what it did for me during my years of service and am humbled by the opportunity to give back in the ways I have been able.

PART I
Original Essays

A S EXPLAINED IN THE INTRODUCTION, eleven eminent historians have contributed original essays for this retrospective, covering a variety of topics and each offering a unique perspective. Because of the eclectic nature of this collection, choosing the order in which they should appear was no simple task and the result is nearly random.

Because, when all else is said and done, battles are fought by individuals—real people whose momentary contributions are the bits of a giant mosaic in space and in time—it is appropriate to begin with Denis Clift's essay that provides several snapshots of the battle, relying on remembrances that are relevant, varied, unique, and—most of all—human. Learned readers may detect a discrepancy or two in these accounts, demonstrating the selective and filtered nature of human memories while lending a degree of authenticity. Serious researchers see this aspect as a stimulant to deeper research, mandating an enhanced verification process that can lead to new interpretations and, in some cases, to a new truth.

Some of the factors that determined how the battle came to pass are detailed and analyzed by Lisle Rose and Milan Vego and are therefore next in order.

Norman Friedman, Trent Hone, Paul Stillwell, and Karl Zingheim are linked by their analysis of Bull's Run, and Kevin Delamer provides a special insight into Kurita's actions off Samar.

Returning to the indispensable role of individuals, the original essay collection concludes with Dave Winkler's focus on two people who were linked by the crucible of battle, and Jim Hornfischer's tribute to the legacy of "ordinary" people who become extraordinary under arduous circumstances.

The result is an eclectic collection of essays that not only offer different perspectives but also prove that no historical topic is ever beyond further insight and interpretation. I look forward to doing this again for the hundredth anniversary!

LEYTE GULF REMINISCENCES
──────── A. Denis Clift ────────

THE BATTLE OF LEYTE GULF, an epic page in the history of World War II, is the victory of thousands of U.S. warriors at sea, ashore, beneath the sea, and in the air—their actions, professional can-do spirit, heroism, and sacrifices. The Japanese committed their carriers and main battle fleet to the action, and they fought hard, determined to turn back U.S. amphibious landings at Leyte and Philippine shores beyond. Mistakes were made on both sides. The Americans rose to the challenge. The U.S. Navy prevailed.

The recollections of those who were in the action—the primary histories—contribute to the formal documentation and analysis in the historical record. Of equal if not greater importance, they capture memories, insights, and color otherwise not available. The following excerpts from six histories are taken from the U.S. Naval Institute's uniquely valuable oral history collection. As the Battle of Leyte Gulf takes shape and unfolds, we hear from:

— Lt. Ernest Schwab on board the submarine USS *Darter* (SS 227)
— Cdr. David McCampbell flying Hellcats from USS *Essex* (CV 9)
— Cdr. Joshua Cooper launching torpedo attacks from USS *Bennion* (DD 622)
— QM Michael Bak Jr. on board the USS *Franks* (DD 554) protecting jeep carriers
— Rear Adm. Gerald Bogan commanding Carrier Division 4 with Task Group 38.2
— Cdr. "Dusty" Dornin, aide to Fleet Adm. Ernest J. King during the battle.

Hitting Bombay Shoal at 19 Knots
Capt. Ernest Schwab, U.S. Navy (Ret.)

In 1943, Lt. Ernest Schwab—U.S. Naval Academy Class of 1939—reported on board a new *Gato*-class submarine, still on the building ways. Following commissioning that October, the USS *Darter* (SS 227) headed out to join the Battle of the Pacific. Cdr. William Stovall was in command, having previously been awarded two Navy Crosses for his patrols on the USS *Gudgeon* (SS 211). Lt. Dennis Wilkinson, future skipper of the USS *Nautilus* (SSN 571) and USS *Long Beach* (CGN 9), was first lieutenant, and Schwab was engineer.

Cdr. David McClintock became CO in June 1944, and by November the *Darter* and the USS *Dace* (SS 247) were on the attack against the Japanese fleet under Vice Admiral Takeo Kurita at the start of the Battle of Leyte Gulf. As Schwab recalled in these edited excerpts of his Naval Institute oral history,

> While we were on the surface, we picked up on radar this huge number of ships coming from the south. Just before dawn, we dived.
> Meanwhile we'd sent off messages to everyone warning them that there was a hell of a lot of ships coming—we counted 20 to 30—big ones. There were several columns there. We lined up and hit the *Atago* with four, five, or six torpedoes, and swung around. We saw another cruiser, the *Takao*, and when we started hitting, the Japanese ships changed course a bit. We just got her stern, didn't sink her, but she stopped dead in the water.
> Just about two seconds later, one column had come right over in front of the *Dace*, setting up perfectly. The *Dace*'s CO Cdr. Bladen Claggett, as I was told, said, "Let the cruisers by; we'll try the battleship." But he got a cruiser, too, the *Maya*.
> They had sixteen or so destroyers with them, and they dropped quite a few depth charges on us. But, when the *Dace* started hitting, that confused them. They missed both of us, and we came up to periscope depth sometime later. There was the *Takao* dead in the water. We had blown up one of its screws, or something. All we had left were some short-range electric torpedoes. That meant we had to get inside of 4,000 yards. Every time we would go in, one of the destroyers would come over, right at us. We'd go down; he'd drop one depth charge, then go away again.
> Finally, McClintock said, "You know, we're not going to get anyplace this way; we can't get close enough." We worked around toward Manila,

figured they would go up there, because there was a dry dock. Instead, they finally got under way, at about six knots, and headed south. We didn't know what had happened to the *Dace*. We kept in touch with the cruiser on the periscope.

Now, you realize, this was October '44, change of the monsoon, and navigation was tricky at best. We were in the Palawan Passage, about twenty miles wide, and we had a dubious navigational position all the time. We had surface radar and were able to tell from the mountains on Palawan roughly what our longitude was, but it was very hard to figure out our latitude, especially getting any star sights, while we were keeping in touch with the cruiser to be sure he wouldn't get away. We got in touch with the *Dace* and arranged to make a combined attack around midnight or one in the morning. We were all set to go in.

We were partially flooded down, making about 19 knots on the surface on our side. I don't know how fast the *Dace* was going on the other side. Just about a couple of minutes before we were supposed to turn in, we hit Bombay Shoal at 19 knots. Just before we hit, I told the captain, "I don't know where I am in latitude, but if we're in the right longitude, we're going to hit a shoal one of these minutes."

The Captain said, "Well shoals aren't any worse than depth charges," and Wham!—we hit. We hit at maximum high tide, and we really hit. We sent out the two-letter code "Aground" to the *Dace*. We had all sorts of classified stuff we started burning. Dennis Wilkinson went over the side in a rubber boat, went all around, and said, "It's horrible." By the time he came back you could see the coral heads coming up.

The *Dace* came over, put a line over to us and tried to tug us off—no luck at all. We decided to abandon ship, set all the demolition charges, including the torpedoes.

The Turkey Shoot
Capt. David McCampbell, U.S. Navy (Ret.)

On 24 October 1944, Cdr. David McCampbell and wingman Ens. Roy Rushing launched in a flight of seven F6F-5 Hellcats from the USS *Essex* (CV 9) to take on Japanese fighters, dive bombers, and torpedo planes menacing U.S. carriers in the Battle of Leyte Gulf. McCampbell would shoot down nine planes, and Rushing would down six. In his 1988 Naval

Institute oral history, McCampbell describes flying above some forty of the enemy planes and then going in for the kill when they broke their orbiting formation.

> So we had the altitude advantage all the time we attacked the Japanese. We zoomed down, would shoot a plane or two. Roy and I each would take one, and I'd tell him which one I was going to take, if it was to the right or to the left, which one it was. By telling him this, that allowed him to know which way I was going to dive, and then allowed him to pull out after we attacked, which gave me freedom to go either way I wanted. This worked very successfully, and he got the news. I'd pick out my plane, then he'd pick out his. We'd make an attack, pull up, keep our altitude advantage, speed, and go down again. We repeated this over and over. We made about 20 coordinated attacks....
>
> Pretty soon, Roy called me. He said, "Skipper, I'm out of ammunition." I called back, and I said, "Well Roy, I've got a little left. Do you want to go down with me for a couple of more runs, or do you want to sit up here and watch the show?"
>
> He said, "Oh no, I'll go down with you." So he followed me down for a couple of more attacks, and then I looked at my gas gauges, and I saw I'd emptied one main tank. I was about on the second one, and I was getting low. By then I was out of ammunition, too, getting low on gas, so I called Roy and said, "Well, we'll go back to the ship. I'm getting low on gas." By now, having followed this flight away from the task group toward Manila, we had gotten pretty far away from the ship. I'd estimate maybe about one hundred miles, give or take a few.
>
> So we headed back to the ship, and when I picked it up on the YE/ZB homing system, I was about 6,000 or 8,000 feet in altitude. I figured it was about 65 miles away, which turned out was about right, based on the length of time it took us to get back to the ship. I called the ship when I first got the YE signal and asked if they could take me as soon as I got back. They said, "Oh yes, come on in." So we kept heading for the ship, and when I got over the ship, I found they had a flight deck full of planes, and I knew that to launch all those planes would take a good 20 minutes, and I didn't have that much gas left.
>
> So I called the ship and told them that, and the admiral called the *Langley* and directed them to launch nine torpedo planes, so they could give me a clear deck to land aboard, which they did. When I saw the deck was clear, I came around and made a pass, but the LSO didn't cut me on

the first pass. They still hadn't cleared the deck properly for landing. So I made a quick turnaround, came back again, and he gave me the cut, and I landed safely. But when I tried to come out of the landing gear, I gave it near full gun, and the engine conked out on me. So I ran out of gas on the deck. They had to push me out of the landing area. I found out from the mech who re-ammunitioned the guns that I had exactly six rounds left in the starboard outboard gun. And they were all jammed. But it worked out all right.

Bearings for Accurate Torpedo Spreads
Rear Adm. Joshua W. Cooper, U.S. Navy (Ret.)

"*Bennion* may have had as remarkable a career as any ship we had," Rear Adm. Joshua Cooper recalls in these edited excerpts from his Naval Institute oral history. "Its pedigree was pretty well established by the fact that the ship was given a Presidential Unit Citation, not while I was in command. It did, in John Paul Jones' words, 'go in harm's way' a lot of times, and managed to get in and out without serious damage." Cooper took command of the new *Fletcher*-class destroyer USS *Bennion* (DD 622) in 1943, headed out to the war in the Pacific, and into the teeth of Leyte Gulf.

Surigao Strait was the high point of the war as far as I was personally concerned. Our D-day landing was October 20th. It was apparent by the 23rd that the Japanese navy was getting set to make an all-out bid to throw us out. We had reports from submarines and fleet aircraft that there were two task forces both headed for Leyte Gulf. One, it was determined, would come from the south through Surigao Strait, and one from the outside, from the open sea.

By the afternoon of the 24th, the situation had crystallized sufficiently for Rear Admiral Jesse Oldendorf to dispose his battleships and cruisers in a formation going around and across Leyte Gulf, putting the heavy ships into a position—the classic position—of crossing the T as the Japanese came up from the south to rout us out.

Our destroyers were organized into three flights of squadron strength. Ships were brought in to make up full squadrons of nine ships. Each squadron was divided into sections of three. We had the unenviable assignment of being in the third flight, and this meant that we waited practically all night to do our thing. It was raining, the visibility was very poor, and by the time our part in the show occurred, any element of surprise was gone.

Our best information came from two radar picket destroyers who were well south near the point where the Surigao Straits turn to the north. From that point on, we had better positions on the Japanese ships, I think, than they did themselves. As they turned up to head in a northerly direction, the first flight of destroyers made torpedo attacks from right, left, and center.

Shortly after this, the battleships and cruisers opened fire. This was followed by the second flight of destroyer torpedo attacks in similar fashion, right, left, and center. Finally, when our turn came, it was about two or three in the morning, and *Bennion* was hard over on the land side of the island of Leyte, trying very hard not to run aground. We finally got the "go" signal, and quickly worked up from five knots to thirty-five. We were darkened ship, but with the drizzle, rain, proximity of land, and shell fire directly over us from our own ships, and sporadic fire from the Japanese ships, it made a real fireworks. Running in close formation at high speed gave us enough to do that our tremendous concentration blocked out the fear syndrome—which had built up to strong proportions during the awful waiting from dusk the night before until two or three in the morning. By the time we went in, we could see our target fairly well from the burning, twisting masses of steel.

This was dramatically described by our young gunnery officer, who is now the Chief of Naval Operations, Lt. James L. Holloway III, who performed an extremely useful function. Even though we were not firing the guns, we did fire all ten of our torpedoes. Holloway, by sight from his director station, was able to give accurate bearings on targets selected by the CIC [combat information center] crew, and was able to furnish data which improved our torpedo solution and also our sense of knowing what we were doing.

At about 3,500 yards, we fired our first spread, then did a countermarch—each ship turning simultaneously, and the rear ship becoming the lead ship. Our section leader was Cdr. Joe Boulware in the USS *Heywood L. Edwards* (DD 663). Our third ship was the USS *Leutz* (DD 481). As we made our turn, we fired our second spread of torpedoes, and I think that one was probably better than the first. We found out the next day that we were only supposed to have fired one spread, save our torpedoes for future use. I am glad we fired them all, because we did better with the second spread.

The only orders we received from Rear Adm. Jesse Oldendorf were to "go on down" and, in view of the rather methodical preparation, that was about all we needed. The admiral's message after the exercise speaks for itself. "Now that the battle phase of our Leyte operation seems to be over, I wish to say to all who had a part in the decisive and epic Battle of the Surigao Strait against the Japanese Navy: well done."

Adm. Thomas Kinkaid went on to say, "The destroyer attacks were executed with remarkable precision and effect. The attacks more than served their purpose of slowing and confusing the enemy. They nearly annihilated him."

Fishtailing on the Franks
QM Michael Bak Jr., U.S. Navy

The son of Russian immigrants, Michael Bak Jr. was raised in New Jersey during the Depression. "I came home one time in my Boy Scouts uniform," he recalled in his Naval Institute oral history, "and one of our Russian relatives berated my parents for allowing me to join the Scouts. She felt that there was a war coming on soon, and I would be the first to be called up because of the uniform."

In late 1942, he enlisted in the Navy, moved through boot camp to quartermaster school at Great Lakes, and then on to the precommissioning crew of the *Fletcher*-class destroyer USS *Franks* (DD 554), fitting out in Bremerton. Following commissioning in July 1943, the *Franks* joined the Battle of the Pacific, screening escort carriers, retrieving downed pilots, and patrolling against submarines. In late 1944, with the Philippine operations coming on, she joined the Seventh Fleet.

The war came into sharp focus for Quartermaster Bak on the morning of October 25, during the Battle of Leyte Gulf. In these edited excerpts from his oral history, Bak recalls the action. The loudspeaker sounded General Quarters.

We ran to our battle stations. I ran to the bridge and looked out, and I saw what looked like toothpicks on the horizon, right across the horizon—many, many ships.

Our carrier planes started taking off. When the Japanese fleet was coming at us, our job was to stay between the carriers and the Japanese ships.

We were going back and forth, sort of fishtailing, because our carriers couldn't go too fast. The Japs were shooting at us and dropping shells around us, 150, 200 yards. We were going right full rudder, left full rudder, right full rudder, and the shells were coming all around us. We were told to go in for a torpedo run. Then, they decided it was crazy to go in. They found a couple of ships had been sunk. We were told to lay a smoke screen between the Jap fleet and the carriers—all the time fishtailing.

I was on the bridge at the quartermaster station, putting entries in the ship's log. The shells were dropping around us. I went under the chart table, which was a ridiculous place to go. Then I was on a long glass, and I couldn't believe you could see these ships so close. I couldn't believe that that fleet had got so close to us without our admirals knowing about it in advance. It was Vice Admiral Takeo Kurita's fleet, the Japanese commander involved.

From about 7:15 to 10:30 that morning, it was several hours of not knowing what was happening. We did see some burning out there. We got a report later that burning was our ships being sunk. If we had held one course, they would have blown us out of the water that day. That's what I liked about our skipper, Cdr. David Stephan. He was out there giving orders, right full rudder, left full rudder.

For some reason or other, later on the Japs turned around and went the other way. They left us when they could have had a kill. They didn't realize what they had. I believe, reading back in history, they thought our destroyers were cruisers.

During all this, the planes were taking off and landing. I remember getting behind these carriers. We had sort of dual duty, fishtailing, trying to pick our pilots out of the water when they crashed or went overboard, and keeping between the Jap fleet and the escort carriers. I saw the smoke and the hit when the *Gambier Bay* went down. The jeep carriers didn't have the maneuverability we had.

In a fight like that, when you're quartermaster, you can see what's going on, but the people below decks can't. The captain would give the results later on to all hands, but never during the battle.

Chasing the Japanese Decoy Force
Vice Adm. Gerald F. Bogan, U.S. Navy (Ret.)

Vice Adm. Gerald Bogan was a naval aviation pioneer, earning his wings in 1925 and joining Fighting Squadron One on the USS *Langley* (CV 1). He would fly from the *Langley*, USS *Lexington* (CV 2), USS *Saratoga* (CV 3), and USS *Yorktown* (CV 5), and in late 1942, take command of the *Saratoga*.

In early 1944, as the march across the Pacific pushed westward, he was promoted to flag and command of Carrier Division 25—the escort carriers USS *Fanshaw Bay* (CVE 70), USS *Midway* (CVE 60), USS *White Plains* (CVE 66), and USS *Kalinin Bay* (CVE 68). That same year, just prior to the Battle of Leyte Gulf, he took command of Carrier Division 4—fleet carriers—and Task Group 38.2. In these edited excerpts from his Naval Institute oral history, he recalls key moments and key issues in the action.

This was right after Formosa. First, they called it the Second Battle of the Philippine Sea, and then MacArthur insisted it be called the Battle of Leyte Gulf. I was in the USS *Intrepid* (CV 11). Rear Adm. Frederick Sherman, in the USS *Lexington* (CV 16) with Task Group 38.3, was to the north. Vice Adm. John McCain, with Task Group 38.1, had just started back to Ulithi to refuel and resupply.

We sent this armed scouting force to the west at 0730 and around 0930 saw this Japanese central force under Vice Admiral Takeo Kurita, which had already lost two cruisers to submarines, the USS *Dace* (SS 247) and the USS *Darter* (SS 227), the day before. Rear Adm. Ralph Davidson [in command of the supporting carrier groups] was called north, and my group made several attacks throughout the day, as this central force came back and around through the Sibuyan Sea. Admiral Sherman's group also sent in one very heavy attack at about 1500. I do not know whether it was as a result of that or the cumulative effects from previous attacks that caused the *Musashi*, a sister ship of the *Yamato* to slow down—with the rest of their force turning around to cover her.

Admiral Halsey got that report and thought they were retreating. Later in the day, Halsey ordered all three groups north at twenty-five knots to attack what turned out to be a decoy force. There were seventeen ships in it, and we had sixty-eight. Capt. Edward Ewen in the USS *Independence* (CVL 22) said they were on course 060 degrees, were coming out through San Bernardino Strait, and navigation lights were turned on.

I thought that Halsey was making one hell of a mistake. I had this message already to send him saying, "Recommend Form Leo (which was Task Force 34, with Vice Admiral Willis A. Lee's fast battleships) leave my group in support and let the other two groups handle the northern force." But when I told him about the lights business, someone on his staff said, "Yes, yes, we have that information." That was a brushoff, as far as I was concerned, and

I wasn't going to say any more. I doubt very much if it would have had any effect, because Admiral Halsey talked to me time after time and justified his decision to go north. Capt. Arleigh Burke, Adm. Marc Mitscher's chief of staff, tried to get him to recommend something to Halsey, but Mitscher, who felt the tactical command had been taken away from him said, "If he wants plans or information from me, he'll ask for it."

Then about 0200 in the morning, 25 October, Admiral Halsey ordered a search made from the *Independence* in my group for these ships. Admiral Mitscher protested, saying he thought that if the planes got in the air, the Japanese radar would discover them and change course. Halsey said, "Launch the search." The Japanese did discover the planes in the air and did change course. Instead of this gun duel which Halsey had envisioned early in the morning, it was nearly 0830 before we could catch them with the planes.

At about 1030, after the second strike, when the thing was practically over, we had sunk all three carriers. The Commander in Chief, Pacific Fleet, Admiral Chester W. Nimitz sent this message to Halsey, "Where is Task Force 34?"—and there was some padding on the end of the message which some kid put on, "the world wonders." And, that just turned Halsey on his ear. "God, why is Nimitz sending me a message like that?"

At 1130, we formed Task Force 34 with my group in support and started back to the Philippines at full twenty-eight knots, refueling destroyers at fourteen knots until they were filled. Of course, Kurita had knocked off the action at about noon and gone west again, after suffering pretty heavy losses. Nobody knows why he turned around, but he did. He'd sunk four little jeep carriers and two destroyers, and if he continued he could have wiped out the landing force at Leyte Gulf. Nobody's ever known why he turned around.

Halsey later said, "I thought that it was Vice Admiral Kinkaid's responsibility to guard that strait, not mine." It's a long story. It will never be resolved, except that I'm clear in my own mind that it was a great mistake on Halsey's part.

King Bawls Out Halsey
Capt. Robert E. Dornin, U.S. Navy (Ret.)

Capt. Robert E. "Dusty" Dornin, U.S. Navy, graduated from the Naval Academy in 1935, a football star, and went on quickly to become one of the fabled submariners in the Battle of the Pacific, serving in the USS

Gudgeon (SS 211) and USS *Trigger* (SS 237)—with two Navy Crosses and four Silver Stars. The *Trigger* under his command was awarded the Presidential Unit Citation.

In 1944, following nine war patrols, he returned to Pearl Harbor and was delighted to be invited to lunch with Adm. Chester W. Nimitz and Vice Adm. Charles A. Lockwood, Commander, Submarines Pacific Fleet. Pleasure turned to shock when the admirals informed him that he had been selected as the aide to Adm. Ernest J. King. "I let them know I wouldn't go," Dornin recalled in these edited excerpts from his Naval Institute oral history. "'What? Are you crazy?' one of them asked. I was told to think it over for twenty-four hours. I did, and then was informed that I had the assignment.... As for the job, I took care of everything, to include the phone calls, that went in and out of Admiral King's office." In October 1944, he was helping King keep track of fast-breaking action in the Battle of Leyte Gulf, including Admiral Halsey's chase of Japanese carriers to the north and Adm. Thomas Kinkaid's plea for heavy-ship help against Japanese battleships and cruisers.

I happened to have the duty that night on the USS *Dauntless* (PG 61), [Admiral King's in-port ship in Washington]. One thing Admiral King had was an order that he was not to be awakened or disturbed during the night. Well, about midnight, King's chief of staff, Admiral Richard "Dickie" Edwards, the number two man in the Navy, came down and showed me this dispatch—Admiral Nimitz's message to Halsey: "Where is, repeat, where is Task Force 34? The world wonders."—and wanted me to show it to Admiral King. And I said, "No, sir, Admiral King does not want to be disturbed." He looked me in the eye and he said, "Dornin, show this dispatch to Admiral King."

So I went in and switched on the light. Admiral King opened one eye like an eagle's eye, and I handed him a few dispatches. He looked at them and then said, "Just what in hell do you want me to do about it, Dornin, at midnight? What do you think I've got Nimitz out there for? Now get out." With that, I turned around and said, "Yes, sir."

Nothing happened for about two days, fortunately. The Japanese for some unknown reason left the area and the invasion was successful. But, when Task Force 34 had come back to anchor and replenish, my buzzer rang. I went in to see Admiral King, who said, "I want to see Admiral Halsey immediately."

"Yes, sir."

With that, I called Vice Adm. Randall Jacobs and told him Admiral King wanted to see Admiral Halsey immediately. He said, "Well, he's out in Ulithi Atoll."

I said, "Sir, I'm only carrying out Admiral King's order."

Admiral Jacobs knew Admiral King well, so he said, "Okay, Dornin."

In a short time, believe me, a very short time, Admiral Halsey showed up and came into the office. I knew him from way back. I was an ex-football player. Halsey was quite a football player himself.

He said, "How are you, Dusty?"

I said, "Just a minute, sir, I'll tell Admiral King you're here." I went in and Admiral King said, "Show him in."

I had hardly gotten out of the door, but, I'm telling you, you talk about reprimands, bawling-outs—when you hear an admiral rip up and down on another four-star admiral, boy, it was insulting, not foul, but the devil's language. I never heard anything in the world like it. I couldn't help but hear it. As a matter of fact, I think everyone on the second deck of the Navy Department heard him. King was fond of Halsey, but he wanted perfection. Frankly, Halsey made a hell of a blunder, and it could have been very costly.

About the Author

A. Denis Clift, the U.S. Naval Institute's vice president for planning and operations, is a former naval officer, editor-in-chief of *Proceedings* magazine, president (1994–2009) of the National Defense Intelligence College, and president emeritus, National Intelligence University. A graduate of Stanford University, he has a master of science from the London School of Economics, and three honorary PhDs. He served two terms, 2000–2005, as a commissioner, Middle States Commission on Higher Education, and as plank-owning presidential commissioner, 1992–2009, on the U.S.-Russia Joint Commission on Prisoners of War Missing in Action.

He was a naval officer in the Eisenhower and Kennedy administrations, on two Antarctic expeditions, including the 1961 Bellingshausen Sea Expedition, authored *Our World in Antarctica* (Rand McNally), and directed production of the film *Portrait of Antarctica*, screened at the Venice Film Festival.

He served in the administrations of eleven successive presidents, including thirteen years in the Executive Office of the President and in the White House, headed President Gerald Ford's National Security Council Staff for the Soviet Union and Eastern and Western Europe, and was assistant for National Security Affairs to Vice President Walter Mondale. From 1991 to 1994 he was chief of staff, Defense Intelligence Agency.

His awards include the National Order of Merit, rank of Knight, Romania, 2009; the President's Rank of Distinguished Executive, 2001; the President's Rank of Meritorious Executive, 1986; the Department of Defense Distinguished Civilian Service Medal; and the Department of Defense Distinguished Public Service Medal. He is the author of five books, including the novels *The Bronze Frog* and *A Death in Geneva*, and the nonfiction works *With Presidents to the Summit* and *Clift Notes: Intelligence and the Nation's Security*.

2

PLANNING THE PENULTIMATE STAGES OF THE PACIFIC WAR

Lisle Rose

IN THE LATE SPRING OF 1943, American military analysts turned their attention to shaping the penultimate stages of the Pacific War. In the South Pacific, Adm. William F. Halsey, under the overall command of Pacific Fleet leader Adm. Chester W. Nimitz, was completing the conquest of the upper Solomon Islands. Simultaneously, Nimitz and his people in Hawaii began preparations for an even more massive island-hopping campaign that would take American sea, air, and land forces through the Gilberts, Marshalls, Marianas, and Palaus to the Philippines. In the Southwest Pacific theater of operations directly north and west of the Solomons, Gen. Douglas MacArthur continued his offensive in the Bismarck Archipelago and along the northern coast of New Guinea, aiming at the Admiralty Islands and eventually Mindanao, the largest southernmost island in the Philippine Archipelago.

Looking beyond the anticipated convergence of MacArthur's forces with those of Nimitz in the next year or so, the Joint Chiefs of Staff (JCS) focused on conquest of a strategic triangle composed of the islands of Luzon and Formosa together with the adjacent China coast with its port city of Amoy (Xiamen). Seizure of this triangle in the 1944–early 1945 time frame would fulfill three objectives. First, it would cut Japan's critical supply lines south down the China Sea to its resource-rich holdings in Southeast Asia. Second, gaining control of the triangle would permit increasingly intensive air and naval bombardments and blockades of the Home Islands in preparation for the ultimate invasions that everyone at the time conceived as essential to end the war. And third, it would allow for use of Chiang Kai-shek's army to help pin down the formidable

Japanese military presence in eastern China, thereby confirming the essential role the Kuomintang government could play in determining the future destiny of East Asia.[1]

Ten months later, the crunching offensives in the Southwest and Central Pacific were approaching the Philippines and key questions required immediate attention. Should MacArthur and Nimitz concentrate all their forces on reconquering the entire Philippine archipelago before moving on to seize Formosa and Amoy, the other two points of the triangle? Was a Philippine offensive of any size and dimension the quickest way to bring the war to Japan's doorstep? What was the best use of America's human and material resources?

By this point, strategic planning had become complex. Each theater commander in Europe, the Pacific, Admiral Louis Mountbatten's Southeast Asia Command, and the China-Burma-India Theater had his own planning staff. Within the Pentagon itself, the JCS could draw on the work of a multitude of combat intelligence and planning staffs, committees, and panels developed since Pearl Harbor by each of the services. Chief of Naval Operations Ernest J. King relied on a planning staff headed by Rear Adm. Charles Cooke, aptly nicknamed "Savvy," while William J. Sebald, a Japanese-speaking lawyer who had practiced in Japan for some years, "pretty much created" his own job as King's chief combat intelligence analyst, basing his work largely on communications intercepts and translations together with "thousands" of often quite informative enemy documents gathered on battlefields throughout the Central and Southwest Pacific. While MacArthur out in Brisbane relied on hundreds of staffers to provide him with intelligence and tactical guidance, Nimitz was decidedly of the "too-many-cooks-spoil-the-broth" school. According to one of his staff, the Pacific Fleet commander was "very strict about keeping the number of people to the minimum consistent with the volume of the work and the requirements of the job." Together, the two staffs—one in Washington, the other in Hawaii—produced impressive work. Ruthven Libby, who served on King's staff, later remarked that "between Admiral King and Admiral Nimitz and 'Savvy' Cooke, Admiral King's chief planner back in Washington, their selection of what points in the Pacific to assault and what points to bypass amounted to nothing short of genius." Another participant in the overall planning process for the Pacific War noted that King "had a very capable staff . . . some of the most intelligent men we had."[2]

While tactical decisions were left to the service commanders and their staffs in the field, final strategic decisions were the ultimate responsibility of the JCS as a corporate whole. Their Joint War Plans Committee (JWPC) was "where really the war plans originated." One member recalled that "the Joint Chiefs didn't do any operational planning, obviously. A high command doesn't do that sort of thing. What they did do was make strategic decisions" based upon daily inputs from the subordinate services. Sebald is particularly emphatic on this point. "Our real objective was to see that the commander in chief and the headquarters staff were fully apprised of the situation of the war in the Pacific, insofar as intelligence was able to inform them."[3]

President Franklin D. Roosevelt's naval aide, Adm. William D. Leahy, chaired the JWPC and, as "the mouthpiece of the President," kept the group firmly in line. "His technique was most interesting," one naval representative remembered.

> [Army Chief of Staff George C.] Marshall, for example, would start discussing some plan of his, something he thought we ought to be doing next, and Leahy would say, "Well, George, I'm just a simple sailor. Would you please back up and start from the beginning and make it simple. Just tell me step one, two and three and so on." Well, Marshall or [Army Air Force head Henry "Hap"] Arnold, or whoever it was kept falling for this thing and they would back up and explain to this simple old sailor. And as they did it—which is what Leahy knew damned well would happen—... they themselves would find out the weakness or misconception or that there was something wrong with it. So he didn't have to start out by saying "This is a stupid idea and it won't work."[4]

By 1944, to the dismay of many in Washington, including Leahy, the JCS and its planners seemed increasingly drawn into the global political as well as military decision-making process.[5] And in the Pacific, military planning itself lay in thrall to one man, Douglas MacArthur. Nimitz and King, despite opposing temperaments, "got along wonderfully well," according to one who observed both closely. The two met privately in San Francisco several times during the war and, according to one of King's chief planners, had reached agreement on operations to follow the Marianas campaign: "an attack on Formosa followed as soon as possible by a landing on the Chinese mainland at places to be chosen after consultation with

General [Joseph] Stilwell," commander of U.S. and Chinese Nationalist forces. "The idea that the Admirals had was to exploit to the fullest extent the strategic position of China and the almost unlimited manpower."[6]

MacArthur would have none of it. The Philippines to which he had publicly pledged to return would be bypassed, its people ignored, forgotten, their simple trust betrayed. Reconquering the archipelago was not the most important objective; it was the only objective. Not only did MacArthur communicate his views by normal channels, he also dispatched his chief of staff, Gen. Richard Sutherland, from distant Australia to Washington, where Sutherland "had told the Joint Chiefs of Staff how General MacArthur felt about future plans."[7]

The mutual dislike between MacArthur and his staff in Australia and Nimitz's people at Pearl Harbor was widely known, making coordination all but impossible. "For instance—we'd send a ship down there loaded with supplies of some kind, which they had to unload and send back to get some more. [MacArthur] wouldn't send them back. He'd keep them down there . . . you couldn't plan accurately" for any future amphibious or resupply operations. And woe betide any one of Halsey's subordinates who allowed one or more of their ships to sail past the "bamboo curtain" separating the South and Southwest Pacific commands.[8] Despite such seething resentments, Nimitz and King both refused to fight publicly with the general. With his own Army and Marine elements under command, Nimitz insisted on cooperation above all. According to one subordinate, "Admiral Nimitz said, 'We've got to get along together. We've got to use everything we have to the best use we can place it.'" King's people observed the same approach: "Admiral King expressed admiration for General MacArthur, and extolled his abilities. I never heard him say anything except to praise the General." Adm. Thomas Kinkaid, whose Seventh Fleet comprised the naval component of MacArthur's Southwest Pacific command, "was really the first that got along with" the general. "He was a very smooth person, like Nimitz was."[9] Nor were the Joint Chiefs inclined to cross their often-fractious Army colleague. According to one staffer, "They realized that they had a very difficult problem on their hands with MacArthur who had formerly been Chief of Staff in the Army. . . . He had a lot of political prestige. The Army men were very loath to ever say 'no' to anything MacArthur wanted." MacArthur knew he could not be fired, there was no place in Washington or the field to send such a widely experienced senior officer. "He would have to be shelved. To shelve MacArthur was impossible. It would have the whole country up in arms." MacArthur's clout was amplified by the fact that he had become the darling of a small but quite vocal fringe of the Republican Party determined to press his presidential candidacy at the 1944 Convention.[10]

Despite this ever-present potential for conflict and confusion, the JWPC had imposed a fairly coherent horizontal structure upon war planning, and on March 11–12, 1944, in "a series of important and at times tense meetings," the JCS formally issued a strategic plan for operations over the next twelve months in the Pacific theater of operations.[11] The following day, Leahy, King, and Nimitz—who had briefly come over from Hawaii—went to the White House to brief the president. Confronted with three of the finest naval minds in American history, with an instinctive naval bias, and with no great personal involvement or investment in the details of Pacific planning to that point, Roosevelt quickly approved. While Nimitz flew back to Hawaii, the strategic plan was formally issued to the two Pacific commands.

The "first major objective of strategy in the Pacific" remained the "Luzon, Formosa and China Coast area." A tentative target date of February 15, 1945, was to be set for the completion of this objective with the subjection of Formosa. Specifically, MacArthur would invade Hollandia—the last major Japanese bastion on the northern New Guinea coast—on April 15, 1944; the great Japanese naval base at Truk in the nearby Caroline archipelago was to be "neutralized and bypassed." Nimitz's forces would invade the Marianas in June and the Palau Islands in September. By November 15, MacArthur and Nimitz would converge on Mindanao, the southernmost large island in the Philippines. Mindful of a recent study by their own Joint War Planning Committee that suggested *either* a rush to Formosa *or* a steady investiture of the Philippine archipelago, the JCS left open the prospect that Luzon might be substituted for Formosa.[12]

However, Nimitz and Halsey (freshly appointed as Third Fleet commander) were becoming smitten with the idea of practically closing down MacArthur's entire Southwest Pacific offensive even before the invasion of Mindanao in favor of concentrating on the Formosa–China Coast operation. There were a number of apparently cogent reasons for this approach. If, possibly, the "Atlantic," (i.e., the European war) was over by October (Normandy was still a month away), then acceleration of the Pacific campaign would be essential to fulfill the mandate of the Anglo-American Combined Chiefs of Staff to end the war against Japan no more than a year after the surrender of Germany. Moreover, at this stage of the war, Soviet Russia could not be expected to enter the Pacific war in order to tie down the formidable Japanese Kwantung Army on the Asian mainland. Nimitz advanced these ideas in a meeting with King and Savvy Cooke, who believed that Formosa could be assaulted with less than the twelve divisions anticipated, perhaps as few as seven. Once Formosa was conquered, the Japanese Home Islands could be successfully blockaded, thereby cutting off the Kwantung Army from reinforcing Kyushu and Honshu as well as denying Japan needed supplies from the south. No costly invasion would be needed as she would be starved into surrender militarily and economically.

"In the discussions that followed, Nimitz" advanced the argument one step further. Perhaps the invasion of Formosa itself could be avoided by gaining "positions on the China coast, whereby supplies and arms could reach the Chinese, thus utilizing Chinese manpower as the ultimate land force in defeating the Japanese *on the continent of Asia*, though, of course, United States forces would be present in numbers as required." While Stilwell would be consulted on the best spots for a landing, Nimitz was inclined to grounds close to Amoy, just across the strait from Formosa. Following the invasion, Nimitz added, "we should plan an advance up the coast of China as far as Shanghai, where there were rail and river transportation facilities inland, but that we should avoid meeting the large [Japanese] Manchurian [i.e., Kwantung] Army." King observed that "only Chinese troops" could pin down whatever Japanese forces were encountered.[13]

According to Halsey, others high up in the Pacific Fleet High Command—including Adm. Raymond Spruance, who alternated command of the battle fleet with Halsey—"favored" the China coast strategy, suggesting that seizure of Nimrod Sound south of Shanghai would provide an excellent base for the invasion of Japan. "Still others," Halsey recalled several years later, "argued for landings on the Shantung Peninsula or at Quelpart Island at the southern end of Korea Strait, or on Korea itself."[14]

Nimitz soon had reason to reconsider such bold thinking. Halsey himself was not wholly on board. While the Third Fleet commander thought that he and Nimitz "agreed completely on [a] long range strategy," they did not. Halsey believed Formosa to be a tough nut to crack. Better to establish "a major base" in the central Philippines that could provide the springboard for a series of leaps to the Japanese Home Islands via the Bonins (Iwo Jima) and Ryukyus (Okinawa).[15] King "strongly recommended by-passing the Philippines entirely" and pushing straight on from the Marianas and the distant Admiralties into Formosa which

Halsey deemed too risky in light of Formosa's size and powerful natural defensive positions.[16]

Finally, China's Kuomintang government was proving a disaster, laced with corruption and hobbled by gross inefficiencies. Despite an earlier commitment to raise thirty new divisions to fight the Japanese, Chiang Kai-shek was husbanding most of his entire army in preparation for a postwar showdown with the Chinese Communists. Dispassionate observers emphasized that "China was becoming progressively demoralized." Not even the prospect of sharing significantly in the final stages of the defeat of Japan could reverse the trend.[17] Washington had already signaled its growing disillusion with Chiang. Roosevelt's strong desire, if not determination, to make China the great postwar stabilizing power in Asia was a dream gone a-glimmering. The JCS had approved Operation Matterhorn, the deployment of eight B-29 bombardment groups to east central China to mount air raids against Japan employing the new, very long-range bombers. But in April 1944, the JCS cut the force in half "due to supply limitations" over the Himalayan "Hump" from India. Even earlier, the Allies had decided on concentrating their limited resources on the reconquest of Burma rather than on defending China. The reduction of that vast country to a secondary theater of war enraged Chiang, prompting him to engage in ever-more bitter clashes with Stilwell.[18] It was becoming increasingly evident that China could not play a significant role in the coming subjection of Japan.

Moreover, Nimitz's planners were beginning to accept Halsey's skepticism about Formosa. Unlike the Filipinos, Formosans had no reason to harbor any great affection for the Americans. The island itself presented many formidable obstacles, not least its size (14,000 square miles) and topography (a broad coastal plain on the west, but rugged mountain ranges filling the eastern half). Could seven divisions—or even a dozen— conquer and hold such a place in a decent time frame?

Early in June, the Joint War Plans Committee presented its superiors with a new and breathtaking proposal. The great Battle of the Philippine Sea, with its "Marianas Turkey Shoot" that downed over 450 Japanese aircraft and its deadly submarine assaults that sank two of Japan's three largest remaining aircraft carriers (Navy fliers accounted for a third light carrier), was still days away. But, dazzled by the months-long success of the rampaging Halsey/Spruance Third and Fifth Fleet carrier task forces, the JWPC now seriously considered "the possibility of speeding up the

[Pacific] campaign." It could be accomplished in two ways, either by accelerating currently scheduled operations or "bypassing objectives currently selected, including Formosa, and choosing new ones, perhaps even Japan itself." According to the most distinguished historian of the JCS, "the suggestion met with general approval," though it apparently did not become JCS policy.[19]

MacArthur replied promptly and vehemently. To bypass the Philippines would not only be an act of military folly but of moral abdication. The United States had lost the Philippines. Its honor demanded a vengeful reconquest and the liberation of 17 million Filipinos, the great majority of whom "remain loyal to the United States and are undergoing the greatest privation and suffering because we have not been able to support or succor them." MacArthur added that if the Joint Chiefs persisted in their folly, "I request that I be accorded the opportunity of personally proceeding to Washington to present fully my views."[20]

Nimitz apparently did not respond formally to the JCS until June 29. When he did, his reply was puzzling to say the least, suggesting that the formidable nature of any conquest of the Luzon-Formosa-Amoy triangle had at last registered with him as well as at least some members of his staff. Just the week before, his flyers and submariners had dealt the Imperial Japanese Navy a shattering blow, practically destroying all but a few pitiful remnants of that once formidable Kido Butai ("Mobile Fleet") that had assaulted Pearl Harbor and roamed the western Pacific and Indian Oceans with impunity. Japan's battle fleet had been reduced to a still-formidable but drastically restricted surface task force. According to Japanese naval historian Masanori Ito, "Warship production in Japan was so inadequate that there was no hope of providing new ships to replace losses. *Zuikaku*, the lone remaining fleet carrier, was joined" by "hermaphrodite carrier-battleships *Ise* and *Hyuga*," three light carriers, and two auxiliaries. The most momentous outcome of the battle, however, was the fatal splitting of the Imperial Navy. "The surface fleet of Admiral Kurita was separated from the remainder of this Mobile Fleet, and sent south to Lingga Roads" nearly two thousand miles away, "because there was not enough fuel for them and the carriers in Japan." The Americans knew it. "Over a period of about six months," William Sebald remembered, "I built up an organization under which one officer was in charge of Japanese naval ships and organizations." Using intercepted communications and some surprisingly valuable information gleaned on Pacific battlefields, Lt. Serge Klotz "had a regular card index, and we had a big map of the whole Pacific, which was, I guess, about 10 feet by 38 feet, and through pins and so forth we kept track of where all the Japanese forces were, our best estimates.... [O]nce a week we sent out a weekly report of the complete estimate of Japanese naval forces," their estimated location, "and, where possible, estimated capabilities."[21]

Nimitz and his intelligence people may not have guessed how conclusive the victory had been or its implications for future operations. The staging of enemy aircraft from the Home Islands through Iwo Jima to the Marianas as battles continued ashore may have misled them about lingering enemy strength. But a four-carrier assault on Iwo just four days after the Fifth Fleet routed the enemy off Saipan was met with no resistance. Nimitz and his admirals definitely ruled the waves. Moreover, within days, their ever-vigilant submariners, together with Philippine observers, reported growing concentrations of enemy naval shipping in the central archipelago and to the south, which clearly suggested a significant division of the Japanese fleet.[22]

Nonetheless, Nimitz's 29 June reply was as crushing in its way as MacArthur's; far from accelerating the existing timetable of conquest, he told the Joint Chiefs "he probably could not achieve the target dates set in the [12] March directive." Even the proposed attack on Mindanao the coming February (1945) followed by a major attack on Luzon through the Lingayen Strait on 1 April now "seemed optimistic." What prompted this burst of pessimism is unclear, but Nimitz did share with many colleagues and the American public in general the belief that the Pacific War would be long and hard; as of spring 1944, the end of the tunnel still seemed distant. One of the admiral's staffers recalled Nimitz's absolute elation in August 1945 at the abrupt cessation of hostilities "because he had predicted previously that it would be late '47 or mid '48 before we would even attempt to invade Japan."[23]

Whether MacArthur or his people saw the Nimitz message, the general promptly exploited it. In early July, he submitted his own plan for the reconquest of the entire Philippine archipelago—"Reno V"—to the JCS. It was, to say the least, a destabilizing document. "In its entirety, Reno V would mean that Formosa, which in current JCS directives was still the objective of the advance across the Pacific, could not be taken as scheduled" by February 15, 1945, "but would have to be postponed" a full eight months "until the following October after the typhoon season."[24]

While apparently not rejecting Reno V outright, the JCS and their planners refused to let go completely of the bewitching thought of just cutting northwest from the Marianas in a series of lightning carrier and amphibious strikes that would soon reach the shores of the Home Islands themselves. Two scenarios for Japan's downfall were produced: either a drive through the Philippines, Formosa, and the Ryukyus (Okinawa) to invasion beaches first on Kyushu then Honshu, or through the Bonins (Iwo Jima) then directly to Kyushu and Honshu.[25]

Clearly a crisis was brewing, though there was still time to reach agreement on a coming timetable. Roosevelt had doubtless been kept informed of at least the outlines of the growing debate through Leahy. The president had already laid plans for a tour of West Coast facilities after stopping briefly at the Democratic Convention in Chicago. Why not extend the trip to Hawaii, including a badly needed relaxation voyage on board cruiser *Baltimore* to Pearl Harbor? Nimitz was there and MacArthur could be summoned. So it was that at the end of July 1944, the three men converged under Oahu's palms and calm breezes.

Despite numerous efforts at projecting a powerful element of drama into the several meetings between the president and his two Pacific theater commanders, the discussions throughout were, according to Leahy who attended them all, "friendly, quiet in tone," even, it would seem, gracious. "It was both pleasant and very informative to have these two men who had been pictured as antagonists calmly presenting their differing views to the Commander-in-Chief."[26] Nimitz remembered that, until the final day, MacArthur's behavior toward him and his Navy colleagues was both cordial and courteous, "complete and genuine."[27] After dinner the first evening, July 26, Roosevelt was wheeled by a large wall map and, after a glance at Mindanao, reportedly said, "'Douglas, where do we go from here?' 'Leyte, Mr. President, then Luzon.'"[28] Nimitz continued to urge Formosa as it "would be easier for the fleet and would expedite the advance against Japan." King had been in Honolulu shortly before the meeting (which he did not attend) shortly before on a grrand tour of the Central Pacific battlefields. He "recalled" for his Pacific Fleet commander "the arguments on both sides" of the Luzon vs. Formosa issue. "Although he did not give Nimitz any definite orders regarding his role in the forthcoming conference, he asked him to think the matter over very carefully before he was called upon to speak." Surely mindful of his CNO's advice, Nimitz nonetheless offered up every argument he could for Formosa. The island was "ideally located to block the flow to Japan of the oil, tin, rubber, quinine and other vital materials of the East Indies area"; it was closer to China with its tantalizing promise of powerful aid from Chiang Kai-shek's army in establishing bomber bases on the coast and, possibly, even a staging area for a direct assault on the enemy's Home Islands. If Chinese aid proved impossible, Formosa was still closer to Japan for bombing and staging purposes than Luzon. Above all, a protracted Philippine campaign would prolong the war unnecessarily at greater cost in American lives and materiel. Doubtless Nimitz reiterated the Navy's long-held view that while a reconquest of the entire archipelago had undoubted "military advantages" and that the plight of the Filipinos was certainly a factor, the liberation of these peoples "could be accomplished more quickly if we would press our offensive closer to Japan itself . . . the sooner that we could strike at the heart of Japan, the sooner Tokyo would surrender."[29]

Yet even as he spoke, Nimitz must have realized he was playing a weak hand. China was rapidly being perceived in Washington as at best a disappointment, at worst an emerging catastrophe. Moreover, *anywhere* that fell into American hands along the archipelagic line from Formosa to Mindanao would be sufficient to cut Japanese supply lines south between the Home Islands and the East Indies. And air bases on Luzon would not be any farther away from Japan than existing bases in the Marianas.

While Nimitz was undoubtedly impressive with his grasp of military and naval strategy, MacArthur proved his equal. According to Leahy, "MacArthur was convinced that the occupation of the Philippines was essential before any major attack in force should be made on Japanese held territory north of Luzon." Just when the general moved beyond military considerations to moral imperative is not wholly clear. According to his biographers, MacArthur on that first night proceeded to pull out all the stops: Filipinos languishing in captivity along with several thousand Americans, all suffering untold "privations"; the "old wounds" of Bataan and Corregidor with their powerful evocation of abandonment. "And if the Philippines alone were not enough, MacArthur admonished that the eyes of all Asia would be watching what we did in the Philippines"—or did not do. Speaking with consistent eloquence and no notes, the general "again and again . . . used the words 'ethical' and 'unethical,' 'virtue' and 'shame,'" to gradually wear Nimitz down and apparently convince his president. Leahy recalled, "As the discussions progressed," Nimitz "admitted that developments might indicate a necessity for occupation of the

Manila area" with its magnificent—if soon to be wreck-cluttered—harbor. Later, in a private meeting, MacArthur allegedly warned Roosevelt that if the archipelago was "abandoned," the voters would undoubtedly repudiate their president in the forthcoming fall national elections. If indeed the general felt impelled to express such a view, it proved unnecessary, for FDR, Leahy, and the rest of the presidential party came away from Pearl Harbor happy if not delighted with the results. Neither Pacific commander had demanded more troops or materiel. Whatever was finally decided, they claimed to have enough resources to do the job. Moreover, both MacArthur and Nimitz agreed that final decisions did not have to be made immediately; the early autumn would do.[30]

An impatient JCS did not agree. Even as the three men sat down in Hawaii, the Joint Staff planners in the Pentagon sent Nimitz a message "requesting views on meeting target date 15 November for LEYTE ISLAND by by-passing objectives or by compressing intervals between presently contemplated operations." The JWPC "express[ed] belief that 1 December is latest target date for LEYTE ISLAND."[31]

Nimitz later told his biographer, E. B. Potter, that MacArthur did not, in fact, adduce any of the political and moral imperatives set forth above until the final night of the conference, when Nimitz himself brought to MacArthur's attention the need to address the matters raised by the JCS message. It was then, according to Nimitz, that the general "blew up and made an oration of some length on the impossibility of bypassing the Philippines, his sacred obligations there," including to the 17 million Filipinos and the redemption of America's military honor, "etc. etc." When MacArthur proceeded to trash the JCS and its planners as armchair strategists who knew nothing of battle and of commitments formed in combat, Nimitz had had enough, replying that these were men striving to fulfill their responsibilities as ardently as anyone else and possessed more information and broader perspectives than any one theater commander.[32]

On his way back to Washington, FDR wrote MacArthur a somewhat cryptic note that nonetheless contained a pledge to see what he could do to get his Southwest Pacific commander's views incorporated as a strategic imperative. MacArthur, believing he had won his president over completely, was euphoric, whispering to a colleague on the flight back to Australia that the Philippines were a go, though not to be publicly announced "for a few days yet."[33] In fact, the president did nothing. According to Potter, Roosevelt "had no intention of imposing the MacArthur-Nimitz Honolulu agreement on the Joint Chiefs of Staff." He let Leahy brief the Chiefs, who were surprised if not dumbfounded to hear that the two Pacific commanders "had no disagreements at the moment" and none that could not be worked out as they arose.[34]

If anything changed as a consequence of the Pearl Harbor conference, it was Nimitz's commitment to Formosa. No less than half a dozen considerations began to work powerfully against any effort to seize all, or even the southern portion, of the island and the port of Amoy across the narrow strait. First, though probably not foremost, Halsey "steadfastly opposed" the Formosa-first plan, now opting for an invasion of Luzon rather than the central Philippines followed by a jump all the way up to Okinawa and then Japan. Second, Army planners argued that despite powerful air and sea resources, the Americans once on Formosa would not enjoy the "protective distance from major enemy bases" that they had in earlier operations. Third, there were thought to be insufficient aircraft available to neutralize all enemy airfields within range of southern Formosa and Amoy. Fourth, experience had indicated that available air and sea forces were insufficient to interdict strong Japanese reinforcement of the Formosan garrison from the mainland. Fifth, Army projections of Japanese troop strength on Formosa were markedly higher than Nimitz's planners had assumed. The Army estimated that it would need *at least* 77,000 additional "service troops" (i.e., stevedores, truck drivers, supply personnel, etc.) and perhaps as many as 200,000 to guarantee a successful lodgment and expansion. Sixth, news of the Pearl Harbor conference was released to the press on August 11 and broadly interpreted as a green light for MacArthur to invade the archipelago. Finally, the general informed the JCS on September 15 that he was ready to accelerate the Philippine schedule immediately. The southern campaign in Mindanao would be abandoned in favor of a direct jump from the Palaus (Central Pacific) and Morotai (Southwest Pacific) to the central Philippines at Leyte on October 20, with Luzon operations to follow several months later.[35]

By this time the only person of consequence to take up the cudgels for Formosa was Ernest King. But even he was weakening. On September 5, the Chief of Naval Operations provided his JCS colleagues with "a long summary of his conclusions." There were only three "realistic courses of action" to bring the Pacific War to a close. First, occupation of the entire Philippine archipelago; second, occupation of southwestern Formosa and Amoy; third, occupation of the southern end of Kyushu.

Conquest of the Philippines, King admitted, could be accomplished with existing resources; taking southern Formosa and Amoy would demand at least a half-million-man invasion force plus 100,000 service troops that King insisted could "probably" be made available. Investing Kyushu could probably be done with the same size force. Formosa and Kyushu operations would entail some risk of failure, "with a certainty of a high cost of life," but would end the war sooner. A Philippine operation would provide at least some of the elements for mounting a prolonged but far less costly blockade and siege of the enemy Home Islands that would eventually result in victory. "My conclusion," King stated, "is that America's least expensive course of action is to continue and intensify the air and sea blockade" of Japan "with an intensification of air bombardment" from the Marianas "of Japan's war industry and at the same time to re-occupy the Philippines. My second choice would be the Formosa-Amoy campaign. My third choice would be Kyushu."[36]

Consensus on future Pacific strategy awaited only the next King-Nimitz meeting in San Francisco, which took place at the end of the month. King at last agreed that a Formosa-Amoy campaign was "impractical." Nimitz accepted Army estimates of "requirements and shortages" and in light of the new realities he proposed what would be the final strategy of the Pacific War. MacArthur would reconquer the Philippines with a Luzon landing tentatively scheduled for mid-December. At the same time, Nimitz said, his Pacific Ocean area forces "could prepare to seize islands in the ... Bonins [i.e., Iwo Jima] on 20 January 1945 and the Ryukyus [Okinawa] on 1 March." In the event, this schedule had to be stretched by a month in the case of both operations. But it was never abandoned or modified.

Finally, Nimitz came to a subject that had hitherto been largely ignored for the past three months since the crushing victory in the skies and seas around the Marianas—the Imperial Japanese Navy. Nimitz told King that he "looked hopefully at the possibility of drawing out the Japanese fleet by these operations" and he pointed out that the Bonins would furnish fields from which fighters could support the B-29s in their long-distance raids on the enemy Home Islands, "a protection much desired by the Army Air Forces."[37]

And so, by early October 1944, the foundations had been firmly set for the conclusion, however protracted or foreshortened, of the Pacific War. Nimitz masterfully balanced and matched his resources and capabilities with his strategic objectives. His only misjudgement was how soon and where the drastically weakened but still threatening Imperial Japanese Navy would react. Whenever and wherever that happened, his sailors would be ready.

About the Author

Lisle Rose was born in Michigan in 1936. He enlisted in the Navy in July 1954 and served on three ships, the bulk of his time being spent as a polar sailor on board (then Navy) icebreaker *Staten Island*, in which he made two cruises to the Arctic and one to Antarctica (Operation DeepFreeze II, 1956–57).

Released from active duty in September 1957, Rose subsequently earned a bachelor's degree in history from the University of Illinois (1961) and a PhD in American history from the University of California, Berkeley, in 1966. Following teaching stints at the Universities of Nebraska and Arizona and Carnegie-Mellon University, he joined the U.S. Department of State in 1972, first as an editor of the *Foreign Relations* series, and then in the Bureau of Oceans and International Environmental and Scientific Affairs. In 1980, he was a member of the U.S. Delegation to the Third United Nations Conference on the Law of the Sea and also worked on Arctic matters and various aspects of international outer space affairs. He climaxed his diplomatic work as one of a two-person U.S. delegation that successfully developed a treaty framework for the Cospas-Sarsat international satellite-based search and rescue system in cooperation with Soviet, French, and Canadian representatives.

Rose retired from the State Department in 1989 to devote himself to writing. Since 1968, he has published fourteen books on U.S. Cold War, naval, and polar affairs, including the three-volume *Power at Sea* (University of Missouri Press, 2006). His latest book is *America's Sailors in the Great War* (Missouri, 2016).

He lives in Edmonds, Washington, with his wife, the historian Harriet Dashiell Schwar.

Notes

1. Robert Ross Smith, "Luzon Versus Formosa," 462–63, online at http://history.army.mil/books/70-7_21.htm. A footnote indicates that this text "is essentially Chapter 1" of Smith, *Triumph in the Philippines*, one of the multivolume "Greenback series" *United States Army in World War II*.

2. William J. Sebald, oral history, 285, 290; Ruthven E. Libby, oral history, 137; Robert Lee Dennison, oral history, 72; Bernard L. Austin, oral history, 354; all included in United States Naval Institute Oral History Program, copies at United States Naval Institute Library, Annapolis, Maryland. Hereafter cited as subject and oral history.
3. Sebald, oral history, 286; Dennison, oral history, 68–69.
4. Dennison, oral history, 70.
5. Dennison, oral history, 463; Steven L. Rearden, *Council of War: A History of the Joint Chiefs of Staff, 1942–1991* (Washington, D.C.: Joint Chiefs of Staff Historical Office, 2012), 40–41.
6. Capt. Henri H. Smith-Hutton, oral history, 441.
7. Smith-Hutton, oral history, 441.
8. Smith-Hutton, oral history, 444; Bernhard H. Bieri, oral history, 134–36.
9. Allen G. Quynn, oral history, 29, in Recollections of Fleet Admiral Chester W. Nimitz oral history.
10. Bieri, oral history, 134, 138; D. Clayton James, *The Years of MacArthur*, 3 vols. (Boston: Houghton, Mifflin Company, 1974–1982), 2:412.
11. Ernest J. King and Walter Muir Whitehill, *Fleet Admiral King: A Naval Record* (New York: W. W. Norton, 1952), 229.
12. Grace Person Hayes, *The History of the Joint Chiefs of Staff in World War II* (Annapolis: Naval Institute Press, 1982), 604; E. B. Potter, *Nimitz* (Annapolis: Naval Institute Press, 1976), 288.
13. The Nimitz-King meeting is recounted in King and Whitehill's *Fleet Admiral King*, 539–42. (Emphasis in original.)
14. William F. Halsey and J. Bryan III, *Admiral Halsey's Story* (New York: McGraw-Hill, 1947), 195.
15. Halsey and Bryan, *Admiral Halsey's Story*, 195.
16. Halsey and Bryan, *Admiral Halsey's Story*, 195.
17. Halsey and Bryan, *Admiral Halsey's Story*, 195; Barbara W. Tuchman, *Stilwell and the American Experience in China, 1911–1945* (New York: Macmillan, 1970), 455.
18. Rearden, *Council of War*, 37.
19. Hayes, *History of the Joint Chiefs*, 605.
20. MacArthur's comment on suffering Filipinos is quoted in Hayes, *History of the Joint Chiefs*, 607; his demand to present his views personally in Washington is quoted in Potter, *Nimitz*, 310, and Hayes, *History of the Joint Chiefs*, 606.

21. Masanori Ito, *The End of the Imperial Japanese Navy: A Japanese Account of the Rise and Fall of Japan's Sea Power*, trans. Andrew Y. Kuroda and Roger Pineau (New York: MacFadden Books, 1965), 91; Sebald, oral history, 288, 292.
22. American Naval Records Society, *Nimitz Grey Book*, 8 vols., 2012, vol. 5, entries 24, 27, 28 June.
23. Hayes, *History of the Joint Chiefs*, 607; James W. Archer, oral history, 22, in Recollections of Fleet Admiral Chester W. Nimitz oral history collection.
24. Hayes, *History of the Joint Chiefs*, 609.
25. Hayes, *History of the Joint Chiefs*, 608.
26. Fleet Adm. William D. Leahy, *I Was There* (New York: Victor Gollancz Limited, 1950), 250.
27. Potter, *Nimitz*, 291–92.
28. Potter, *Nimitz*, 317.
29. King and Whitehill, *Fleet Admiral King*, 567; Potter, *Nimitz*, 317–18; Leahy, *I Was There*, 229, 250.
30. Leahy, *I Was There*, 250–51; Thomas J. Cutler, *The Battle of Leyte Gulf* (New York: Pocket Books, 1994), 37; William Manchester, *American Caesar: Douglas MacArthur, 1880–1964* (Boston: Little, Brown, 1978), 369; William B. Hopkins, *The Pacific War: The Strategy, Politics, and Players That Won the War* (Minneapolis: The Zenith Press, 2008), 242–43.
31. *Nimitz Grey Book*, vol. 5, entry 28 July 1944.
32. Potter, *Nimitz*, 291–92.
33. Cutler, *Battle of Leyte Gulf*, 37–38; Hayes, *History of the Joint Chiefs*, 611; Leahy, *I Was There*, 250–51. MacArthur's euphoric mood is recounted in Hopkins, *Pacific War*, 242.
34. Potter, *Nimitz*, 321.
35. Smith, "Luzon Versus Formosa," 471–72.
36. Quoted in Hayes, *History of the Joint Chiefs*, 618–19.
37. Hayes, *History of the Joint Chiefs*, 623.

3

ALLIED PLANS AND OPERATIONAL ART

Milan Vego

THE LEYTE OPERATION WAS THE FIRST major joint/combined operation in the Philippines Campaign (October 1944–August 1945). Most of the operational planning for the Leyte operation was conducted by Gen. Douglas MacArthur's General Headquarters (GHQ), Southwest Pacific Area (SWPA), and Gen. Walter Krueger's Sixth Army Headquarters in late summer of 1944. Vice Adm. Thomas C. Kinkaid, Commander, Allied Naval Forces (CANF), and Gen. C. Kenney, Commander, Allied Air Forces (CAAF), drafted plans for the respective major operations. In addition to his position as CANF, Admiral Kinkaid was also Commander, U.S. Seventh Fleet, and Commander, Central Philippines Attack Force (CTF 77). Hence, he was also a major tactical commander. This in turn created the potential for neglecting his basic responsibilities as commander of the Allied Naval Forces.[1] Adm. Chester W. Nimitz's headquarters of Pacific Ocean Area (POA)/U.S. Pacific Fleet in Pearl Harbor, Hawaii, and Adm. William F. Halsey's staff of the Third Fleet Staff drafted their own plans in support of the Leyte operation.

CINCSWPA Plans

The first version of the plan for the Philippine campaign (codenamed Operation Musketeer I) was issued on 10 July 1944. The operational idea was to capture a series of positions along the east coast of the Philippines to serve as bases for the final attack on Luzon. The campaign plan Musketeer I consisted of a series of major and some minor operations (codenamed King, Love, Mike, and Victor).[2] The plan envisaged capturing

Sarangani Bay on 15 November (Operation King I), followed by landing on Leyte on 20 December (Operation King II). The plan provided for the capture of air and naval bases in central Luzon in January and February 1945 (Love operations) and some other important positions on Luzon in April and May 1945 (Mike operations). It also included a series of operations aimed to reduce enemy garrisons in bypassed parts of Mindanao and the Visayas (Victor operations).³

Operational sequencing outlined in the Musketeer I campaign plan was subsequently discussed in a series of meetings held at Brisbane, Australia, between early July and September 1944 (codenamed Wideawake). Representatives of the GHQ/SWPA, and the subordinate headquarters prepared a series of staff studies covering the planned operations. After the July conferences at Brisbane and Pearl Harbor, the Musketeer I campaign plan was revised in accordance with arrangements made for the allocation and use of amphibious shipping, anticipated fleet support, and the availability of ground forces.

The second version of the Philippines Campaign plan (Musketeer II) was issued on 29 August 1944. The ultimate (strategic) objective was to destroy or contain enemy forces in the Philippines, provide air support, and secure bases for further operations. It was also aimed to reduce the Japanese strength by destroying installations in the eastern Netherlands East Indies (NEI), and northern Borneo–South China Sea areas. The SWPA's forces would "reestablish and defend the constituted government of the Philippine Islands." The planners assumed that the enemy would make "a major national effort" to defend the Philippines. The principal concentrations of the enemy ground forces would be in Mindanao, central Visayas, and central Luzon. The island of Leyte would be defended by at least one infantry division. The SWPA's planners assumed that the Japanese would maintain strong land-based air forces in the Philippines-Formosa area. Another planning assumption was that the Allies would render enemy airpower in the Philippines ineffective by 20 February 1945 (target date for invasion of Luzon).⁴ The planners also assumed that the full support of the U.S. Pacific Fleet would be available not only for securing a foothold on the eastern coast of the Philippine archipelago but also in supporting the invasion of central Luzon.⁵

The Musketeer II plan had different operational sequencing of intermediate objectives from the first version of the plan. It envisaged two preliminary operations: King I (amphibious landing at Sarangani Bay) and King III (airborne landing at Misamis Oriental) to take place on 15 November and 7 December, respectively. They would be followed with Operation King II on 20 December 1944, which aimed to capture the Leyte Gulf area.[6]

The Love series of operations aimed to capture Aparri on 31 January 1945 and Mindoro on 15 February. Afterward, Aparri and Mindoro would provide air bases and logistical facilities in support of operations in central Luzon. The main Allied forces would land at Lingayen Bay on 20 February 1945 (Operation Mike I). Another, smaller landing would take place (if necessary) at Dingalan Bay on 4–15 March (Operation Mike II). The Allied forces would capture the Manila area and the central plain and then secure the remaining area of Luzon.[7] A series of smaller landings would be conducted to capture bypassed positions (Victor operations).[8]

The primary reason for selecting Leyte as the initial operational objective in the Philippines Campaign was the Allied belief that the island, with its large and fertile Leyte Valley, offered a favorable place for the construction of airfields from which large-scale attacks could be launched against Luzon and the rest of the Philippines and China. However, Leyte was later deemed unsuitable for the construction of a large number of airfields and air facilities. The Allied planners correctly believed, however, that Leyte would provide an excellent anchorage together with sites for supply bases.[9]

At the Allied Second Quebec Conference (codenamed Octagon) on 12–16 September 1944, the Combined Chiefs of Staff (CCS) twice changed the timetable for Pacific operations. MacArthur's forces would capture Morotai and Nimitz's forces would seize Peleliu in September. Admiral Nimitz's POA forces would invade Yap and Ulithi in October and then move into Talaud (north of Sulawesi Island). In November, MacArthur would seize Sarangani Bay. In December, MacArthur and Nimitz would jointly capture Leyte; followed by the landing on Luzon or Formosa. The second change was prompted by events in the Pacific. Aircraft of the Third Fleet struck Yap and the Palau islands on 7 and 8 September and for the next two days, Mindanao as well. In the wake of these attacks, Adm. William F. Halsey, Commander, Third Fleet, informed Nimitz and MacArthur that few serviceable Japanese aircraft were left in the Philippines; the bulk of the enemy oil supplies were destroyed; there was no shipping left to sink; and, in his view, the entire area was wide open for an Allied attack. He recommended that the Pacific Fleet and the Seventh

Fleet jointly invade Leyte on 20 October—two months ahead of schedule. Nimitz on his part recommended that the intermediate operations against Yap, Talaud, and Sarangani Bay be canceled, as Leyte could be captured easily and without any intermediate operation.[10] On 15 September, the highest Allied political and military leaders met at Quebec and took both commanders' suggestions. They decided to cancel the intermediate operations for seizing Yap, Talaud, and Sarangani, and directed MacArthur and Nimitz to coordinate their plans and invade Leyte on 20 October. In order not to overshadow the D-Day for the Normandy invasion, MacArthur designated the day of the Leyte invasion as A-Day.[11] He reportedly said that Leyte would be "the anvil against which I hope to hammer the Japanese into submission in the central Philippines—the springboard from which I could proceed to the conquest of Luzon or the final assault against Japan itself."[12]

In retrospect, the strategic decision to invade Leyte first instead of Mindanao was a bold but very risky move. MacArthur's forces would be inserted into the central part of the Philippine archipelago and thereby obtain a commanding position to neutralize the enemy's airpower on Luzon, thus isolating the enemy forces on Mindanao. By canceling the Sarangani operation, the potentially long and costly struggle for control of Mindanao would be avoided. Another advantage of advancing the target date was to deny the enemy enough time to prepare his defenses, and especially to reconstitute the combat potential of his carrier forces. Because Leyte was located beyond the effective range of the SWPA's land-based aircraft, it was critical that the U.S. Third Fleet provide reliable and timely cover and support. Yet advancing the original date for the Leyte operation by about two months was bound to create rather serious problems for the Allied operational planners and complicate logistical support and sustainment.

GHQ/SWPA Plans

In his Operations Instruction No. 70 issued on 21 September, MacArthur directed that SWPA forces covered and supported by the Third Fleet would reoccupy the Philippines by capturing positions in the Leyte and western Samar areas, and establish naval, air, and logistic facilities for the support of future operations.[13] Leyte's northwestern coastal plain was selected as the best for landing because the eighteen-mile-long stretch of coast between Dulag and San Jose would allow for the early capture of the critically important Tacloban airfield. It would also enable the Allies to control the San Juanico Strait and bring landing forces within striking distance of the Panaon Strait, some seventy miles south of the main landing beaches. Another factor in selecting the Dulag–San Jose area was an intelligence estimate that suggested that the beaches were not heavily defended, though the enemy had prepared some fortifications along the inland road net.[14]

MacArthur specified that the Sixth Army, supported by the Allied naval and air forces, would capture the Tacloban and Dulag areas. Homonhon and Dinagat Islands would be seized prior to the main assault to give amphibious shipping uninterrupted access to Leyte Gulf. The Panaon Strait would be captured to allow Allied forces to operate in the Camotes Sea. Another objective was to obtain control of the San Juanico Strait to allow passage of the Allied naval forces for operations in the Samar Sea. Successive objectives included capturing the remainder of Leyte Island, occupying and consolidating control over the western part of southern Samar, and seizing positions that would allow the opening of Surigao Strait for Allied ships. In the next phase, the Sixth Army would consolidate control over Samar, destroy or contain hostile garrisons in the Visayas, assume control and direct the operations of the Filipino forces in the Leyte-Samar area, occupy and defend sites for radar and air warning installations, and establish air facilities in Leyte.[15]

GHQ/SWPA's operational idea for the Leyte landing was not innovative: a frontal attack on the enemy's positions on the eastern coast of Leyte followed by advances on a broad front inland to seize the rest of the island. The risks in this were low, but so were the potential gains. The combination of the difficult mountainous and forested terrain, the high possibility of typhoons with their attendant torrential rains, and the enemy's stubborn resistance made it more likely that the Allied progress on land would be slow. It would progressively call for larger forces to be committed on the island. The situation would be even more complicated for the Allies if the Japanese decided to pour large numbers of troops into Leyte from the adjacent islands. The only large port on the western coast of the island that could be used for such purposes was Ormoc. Hence, it was critical that the Allied forces prevent the Japanese from using Ormoc and adjacent beaches as destination points for the transport of their troops and materiel to Leyte. The chances of achieving a relatively quick capture of Leyte would have been much greater if MacArthur's operational idea included landing in Ormoc Bay, carried out sometime after the main landings at Tacloban and Dulag. This turning maneuver from across the sea would essentially have sealed the fate of the enemy defenders because they would have been cut off from any large-scale reinforcements from the adjacent islands. Such a maneuver would have been riskier than a slow advance across the island, but would have resulted in a much shorter operation and lower Allied losses in personnel and materiel.

Sixth Army Plans

Planning for the ground phase of the Leyte operation was complicated because precise information on the island's topography was sorely lacking. This was somewhat surprising, because the United States had governed the area for more than forty years.[16] Moreover, the Allied planners had several months to obtain detailed and reliable information about the island prior to the invasion. General Krueger issued his field order for the Leyte operation on 23 September 1944. He was formally Commander, Assault Task Forces and also Commander, Ground Assault Forces (Sixth Army). Krueger's operational idea for the landing envisaged four main phases of the operation (see Map 1). In Phase I, the 6th Ranger Infantry Battalion would capture three islands controlling the eastern approaches to Leyte Gulf on 18 October (A-2 Day). This phase also included clearing mines in Leyte Gulf. The landings on Homonhon and Dinagat islands would be carried out on A-3, or one day earlier than initially planned, to ensure sufficient time for clearing mines in Leyte Gulf. The 21st Infantry Regiment (IR) was directed to provide two rifle companies to reinforce the 6th Ranger Infantry Battalion on Homonhon and Dinagat islands from A-3 to A-1 inclusive.[17]

The main landings were planned to take place in Phase II (A-Day to A+6) of the operation. The aim was to occupy the Tacloban-Dulag area and also establish local air control there. Specifically, on A-Day, X Corps would land at the northern end of Leyte Gulf to quickly capture Tacloban and its airfield on Cataisan Point, Palo airfield. It would also establish control of the San Juanico Strait, and then advance through the Leyte Valley to Carigara (on the north-central coast of Leyte). Both shores of the Panaon Strait would be captured to allow small craft access into the Camotes Sea. Control of the San Juanico Strait would allow Allied light naval forces access to the Samar Sea.[18] At the same time, the XXIV Corps would land about fifteen miles south of X Corps, near Dulag, and rapidly advance to seize the Dulag-Burauen-Dagami-Tanauan area with its airfields and then capture Abuyog. It would then advance across the island to Baybay on the west coast.[19]

The wide separation between the landing beaches of the two corps was dictated by the need to allow sufficient maneuvering room for large numbers of transports and fire support ships. In addition, the need to seize control of the roads connecting Dulag and the Burauen airfield area with Dagami and Tanauan, and to quickly reach the Burauen airfield, dictated the selection of the Dulag beaches for the landing of the XXIV Corps.[20]

In Phase III (A+7 to A+11), X and XXIV Corps would advance separately through the mountains to clear enemy forces from the Ormoc Valley and the west coast. At the same time, Allied troops would land on western Samar and establish a foothold there.[21] Surigao Strait would be open to allow naval movements into the Camotes Sea and adjacent waters.

In Phase IV (after A+12; no ending date was provided) of the operation, the Sixth Army would initiate an overland advance and conduct minor amphibious landings as the situation dictated, aimed at destroying or containing the enemy forces in northern Samar or the central Visayas threatening the development of the Allied facilities in the Leyte area. The length of this phase was left undetermined.[22]

After A+3 Day, the 32nd Infantry Division (ID) and the 77th ID would embark on twenty-four-hours' notice to reinforce Sixth Army elements in the landing objective area. However, neither division could arrive in the objective area before mid-November because of the lack of amphibious lift. The selection of an Army floating reserve for possible employment in the zone of either corps also presented a problem because it had to be drawn from one of four divisions to be employed on A-Day. Finally, a decision was made that the 96th ID would provide one regiment to serve as a floating reserve.[23]

Plans for Allied Naval Forces

Task Force (TF) 77 consisted of two major task forces: the Northern Attack Force (TF 78) and the Southern Attack Force (TF 79). Other elements of the invasion force were Bombardment and Fire Support Group (TG 77.2); Close Covering Group (TG 77.3); Escort Carrier Group (TG

77.4); Minesweeping and Hydrographic Group (TG 77.5); and Beach and Demolition Group (TG 77.6). Also taking part in the Leyte operation were TF 71 Submarines West Australia, TF 72 Submarines East Australia, and TG 70.1 Motor Torpedo Boats (MTBs).

Admiral Kinkaid issued two plans for the Leyte operation. Operation Plan No. 12-44 for the Allied Naval Forces of 25 September was based on MacArthur's Operations Instructions Nr. 70. It was rather short (seven pages) and contained only one annex. Operation Plan No. 13-44, issued on 26 September for TF 77, was much longer and more detailed.[24] Operation Plan 12-44 directed that Allied naval forces transport and establish landing forces in the Leyte-Surigao area and provide air protection for convoys and naval task forces. Direct air support for the landing would be provided in coordination with Commander, Third Fleet, and Commander, Allied Air Forces. The Allied Naval Forces were also directed to arrange direct air support and cover with carrier aircraft of minesweeping and preliminary landings in the Leyte Gulf area between A-2 and the time escort carriers assumed the tasks of direct support on A-Day. Direct air support would be the responsibility of General Kenney after land-based fighters and light bombers were established in the Leyte area. Allied Naval Forces would also be responsible for escorting and protecting Allied ships into the Leyte Gulf and Samar area and establishing forces to support current and future operations in Visayan waters.[25]

Operation Plan 13-44 Central Philippines Attack Force, issued on 26 September 1944, was a tactical plan. It repeated in large part the scheme of maneuver explained in the Sixth Army's plan. The XXIV Army Corps (7th ID, 96th ID), the X Army Corps (1st Cavalry Division, 24th ID), and the 98th Ranger Battalion were designated landing forces. The XXIV Army Corps was the landing force of the Southern Attack Force under Vice Adm. Theodore S. Wilkinson, while the X Army Corps provided the landing force for the Northern Attack Force under Rear Adm. Daniel E. Barbey. Both forces would be under Kinkaid's command. Each force would depart mounting areas and rendezvous as directed, en route to the objective area. Both forces would land the main elements as nearly simultaneously as practicable at H-hour on A-Day (20 October).[26]

Plan 13-44 also included the tasks of the Third Fleet in support of the Leyte operation. Among other things, Third Fleet was to strike targets in the Luzon-Bicol area and the Leyte-Cebu-Negros area in support of the landing in the Leyte area. Third Fleet would operate in "strategic" (actually operational in today's terms) support of the operation and carry out strikes as the situation at the time required.²⁷

In Operation Plan 12-44, Kinkaid directed TF 71 (West Australia) and TF 72 (East Australia) submarines to continue to present missions to the fullest extent practicable and to station strong offensive and reconnaissance patrols and lifeguard submarines in accordance with the instructions to be issued by Commander, Seventh Fleet. In general, submarines would "interdict and report enemy surface forces in the approaches to our movement routes and objective area." In his dispatch on 9 October, Kinkaid specified that TF 71 and TF 72 would conduct "strategic" patrols and "offensive reconnaissance" across the most likely lines of advance by enemy surface forces. Specifically, TF 71 would maintain "strong patrols" in the Makassar Strait and along the western entrances to the Celebes and Sulu Seas. In coordination with submarines of the Pacific Fleet (TF 17), they would also maintain "strong" patrols in the Hainan–Northern Luzon area and provide prompt and early warning on the movements of enemy forces. The submarines of TF 72 (East Australia) had the task of conducting "strong" offensive reconnaissance, providing lifeguard service, and reporting and interdicting enemy surface ships close to Allied routes and in the approaches to the landing objective area.²⁸

TF 71 had too few submarines to accomplish its assigned missions. This was the reason why some of the most important straits and passages guarding the western approaches to the Philippines were left uncovered. Among other areas, the Linapacan (northwest Palawan) and Mindoro straits, the Verde Passage, the approaches to the Sulu Sea and to the Celebes Sea, and the Hainan-Luzon area were not covered. More serious, no TF 71 submarines were deployed to monitor the Lingga-Singapore area. Yet they *were* able to cover the western approaches to the Philippines and the critically important Lingga-Singapore area if antishipping patrols were reduced to the minimum.²⁹

Allied Air Forces Plans

MacArthur's Operations Instruction No. 70 covered only in broad terms the employment of Allied Air Forces for the Leyte operation. The details were left to General Kenney. In his Letter of Instruction No. 71, issued on 24 September, Kenney designated the Fifth Air Force as the air assault force, with the Thirteenth Air Force and the RAAF providing support as necessary. The Fifth Air Force was commanded by Maj. Gen. E. C. Whitehead (Air Corps), USA, with headquarters at Owi, Schouten Islands, while the Thirteenth Air Force was under Maj. Gen. St. Clair Streett (AC), USA, with headquarters at Noemfoor, New Guinea. After 1 November 1944, the Fifth Air Force HQ moved to Morotai.[30] In addition, the Northern Solomons Air Group (TG 70.9) (Torokina, Bougainville), Royal Australian Air Force Command (RAAFC) (Brisbane), and Air Force, Seventh Fleet (TF 73) (AV 7 *Currituck* at Manus) also took part in supporting the Leyte operation.

In the same letter of instruction (No. 71), Kenney directed that the primary mission of the Allied Air Forces was the neutralization of hostile naval and air forces in the Philippines archipelago in coordination with Third Fleet carriers. After A-9 Day, these efforts would be intensified in the western Visayas and the Mindanao area. Secondary missions included aerial reconnaissance and the protection of the Allied convoys and naval forces. Kenney stipulated that Allied Air Forces would assume direct support of the operation in the Leyte-Samar area after fighters and light bombers were established on Leyte. In the meantime, they would continue destroying hostile naval and air forces and shipping in the Arafura and Celebes Sea area and striking targets on northeastern Borneo and the Sulu archipelago. Other missions of the Allied Air Forces were to deny the enemy the use of naval facilities in the Sulu archipelago and to protect the western flank of the operation.[31]

Kenney's plan was modified in his Operations Instruction No. 6, issued on 29 September. He specified that prior to A-2 (not after A-9 Day as originally planned), the Fifth Air Force would neutralize the western Visayas and Mindanao and destroy enemy air and surface forces and shipping in the Celebes Sea. The task of the Thirteenth Air Force was to conduct aerial reconnaissance and destroy hostile air forces and installations in the bypassed areas. The latter would establish an air blockade of Makassar Strait and prepare to relieve the Fifth Air Force. Another change in the plan was issued on 4 October. Among other things, the Fifth Air Force was directed, starting on A-10 Day, to neutralize Japanese air forces and shipping in the Mindanao area south of latitude 08° 45' N. After heavy bombers were based on Morotai, these efforts would be extended to encompass the Visayas, but exclude the Leyte and Samar areas. However, after the departure of escort carriers, Leyte and Samar would be included in these efforts as well. Another change was to initiate strikes against the Brunei area of Borneo "at the earliest practicable date."[32]

The Northern Solomons Air Group and RAAFC were directed to protect bases in the rear area and destroy enemy forces in bypassed areas. The RAAFC, in cooperation with the Thirteenth Air Force, would maintain an air blockade of the Banda Sea between Timor and Ceram, destroying enemy installations and sources of war materials in the eastern part of the Netherlands East Indies, and conducting antisubmarine patrols.[33]

CINCPOA's Plans

Planning for the Leyte operation was conducted in the Hawaii headquarters of Commander in Chief Pacific Ocean Areas (CINCPOA), in conjunction with the staffs of Third Fleet and Task Force 38 (TF 38—Third Fleet's carrier strike force). The Third Fleet's broad mission, as stated in MacArthur's Operations Instruction, was to provide cover and support to contain and destroy the enemy fleet. Specifically, the Third Fleet would take out hostile air and sea forces in the Formosa, Luzon, Visayas, and Mindanao areas from A-9 through A-3, and from A-Day through A+30, if necessary. It was also directed to destroy enemy ground defenses and installations and shipping in the landing area and adjacent areas from A-2 until escort carriers could assume the mission of direct support.[34]

In Operation Plan 8-44, issued on 27 September, Nimitz directed POA forces to support SWPA forces in the central Philippines. However, he made some important changes in paragraph 2 (Mission) of his plan. Believing it critically important that the major part of the Japanese fleet be destroyed, he directed the Western Pacific Task Forces (under Halsey) to "destroy enemy naval and air forces in or threatening the Philippines Area and protect air and sea communications along Central Pacific axis." The most controversial part was subparagraph X-Ray of paragraph 3 (Execution), which stated that "in case opportunity for destruction of major portion of the enemy fleet offer[s] or can be created, such destruction becomes the primary task."[35] This change explains the reasons for Halsey's later decision to abandon guarding San Bernardino Strait, which subsequently led to the battle off Cape Engano. Nimitz was telling Halsey that he should destroy enemy naval and air forces threatening not only the Philippines, but almost anywhere else, too—*so long* (author's italics) as their destruction contributes to the protection and support of SWPA's forces.

This was a caveat that Halsey should have taken into account when making the decisions in the course of the execution of the operation.[36]

Nimitz, in fact, had the same view on the critical importance of destroying the major part of the Japanese fleet in issuing the plan for the invasion of the Palaus in August 1944. Then he gave Halsey an almost identical mission.[37] Unlike other directives issued by CINCPOA's staff, this directive to the Third Fleet did not include a number or a letter designation. Some historians speculate (without providing evidence) that aviators on Nimitz's staff added the wording to give Halsey freedom to do what Adm. Raymond A. Spruance supposedly failed to do in the Battle of the Philippines Sea—destroy the major part of the enemy fleet. Yet even if that was true, this did not replace the original mission of providing cover and support to the landing at Leyte, because it did not specify that the destruction of the enemy fleet was Halsey's sole and most important mission.[38] Whatever the case may have been, adding a new task to task(s) already assigned considerably complicated the execution of the assigned missions and opened the way for all possible interpretations on the part of Halsey and his staff.

Based on CINCPOA's Plan 8-44, Admiral Halsey issued his Operation Order 21-44 on 4 October 1944. He repeated the task of destroying the enemy fleet by employing his entire force. Halsey also directed that after fueling on 19 October, four carrier task groups of TF 38 would join off Samar, "from where all groups [would] support landing operation at Leyte as later directed, and as coordinated by the Commander, Seventh Fleet." This mission was in accordance with the agreement between Nimitz and Macarthur through their respective planners: the Third Fleet, including four carrier groups, would provide "strategic" (operational) cover and support for King II on D-1 and afterward.

Halsey stressed that cooperation with other forces should not discourage employment of Third Fleet carrier forces to attack enemy forces within their range. He envisaged that TF 34 (Heavy Surface Striking Force) would be initially deployed in the most probable direction of the enemy fleet and would be provided with adequate air cover. TF 38 would search for the enemy, provide air cover, launch strikes, and be prepared to coordinate strikes with TF 34. Halsey highlighted that "every attempt should be made to create [a] situation in which the enemy may be attacked by a predawn or dawn strike when TF 34 is in position to engage decisively at an early date." TGs 35.1 and 35.2 (Light Surface Striking Forces) would defend aircraft carriers against surface attack. If ordered, these two groups would support TF 34 or attack enemy forces.[39]

The Third Fleet's Plan 21-44 for providing distant (or operational) cover and support for the King II Operation also included a section on striking Okinawa, Formosa, Luzon, and the Visayas. The objective was to inflict maximum damage on enemy air and surface forces and ground installations. In modern terms, this objective constituted *operational fires*—a series of attacks and strikes aimed to prevent the arrival of the enemy's forces and logistical supplies to the areas where a major operation or campaign is being conducted. Another purpose was to isolate the central Philippines from the rest of the Japanese-controlled areas in the western Pacific. The planned employment of the Third Fleet amounted to a major offensive naval operation aimed at accomplishing an operational objective—establishing a virtual blockade of the northern and northwestern approaches to the Philippines.

The plan specifically directed that TF 38, after refueling on 7 October, would proceed to a launching position on 9 October. All four carrier groups would attack selected targets on Okinawa starting at dawn on 10 October. After completing refueling the next day, TF 38 would arrive at a position southeast of Formosa and conduct a feint toward Luzon by carrying out a fighter sweep of the northern Luzon area. On 12–13 October, all four carrier groups would conduct sustained strikes on Formosa. After arriving at the next refueling area at about 0700 on 15 October, three carrier groups (TGs 38.2, 38.3, 38.4) would strike the Luzon-Bicol area during the next two days. TG 38.1 would sail to a position off Samar from which to strike the Visayas for three days, starting on 16 October. Upon completing the strikes on Luzon on 17 October, TG 38.4 would join TG 38.1 off Samar, and they would jointly attack the Visayas area the next day. After refueling that day, two carrier groups (TG 38.2; TG 38.3) would proceed to the area eastward of Samar and then strike targets in the Visayas on 20 October. Afterward, all four groups would concentrate off Samar and provide support to the landing at Leyte as directed and coordinated by Commander, Seventh Fleet. Among other things, the plan stated that TG 30.5 would conduct a long-range search from the Marianas and Kossol Passage to intercept and destroy enemy search aircraft in the vicinity of TF 38 on 8 and 9 October, and, if possible, also on 10 October. TF 59 (Forward Area, Central Pacific Force) would carry out its assigned mission, but maximum efforts would be spent in striking targets on the Volcano and Bonin islands on 8–10 October inclusive.[40]

The Third Fleet staff prepared a plan to deceive the Japanese about the real purpose of TF 38's attack on Okinawa. Operation Order 20-44, issued on 3 October, envisioned the bombardment of weakly defended Marcus Island by TF 57 (Shore Based Air Force, Forward Area) and TF 59 on 10 October to create a diversion. Specifically, the bombardment would be conducted by the newly formed TG 30.2 (three cruisers and six destroyers). CINCPOA's intelligence assessment concluded that the enemy had no aircraft on the island. TF 59 would conduct aerial daylight reconnaissance over Marcus on 7 and 8 October. The plan envisaged TG 30.2 departing from Saipan and reaching the vicinity of Marcus in the early morning of 9 October. In case aerial reconnaissance revealed substantial reinforcements of enemy aircraft, the diversionary bombardment would be canceled, and the task group would return to Saipan.[41] However, this plan was directed against too small an objective to cause the enemy to react even tactically, not to say operationally. Also, the forces assigned to the task were too small to give the enemy much to worry about.

CINCPOA's Submarines

Nimitz directed that Adm. Charles A. Lockwood, the commander of TF 17 (Submarines), would support the Leyte operation, both during the preliminaries and its execution, by intercepting, reporting, and destroying enemy forces approaching the area of operations or retiring from it; destroying enemy merchant ships; and performing lifeguard duties. These tasks were not in fact new. In early 1943, Nimitz directed TF 17 to inflict maximum damage on enemy ships and shipping by offensive patrols at enemy shipping focal points; to plant offensive minefields in suitable enemy waters to destroy enemy ships; and to force the enemy to adopt countermeasures.[42] Lockwood specified that TF 17 would support the Leyte operation by establishing and maintaining patrols on the Formosa-Luzon line and off Tokyo Bay and Sasebo. TF 17 submarines were directed to patrol waters where profitable targets might be expected and where ships trying to escape TF 38's carrier strikes might be encountered. He also established a submarine patrol (HYZ Patrol) to cover the Ryukyus area.[43] In his operation order issued on 25 September, Lockwood directed TG 17.17 to conduct offensive patrols in empire waters, destroying enemy forces and reporting on the movement of important naval vessels. The task group would prevent undetected sorties of enemy task forces through Bungo-suido (channel separating the islands of Kyushu and Shikoku). The same order directed that six boats would sortie on 7 October to their respective patrolling areas in the Formosa Rotating Patrol (known as "Convoy College"). Another six boats were ordered to sortie on 26 October to the same patrolling area. Six other boats would depart between 21 and 30 October to their patrolling area in the China Rotating Patrol (codenamed "Maru Morgue"). One boat was scheduled for a sortie to the Bonin Rotating Patrol ("Dunkers Derby") on 16 October and another boat to a subarea of the "Hit Parade" (south of Kyūshū-Honshū) patrolling area on 26 October.[44]

On 28 September, Halsey expressed his unease to Nimitz about the TF 17 submarines' dispositions for the pending Leyte operation. He was especially concerned that the approaches to the Kii Channel and Shimonoseki Strait were left unguarded. On the other hand, TF 17 submarines deployed off Yokosuka and Sasebo operated too close to the shore for establishing contacts and trailing enemy ships, because of the proximity of the Japanese shore-based aircraft. Halsey was also worried about a large gap in the submarine dispositions between the China and the Formosa rotating patrolling areas. These weaknesses in the submarine dispositions could result in the enemy fleet reaching open waters without Halsey receiving timely information on its movements.[45]

Conclusion

Planning for the Leyte operation by the operational-strategic and operational levels of command followed standard U.S. procedures. The basic plans were short and succinct. Details on the key aspects of the basic operation plan were explained in some detail in annexes. The operational idea (or scheme of maneuver in U.S. terms) for the Leyte operation was not bold and innovative. This, in turn, precluded a quick capture of the island of Leyte. Perhaps if the main landing in Leyte Gulf had been combined with a supporting attack aimed to capture the port of Ormoc on Leyte's western coast, the protracted struggle to consolidate operational success accomplished by the end of the amphibious phase of the main landing would have been avoided. Because the Japanese were able to bring fresh troops to Leyte by using mainly Ormoc as a port of debarkation, the island was not secured until Christmas 1944. Plans of SWPA's service component commanders were prepared based on General MacArthur's plans. However, Admiral Kinkaid was also involved in planning for the employment of major tactical forces (Central Philippines Attack Force). The reason was that he was not only an operational but also a major tactical commander.

The single biggest problem in planning for the Leyte operation was the lack of unity of command at the operational-strategic levels. General MacArthur did not have operational command over the Third Fleet and other POA forces taking part in the operation. There was not a single operational plan issued by one overall commander. Both MacArthur and Nimitz issued separate operational plans. This was the major reason for a disconnect between the mission given by Admiral Nimitz to Halsey and General MacArthur's need for distant cover and support by the Third Fleet. This, in turn, was one of the key elements in Halsey's decision to move northward with the entire TF 38. In so doing, he uncovered San Bernardino Strait and potentially exposed Allied forces in the Leyte Gulf to attack by the powerful Japanese heavy surface force led by Vice Admiral Takeo Kurita. That the worst did not happen, because Kurita turned away when he was on the verge of victory in the Battle off Samar on 25 October 1944, did not justify unsound command arrangements between SWPA and POA in the Leyte operation. But the responsibility for that situation lay not with MacArthur and Nimitz but with the highest politico-military leadership in Washington, D.C.[46]

About the Author

Milan Vego is the Admiral R. K. Turner Professor of Operational Art in the Joint Military Operations (JMO) Department of the U.S. Naval War College in Newport, Rhode Island. He is a Croatian native of Čapljina, Herzegovina. Dr. Vego is a graduate of the former Yugoslav Naval Academy (1961) and Torpedo Tactical School (1966). He is also a licensed Master Mariner (1973). He holds a BA in modern history (1970), an MA in U.S./Latin American history (1973) from Belgrade University, and a PhD in modern European history from George Washington University (1981). Dr. Vego served for twelve years as an officer in the former Yugoslav Navy and for three years as a second officer (deck) in the former West German merchant marine before obtaining political asylum in the United States in 1976. He became a naturalized citizen in 1984. Dr.

Vego was an adjunct professor at George Washington University (1983), the former Defense Intelligence College (1985–91), and the War Gaming and Simulations Center, National Defense University, Washington, D.C. (1989–91) before joining the Naval War College faculty in August 1991. He was a senior fellow at the Center for Naval Analyses, Alexandria, Virginia (1985–87), and the former Soviet Army Studies Office (SASO), U.S. Army Combined Center, Fort Leavenworth, Kansas (1987–89). Dr. Vego is the author of thirteen books, including *The Battle for Leyte, 1944: Allied and Japanese Plans, Preparations, and Execution* (Naval Institute Press, 2006). His latest book is *Maritime Strategy and Sea Denial: Theory and Practice* (Routledge, Taylor & Francis Group, 2019). Dr. Vego is also the author of numerous articles and essays published in professional journals and magazines.

Notes

1. Richard W. Bates et al., *The Battle for Leyte Gulf, October 1944: Strategical and Tactical Analysis*, vol. 2, *Operations from 0719 October 17th until October 20th (D-Day)* (Newport, RI: Naval War College, 1955), 14.
2. USSBS (Pacific), *The Employment of Forces under the Southwest Pacific Command* (Washington, D.C.: Military Analysis Division, February, 1947), 37; Wesley F. Craven and James L. Cate, *The Army Air Forces in World War II*, vol. 5, *The Pacific: Matterhorn To Nagasaki, June 1944 to August 1944* (Washington, D.C.: Office of Air Force History, reprint, 1983), 282.
3. Craven and Cate, *The Pacific*, 282–83.
4. "Basic Outline Plan for Musketeer II," 29 August 1944, Box 378: Southwest Pacific Area, July 1944–September 1944, RG 38: *Plans, Orders & Related Documents*, National Archives and Records Administration (NARA), College Park, MD, 1–2.
5. USSBS (Pacific), *The Employment of Forces under the Southwest Pacific Command*, 38.
6. "Basic Outline Plan For Musketeer II," 4–5.
7. "Basic Outline Plan For Musketeer II," 6–8; Craven and Cate, *The Pacific*, 285.
8. "Basic Outline Plan for Musketeer II," 9.
9. M. Hamlin Cannon, *United States Army in World War II, The War in the Pacific, Leyte: The Return to the Philippines* (Washington, D.C.:

Center of Military History, United States Army, 1954, reprinted 1987), 3, 1, 15.
10. Samuel E. Morison, *Two-Ocean War: A Short History of the United States Navy in the Second World War* (Boston: Little, Brown, 1963), 422; Cannon, *Leyte*, 8–9.
11. Cannon, *Leyte*, 9; Edward J. Drea, *MacArthur's Ultra: Codebreaking and the War Against Japan, 1942–1945* (Lawrence, KS: University Press of Kansas, 1992), 158; Morison, *Two-Ocean War*, 423.
12. Gavin Long, *MacArthur as Military Commander* (London: B. T. Batsford, and Princeton, NJ: D. Van Nostrand Company Inc., 1969), 151.
13. Annex III, GHQ, Southwest Pacific Area, Operations Instruction No. 70, 21 September 1944, Air Evaluation Board, S.W.P.A, *Leyte Campaign, Philippines 1944* (June 1945), Folder 2-2263-1B, Box 138.8-53, 1944, Air Force Historical Research Agency (AFHRA), Maxwell AFB, AL, 286–87.
14. Douglas MacArthur, *Reminiscences: General of the Army Douglas MacArthur* (New York: McGraw-Hill, 1964), 212.
15. Annex III: GHQ, Southwest Pacific Area, Operations Instruction No. 70, 21 September 1944, Air Evaluation Board, S.W.P.A, *Leyte Campaign, Philippines 1944* (June 1945), Folder 2-2263-1B, Box 138.8-53, 1944, Air Force Historical Research Agency (AFHRA), Maxwell AFB, AL, 286–87.
16. Report on Intelligence Activities of the Joint Staff, CincPac-CincPOA, 29 August 1945, History of the Joint Intelligence Center, Pacific Ocean Areas, and the Advance Intelligence Center, CincPac-CincPOA, Reel 1, M392, *Military Intelligence in the Pacific, 1942–46: Bulletins of the Intelligence Center, Pacific Ocean Area, and the Commander-in-Chief, Pacific Ocean Area*, 1.
17. Sixth United States Army HQ, *Report of the Leyte Operation, 17 October 1944–45, December 1944* (June 1945), Folder 2-2263-1B, Box 138.8-53, 1944, Air Force Historical Research Agency (AFHRA), Maxwell AFB, AL, 23.
18. "Forces under Vice Admiral Thomas C. Kinkaid to support elements of the United States Sixth Army in the Seizure and Occupation of the Leyte Area," Operation Plan 13-44, 26 September 1944, Box 66, Seventh Fleet Sep 44, RG 38, Operations Plans, Orders & Related Documents, World War II, NARA, 19–20.

19. Walter Krueger, *From Down Under to Nippon: The Story of Sixth Army in World War II* (Washington, D.C.: Combat Forces Press, 1953), 150.
20. Krueger, *From Down Under to Nippon*, 150.
21. Robert C. Anderson, *Leyte* (Washington, D.C.: U.S. Government Printing Office, CMH 72-27, 1994), 12; Craven and Cate, *The Pacific*, 348-49.
22. "Summary of Plan for King II opn," 21 Sep 44, No. 6767, GHQ Southwest Pacific Area, HRIC, Box 1826, RG 496, Records of General Headquarters Southwest Pacific Area and United States Army Forces, Pacific, NARA; "Forces under Vice Admiral Thomas C. Kinkaid to support elements of the United States Sixth Army in the Seizure and Occupation of the Leyte Area," Operation Plan 13-44, 26 September 1944, Box 66, Seventh Fleet Sep 44, RG 38, Operations Plans, Orders & Related Documents, World War II, NARA, 20.
23. Sixth United States Army HQ, *Report of the Leyte Operation, 17 October 1944–25 December 1944*, Sixth United (28 November 1945), 23.
24. "Plan for the Seizure and Occupation of Leyte Gulf," Nr. 6788, GHQ Southwest Pacific Area, HRIC, Box 1826, RG 496, Records of General Headquarters Southwest Pacific Area and United States Army Forces, Pacific, NARA: Operation Plan 12-44, 25 September 1944, Folder CTF 70 Operation Orders, Box 53, RG 23: Record Group 23: *World War II, Battle Evaluation Group, 1946–1956* (BEG), Naval Historical Collection (NHC), Naval War College, Newport, RI; Air Evaluation Board, S.W.P.A, *Leyte Campaign, Philippines 1944*, 302.
25. Air Evaluation Board, S.W.P.A, *Leyte Campaign, Philippines 1944*, 287-78; Commander Allied Naval Forces, Southwest Pacific Area, Vice Admiral Kinkaid, USN, "Forces under Vice Admiral Thomas C. Kinkaid, USN to Transport and Land the Sixth Army USA Ashore on Leyte Island to Take Part in the Reoccupation of the Philippines Islands," Folder Seventh Fleet (Sept–Oct 1944), Box 66, Naval Operational Archives, Naval Historical Center; Washington Navy Yard, Washington, D.C., Operation Plan 12-44, 25 September 1944, Folder CTF 70 Operation Orders, Box 53, RG 23: BEG, NHC.
26. "Forces under Vice Admiral Thomas C. Kinkaid to Support Elements of the United States Sixth Army in the Seizure and Occupation of the Leyte area," Operation Plan 13-44, 26 September 1944, Box 66, Seventh Fleet Sep 44, RG 38, Operations Plans, Orders & Related Documents, World War II, 19.

27. "Forces under Vice Admiral Thomas C. Kinkaid to Support Elements of the United States Sixth Army in the Seizure and Occupation of the Leyte area," Operation Plan 13-44, 26 September 1944, Box 66, Seventh Fleet Sep 44, RG 38, Operations Plans, Orders & Related Documents, World War II, NARA, 20.
28. "Submarine Operations," Annex "H" to Operation Plan 13-44, 26 September 1944, Seventh Fleet Operations, Box 66, RG 23; BEG, NHC; Richard W. Bates et al., *The Battle for Leyte Gulf, October 1944: Strategical and Tactical Analysis*, vol. 1, *Preliminary Operations until 0719 October 17th including Battle off Formosa* (Newport, RI: U.S. Naval War College, 1953), 71.
29. Bates et al., *Preliminary Operations*, 195–96.
30. Bates et al., *Preliminary Operations*, 32; HQ Allied Air Forces, Southwest Pacific Area, Operations Instruction No. 71, 24 September 1944, Air Evaluation Board, S.W.P.A., *Leyte Campaign, Philippines 1944*, Box 138.8-53, 1944, AFHRA, 292; Craven and Cate, *The Pacific*, 351.
31. GHQ, Southwest Pacific Area, Operations Instruction No. 70, 21 September 1944, Air Evaluation Board, S.W.P.A, *Leyte Campaign, Philippines 1944* (June 1945), Box 138.8-53, 1944, AFHRA, 288; Letter of Instruction, No. 71, FEASC, King–II, 20 October–11 November 1944, Folder 721.804-721. 8671 1943–1945, Box 10, AFHRA, 1, 12.
32. GHQ, Southwest Pacific Area, Operations Instruction No. 70, 21 September 1944, Air Evaluation Board, S.W.P.A, *Leyte Campaign, Philippines 1944*, (June 1945), Box 138.8-53, 1944, AFHRA, 288; Letter of Instruction, No. 71, FEASC, King–II, 20 October–11 November 1944, Folder 721.804-721. 8671 1943–1945, Box 10, AFHRA, 1; "5th USAAF Operations Instructions No. 6, 29 September 1944," Folder L, Box 56, RG 23; BEG, NHC, 1.
33. "Commander Allied Air Forces Plan for Support of King II," 8 October 1944, Nr. 6881, GHQ Southwest Pacific Area, HRIC, Box 1827, RG 496 Records of General Headquarters Southwest Pacific Area and United States Army Forces, Pacific, NARA.
34. Annex III: GHQ, SWPA Operations Instruction No. 70, 21 September 1944, Air Evaluation Board, S.W.P.A, *Leyte Campaign, Philippines 1944* (June 1945), Box 138.8-53, 1944, AFHRA, 286.
35. CINCPOA Operations Plan 8-44, 27 September 1944, Folder: CINCPOA, Box 33, Operational Archives, Naval Historical Center, Washington Navy Yard, Washington, D.C.

36. "Submarine Operations," Annex "H" to Operation Plan 13-44. Commander, Seventh Fleet. Operation Plan 13-44, 26 September 1944, Seventh Fleet Operations, Box 66, RG 23: BEG, NHC.
37. In contrast to Halsey, Spruance did not have Nimitz's clause in his operation order in support of the invasion of the Marianas in June 1944. In the Battle of the Philippine Sea, Spruance went out to seek the enemy but, making no contact, turned back to perform his primary duty of covering the amphibious operation at Saipan. However, in informal discussions at Pearl Harbor, Spruance was strongly criticized by some naval aviators both for turning east when he did, and for not pursuing the Japanese fleet after he had destroyed its air groups; Samuel E. Morison, *History of United States Naval Operations in World War II*, vol. 12, *Leyte, June 1944–January 1945*, (Boston: Little, Brown, 1984; first printed 1958), 59.
38. Comdr. Western Pacific Task Forces (Adm. Halsey), "Battle Plan Nr. 1-44, 9 Sept 44," Nr. 6681, GHQ, Southwest Pacific Area, HRIC, Box 1826, RG 496, Records of General Headquarters Southwest Pacific Area and United States Army Forces, Pacific, NARA; Bates et al., *Preliminary*, 17; Elmer B. Potter, *Nimitz* (Annapolis, MD: Naval Institute Press, 1976, reprinted 1987), 325–26.
39. Commander Third Fleet, "Commander Third Fleet Operation Plan No. 21-44 (4 October 1944): Forces Under Admiral W. F. Halsey, USN, to Conduct Air Strikes in Okinawa, Formosa, Luzon, and the Visayan Island in Support of Landing on and Occupation of Leyte," Box 57, Operational Archives, Naval Historical Center, Washington Navy Yard, Washington, D.C.; "Conference Between Representatives of the Southwest Pacific Area and CINCPOA, 19–21 September 1944," September 23, 1944, Box 164: Strategic Plans, Operational Archives, Naval Historical Center, Washington Navy Yard, Washington, D.C.
40. Third Fleet, Operation Plan No. 21-44, 4 October 1944; Third Fleet (1944), Box 57, Naval Operational Archives, Naval Historical Center, Washington Navy Yard, Washington, D.C., 2–5.
41. "Operation Order 20-44: Forces Under Vice Admiral W. F. Halsey, USN, to Conduct Air Strikes Against Marcus Island, 10 October 1944, 3 October 1944," Box 57, Third Fleet (1944), Operational Archives, Naval Historical Center, Washington Navy Yard, Washington, D.C.
42. Bates et al., *Preliminary Operations*, 159.

43. "Submarine Operations," Annex "H" to Operation Plan 13-44, Seventh Fleet Operations, Box 66, RG 23: BEG, NHC; Theodore Roscoe, *United States Submarine Operations in World War II* (Annapolis, MD: United States Naval Institute, 1965), 410.
44. U.S. Pacific Fleet, Submarine Force, TF 17, Operation Order Nr. 328-44, 25 September 1944, Box 55, RG 23; *World War II, Battle Evaluation Group, 1946–1956*, NHC, 2–4.
45. Edwin P. Hoyt, *How They Won the War in The Pacific: Nimitz and His Admirals* (New York: Weybright and Talley, 1970), 424.
46. See Thomas J. Cutler, "MacArthur, FDR, and the Battle of Leyte Gulf," *Naval History*, October 2009, for further explanation/discussion.

4

THE PRINCIPLE OF THE OBJECTIVE AT LEYTE GULF

Norman Friedman

Admiral Halsey's run north to attack the Japanese decoy force is the great puzzle of Leyte Gulf. By doing so he exposed the invasion shipping to destruction by a Japanese surface force his fliers had damaged, but hardly destroyed, in the Sibuyan Sea the previous day. This force turned back, but then turned again toward Leyte Gulf. When it got there, it encountered only the escort carriers and their screening "small boys." The epic stand of these ships saved the invasion shipping; miraculously they drove off the most powerful surface action group the Imperial Japanese Navy could then muster. When Taffy 3, the escort carrier group, called for help, Admiral Nimitz at Pearl Harbor asked why Halsey had not detached his fast battleships, which would have been organized as Task Force 34. Due to a code-room error, Halsey received Nimitz's message as "The world wonders where is Task Force 34," and reversed course. Damage to the Japanese decoy force was more limited than it might have been, and Halsey arrived too late to engage the surface force. What had happened?

Halsey had attended the Naval War College and had, presumably, absorbed the decision-making principles it taught. Its standard exercise was to issue basic orders. Each student produced his own "Estimate of the Situation," containing an interpretation of the order giving priorities to various aspects, and then listed enemy courses of action before listing his own and making a decision as to which to adopt. In games, the college staff officer assigned to a game collected the students' estimates and produced one estimate to guide each side in the game. In one of the games, for example, students envisaged an attack on an island. The enemy's fleet might interfere. How should the U.S. commander balance the success of the attack against the possibility of destroying the enemy's fleet? He could protect the invasion shipping by keeping his own fleet close to the island, or he could steam off to fight the enemy's fleet. In that case he would risk an attack on the invasion shipping by either part of the enemy fleet or even by the whole enemy fleet if it managed to evade him. The College forced students to decide what priorities their orders implied. That was the key question in both the Battle of the Philippine Sea (June 1944) and the Battle of Leyte Gulf (October 1944). The decisions made, first by Spruance in June and then by Halsey in October, must surely be understood against a background of the larger U.S. strategy they absorbed at Newport, tempered by later decisions.

The college forced students to think about the whole shape of a possible war, usually against Japan. That meant beginning with the endgame, the action that would force the Japanese to accept defeat. Everything else followed from that understanding. In every game played out between the world wars involving Japan, the decisive act was a blockade that would strangle that country.

World War I had shown how a battle fleet could act as a shield by protecting the weaker ships enforcing a blockade or protecting convoys. That had been the ultimate significance of the Grand Fleet. Without it, the Germans could have wiped out convoys—as two fast German cruisers actually did in November 1917. Conversely, by its existence the German fleet had shielded wartime U-boat bases from British attacks at source. By its existence it had prevented the British from mounting an effective blockade to cut Germany off from vital resources in Scandinavia, such as Swedish iron ore. The postwar critique of Adm. John Jellicoe's failure to destroy the German High Seas Fleet at Jutland was that victory would have doomed the Germans; it would have made all sorts of flanking operations possible.

For U.S. naval officers at Newport looking back, the point of the critique was that without a dominant fleet Japan would have no shield against the blockade that would strangle her.

When we look back at the Pacific War, we see an island-by-island fight, culminating in the reconquest of the Philippines followed by attacks on islands closer to Japan, which were wanted as bases for invasion. That is not how the war was visualized earlier. To U.S. naval strategists, the key target was not this or that bit of land. It was Japan itself, shielded by the Japanese fleet. If the fleet was destroyed, the war-ending blockade could be mounted.[1] Through the mid-1930s, the U.S. war plan envisaged movement of the fleet directly from Pearl Harbor to the Philippines, in the expectation that it could arrive before the Japanese army overran the islands. The approach of the fleet would force the Japanese to fight a decisive battle near Japan. This strategy was called the "through ticket to Manila." It emphasized the central role of a battle to destroy the Japanese fleet. However much of the Philippines the Japanese seized before the fleet arrived, they would have to disgorge once their fleet was gone. The Japanese, incidentally, became aware of the U.S. war plan by carefully observing our maneuvers (as we observed theirs).[2]

In 1933 the College fought a "through ticket" game, partly to test the new war plan. At the time, the War College was at least as much war-planning laboratory as educational institution. It had a commentator, Capt. W. R. van Auken, whose job it was to extract lessons from games. This time, as usual, the U.S. fleet came out ahead in the battle, which was fought near the Philippines. By that time the Japanese had conquered Manila, which had the only U.S. drydock and repair facility west of Hawaii (there was no question of cooperating with the British and using Singapore). The U.S. Navy had identified various sheltered anchorages in the southern Philippines in which the fleet could shelter after its run from Hawaii. Van Auken pointed out that their safety was illusory. In the big battle, most of the U.S. ships emerged afloat but with serious underwater damage. They would sink to the bottom as soon as their pumps stopped. Japanese ships with equivalent damage could be repaired in Japan. A follow-on game, in which the ships had been miraculously repaired, also ended badly. The results of the game were considered so important that they were sent directly to the Chief of Naval Operations. This seems to have been unique.[3]

The result of the 1933 game forced a shift to a step-by-step advance. The "through ticket" had subjected the fleet to air attack as it passed through the chains of islands that had been mandated to Japan after World War I. That problem had, incidentally, boosted interest in fleet carriers and also in high-performance naval fighters. In a step-by-step advance, air bases would be set up on islands the fleet seized. Bombers based on them would neutralize island air bases farther afield.[4] Step-by-step could also provide the fleet with support and repair facilities beyond Hawaii. Before 1941 it was assumed that a base would actually be built; but after Pearl Harbor, fully mobile facilities, including very large floating drydocks, were produced.

Understanding this shift helps explain Halsey's actions at Leyte Gulf. The shift required the U.S. Navy to seize island after island, but it did not change the underlying perception that such seizures were no more than a means to an end. The end was still the strangulation of Japan; and to do that, the U.S. Navy had to destroy the Japanese fleet. The fleet, not particular islands, was the objective. It was always understood that the Japanese would husband their weaker battle fleet, and a very important question was how to force it to accept battle.[5] That had been the key problem the British had faced in World War I.

It appears that the Japanese gained insight into the shift in U.S. naval strategy, despite U.S. security measures. When they faced the "through ticket," they envisaged a decisive battle somewhere near Japan. To fight it they needed combatants but relatively little in the way of a fleet train. Despite U.S. belief that the mandated islands would be fortified and turned into air bases, until the late 1930s that was not done, because it would have been an undue diversion of valuable resources.[6] Only at that time did the Japanese become interested in the sort of land-based air attacks that already played prominently in contemporary U.S. thinking. That may have been due to their own development of long-range land-based naval bombers, beginning with the Mitsubishi G3M ("Nell"). In 1941 the Japanese had a land-based naval air fleet as well as their concentrated carrier air force. This was, among other things, the force that sank HMS *Prince of Wales* and *Repulse* off Malaya in December 1941.

In 1940, the Japanese naval war plan changed. The focus shifted to an outer line of defense based on the Mandates. The fleet would fight much farther forward, which meant that it needed more auxiliaries and the ability to sustain itself far from home. That made sense, because once the U.S. fleet gained its first island base, it could project itself forward. The idea of an outer defense perimeter is usually associated with the conquests of 1941–42, but that makes little naval sense. Navies are concentrated and mobile; to adopt a defensive perimeter is to weaken naval power, probably decisively. It is certainly to accept local inferiority. The Japanese adopted a new form of mobility suited to their new strategic problem. They might find it difficult to concentrate ships wherever the U.S. fleet struck, but they could shuttle land-based aircraft from island to island.

The important change after Pearl Harbor was that carrier forces became dominant. Before the war, U.S. (and, incidentally, Japanese) naval aviators believed that as long as the enemy's carriers survived, they were under constant threat. Carrier duels were common in prewar, full-scale exercises. Yet carriers were also vulnerable to attacks by surface ships. That reality had been demonstrated graphically in 1940 when two German battlecruisers sank HMS *Glorious*.

The immediate context in the Philippines in October 1944 was the previous major engagement, the Battle of the Philippine Sea that June. The island seized, Saipan, was so close to Japan that their fleet could be expected to come out to defend it. Indeed, it was so important that when it fell, so did the current Japanese administration. U.S. commander Adm. Raymond F. Spruance could either concentrate on the invasion force or he could leave the invasion to its fate and seek decisive action against the Japanese. He chose to concentrate on the invasion. The Japanese tried to destroy his force using their carrier aircraft—which Spruance's fliers wiped out in the "Turkey Shoot" of the Battle of the Philippine Sea. This victory, we now know, wiped out nearly all of the remaining trained Japanese carrier aviators. Although the Japanese carriers survived, they would be useless for some considerable time. The Americans did not know that. The pilots returning to the U.S. carriers did not feel that they had just won a decisive victory, because they had been unable to sink the Japanese carriers. We now know that there was no training pipeline that could quickly replace those dead pilots, but that seems not to have been so obvious at the time. In the U.S. aviators' world, pilots were quickly replaced by a massive training machine.[7]

It seemed at the time that the Japanese carriers were anything but impotent. Even if they were encountered with few aircraft on board, they represented a potential that had to be eliminated.

Presumably Nimitz had seen Saipan as a way of drawing out the Japanese fleet so that it could be destroyed. Once that happened, the United States would gain enormously in freedom of action. No particular island was nearly as important. After Saipan, Admiral Halsey took over the fleet, which changed designation to Third Fleet. Admiral Spruance and his staff were detached to plan the operation after the Philippines. Halsey's orders for the next invasion, at Leyte Gulf, included the instruction that if he had to choose between protecting the invasion and destroying the Japanese fleet, his priority should be the enemy fleet.[8] That was absolutely consistent with previous U.S. naval thinking. Particular places were convenient but not decisively so. The Japanese had only one fleet to lose.

From a U.S. point of view ideally the Japanese would have concentrated their fleet so that it could be destroyed in a single battle. At Leyte Gulf, however, they split into three groups. Since the Japanese fliers had been wiped out at the Philippine Sea, the most powerful was a surface action group. Its main target was the invasion shipping in Leyte Gulf. A second, weaker surface force would come from the south, through Surigao Strait. A third force, built around the carriers, came down from the north to decoy the U.S. force covering the invasion and uncover it for the heavy attack force.

Halsey's pilots found the two surface action groups first, and pilots' reports indicated that they had badly damaged the battle force coming from the west. It is generally assumed that Halsey erred badly in believing his pilots' reports. His staff rejected reports from search aircraft, particularly from the night carrier *Independence*, that the Japanese surface action group was passing back toward Leyte Gulf, where it would threaten the invasion shipping. That is typically described as gross arrogance; his staff was not interested unless Halsey asked. Just why Admiral Halsey did not want to hear the reports is one of the mysteries of the battle.

When the Japanese split their force into three groups, Halsey had to decide what it meant to destroy the Japanese fleet. He could not simultaneously destroy all three, although pilots from his four task groups did attack all of them at one time or another. Probably the central reality was that Halsey had witnessed the rise of carrier aviation in the Pacific, to the point where heavy gun ships were almost an auxiliary. The core Japanese fleet was the carriers. Battleships could certainly inflict damage as long as they survived, but they were generally at the mercy of aircraft. During the day action, U.S. carrier pilots thought they had damaged much of the Japanese force.[9] Halsey probably considered the carriers—which he did not know lacked aircraft—far more important. They had been the target at Philippine Sea. Much is typically made of Halsey's naïveté in believing the pilots who had attacked the big Japanese surface action group, but that may well be irrelevant.

Moreover, much of what had to come ashore at Leyte Gulf had already done so. If the Japanese battleships managed to attack the anchorage, they could certainly do serious damage, but it was most unlikely that they could abort the landing. It had already gone too far. They might cause enough damage to slow down whatever advance the army hoped to make, but that was acceptable: the Philippines were not nearly so important as the dominance that could be achieved by wiping out the Japanese carrier force. After all, Halsey had been at Guadalcanal, where the U.S. force ashore had survived devastating Japanese surface attacks. Even without the fast carriers, the U.S. force at Leyte Gulf was considerably stronger.

Halsey could not be at all sure that the Japanese surface strike group was not going to be directed against his fast carriers. For the Japanese, too, the destruction of the U.S. fleet was much to be desired. Halsey's carriers were at once the most powerful U.S. weapon *and* the most valuable U.S. target. Without their battleships, they would be extraordinarily vulnerable, particularly at night near islands behind which Japanese capital ships might hide. The Japanese had already tried and failed to do so, using shore-based aircraft. To Halsey, the bare existence of a heavy Japanese surface force probably justified keeping all of his fast battleships with his carrier force. He could not bet that the Japanese would not see things that way. The only evidence to the contrary was a remarkable document that Third Fleet intelligence had obtained at Ulithi on 6 October. It was the March 1944 Japanese plan for the next big naval battle, the Z-plan.[10] It mentioned transports as the primary target of a surface action group, but there were considerable caveats. It does not appear that U.S. naval intelligence had much in the way of illuminating documentation. That seems to have come from the wreck of the cruiser *Nachi*, sunk in the Philippines on 5 November 1944.[11]

Halsey rarely discussed Leyte Gulf afterward, although at times he did say that he had taken his battleships with him because they were an essential part of his command. It appears that Task Force 34 had been envisaged as a battle line working with the carriers to sink ships their aircraft crippled; air attacks were far more likely to cripple than to kill. Halsey probably never imagined them as a separate command far from his fast carriers, and he must have been surprised that Nimitz wrote what he did.

It all came down to the question everyone at Newport was asked: What was the objective?

About the Author

Norman Friedman has published more than forty books, most of them concerned with the intersection of defense policy, strategy and tactics, and technology. They include design histories of most U.S. warships and many of their Royal Navy equivalents, and a history of naval command and control and information warfare, *Network-Centric Warfare*. Dr. Friedman's Cold War history, *The Fifty-Year War*, received the Westminster Prize awarded by the Royal United Service Institute as the best military history book of its year; his *Fighting the Great War at Sea* received the Lyman Award from the North American Society of Oceanic Historians; and his *Seapower as Strategy* received the Samuel Eliot Morrison Award given by the Naval Order of the United States. Works written under government contract include a history of U.S. Navy air defense missiles and a history of the joint program to develop the MRAP (mine resistant, ambush protected) vehicle. Other works include a history of interwar gaming at the Naval War College and a forthcoming history of British submarines. Dr. Friedman spent over a decade at a prominent defense-oriented think tank, another decade in the office of the Secretary of the Navy, and two years in the Marine Corps Headquarters. He writes a monthly column on "World Naval Developments" for Naval Institute *Proceedings*, and has published numerous articles in other defense journals. Dr. Friedman received his PhD in theoretical physics from Columbia University.

Notes

1. References to prewar gaming at the Naval War College are based on this author's book *Winning the Next War: Learning How to Fight the Pacific War*, forthcoming from the U.S. Government Printing Office (GPO). The book was based on, among other things, a review of all surviving game material, and also on much other material on Naval War College methodology.

    U.S. joint war planners of the late 1920s recognized that the Japanese might not accept this reality. They could not imagine that the United States would ever raise an army large enough to invade Japan. Instead, the alternative war-ending measure was aerial bombardment of Japan, whose flimsy cities were considered particularly vulnerable to fire-bombing. The same naval campaign that would support the blockade would support the bombing attack, because it required the capture of island bases near Japan. This nuance explains why, by 1929, plans to convert existing merchant ships into warships included aircraft transport for the army bombers.

2. U.S. analysis of the Japanese 1930 maneuvers revealed that they understood the U.S. war plan and had learned how to counter it. That was why the U.S. Navy could not offer any viable offensive option when the Japanese seized Manchuria in 1931. For the discovery of the Japanese success, see the prewar history of U.S. naval signals intelligence prepared by the Naval Security Group: SRH-355 (Pt. I), compiled by Capt. J. S. Holtwick Jr. USN (Ret.), and dated June 1971, in RG 457, SRH Box 108 in NARA II.
3. This was the "big game" (Operations IV) of 1933. Adm. Luke McNamee, president of the Naval War College, sent the analysis and summary of the game to CNO. From 1935 on, the War College's big Blue-Orange games always included the seizure or defense of a Pacific island.
4. The first big war game to reflect the new strategy was Operations III of May 1935 for the Class of 1935. In this scenario, Orange (Japan) almost immediately seized the Philippines while blockading Chinese ports and maintaining a large army in Manchuria to guard against the Soviets. Blue began its offensive by capturing Truk. Blue strategy was to consolidate its position in the Eastern Pacific, then establish its fleet in the Mandates, and then to move west to cut Orange sea lanes. This was not too far from what the United States actually did beginning in 1943 in its Central Pacific offensive. The game was part of the second phase, the establishment of U.S. superiority in the Mandates. In this game, Blue turned Truk into an intermediate fleet base. Blue assumed that Orange would hold its fleet back, resisting the seizure of Guam, Saipan, Yap, and Palau (in succession) with submarines. The fleet battle was played as Tactical Problem IV. This exercise brought out the problems of supporting an amphibious assault: the Blue fleet remained within one hundred miles of Guam for ten days, in the view of the War College analysis group, unnecessarily risking attrition by submarines, aircraft, and destroyers. During the landing, an Orange submarine torpedoed two Blue battleships. An associated game showed how vulnerable carriers could be to land-based aircraft if they had to remain within range. The tactical game was innovative: it embodied the new perception that any modern battle would probably begin with air strikes by each side at the earliest possible moment, if for no other reason than to avoid having its aircraft found on deck and wiped out. The new factor in 1944 was radar-directed fighter air defense.

5. The prewar context was the belief that ultimately the enemy's battleships had to be destroyed. Carriers were essential, but it was widely doubted that they could sink enemy battleships, because their dive-bombers could not penetrate thick deck armor, and their torpedo bombers had too poor a chance of hitting. The dive-bomber problem persisted through World War II, and the only battleships sunk by carrier torpedo bombers, the big Japanese *Yamato* and *Musashi*, succumbed to attacks on a far larger scale than could have been imagined prewar. In games, the Japanese were willing to risk their carriers and their lightly protected fast battleships (*Kongo* class), but not their main battle line. By 1944, perception had flipped, and carriers were considered the key capital ships on both sides. Note that in 1941 U.S. Pacific commander Adm. Husband Kimmel was interested in raiding the Marshalls as a means of forcing the Japanese fleet into battle.
6. According to David C. Evans and Mark R. Peattie, *Kaigun: Strategy, Tactics, and Technology in the Imperial Japanese Navy 1887–1941* (Annapolis: Naval Institute Press, 1997), 465, in 1936 the Japanese navy began to consider basing much of its land-based airpower in the Mandates; by 1941 there were eleven complete air bases in Micronesia. During the late 1930s the Japanese considered the air bases as a tripwire behind which attacks could be launched against an intruding U.S. fleet. This was much what U.S. war planners had expected when they worked out the "through ticket," the surprise being that the Japanese waited so long to set up the air bases. According to Evans and Peattie, by 1940, however, the strategic advantage offered by the bases had led the Japanese to move the location of the decisive naval battle to east of the Marianas, the air units on the islands participating. I interpret the shift more as Japanese realization of a shift in U.S. naval strategy.
7. As indicated by the reaction to an initial report that the 1st Mobile Fleet—the carrier force—was coming toward the Philippines. Carl Solberg, *Decision and Dissent: With Halsey at Leyte Gulf* (Annapolis: Naval Institute Press, 1995), 100. Solberg was one of Halsey's intelligence officers. The Japanese were also concentrating land-based aircraft, and there seemed to be no shortage of them. Solberg's account shows that Halsey's staff considered the Japanese carriers fully capable at this time.

8. The War College tried a scenario something like Leyte Gulf in its Operations I game played in October 1934 for the Class of 1935; this problem is in the files of the OpNav War Plans Division (at NARA II, College Park) but not in the archives of the Naval War College. Blue is trying to consolidate a position in the southern Philippines, which required it to protect incoming supply convoys. Orange's fleet is fairly intact, and it can divide Blue by forcing it to deal with multiple threats. In this case the game ended badly for Blue. Neither Spruance nor Halsey was in the Class of 1935 (Halsey was in the Class of 1933); but for the Class of 1936, Spruance was in the Tactics and Minor Strategy faculty for the Junior Class. No surviving game seems to reflect the situation Spruance faced at Saipan in 1944.

9. The attack on the surface action group had, it happened, demonstrated a weakness in U.S. carrier strike tactics. Each task group attacked as a unit, and in each attack there was a strike coordinator. In theory, that ensured that attacks would be properly distributed over the enemy formation. For some reason none of the coordinators caused pilots to spread their attacks properly. They concentrated on *Musashi*, and they kept hitting as she took what turned out to be fatal damage. Also, the task groups attacked one by one. There was no overall coordinator to make sure that the next task group shifted to another target. It is also possible that smoke from the burning battleship distorted coordinators' view of the target. It was not even obvious to the pilots that *Musashi* had been sunk. This problem of coordination across the whole striking force is reminiscent of a classic problem of the battleship era: how to make sure fire was distributed over the whole of the enemy's fleet. For example, at Dogger Bank, Beatty's ships concentrated on the unfortunate SMS *Blucher* and thus failed to destroy the rest of the enemy force (even so, a few hits almost sank SMS *Seydlitz*). It is not at all clear that the U.S. Navy had addressed the air version of this issue before Leyte Gulf. The next opportunity for massive air attacks against a surface force came off Okinawa, when *Yamato* and her consorts were sunk—thanks largely to the presence of a multitask group strike leader who could allocate attacks.

10. Z presumably because at Tsushima, Togo flew a Z flag. It had been drawn up by Admiral Mineichi Koga, CinC Combined Fleet. On 31 March Koga's and an accompanying airplane crashed into the sea at Davao in the southern Philippines; Philippine guerillas found

documents in the wreckage, including the red-bound Z-plan. It went to MacArthur's Southwest Pacific Headquarters, was translated, and provided to Third Fleet. The translation is dated 23 May 1944. A copy is in the collection of Japanese naval documents in NARA II (Box 60). According to Solberg, 122, it was later understood to have been the basis for the A and Sho Plans devised to defend the Philippines. The Z Plan emphasized the use of land-based aircraft and included the use of a surface attack force to destroy transports. As written, it was an attempt to maintain control of a defensive perimeter running from the Kuriles through the South Sea islands, the Marianas and Carolines, and Western New Guinea. It would "seek out and destroy enemy airplane carriers with the major portion of our air strength, to ensure control of the air before directing our main attack against transport convoys (under certain circumstances enemy transport convoys may be attacked and destroyed first). Coordinating our plans with the aforesaid air attack, to strike suddenly with our surface forces, and annihilate enemy transports or the enemy fleet near vital areas." Enemy troops who landed were to be destroyed at the water's edge. The paper listed possible areas of preparedness and of operations, one of which was the Marianas (including Saipan). It also listed six different methods of operation, three of which (Nos. 4, 5, and 6) were suited to the Marianas, and four types of operations, including surface strike (carried out with 1 KdF as nucleus force). Clearly the translators did not know what 1 KdF was, but it was probably the two *Yamatos*. According to a tabulation of action to be taken when the enemy was attacking, the surface battle forces were to make enemy transport convoys their primary objective, making a sudden attack near the vital areas held by the Japanese. Solberg and others in Halsey's intelligence cell were struck by the idea of using a surface action group to attack the transports.

11. These are in the same record group as the Z-Plan. They are a remarkable trove, translated in 1945. There do not seem to be any tactical handbooks recovered before the *Nachi* sinking, and nothing comparable to the Z-Plan.

HALSEY'S DECISION
Trent Hone

Introduction

AT ABOUT 1655 LOCAL TIME ON 24 October 1944, Adm. William F. Halsey Jr., commander of the U.S. Navy's Third Fleet, received word from his northernmost carrier group, Rear Adm. Frederick C. Sherman's Task Group (TG) 38.3, that a Japanese carrier force had been sighted east of the island of Luzon, about 150 miles to the north. This "Northern Force" was reported to consist of twenty-four ships; it was in a prime position to make flank attacks on Halsey's forces.[1] As additional contact reports augmented the initial one, he assessed the situation; Halsey was gratified that the enemy carriers had finally been located.

Throughout the day, Halsey had concentrated the carrier task forces of Vice Adm. Marc A. Mitscher's Task Force (TF) 38—Sherman's TG 38.3, Rear Adm. Gerald F. Bogan's TG 38.2, and Rear Adm. Ralph E. Davison's TG 38.4—around the eastern exit to San Bernardino Strait. Their pilots subjected the Japanese "Center Force" to powerful air attacks while it approached the strait via the Sibuyan Sea. They sank the large battleship *Musashi*, the flagship of the Center Force's commander, Vice Admiral Kurita Takeo. The battleships *Yamato*, *Nagato*, and *Haruna* were damaged; the heavy cruiser *Myoko* had been forced to withdraw. At 1400, TF 38 planes had observed the Center Force turning about and retiring. According to the best estimates of the aviators, it had been damaged so severely that it was no longer a serious threat.[2]

To the south, the Japanese "Southern Force" was approaching Surigao Strait, apparently intent on entering Leyte Gulf through those narrow waters. Planes from Davidson's TG 38.4 had attacked it that morning, but

Halsey's orders to concentrate against the Center Force had prevented further strikes. Halsey was confident that the commander of the Seventh Fleet, Vice Adm. Thomas C. Kinkaid, was prepared to meet this force and defeat it.[3] Kinkaid delegated destruction of the Southern Force to Rear Adm. Jesse B. Oldendorf, who set a well-crafted trap. Of the three Japanese forces converging on Leyte Gulf, only the newly sighted Northern Force was unaccounted for; it appeared to be the most threatening of all.

This was the situation confronting Halsey when he made one of the most controversial decisions of World War II. Estimating the Northern Force as "the most formidable threat to Allied operations in the Pacific, both present and future," at 1950, Halsey ordered his carrier group commanders to coalesce into a single powerful striking force.[4] They would head north, close with the recently sighted Japanese force, and attack. Halsey's intention was to destroy Imperial Japan's remaining naval forces and win a decisive victory. It would not work out as he planned.

Pacific Fleet Plans

Halsey's decision was informed by the established orders and plans of the Pacific Fleet. Halsey's immediate superior was Adm. Chester W. Nimitz, who commanded both the Pacific Fleet (as CINCPAC) and the Pacific Ocean Areas (as CINCPOA). Nimitz tended to provide clear, high-level instructions for his subordinates and generally refrained from interfering with commanders on the spot; he assumed they had a clearer sense of context and access to more timely information. The Central Pacific drive, which seized Japanese positions in the Gilberts, Marshalls, Marianas, and Palaùs before the assault on Leyte, was governed by the Granite Campaign Plan. Drafted by Nimitz in December 1943, and issued in January 1944, this plan outlined several objectives. Two of the most important were to maintain "unremitting pressure" on Japan and "destroy the Japanese Fleet at an early date."[5] These emphases were reinforced in subsidiary plans, especially those for the invasion of Leyte.

In June 1944, an opportunity to strike a decisive blow against the Japanese Fleet appeared. While Adm. Raymond A. Spruance's Fifth Fleet was invading Saipan, Vice Admiral Ozawa Jisaburo's Mobile Fleet attacked. Spruance deftly covered the invasion forces with his carrier groups and intercepted a series of long-range Japanese strikes. The "Marianas Turkey Shoot" devastated the Imperial Japanese Navy's (IJN's) carrier air power, but, at the time, the victory felt incomplete. Spruance's failure to close with and decisively defeat the enemy carrier forces was criticized.[6] Nimitz altered his instructions for future operations.

A new sentence entered CINCPOA Operational Plans in July, during the preparation for the invasion of the Palaus. It read, "In case opportunity for destruction of major portion of the enemy fleet offers or can be created, such destruction becomes the primary task."[7] Nimitz did not want the Japanese to escape again. He repeated this direction in CINCPOA Operation Plan 8-44, issued on 27 September 1944, which governed the Leyte operation. Operation Plan 8-44 emphasized Granite's dual objectives and forced Halsey to balance them. His main objective was to "maintain and extend unremitting military pressure against Japan," but if an "opportunity for destruction of major portion of the enemy fleet" appeared, it would become his primary task.[8]

Halsey was an aggressive commander. He was predisposed to seek action with the enemy. Reflecting Nimitz's shift in emphasis in the beginning of August, Halsey had stressed to his forces that they should "utilize every opportunity which may be presented or created to destroy major portions of the enemy fleet."[9] In October, he modified his instructions to reflect Nimitz's new language.[10] One of the reasons he adopted such an aggressive stance was his assumption—shared by many in the Pacific Fleet—that the Japanese would not fight for the Philippines; if decisive action was to occur, Halsey was expected to have to seek it out.[11]

Third Fleet's Battle Plan

If the opportunity arose, Halsey would be well prepared for fleet action. He issued detailed instructions outlining his preferred battle plan. When "contact with the enemy fleet or a major portion thereof becomes a probability," he would put it in motion. Halsey's intent was to close with the enemy at night and bring about a "decisive engagement." As the Third Fleet approached the enemy, a powerful surface action group, TF 34, would separate from the carrier task forces and come together under Vice Adm. Willis A. Lee. It would take a position seventy-five miles ahead of the main formation. Vice Admiral Mitscher, commander of TF 38, would operate the carrier groups in support. At dawn, a coordinated attack by the guns of Lee's battle line and the strike planes of the carrier groups would shatter the enemy formation.[12] For decades, the Navy had anticipated using coordinated attacks by carrier planes and surface gunfire in decisive battle.[13] Halsey's plan developed this tactic to its most sophisticated form.

Lee expected TF 34 to comprise six battleships (three heavy cruisers, three light cruisers), and twelve destroyers would operate on their flanks while a carrier TG provided air cover and close support. If circumstances required it, Lee would form a smaller "Special Group" based around his two fastest battleships, the *Iowa* (BB 61) and *New Jersey* (BB 62). This was TG 34.5; its purpose was to pursue and destroy any enemy ships that attempted to withdraw.[14]

Japanese Plans

American planners were incorrect in their estimates of Japanese intentions. Admiral Toyoda Soemu, commander of the Combined Fleet, recognizing the threat to the empire's supply lines, had resolved to fight to defend the Philippines. In early August 1944, Toyoda and his staff worked through preliminary plans for thwarting an American assault on the archipelago. The initial plan expected the First Diversionary Attack Force, with the bulk of the IJN's remaining battleships, to approach the enemy fleet under cover of land-based air, decisively defeat it, and then destroy the American landing forces. The Sho plans, later evolutions of this concept, were developed in September. They envisioned using the Mobile Force, with the IJN's remaining carriers, to draw the American fleet north. The Mobile Force would approach from Japan, enter the Philippine Sea, and distract the American carriers, clearing the way for the First Diversionary Attack Force to shatter the invasion fleet.[15] When, on 18 October, the Imperial General Headquarters received word that landings on Leyte were imminent, they put the Sho-1 plan in motion.[16]

The First Diversionary Attack Force, under Vice Admiral Kurita, would advance through San Bernardino Strait and destroy enemy invasion forces on X-Day. One or two days prior to that, the Mobile Force, led by Vice Admiral Ozawa, would lure the enemy carrier forces north. Land-based planes would concentrate in the Philippines and seek out the enemy carriers. X-Day was tentatively set for 24 October. It was later pushed back a day to allow time for Kurita to refuel in Brunei Bay. While there, he and his staff reviewed a recommendation from Combined Fleet Headquarters to split his forces into two groups. The first would attack through San Bernardino Strait while the second came through Surigao Strait. After considering the problem, Kurita and his staff agreed to this division of forces.[17]

Reacting to Japanese Moves

Halsey, unaware that the Japanese were moving toward the Philippines in force and conscious of the need to prepare for an upcoming series of strikes on the Japanese Home Islands, detached two of his four carrier groups (TG 38.1 and TG 38.4) on 21 October so that they could rest and rearm at Ulithi. TG 38.2 and TG 38.3 remained off the Philippines. Kinkaid was far less sanguine. His alertness was justified as contact reports began to come in from submarines and aircraft. By the morning of 23 October, Kinkaid had concluded that the Japanese were approaching Leyte in force; he prepared his command to fight them off, assuming that "any major enemy naval force approaching from the North will be intercepted and attacked by Third Fleet covering force."[18]

Halsey began to realize that the developing situation might overmatch the Third Fleet's remaining forces. During a staff meeting on 23 October, he concluded that he needed one more carrier group and all six of his battleships. He recalled TG 38.4, which had the battleships *Washington* (BB 56) and *Alabama* (BB 60) as well as the carriers *Franklin* (CV 13), *Enterprise* (CV 6), *San Jacinto* (CVL 30), and *Belleau Wood* (CVL 24). Halsey also realized that he needed to search more thoroughly to the west; he arranged his three TGs so that they could cover the approaches through the Philippines, including the Sibuyan and Mindanao seas. TG 38.3 was positioned east of Polillo Island, TG 38.2 patrolled off San Bernardino Strait, and TG 38.4 moved southeast of Samar.[19]

Searches on the morning of 24 October revealed the advance of Kurita's First Diversionary Attack Force. Both elements of it were sighted. The San Bernardino group—referred to as the Center Force in U.S. Navy reports—was quickly estimated by Halsey to be the greatest threat. He ordered TG 38.1 to return to the Philippines and concentrated his other task groups for strikes against the Center Force. A series of powerful attacks sank Kurita's flagship *Musashi* and damaged other ships. By midafternoon, he had reversed course to seek some relief from the Third Fleet's aerial onslaught. Halsey's rapid concentration left the Southern Force—Kurita's Surigao group—largely unscathed. Halsey left it to Kinkaid.

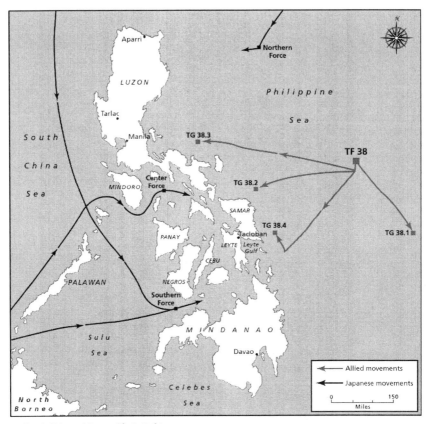

Halsey's Dispositions. *Chris Robinson*.

During the day, the light carrier *Princeton* (CVL 23), part of Sherman's TG 38.3, was struck by a bomb that penetrated the flight deck, entered the heart of the ship, and exploded. As Samuel Eliot Morison recounted: "The blast entered the hangar deck, which was soon roaring with burning gasoline. The flames greedily licked through open bomb bay doors on six TBFs that had been struck below, enveloping their loaded torpedoes, which exploded one by one, tossing the 25-foot square elevator masthead-high—whence it fell back into the pit—and blowing the after elevator onto the flight deck."[20]

The *Princeton*'s crew made progress against the conflagration until that afternoon when the torpedo stowage exploded, blowing off her stern. The small carrier was doomed. The cruiser *Birmingham* (CL 62), alongside to help fight the fires, was showered with lethal debris; many of her crew were killed. The event was a powerful reminder of the potential lethality of Japanese land-based planes. Halsey noted it accordingly.[21]

Meanwhile, Vice Admiral Ozawa was working hard to draw the American carriers away from Leyte Gulf. His planes first sighted Halsey's TG 38.3 that morning, at about 0700, when Ozawa's force was roughly 350 miles away. He decided to close to 150 miles, well within the range of American search planes, before launching a strike. By 1145, his first group of attack aircraft was taking to the air.[22] These were intercepted by Rear Admiral Sherman's combat air patrol, which mistook them for land-based planes. At 1430, Ozawa detached a surface action group under Rear Admiral Matsuda Chiaki with the battleships *Ise* and *Hyuga*, and escorting light forces. It was intended to attract Halsey's attention and draw attacking aircraft away from Ozawa's carriers. If he could get close enough, Ozawa expected Matsuda to join Kurita's forces in a surface action. The Third Fleet remained unaware of Ozawa's presence throughout these moves.

However, Rear Admiral Sherman, commander of TG 38.3, suspected the Japanese carriers were to the north. Halsey's instructions failed to acknowledge the potential threat from that direction, so Sherman obtained permission from Vice Admiral Mitscher, who was in TG 38.3 on board the carrier *Lexington* (CV 16), to search northward.[23] Sherman's planes took off at 1405. At about 1540, one of them finally detected Ozawa's force by sighting Matsuda's ships. Another plane found the rest of Ozawa's group about an hour later. The presence of the Japanese carriers was finally revealed; by 1655, the information had reached Halsey.

In the meantime, Halsey had been reacting to enemy moves. At 1640, he issued orders based on his standing battle plan. If the Central Force continued its progress it would emerge through San Bernardino Strait that night. He prepared to attack it with a smaller version of his major surface striking force, TF 34, by combining ships from TG 38.2 and TG 38.4. The ships in Sherman's TG 38.3 were too far away to concentrate in time.

> Battle Plan. BatDiv 7, MIAMI, VINCENNES, BILOXI, Desron 52, less STEVEN, PORTER, from TG 38.2 and WASHINGTON, ALABAMA, WICHITA, NEW ORLEANS, DesDiv 100, PATTERSON, BAGLEY from TG 38.4 will be formed as TF 34 under V.Adm. Lee, Commander Battle Line. TF 34 engage decisively at long ranges. CTG [Commander, Task Group] 38.4 conduct carriers of TG 38.2

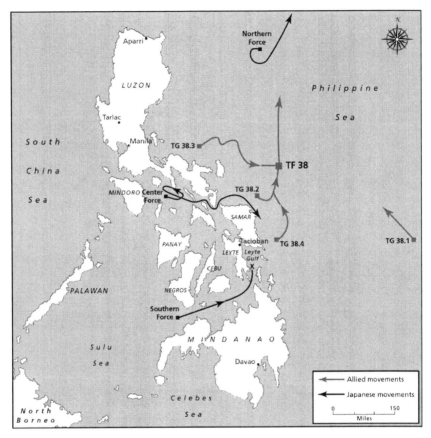

Halsey's Concentration. *Chris Robinson.*

and TG 38.4 clear of surface fighting. Instructions for TG 38.3 and TG 38.1 later. Halsey OTC [Officer in Tactical Command] in NEW JERSEY.[24]

These instructions gave Vice Admiral Lee a force of four battleships—*Iowa, New Jersey, Washington,* and *Alabama,* five cruisers, and fourteen destroyers.[25] The order was sent via shortwave radio so that Admiral Nimitz, included as an informational addressee, could receive it. Although it was not sent to Kinkaid, he intercepted it. Neither of them received the follow-up, which Halsey sent by voice radio. It indicated, "If the enemy sorties, TF 34 will be formed when directed by me."[26] Halsey's instructions were a preparatory order, but Nimitz and Kinkaid believed that TF 34 had been formed and was waiting to ambush the Center Force.

The Decision

Halsey's preparatory instructions were soon overtaken by events. The sighting of the Japanese carriers offered an opportunity to eliminate the IJN's remaining strike forces. Rear Admiral Sherman's attitude accurately reflected the developing situation: "As the sun went down, the situation was entirely to my liking and I felt we had a chance to completely wipe out a major group of the enemy fleet including the precious carriers which he could ill afford to lose."[27] The "opportunity for destruction of major portion of the enemy fleet" had appeared. It was up to Halsey and his subordinates to determine how best to carry it out.

Halsey had built a reputation and public persona through bold, aggressive leadership in the South Pacific. He had won the Guadalcanal Campaign and led the successful offensive up the Solomon Island chain, helping to isolate the Japanese stronghold at Rabaul and subjecting their forces to substantial attrition. As a theater commander in the South Pacific, Halsey had commanded from shore bases, operating through his subordinates with clear, direct instructions. Time and distance forced him to temper his stance and delegate action to others. Command of the Third Fleet changed this paradigm. At sea, on the flag bridge of the battleship *New Jersey*, Halsey could directly intervene in the movements of his ships and planes. His aggressive disposition led him to downplay the responsibilities of fleet command and direct the movements of ships as if he were a task force commander. Halsey's staff, which he brought over with him from the South Pacific, was personally enamored with his style of leadership. They did little to check these tendencies. As a result, the responsibilities of Vice Admiral Mitscher, commander of TF 38, were curtailed, dampening his initiative.

This would lead to an unfortunate decision on the evening of 24 October. Halsey's staff lacked the necessary expertise with carrier warfare to thoroughly analyze the developing situation. They failed to check their admiral's predispositions or make use of alternative sources of information.[28] In a lengthy discussion, Halsey's fear of Japanese land-based air predominated. He dismissed the idea of leaving TF 34 and a supporting carrier group to guard San Bernardino Strait as too dangerous. He refused to entertain courses of action that divided his forces; instead, he stressed the importance of keeping TF 38 together to annihilate the IJN carriers.[29] Halsey's staff was unable to force an effective analysis of alternatives or prompt a consultation with subordinates; the admiral was set on taking the whole force north. "When . . . one staff member dissented from the admiral's decision, Halsey overruled further debate."[30] By 1950, he had resolved to go after the enemy carriers.

His subordinates were surprised by this decision. Several, once they fully realized its implications, offered alternatives or new information that called it into question. At 2005, a plane from TG 38.2's light carrier *Independence* (CVL 22) transmitted a sighting report: Kurita's Center Force had turned around and was heading east once again. Rear Admiral Bogan discussed the situation with his flag captain, Capt. Edward C. Ewen. Both were convinced the Center Force would emerge from the strait the next day. Bogan called Halsey over the TBS radio and received a curt dismissal.[31] Bogan had apparently been working on a recommendation to send TG 38.3 and TG 38.4 north while TG 38.2 and TF 34 guarded the strait, but decided against sending it.[32] In the meantime, Vice Admiral Lee was analyzing the developing situation. He became convinced the Northern Force was a decoy and Kurita's surface action group was the real threat. Before sundown, he sent a visual signal to Halsey offering this perspective.[33] Lee received an acknowledgment, but nothing more. After the report from the *Independence*'s plane came in, Lee transmitted a TBS message indicating he was "certain" the Center Force was going to come out and fight.[34] Halsey does not appear to have factored these inputs into his decision.

Halsey and his staff also failed to consult with his senior task force commander, Vice Admiral Mitscher, or his staff, which had gained extensive experience commanding the large, distributed, fast carrier task forces.[35] Much like Nimitz and Kinkaid, Mitscher assumed that Halsey's orders on the evening of 24 October would lead to two separate engagements, one with TF 34 off San Bernardino Strait and another with the remaining forces of TF 38 farther north. Dividing his forces this way would have allowed Halsey to engage both IJN groups simultaneously. Once Mitscher's chief of staff, Commo. Arleigh Burke, realized that this was not the case and that the entire force was heading north, he woke Mitscher and urged him to press Halsey to pursue an alternative. Mitscher refused, saying, "If he wants my advice, he'll ask for it."[36] Halsey's tendency to operate as his own task force commander had shunted Mitscher and his talented staff aside.[37]

When Halsey put his plan in motion at 1950, he radioed Kinkaid: "Strike reports indicate enemy heavily damaged. Am proceeding north with three groups to attack carrier forces at dawn."[38] Although the meaning of this was clear to Halsey, Kinkaid mistakenly assumed that TF 34 had already been formed and was positioned to guard the northern flank of Leyte Gulf. At Pearl Harbor, Nimitz came to the same conclusion. Halsey's imprecise communications and decision to move all of his forces north created a major misunderstanding.

The Reasoning

By midnight on 24 October, Halsey was racing north with his three carrier task groups. He assumed that the Center Force was so damaged that it would offer no threat to Kinkaid, but Halsey did not have to choose one threat over the other. The Third Fleet had sufficient fighting strength to deal with both enemy forces simultaneously. When planes from Rear Admiral Sherman's TG 38.3 sighted Ozawa's force, Commodore Burke recommended to Mitscher that he detach TG 38.3's battleships *Massachusetts* (BB 59) and *South Dakota* (BB 57), along with supporting cruisers and destroyers, to seek a night surface action with Ozawa's group. Burke was a surface warfare officer who had repeatedly triumphed over the Japanese in night battles in the Solomons. He knew that modern radars and the Combat Information Center would give his ships a decisive advantage at night. Mitscher agreed with the idea and ordered Sherman to prepare plans for the mission.[39]

Halsey's order to concentrate superseded these instructions and deprived subordinate commanders of the opportunity to exploit the situation on their own initiative.[40] That was unfortunate, because new tactical instructions issued the year before had been developed to cover these kinds of situations. PAC-10, *Current Tactical Orders and Doctrine, U.S. Pacific Fleet*, and its successor USF-10A, *Current Tactical Orders and Doctrine, U.S. Fleet*, provided a suite of battle plans for task forces of various sizes and compositions, giving the Pacific Fleet unprecedented flexibility.[41] They created the ability to quickly respond to a variety of different circumstances with clear plans and orders that would lend cohesion in battle; Vice Admiral Lee regularly referenced them as a basis for his instructions.[42] Had Sherman sent the *Massachusetts* and *South Dakota* against Ozawa, they would have fought using the plans in USF-10A.[43]

That course of action—sending TG 38.3 against Ozawa while TG 38.2 and TG 38.4 guarded San Bernardino—would not only have allowed

Halsey to engage both enemy groups simultaneously, it also would have initiated combat with the Northern Force earlier. Other combinations were possible, such as sending two carrier groups north while the four-battleship configuration of TF 34 and a supporting carrier group remained behind. Regardless of the specific arrangement, a powerful surface action group could have intercepted Kurita in the early morning, striking in concert with carrier planes. Mitscher could have led a similar fight farther north against Ozawa. Halsey could have divided his force and relied on decentralized decision-making to act more rapidly against the IJN, decisively defeating both enemy forces. He failed to do so. Why did he not pursue these alternatives?

The evidence suggests three primary factors led to Halsey's decision. The first was that the Third Fleet had no defined battle plan for simultaneous action in separate locations. Halsey assumed that a single major action would occur. In that battle, TF 34 would be the fleet's surface striking force and TG 34.5 would pursue any fleeing enemy vessels.[44] There was no contingency plan for operations against two roughly equivalent Japanese forces. These plans built on assumptions the Navy embraced throughout the interwar period (1919–39). Concentration was essential to prevent defeat in battle. The *War Instructions* made this clear: "An adequately superior force should be concentrated at the decisive point. The forces detailed for tasks, which do not permit them to support the operations or the action at the decisive point, must be kept to a minimum. The pressure at the decisive point should be brought to bear with full effect and with dispatch."[45]

This is exactly what Halsey intended to do. The predilection of the Japanese to divide their forces and attack from multiple directions had strengthened the Navy's belief in the importance of concentration; during the Battle of the Philippine Sea in June, Vice Admiral Spruance minimized losses by keeping his forces concentrated in the face of Japanese aerial attacks.[46] Halsey, cognizant of the threat of Japanese land-based planes, intended to do the same. Accordingly, he kept the Third Fleet concentrated as it moved north and prepared for battle.

The second explanation is that Halsey and his staff had difficulty effectively commanding such a large and distributed collection of forces from the flagship *New Jersey*. While afloat, Halsey's aggressive nature predisposed him to act as a task force commander; he downplayed the greater responsibilities of fleet command and avoided searching for information beyond that which he expected to receive. Early in the war, Admiral Nimitz and many of his subordinates recognized the value of commanding from ashore, where communication facilities were superior and radio silence unnecessary. Shore commands had the additional advantage of being removed from the chaos and confusion of naval battles; admirals and their staffs could rest more consistently. They could also track developing situations, assess alternatives, and direct their forces more effectively. This approach had served Halsey well in the Solomons, but he lacked these advantages when operating with TF 38. As a result, he slipped out of his role as an operational commander and became focused on the tactical mission.[47] Halsey and his staff failed to recognize the Japanese ruse, despite warnings from subordinates and intelligence that the IJN would make the transport forces their primary target.[48]

Finally, Halsey and his subordinates were tired.[49] They had been at sea almost two months. TF 38 began supporting the invasion of the Palaus on 31 August with strikes on the Bonins and Yap. Strikes against the Visayas followed. In mid-September, large-scale attacks on the Philippines convinced Halsey that plans for the invasion of Leyte could be accelerated; they were, but this left little time for rest or to absorb lessons. From 9 to 17 October, TF 38 struck Formosa, the Ryukyus, and targets in the Philippines. The assault on Leyte immediately followed. By the evening of 24 October, Halsey had been "without sleep for nearly two days."[50] The Third Fleet had kept the pressure on the Japanese, but the admiral and his men were fatigued from the effort. This made it more likely that they would default to established plans, fall into entrenched habits, and fail to respond creatively to Japanese moves.

Once Halsey had concluded that the Center Force was no longer a significant threat—he later argued that he believed that "even if the Center Force did sortie from San Bernardino Straits, its fighting efficiency had been too greatly impaired to be able to win a decision against the Leyte [Invasion] forces"—it was natural for him to take his entire force north to seek battle with Ozawa.[51] On 25 October, Halsey sent a communication to Nimitz, MacArthur, and Kinkaid explaining his decision. It stated in part:

> To statically guard San Bernardino Strait until enemy surface and carrier air attacks could be coordinated would have been childish so three carrier groups were concentrated during the night and

started north for a surprise dawn attack on the enemy carrier fleet. I considered that the enemy force in Sibuyan Sea [Center Force] had been so badly damaged that they constituted no serious threat to Kinkaid and that estimate has been borne out by the events of the 25th off Surigao. The enemy carrier force was caught off guard there being no air opposition over the target and no air attack against our force.[52]

Halsey's rationalization is valuable for what it does not say. His failure to capitalize on the initiative of his subordinates and inability to assess all available sources of information had cost him the opportunity to fight both IJN forces simultaneously and win a decisive victory.

The Plan in Action

Mitscher's planes sighted Ozawa at 0710; the Northern Force was much farther away than anticipated. During the night, Halsey had reduced speed to put his battle plan in action. As the battleships, cruisers, and destroyers separated from their respective task forces and came together as TF 34, the fleet slowed. There would be no coordinated strike of carrier planes and surface gunfire at dawn. Instead, swarms of planes concentrated on the Japanese ships in a series of powerful strikes. Light carrier *Chitose* was the first to succumb. The carrier *Zuikaku*, veteran of the Pearl Harbor attack, was torpedoed, bombed, and sunk. Light carrier *Zuiho* followed her down. The light carrier *Chiyoda* caught fire and was abandoned; Halsey's cruisers sank her that afternoon. The hybrid battleship-carriers *Ise* and *Hyuga* survived the air strikes. They would have been perfect targets for TF 34, but Lee's battleships never got into range.

Earlier that morning, as Rear Admiral Oldendorf's ships were defeating the IJN's Southern Force, Kinkaid called a conference to discuss the situation. He wanted to be sure he and his staff were not overlooking anything. Kinkaid's operations officer, Capt. Richard H. Cruzen, pointed out that they lacked definitive evidence that TF 34 was guarding the exit to San Bernardino Strait. He recommended they ask Halsey about it directly; Kinkaid agreed. A message was sent at 0412. Halsey did not receive it until 0648 and he did not respond until 0705.[53]

While these messages were being exchanged, the ships of Rear Adm. Thomas L. Sprague's TG 77.4, part of Kinkaid's escort carrier group, sighted Kurita's Center Force, bearing down on them off Samar. Rear Adm.

Clifton A. F. Sprague's TU 77.4.3—callsign "Taffy 3"—was nearest the enemy. At about 0700, Kurita's battleships opened fire. In a desperate fight, the diminutive carriers and their escorts fought a delaying action, damaging three heavy cruisers for the loss of two escort carriers, two destroyers, and a destroyer escort.[54]

The surprise appearance of Kurita's powerful force off Samar alarmed Kinkaid. At 0707, he sent a plain-language transmission to Halsey saying that enemy battleships and cruisers were firing on Rear Adm. Clifton Sprague's TU 77.4.3. Halsey did not receive it until 0822. A series of additional requests reached Halsey out of order as Kinkaid and Clifton Sprague repeatedly asked for assistance. At 0727, Kinkaid explicitly requested help from Lee's battleships. By the time Halsey read that message, he had already ordered Vice Adm. John S. McCain's TG 38.1 to assist; Halsey let Kinkaid know help was coming at 0927 but remained focused on his mission to destroy the Northern Force. He kept Lee's TF 34 with him.[55]

At 1000, Halsey received a query from Admiral Nimitz, who had been monitoring the situation. Nimitz was aware of the surprise appearance of the Center Force and the desperate fight of Taffy 3. He was hesitant to interfere with commanders on the spot, but was surprised that TF 34, which he believed had already been formed, was out of position. He suspected that TF 34 was probably with Halsey, engaging the Northern Force, but he sent a message to determine its whereabouts and suggest to Halsey that it might be in the wrong place.[56] The message was encoded and sent as: "Turkey Trots to Water. From CINCPAC. Where is, repeat, where is TF 34. The world wonders." Nonsense padding appeared at the start and end of the message, but because the padding at the end made sense in context, it was not removed by the signalmen aboard the *New Jersey*. When Halsey read, "the world wonders," he took it as a sarcastic comment on his leadership and was livid.[57] But the prompt did cause Halsey to reassess the situation. At 1015, he ordered the bulk of TF 34 to head south with TG 38.2 in support.[58] By then Kurita had already made the decision to retire. Lee's ships would arrive off San Bernardino too late to catch them.

Conclusion

Halsey's decision to take his whole force north prevented him from winning a decisive victory over the IJN. He had sufficient force to defeat both the Center Force and the Northern Force simultaneously. Had Halsey retained focus on his responsibilities as a fleet commander, made more effective use of the initiative of his subordinates, and created an atmosphere of decentralized decision-making, he might have won an unparalleled victory. However, his fatigue, his predisposition for aggressive action, and the inexperience of his staff combined with a tactical doctrine that emphasized the importance of concentration prevented him from considering alternative courses of action. The Battle of Leyte Gulf was a significant victory in spite of these shortcomings, but Halsey's performance deserves critical analysis; his decision to concentrate and head north prevented Leyte from being the decisive action he sought. If Halsey had made more effective use of his subordinates and created a command environment that fostered their initiative, he could have won an overwhelming victory.

About the Author

Trent Hone is an award-winning naval historian and a managing consultant with Excella in Arlington, Virginia. He is an expert on U.S. Navy tactics and doctrine. He co-authored *Battle Line: The United States Navy, 1919–1939* and has written chapters for several books, including *To Crown the Waves: The Great Navies of the First World War* and *On Seas Contested: The Seven Great Navies of the Second World War*. His article "U.S. Navy Surface Battle Doctrine and Victory in the Pacific" was awarded the U.S. Naval War College's Edward S. Miller Prize and the Naval History and Heritage Command's Ernest M. Eller Prize. His essay "Guadalcanal Proved Experimentation Works" earned second place in the 2017 Chief of Naval Operations Naval History Essay Contest. Hone regularly writes and speaks about the Navy's organizational learning, doctrine, strategy, and how the three interrelate. His latest book, *Learning War: The Evolution of Fighting Doctrine in the U.S. Navy, 1898–1945*, brings a new and valuable perspective that explains how the Navy improved its tactical doctrine before and during World War II. It was published by the U.S. Naval Institute in June 2018.

Notes

1. *Report on the Operations of Western Pacific Task Forces and the THIRD Fleet,* Commander THIRD Fleet, 25 January 1945, 11, Box

41, *World War II Action and Operational Reports,* Record Group 38, Records of the Office of the Chief of Naval Operations [hereafter: RG 38], National Archives and Records Administration [hereafter: NARA], Washington, D.C.
2. *Report on the Operations of Western Pacific Task Forces and the THIRD Fleet*, 11.
3. *Report on the Operations of Western Pacific Task Forces and the THIRD Fleet*, 11.
4. Milan Vego, *The Battle for Leyte, 1944: Allied and Japanese Plans, Preparations, and Execution* (Annapolis, MD: Naval Institute Press, 2006), 278; Clark G. Reynolds, *The Fast Carriers: The Forging of an Air Navy* (Annapolis, MD: Naval Institute Press, 1968), 268.
5. "Preliminary Draft of Campaign—Granite," Commander-in-Chief, United States Pacific Fleet, 27 December 1943, Box 24, *World War II Plans, Orders, and Related Documents*, RG 38, NARA; "Campaign Plan Granite," Commander-in-Chief, Pacific Ocean Areas, 15 January 1944, *Strategic Plans Division Records*, RG 38, NARA.
6. Samuel Eliot Morison, *History of the United States Naval Operations in World War II* (Boston, MA: Little, Brown, 1984), 12:59; Reynolds, *Fast Carriers*, 204–10; Vego, *The Battle for Leyte, 1944*, 290.
7. "Operation Plan No. 6-44, CINCPOA," 21 July 1944, Box 41, *World War II Action and Operational Reports*, RG 38, NARA.
8. "Operation Plan No. 8-44, CINCPOA," 27 September 1944, Box 41, *World War II Action and Operational Reports*, RG 38, NARA; Vego, *The Battle for Leyte, 1944*, 126.
9. "Operations Plan No. 14-44, Third Fleet," 1 August 1944, Box 57, *World War II Plans, Orders, and Related Documents*, RG 38, NARA; Vego, *The Battle for Leyte, 1944*, 127.
10. "Operations Order No. 21-44, Third Fleet," October 1944, Appendix C to *Report on the Operations of Western Pacific Task Forces and the THIRD Fleet*, Commander THIRD Fleet, 25 January 1945.
11. Vego, *The Battle for Leyte, 1944*, 100–103.
12. "Battle Plan No. 1-44, Commander Third Fleet," 9 September 1944, Box 57, *World War II Plans, Orders, and Related Documents*, RG 38, NARA.
13. Trent Hone, *Learning War: The Evolution of Fighting Doctrine in the U.S. Navy, 1898–1945* (Annapolis, MD: Naval Institute Press, 2018), 92–162.

14. "Operation Order No. 13-44, ComBatPac," Addendum No. 1, 16 October 1944, Box 224, *World War II Plans, Orders, and Related Documents*, RG 38, NARA.
15. Vego, *The Battle for Leyte, 1944*, 55–58.
16. Vego, *The Battle for Leyte, 1944*, 197–98.
17. Vego, *The Battle for Leyte, 1944*, 211–15.
18. "Operation Plan No. 13-44, Commander Allied Naval Force, Southwest Pacific Area," 26 September 1944, Appendix 2 to Annex E, Box 66, *World War II Plans, Orders, and Related Documents*, RG 38, NARA; Vego, *The Battle for Leyte, 1944*, 115.
19. Richard W. Bates, *The Battle for Leyte Gulf, October 1944: Strategical and Tactical Analysis*, vol. 3, *Operations from 0000 October 20th (D-Day) until 1042 October 23rd* (Newport, RI: U.S. Naval War College, 1957), 771–72.
20. Morison, *History of the United States Naval Operations in World War II*, 12:178.
21. *Report on the Operations of Western Pacific Task Forces and the THIRD Fleet*, 10.
22. Vego, *The Battle for Leyte, 1944*, 276–77.
23. Bates, *The Battle for Leyte Gulf, October 1944*, 3:773.
24. Command Summary of Fleet Admiral Chester W. Nimitz, "Graybook," COM 3RD FLEET Serial 240612, 24 October 1944, 5:2242.
25. "Report of Operations of Task Force Thirty-Four During the Period 6 October 1944 to 3 November 1944," Commander Task Force Thirty-Four, 14 December 1944, 5–6, Box 135, *World War II Action and Operational Reports*, RG 38, NARA.
26. Vego, *The Battle for Leyte, 1944*, 260.
27. Sherman Action Report, 0090, 2 December 1944, quoted in Reynolds, *Fast Carriers*, 267.
28. Vego, *The Battle for Leyte, 1944*, 291.
29. Reynolds, *Fast Carriers*, 267.
30. Clark G. Reynolds, "William F. Halsey, Jr.: The Bull," in *The Great Admirals: Command at Sea, 1587–1945*, edited by Jack Sweetman (Annapolis, MD: Naval Institute Press, 1997), 496.
31. Morison, *History of the United States Naval Operations in World War II*, 12:195.
32. Vego, *The Battle for Leyte, 1944*, 280.
33. Reynolds, "William F. Halsey, Jr.," 496; E. B. Potter, *Admiral Arleigh Burke* (Annapolis, MD: Naval Institute Press, 1990), 206.

34. Morison, *History of the United States Naval Operations in World War II*, 12:195; Vego, *The Battle for Leyte, 1944*, 280.
35. Clark G. Reynolds, *Admiral John H. Towers: The Struggle for Naval Air Supremacy* (Annapolis, MD: Naval Institute Press, 1991), 493.
36. Potter, *Burke*, 207; Reynolds, *Fast Carriers*, 270; Morison, *History of the United States Naval Operations in World War II*, 12:196.
37. Vego, *The Battle for Leyte, 1944*, 291.
38. "Graybook," COM 3RD FLEET Serial 241124, 24 October 1944, 5:2243.
39. Potter, *Burke*, 204.
40. Potter, *Burke*, 204.
41. *Current Tactical Orders and Doctrine, U.S. Pacific Fleet*, PAC-10, Commander-in-Chief, U.S. Pacific Fleet, June 1943, Box 61, *U.S. Navy and Related Operational, Tactical, and Instructional Publications*, Entry 337, RG 38, NARA; *Current Tactical Orders and Doctrine, U.S. Fleet*, USF-10A, Commander-in-Chief, United States Fleet, 1 February 1944, Box 16, *World War II Bates-Leyte Collection*, RG 38, NARA.
42. *General Tactical Instructions, United States Navy*, FTP-188, 1940, 14–10 through 14–15, Box 108, *World War II Command File*, Naval Historical Center Archives, Washington, D.C.; "Operation Order No. 13-44, COMBATPAC," 6 October 1944, Box 224, *World War II Plans, Orders, and Related Documents*, RG 38, NARA; "Operation Plan No. 1-44, COMBATPAC," 12 April 1944, Box 223, *World War II Plans, Orders, and Related Documents*, RG 38, NARA; "Operation Plan No. 10-44, COMBATPAC," 26 August 1944, Box 224, *World War II Plans, Orders, and Related Documents*, RG 38, NARA.
43. Hone, *Learning War*, 250–99.
44. "Battle Plan No. 1-44, Commander Third Fleet," 9 September 1944; "Operation Order No. 13-44, ComBatPac," Addendum No. 1, 16 October 1944.
45. *War Instructions, United States Navy*, FTP-143, 1934, 19, Box 108, *World War II Command File*, Naval Historical Center Archives, Washington, D.C.
46. Capt. Wayne P. Hughes Jr. (Ret.), *Fleet Tactics and Coastal Combat* (Annapolis, MD: Naval Institute Press, 2000), 105–8.
47. Vego, *The Battle for Leyte, 1944*, 20, 290–91.
48. "Captured Enemy Operation Order, Z Ops," 28 May 1944, Box 29, *World War II Plans, Orders, and Related Documents*, RG 38, NARA.

49. Reynolds indicates Halsey went to sleep "exhausted" immediately after committing the Third Fleet to run to the north. See Reynolds, "William F. Halsey, Jr.," 496.
50. Reynolds, *Fast Carriers*, 268.
51. *Report on the Operations of Western Pacific Task Forces and the THIRD Fleet*, 11.
52. "Graybook," COM 3RD FLEET Serial 251317, 25 October 1944, 5:2392.
53. Vego, *The Battle for Leyte, 1944*, 268–69.
54. Morison, *History of the United States Naval Operations in World War II*, 12:242–88; James D. Hornfischer, *The Last Stand of the Tin Can Sailors: The Extraordinary World War II Story of the U.S. Navy's Finest Hour* (New York: Bantam Books, 2009).
55. Morison, *History of the United States Naval Operations in World War II*, 12:293–94; Vego, *The Battle for Leyte, 1944*, 282–83.
56. E. B. Potter, *Nimitz* (Annapolis, MD: Naval Institute Press, 1976), 338–40.
57. Vego, *The Battle for Leyte, 1944*, 283.
58. Vego, *The Battle for Leyte, 1944*, 283; Morison, *History of the United States Naval Operations in World War II*, 12:329.

6

"WHERE IS TASK FORCE 34?"
The Frustration of Admiral Lee
Paul Stillwell

VICE ADM. WILLIS LEE HAD BEEN PREPARING for the Battle of Leyte Gulf his entire professional life. Even before he graduated from the Naval Academy in 1908, he had developed a keen interest in gunnery. One year he accomplished the unparalleled feat of winning national championships in both rifle and pistol. In 1914, as a crew member of the battleship *New Hampshire*, he went ashore with a rifle as part of the ship's landing party at Vera Cruz, Mexico. When he was a member of the U.S. rifle team at the 1920 Olympic Games, he won seven medals. In the 1920s, he commanded four-stack destroyers and was known for his tactical and ship-handling prowess. Lee was also gifted in mathematical ability. By using a small device pulled from his pocket, he could usually solve station-taking trigonometry problems before watch standers did.

Curiously, even though Lee was a gunnery expert, he did not get a postgraduate degree in ordnance engineering. Essentially his postgraduate education came at sea. His focus was on using guns, rather than designing and building them. Because of all his destroyer service in the 1920s, he had missed the billet of battleship gunnery officer that was a standard for up-and-coming surface officers of the era. By the time he reported to the battleship *Pennsylvania* in the early 1930s, he was a commander and too senior to be gunnery officer. Instead he took over as navigator of the ship and was later the executive officer. The latter was casting against type because the fleet flagship required spit and polish, and Lee tended toward the unkempt in his personal appearance.

His tours ashore during the 1930s were in the Fleet Training Division (OP-22) in the Navy Department in Washington. The training was not for personal skills but for the collective performance of ships' crews in improving battle readiness. That involved monitoring gunnery and engineering exercises and the results of annual war games, known as fleet problems. A constant challenge during the period was dealing with the changes necessitated by the ever-increasing role of aircraft in naval warfare. The battle line still had primacy in the fleet, but airplanes were no longer just for scouting to find the enemy. The development of dive-bombing, and the growing number of carriers being built, brought about an offensive role for aircraft—to seek out and attack the enemy, perhaps even before opposing battle lines came in contact.

Another irony, added to his not having served as a battleship gunnery officer, was that he never commanded an individual battleship. In 1936, after being promoted to captain, he was too junior for a battleship. Instead, he became skipper of the light cruiser *Concord*, which was commissioned in 1923. Her intended role was as a scout cruiser. She had a designed speed of thirty-five knots, so she could scout ahead of the battle fleet in search of enemy combatants. Even though the ship was barely a teenager by the time Lee went on board, she was hopelessly outmoded. She had a main battery of twelve 6-inch guns, but scouting aircraft could far outrange her. Lee was well aware of the new reality and concentrated his efforts on her meager antiaircraft (AA) battery, trying to find ways to make it more effective. She was homeported in San Diego, California, and one shipmate recalled that the Sunday newspaper might go unread because Lee was instead poring over data and trying to improve the ship's AA capability.

After two years as skipper, Lee was relieved but remained on board the *Concord*, which was the flagship for Commander Cruisers Battle Force/Cruiser Division Three. Lee became operations officer to Rear Adm. Harold R. Stark. Since Stark had white hair and the staff consisted of seven officers, the group received a nickname from a movie that had been recently released: *Snow White and the Seven Dwarfs*. Soon the command received a huge upgrade in capability. Light cruisers of the *Brooklyn* class began joining the fleet. Each was equipped with five triple turrets of rapid-fire 6-inch guns. After a time, the admiral and staff moved to one of the new ships—the USS *Honolulu*.

In August 1939, Admiral Stark was promoted to four stars and became Chief of Naval Operations. He took with him to Washington some of his cruiser staff members, including Captain Lee. As he had in his previous shore tours, Lee gravitated to the Fleet Training Division of OpNav and became its assistant director. One month after Stark took over, World War II began in Europe with Germany's invasion of Poland and declarations of war by Britain and France. Now the focus of Lee's division shifted from monitoring exercises in the fleet to active preparation for combat.

For Lee that meant working with the Bureau of Ordnance and the Bureau of Ships to outfit as many combatants as possible with antiaircraft guns. The standard light AA guns were the unreliable 1.1-inch weapons. Soon the Navy began installing large numbers of 20-millimeter and 40-millimeter guns to augment the heavier 5-inch weapons. Lee was technically oriented and understood the big advantage conferred by radar, which was just beyond its fledgling stage. It would be another big help in solving the antiaircraft problem. He visited shipyards to view wooden mockups of such things as plotting rooms that were going into the new ships. The Japanese attack on Pearl Harbor in December 1941 added still more urgency to the task. By then Lee had been selected for rear admiral and moved up to head OP-22. After Adm. Ernest J. King became commander in chief of the U.S. Fleet on 30 December 1941, Lee moved to his staff as assistant chief of staff for readiness.

His first wartime sea duty began in August 1942 when he boarded the new fast (27-knot) battleship *South Dakota* and took residence in her flag quarters as the commander of Battleship Division Six. Previously the 27-knot *Washington* and her sister *North Carolina* had been serving in the Atlantic and overseas in support of Britain's Royal Navy. Lee was the first U.S. flag officer to take a division of fast battleships to the Pacific. The initial destination was the Nukualofa anchorage of Tongatabu in the Friendly Islands of the South Pacific. Alas, on 6 September, two days after her arrival, the *South Dakota* scraped her hull on an uncharted coral pinnacle and suffered extensive damage. She had to head for Pearl Harbor for repairs and a considerable beefing up of her antiaircraft guns. After a brief delay, Lee transferred to the USS *Washington*, which became his favorite flagship during the war. Lt. Dave Gray, later assistant ops officer on his staff, explained that Lee liked the setup in which the *Washington*'s combat information center was directly abaft the flag bridge and thus in direct touch with the flow of information. By contrast, in the *South Dakota*, CIC was inside the armored box lower in the ship.[1]

In August of 1942 members of the 1st Marine Division had landed on the islands of Guadalcanal and Tulagi in the Solomons chain. In the months that followed, U.S. and Japanese forces engaged in a bitter struggle as the latter tried to retake Henderson Field, the island's airstrip. The campaign involved heavy fighting at sea, in the air, and on land. The Japanese made frequent attempts to reinforce manpower while also hitting the island with aerial bombing and heavy surface naval bombardment. The latter was known as the "Tokyo Express." The frequent nocturnal raids were hard on morale. On the night of 12–13 November, a force of U.S. cruisers and destroyers fended off a planned bombardment but at a heavy loss in ships and men.

Two nights later, another bombardment group approached. Vice Adm. William Halsey Jr., Commander, South Pacific Force, ordered a cobbled-together team of four destroyers and two battleships to intercede. Lee, on board the *Washington* as the commander of Task Force 64, had tactical command. The second battleship was the *South Dakota*. The American ships made a clockwise circuit around Savo Island, adjacent to Guadalcanal, and then encountered a multipronged Japanese attack. The *Washington* relied on radar fire control, which the Japanese did not have. With torpedoes and optical fire control of guns, the Japanese put three of the four U.S. destroyers out of action. The *Preston* and *Walke* sank that night, and the *Benham* did so the following day. Only the *Gwin* survived. The *South Dakota* was riddled with gunfire. The *Washington*, under Lee's direction, inflicted fatal damage on the destroyer *Ayanami* and battleship *Kirishima*; she herself escaped unscathed. Lee credited radar for the victory. The Guadalcanal campaign had a few more spasms of combat after that battle, but Lee's victory had essentially ended Japanese hopes of retaking the island.

In April 1943, Lee was elevated to commander, Battleships Pacific, in part an administrative role as type commander for both old and new ships. But he still remained on scene in the *Washington* with the expectation that he would take tactical command if and when the Japanese heavy ships came out to pose a challenge. For more than a year, they did not, so it was largely a matter of watching, training, and waiting. The surface ship action had moved to the northern Solomons, which did not offer sea room for battleships. Indeed, the area around Savo and Guadalcanal did not either, but in late 1942 the use of battleships was a last-ditch means of dealing with a dire situation.

In late 1943, under the leadership of Adm. Chester Nimitz, Commander in Chief, Pacific Fleet, the U.S. Navy embarked on the Central Pacific offensive. In essence it was a matter of island hopping—invading at the edges of the Japanese empire. The key ships were the fast attack carriers and the amphibious craft that carried Marines and soldiers to their objectives. The task of shore bombardment fell to the old, slow U.S. battleships. The new battleships became tethered to the fast carrier task forces because they had the speed to keep up with them and because the forests of antiaircraft guns on their decks provided close-in protection for the vulnerable aircraft carriers. In effect, Lee became a passenger in his flagship, because the officer in tactical command was the commander of the fast carrier task force. By early 1944 that was Vice Adm. Marc Mitscher, Commander, Task Force 58. Lee continued to go along for the ride because of the possibility that heavy Japanese surface ships would emerge to challenge the American offensive. If that situation came about, the plan was to detach Lee's ships as a separate task force that would move away from the carriers to engage the enemy.

Such a possibility came up in June 1944 when U.S. forces landed at Saipan in the Marianas chain. The Marianas were within the Japanese defensive perimeter, and that was sufficient provocation for the Japanese navy to come in force to oppose the invasion. By that time in the war, Japan no longer had the top-notch pilots of 1941–42. The newer men had much less training and experience. On 19 June the Japanese sent waves of planes to attack the American ships. The U.S. air groups outmanned them and outgunned them. That day the Japanese lost nearly 350, planes shot down in an event that soon came to be known as the "Great Marianas Turkey Shoot."

The question that faced Adm. Raymond Spruance, Commander, Fifth Fleet, was whether to send his forces west to attack and destroy Japanese warships. Spruance, who had been the victor at the Battle of Midway in June 1942, was cautious. He feared that the Japanese might try an end run and send in ships to attack the U.S. troops ashore on Saipan. Admiral Mitscher, the carrier commander, had as his chief of staff Commo. Arleigh Burke, who had proven to be an excellent tactician in destroyer operations in the Solomons. As a surface warrior, he wanted to constitute Lee's proposed task force of heavy combatants to head west to take on the Japanese at night. He thus persuaded Mitscher to invite Lee to engage.[2]

Lee demurred in an emphatic response: "DO NOT RPT NOT BELIEVE WE SHOULD SEEK NIGHT ENGAGEMENT. POSSIBLE

ADVANTAGES OF RADAR MORE THAN OFFSET BY DIFFICULTIES OF COMMUNICATIONS AND LACK OF TRAINING IN FLEET TACTICS AT NIGHT. WOULD PRESS PURSUIT OF DAMAGED OR FLEEING ENEMY, HOWEVER, AT ANY TIME."[3] Admiral Lee doubtless recalled the confused close-quarters action off Guadalcanal and that the Japanese were skilled at night operations. Added to that, as he wrote Mitscher, his ships had not had the opportunity to train together because they had been absorbed into the carrier screens. Spruance quickly endorsed Lee's position, because it fit in with his own thinking. The chase after Japanese ships far to the west was mounted on 20 June by Mitscher's carrier pilots. They were partially successful but had only limited time to attack because of the long range and fuel limitations.

Because the battle line had not had a chance to maneuver together and thus was probably rusty in surface tactics, it was comparable to a football team that had been playing only defense and hadn't worked on its offensive plays. In August Admiral Halsey embarked in the flagship *New Jersey* as he took command of the Third Fleet. Since Halsey didn't want another missed opportunity, he directed that the battleships practice, and they did so after leaving Manus Island on 5 September.

Lee, on board the *Washington*, was designated commander of Task Group 38.5 and had tactical command for several days of operations. Halsey sent some officers from his staff to confer with Lee on plans. Six of the fast battleships maneuvered in company, including Halsey's flagship *New Jersey*. She and her sister *Iowa* had joined the Pacific Fleet in early 1944 and were rated at thirty-three knots—six knots faster than the two previous classes. The other ships that underwent the September training were the *Alabama, North Carolina, Massachusetts,* and *South Dakota.* The role of fast battleships in a fleet action would be to race ahead of the carriers and pick off cripples that had been damaged by carrier aircraft. The tactical exercises included rotating the formation axis, changing cruising dispositions, and varying speeds. Lt. Carl Solberg, an air intelligence officer on Halsey's staff, observed that the massing of the dreadnoughts jump-started morale: "The men on *New Jersey* drilled with shining eyes. Their time was at hand."[4]

One of the keys to U.S. success in the Pacific War was the ability of code breakers to decipher the contents of Japanese radio messages and thus divine their intentions for upcoming operations. The results of the code breaking came under the term Ultra. The most notable example was in

1942, when Adm. Chester Nimitz dispatched a force of American aircraft carriers that was able to ambush a large Japanese task force that planned to attack and occupy Midway Island. The American victory was a major turning point of the entire Pacific struggle—enabling U.S. forces to shift from defense to the offense. Later, in 1943, code breakers had advance word of the itinerary of Admiral Isoroku Yamamoto, Commander in Chief, Combined Fleet, during a visit to the Solomon Islands. Army Air Forces fighters shot down Yamamoto's plane and killed the admiral who had been a key architect of the attack on Pearl Harbor. American submarines sank many Japanese merchant ships because they had been tipped off about the routes of convoys.

Unfortunately, the American code breakers were not able to provide advance word on the overall scheme for Leyte Gulf. Years after the war, one of Halsey's intelligence officers wrote, "When Third Fleet went to sea the admiral continued to receive daily ULTRA dispatches from Nimitz's basement eavesdroppers filled with invaluable if sketchy clues as to enemy moves. But it must be emphasized that never during the battle for Leyte was it possible to read the command messages of the Imperial Fleet."[5]

As other essays in this volume report, the Japanese effort to disrupt the American landings on the island of Leyte was a three-pronged effort. The Sho ("To Conquer") plan called for a force of battleships, cruisers, and destroyers under Vice Admiral Takao Kurita to thread its way through the Philippine archipelago via the Palawan Passage, the Sibuyan Sea, and the San Bernardino Strait to attack the landing force. A northern force, under Vice Admiral Jisaburo Ozawa, composed of aircraft carriers, converted battleships, and smaller ships, would operate to the north as a decoy force to draw the Third Fleet away from San Bernardino Strait. The carriers had so few effective planes on board that the plan made this essentially a suicide mission. Two more groups of surface ships were to approach from the south. They were commanded by Vice Admirals Shoji Nishimura and Kiyohide Shima.

Things did not go well for the center force. At the outset the U.S. submarine *Darter* sank Kurita's flagship, the heavy cruiser *Atago*, on 23 October. The admiral was forced to seek a new flagship, in this case the super battleship *Yamato*. The *Yamato* and her sister *Musashi* were behemoths, displacing some 72,000 tons apiece and each mounting nine 18.1-inch guns. They had been on the sidelines during the early part of the war, the specifics of their capability known only vaguely by U.S. intelligence.

Things got worse on 24 October as the force transited eastward across the Sibuyan Sea. Planes from Mitscher's Task Force 58 pummeled the ships relentlessly during daytime attacks. Kurita's ships had no air cover. The planes also went after Japanese aircraft that flew from land bases. The scope was not as vast as at the Marianas, but the results were again one-sided. Cdr. David McCampbell was air group commander for the carrier *Essex* and supposedly consigned to coordination duties. But some of the land-based planes constituted too much of an immediate threat, so he jumped into his F6F Hellcat fighter, which was only partially fueled. He had a day for the record books, shooting down a total of nine enemy planes in one flight, a feat for which he later received the Medal of Honor.

The U.S. carrier planes mortally wounded the *Musashi* that afternoon with an overwhelming combination of armor-piercing bombs and torpedoes. The *Yamato* was also hit but survived. At 1530, Kurita turned his force west to get away from the pounding his ships were taking and to get some room to maneuver. At 1715, by which time the aerial attacks had ceased, Kurita reversed course, and his ships again headed east to carry out their mission in Leyte Gulf. Years later, Kurita's chief of staff, Rear Admiral Tomiji Koyanagi, wrote of a fascinating what-if. He said that if the U.S. planes had maintained surveillance, Admiral Halsey could have ignored Ozawa's carrier force and set up his ships outside San Bernardino Strait for an ambush. Wrote Koyanagi, "If he had done so, a night engagement against our exhausted forces would undoubtedly have been disastrous for us."[6]

Meanwhile, the southern arm, under Nishimura and Shima, steamed through the Sulu Sea with the objective of breaking through Surigao Strait into the gulf. In this case, lying in wait was a layered force of U.S. PT boats, destroyers, cruisers, and battleships under Commander, Task Group 77.2, Rear Adm. Jesse Oldendorf. The night battle was disastrous for the Japanese. The American heavy ships had the tactical advantage of crossing the Japanese T, that is, the Japanese ships were in column formation so that only their forward guns could bear. The Americans were in a perpendicular column so that all their turrets turned broadside could fire at the Japanese. Among the losses were the battleships *Fuso* and *Yamashiro*; the only survivor of the ambush was the destroyer *Shigure*.

Oldendorf's battleships (nearly all Pearl Harbor survivors), cruisers, and destroyers were attached to the U.S. Seventh Fleet, commanded by Vice Adm. Thomas C. Kinkaid. Their intended main role was to support the assault force on Leyte. The fact that they were available when the southern prong showed up was fortuitous and eliminated the Nishimura and Shima ships from any further role in the conflict. Far from fortuitous was the lack of an overall U.S. command structure for the battle. Halsey's Third Fleet was an independent entity. The amphibious force was detailed to handle the landings, while Halsey maintained command of Task Force 38, the carriers and associated ships. In effect, he shoved Mitscher aside and maintained tactical command of Task Force 38. His assigned mission was to protect the landing force, but Admiral Nimitz had given him the additional option of going after the Japanese carriers if they appeared. The aggressive Halsey chose to make attacking the defanged carriers his principal mission.

At 1512, before the Japanese turned west in the Sibuyan Sea, Halsey sent out by radio message a battle plan that aimed to set up Task Force 34 under Lee with four fast battleships, seven cruisers, and nineteen destroyers. Though Kinkaid was not an addressee on the message, his communicators intercepted it, thus leading to Kinkaid's assumption that Lee's force would be ready to take on Kurita's remaining ships. What he didn't know was that Halsey's message was a contingency plan for an uncertain future time, not an order to be executed. Halsey informed Kinkaid that he was taking the carrier force north, but his message was so vaguely worded as to be unclear about Lee's force. In fact, Halsey took the entire Task Force 38, including Lee's ships, to the north in order to avoid dividing his assets.

Most of the U.S. carriers were capable of flight operations only in daylight. One light carrier, the *Independence*, had a night-capable squadron and sent out reconnaissance planes on the night of 24–25 October. Reports back to the ship indicated that Japanese navigation lights were burning en route to San Bernardino Strait, showing the way for Kurita's ships to steam there. Rear Adm. Gerald Bogan, Commander. Task Group 38.2, called the *New Jersey* with a message to Halsey recommending that he activate Task Force 34 and send it to San Bernardino Strait, with Bogan's group along to provide air cover. A member of Halsey's staff brushed him off. It would have been a superb plan, allowing Halsey to have his cake and eat it too. But he resoundingly rejected the idea of dividing his assets.

Lee's staff was concerned that the Ozawa force was a decoy, that Kurita's force was headed east, and that Task Force 34 should be left to guard the strait. Lee's aide was Lt. Guilliaem "Gil" Aertsen; he had been with Lee since late 1942 and was treated almost as a surrogate son by the childless Lee. Before darkness fell, Aertsen recalled, Lee sent a flashing light message to Halsey to share his views about the coming battle. The only response was the simple word "Roger," indicating that the message had been received.[7] After dark, once the *Independence* reconnaissance reports arrived on board the *Washington,* Lee sent a voice message to Halsey and pushed his belief that Kurita was coming. No response came from the *New Jersey.* Lee was not the assertive type, and that was his last attempt to alert the single-minded Halsey. As Aertsen said of Lee, "He wasn't a heckler, as such."[8]

Mitscher, having been ousted from tactical command, had become the same sort of passenger as Lee. Commodore Burke took the *Independence* reports and woke up Mitscher to suggest that he urge Lee's force be activated. Mitscher asked if Halsey had the spotting report. Assured that he did, Mitscher said, "If he wants my advice he'll ask for it." Thus, presumably, Halsey assumed that Kinkaid's ships were guarding the strait, and Kinkaid assumed that Lee's were. In some cases, two wrongs can make a right. In this case two wrongs led to disaster for the Americans.

Meanwhile, Halsey and the entire Task Force 38 were under way through the night. Even as Japanese ships were being chewed up in Surigao Strait, Halsey ordered the formation of Task Force 34, which was to move out ten miles ahead of the carriers. It was a time-consuming task to withdraw the heavy ships from the carrier formations. As historian Clark Reynolds wrote, "Lee liked this close maneuvering at night even less than did Mitscher, and he ordered all his battleships to change to a different fixed course and slow to 15 knots, thus drawing them out of formation in a painfully slow but safe manner."[9]

By this time in the war, in response to an order from Adm. Ernest King, surface flag officers were assigned aviation chiefs of staff and vice versa. Up to then, Lee had relied on surface officer Capt. Bill Jennings in the role. Now, instead, he had Commo. Thomas Jeter, formerly a carrier skipper. Jeter didn't want to be in a battleship, and Lee didn't want him there either. Jeter urged Lee to speed up the process, but Lee maintained the cautious approach.[10] Once the ships were extricated, they moved out ahead. On his watch station in *Washington*'s sky control on the morning of 25 October was Lt. Cdr. Ned Mathews, staff combat intelligence officer. At the first glimmer of dawn, he remembered, the battleships fanned out to form a line abreast as they prepared to engage. Their forward turrets would be able to shoot on a wide front.[11]

WHERE IS TASK FORCE 34?

That same morning, with Lee's ships heading north, three small task units were operating to the east of San Bernardino Strait. They were part of Kinkaid's Seventh Fleet. The northernmost was Task Unit 77.4.3, known as Taffy 3. It was under the command of Rear Adm. Clifton A. F. Sprague, embarked in the escort carrier *Fanshaw Bay*. Taffy 3 comprised six small escort carriers, three destroyers, and four destroyer escorts. Their role was to provide support to the landing forces on Leyte. As the men on board the ships looked to the west, shapes like toothpicks appeared on the horizon. They were the topmasts of Admiral Kurita's force. At 0658, even before their hulls were above the horizon, the Japanese ships opened fire, dropping large-caliber rounds in among the ships of Taffy 3. Elsewhere in this book is a much more detailed account of the ordeal of the small ships and their heroic resistance.

As would be expected, news of the battle off the island of Samar soon reached Admiral Kinkaid. It came as a considerable surprise, because he expected Lee's battleships were there, not the light force that bore the brunt of Kurita's attack. Within a few minutes, shortly after 0700, Kinkaid sent a message to Halsey about the events in progress. He also posed a question that came as a surprise to Halsey: "Is TF 34 guarding San Bernardino Strait?" A later message to Halsey said, "Urgently need fast BBs Leyte Gulf at once." At 0900 Kinkaid's message to Halsey said, "Our CVEs being attacked by 4 BBs, 8 cruisers, plus others. Request Lee cover Leyte at top speed. Request fast carriers make immediate strike." The final plea was a desperate one, sent in plain language rather than taking time to encode it: "Where is Lee? Send Lee."[12]

Kinkaid's messages also attracted the attention of Admiral Nimitz in Hawaii. His normal approach, as fleet commander in chief, was to leave the tactical decisions to the commanders on scene, presumably because they had a better knowledge of the situation than he. As did Kinkaid, Nimitz had concluded that Halsey had left Task Force 34 at San Bernardino Strait, but clearly something was amiss.

At the direction of Nimitz, his war plans officer, Rear Adm. Forrest Sherman, drafted a message to Halsey, the substance of which was, "WHERE IS RPT WHERE IS TASK FORCE THIRTY FOUR." However, in those days of Morse code and manual encoding and decoding, it was standard practice to put nonsense padding at the beginning and end of messages to foil possible enemy decryption. The decoder on board the *New Jersey* quickly stripped away "TURKEY TROTS TO WATER" but left

"THE WORLD WONDERS" at the end. When Halsey read the message as delivered to him, he took the unintended second sentence as a sarcastic jibe and flew into a rage.

Concluding that he had to do something, Halsey detached Lee's force to head south, along with Bogan's Task Group 38.2. That combination was what Bogan had suggested the night before, only to be rebuffed. Included in Lee's force was Halsey's flagship *New Jersey*. It had to be irksome for him to leave the scene of the carrier action he had so yearned for. And, in retrospect, it may have been irksome for Lee as well.[13] Ozawa's force included two old battleships, *Ise* and *Hyuga*, that had been retrofitted with flight decks aft. They still retained their big guns forward and had powerful antiaircraft batteries. Mitscher's carrier planes sank the large carrier *Zuikaku*, the last surviving carrier from the six that hit Pearl Harbor in 1941. Also sunk were the light carriers *Chitose*, *Zuiho*, and *Chiyoda*, a cruiser, and two destroyers. But the old "hermaphrodite" battleships survived.

Coordinating the attack from overhead that day was Commander McCampbell, the *Essex* air group commander who had shot down nine planes the day before. At one point during the morning he saw from his aerial perch both the Japanese and American fleets steaming toward each other. He estimated that the enemy fleets got within about thirty miles of each other. And then, in response to Halsey's signal, Lee's big ships turned south at 1115 to head for San Bernardino Strait. At the time McCampbell wondered why they had reversed course. Only later did he learn of the message from Nimitz to Halsey.[14]

Heading south with Lee, in addition to his flagship *Washington*, were the two 33-knot ships, *Iowa* and *New Jersey*, and three more of the 27-knot fast battleships, *South Dakota*, *Massachusetts*, and *Alabama*; supporting cruisers and destroyers; and Bogan's Task Group 38.2. The force was delayed for two hours while fueling destroyers. In the meantime, shortly before noon on 25 October, Kurita ordered his center force to turn around and steam north and thus leave the transports unmolested. Around 1925, his ships prepared to enter San Bernardino Strait and head west. In the late afternoon, Halsey had sent the two fastest battleships, *Iowa* and *New Jersey*, ahead of the rest of Task Force 34, steaming in company with three cruisers and eight destroyers. Rear Adm. Oscar Badger commanded this Task Group 34.5, leaving Lee's slower ships behind. Badger's group did not arrive at the strait until around 0100 on 26 October. The Japanese heavy ships were long gone.

Writers have put forth a number of possible explanations for Kurita's decision to give up the fight: severe fatigue after his ships underwent three days of attacks; the mistaken belief that the plucky escort carriers and destroyers constituted Halsey's force of big carriers; the belief that the American transports had already disgorged their troops and cargoes to the shore; heavy fuel consumption during high-speed maneuvering; the desire to preserve his fleet; and a reluctance to sacrifice still more men and ships. Kurita's chief of staff, Koyanagi, said the overall plan was flawed and would have constituted a suicide order for Kurita. He did offer a tantalizing tidbit: "Giving up pursuit [of the escort carriers and destroyers] when we did amounted to losing a prize already in hand. If we had known the types and number of enemy ships, and their speed, Admiral Kurita would never have suspended the pursuit, and we would have annihilated the enemy."[15]

Monday-morning quarterbacking was inevitable. Historian Clark Reynolds opined, "If TF 34 had been detached a few hours earlier, after Kinkaid's first urgent request for help, and had left the destroyers behind, since their fueling caused a delay of over two hours and a half, a powerful battle line of six modern battleships under the command of Admiral Lee, the most experienced battle squadron commander in the Navy, would have arrived off San Bernardino Strait in time to have clashed with Kurita's Center Force.... There is every reason to believe that Lee would have crossed Kurita's T and completed the destruction of Center Force."[16]

Admiral Kinkaid added a bitter postscript in commenting on an account of the battle written by newspaperman (and Naval Academy graduate) Hanson W. Baldwin. Kinkaid's comments were essentially parallel to those of Reynolds. He wrote of the benefits in terms of Lee's force being in a more advantageous position if it had been sent south when Halsey received Kinkaid's first call for support. He added, "The net result of all this was that the six strongest battleships in the world—except the *Yamato* and *Musashi*—steamed about 300 miles north and 300 miles south during 'the greatest naval battle of the Second World War and the largest engagement ever fought on the high seas'—and did not fire a single shot. I can well imagine the feelings of my [Naval Academy] classmate, Lee."[17]

One who did not have to imagine them was Lee's aide, Lieutenant Aertsen. He summarized the difference between the Marianas tactical situation and that at Leyte Gulf. In June, as Lee explained to him, the enemy was retreating and did not constitute a threat. In October the Japanese were approaching and were indeed a threat.

The outcome of the battle generated many what-ifs, including one that has tantalized battleship enthusiasts for decades—what would have been the outcome of a gunnery duel between the ultimate Japanese battleship and the ultimate U.S. battleship? Scholars Thomas Hone and Norman Friedman took on that challenge in a 1983 professional note in *Proceedings*. They concluded that Lee would have attempted to get in hits at long range because the U.S. ships had the superior Mark 8 fire control radar while the Japanese used optics. The *Yamato*'s heavy armor provided little protection beyond 35,000 yards. Thus the U.S. ships would have fired from over the horizon and won.[18] A subsequent letter to the editor came from Vice Adm. Lloyd Mustin who served during World War II as Lee's gunnery, radar, and combat information center officer. He argued that the capability of the Mark 8 radar to distinguish targets at a distance was even better than Hone and Friedman believed, because he had seen the results at sea. In sum, Mustin concurred that with Lee at the helm the outcome would have been the same, a U.S. victory.[19]

About the Author

Paul Stillwell graduated from Drury College in 1966 with a bachelor's degree in history and in 1978 from the University of Missouri-Columbia with a master's in journalism. A Vietnam War veteran, he served on board the tank landing ship *Washoe County* from 1966 to 1969. In 1969, as a lieutenant, Stillwell was the assistant combat information center officer of the battleship *New Jersey* during operations in the Eastern Pacific. In the process he learned that a quarter century earlier, during different periods in 1944, both Admiral Lee and Admiral Halsey had used the *New Jersey* as flagship. Stillwell retired as a commander in the Naval Reserve in 1992, following thirty years of service. His final active duty was in 1988, when he was sent to the Persian Gulf as a historian to document the Navy's role in Operation Earnest Will during the Iran-Iraq tanker war.

Stillwell was on the staff of the Naval Institute from 1974 to 2004 and continues to do freelance oral history work for the organization. During his time on the staff, he served several editorial roles with *Proceedings*, was editor of the annual *Naval Review*, was the founding editor in chief of *Naval History* magazine, and served as director of oral history and the history division. For twenty-three years he wrote a column titled "Looking Back" for *Naval History*. All told, he is author, coauthor, or editor of twelve books. Among them is *The Golden Thirteen: Recollections of the First Black Naval Officers*, which was selected by the *New York Times* as one of the notable books published in the field of history in 1993. Stillwell is the recipient of the Navy League's Alfred Thayer Mahan Award for Literary Achievement, the Naval Institute's Book Author of the Year Award, and the Naval Historical Foundation's Dudley Knox Award. He has written four books on battleships and is in the process of writing a book-length biography of Vice Adm. Willis A. Lee. He and his wife Karen live in Arnold, Maryland. They are the parents of three sons: Joseph, Robert, and James.

Notes

1. David S. Gray, letter to author, 18 January 1980.
2. Arleigh A. Burke, interview with author, 15 September 1976.
3. Samuel Eliot Morison, *History of United States Naval Operations in World War II*, vol. 8, *New Guinea and the Marianas* (Boston: Little, Brown, 1953), 244.
4. Carl Solberg, *Decision and Dissent: With Halsey at Leyte Gulf* (Annapolis: Naval Institute Press, 1995), 17; USS *New Jersey* (BB 62) deck log, 1944.
5. Solberg, *Decision and Dissent*, 37.
6. Rear Admiral Tomiji Koyanagi, "With Kurita in the Battle for Leyte Gulf," U.S. Naval Institute *Proceedings*, February 1953, 124.
7. Samuel Eliot Morison, *History of United States Naval Operations in World War II*, vol. 7, *Leyte* (Boston: Little, Brown, 1953), 195–96.
8. Guilliaem Aertsen, interview with author, 8 April 1979.
9. Clark G. Reynolds, *The Fast Carriers: The Forging of an Air Navy* (New York: McGraw-Hill, 1968), 270.
10. Reynolds, *Fast Carriers*, 270–71.
11. Edward J. Mathews, interview with author, 22 June 1977.
12. Thomas J. Cutler, *The Battle of Leyte Gulf* (New York: HarperCollins, 1994), 237–38.
13. Quoted in Hanson W. Baldwin, *Sea Fights and Ship Wrecks* (Garden City, NY: Hanover House, 1955), 170.
14. Capt. David McCampbell, interview with author, 16 July 1987, Naval Institute oral history, 209–10.

15. Koyanagi, "With Kurita in the Battle for Leyte Gulf," 125–29.
16. Reynolds, *Fast Carriers*, 330.
17. Baldwin, *Sea Fights and Ship Wrecks*, 170.
18. Thomas Hone and Norman Friedman, "*Iowa* vs. *Yamato*: The Ultimate Gunnery Duel," U.S. Naval Institute *Proceedings*, July 1983, 122–23.
19. Lloyd M. Mustin, "Comment and Discussion," U.S. Naval Institute *Proceedings*, November 1983, 98–99.

7

SIBUYAN SEA
The Price of Daring
——— *Karl Zingheim* ———

During the morning and afternoon of 24 October 1944, carrier aircraft from Adm. William F. Halsey's Third Fleet attacked Vice Admiral Kurita Takeo's powerful task force of five battleships, nine cruisers, and thirteen destroyers as they transited the Sibuyan Sea in the central Philippines to attack the invasion shipping off Leyte. Despite enjoying aerial supremacy, and losing just eighteen aircraft, Halsey's fliers succeeded only in sinking the battleship *Musashi* and crippling the cruiser *Myoko*. This failure of Halsey's carrier aircraft to destroy, or at least repulse, Kurita's heavy ships west of Leyte descended from a cascade of calculated risk, intelligence misinterpretations, and misfortune. It also contributed to one of the most controversial command decisions of the Pacific War.

The principal American problem during the Sibuyan Sea action was the inability to mass their attacking air groups to overwhelm Kurita's ships. Ironically, this stemmed from Halsey's own bold recommendation weeks earlier to cancel the invasion of Mindanao and advance on Leyte. Though it accelerated the offensive, this change meant that newly captured Morotai, some 540 miles from Leyte, was the nearest air base, with three other facilities just under one thousand miles away.[1] Accordingly, Halsey's carrier air groups were not only the roaming offensive air cover for the invasion, but were on hand to provide direct support for the landings as well.[2] This mission duality forced him to keep carriers near the Japanese air bastion around Manila as well as off Leyte. By the time the Leyte Gulf battle coalesced, the Third Fleet's carrier task groups stretched across the length of the Philippines. Without robust land-based reconnaissance, Halsey was obliged to divert nearly one hundred fighters as well as fifty-eight dive-bombers to search for approaching Japanese ships within the vast archipelago on 24 October.[3]

A corollary to Halsey's dilemma was his reliance on submarine sightings to inform his intelligence estimates while the enemy ships were only two days' steaming from Leyte. Necessarily vague on force compositions, these reports prompted staff discussions on board the flagship *New Jersey* that concluded the Japanese navy was likely reestablishing a "Tokyo Express"–style reinforcement and harassment scheme from the Solomons campaign. Sighting reports of battleships, though, prompted the recall of Rear Adm. Ralph Davison's Task Group 38.4 from its journey rearward for rest in order to have all the available fast battleships on hand.[4] However, Vice Adm. John S. McCain's Task Group 38.1, containing five carriers and 326 embarked aircraft, continued eastward toward Ulithi.[5]

Contact occurred at 0820 when an *Intrepid* SB2C Helldiver's radar detected ships south of Mindoro. Visual inspection revealed four battleships, eight cruisers, and thirteen destroyers headed northeast, into the Sibuyan Sea.[6] With doubts about Japanese intentions settled, at 0827 Halsey directed Davison's task group off Samar to join on Rear Adm. Gerald Bogan's Task Group 38.2 off the San Bernardino Strait exit, and four minutes later, for all three task groups, including Rear Adm. Frederick C. Sherman's Task Group 38.3 off central Luzon, to attack. McCain's task group was recalled, but would play no part in the coming action.[7] However, two misfortunes hampered Halsey's ability to overwhelm Kurita's ships that day.

The first arose from Halsey's aggressive conduct of the preliminary raids across the western Pacific: just as the Leyte campaign began in earnest, his air groups were worn down. A rotation plan called for having two task groups supporting the Leyte landings and was in midstride when the Japanese navy deployed.[8] The upshot for the looming Battle of Leyte Gulf was that the closest task group to Kurita's oncoming ships was Bogan's 38.2, containing just the fleet carrier *Intrepid* and the light carrier *Cabot*, as well as *Independence*, a night carrier. The other two task groups contained a pair of fleet carriers and two light carriers apiece with daytime air groups.

Halsey's other misfortune was borne on Japanese wings. Vice Admiral Fukudome Shigeru, commanding the Sixth Base Air Force, decided the best way to support Kurita's mission was to sustain a maximum effort against the Third Fleet's carriers, which instead was Sherman's task group off Luzon.[9] Nearly one hour before word of Kurita's sighting arrived, radars detected the first in a string of large incoming raids.[10] Sherman reinforced his combat air patrol and kept his bombers on the hangar decks as his ships fought off the sporadic but persistent attackers. Though Japanese formations were cut to ribbons, a lone dive-bomber planted its bomb on the light carrier *Princeton*, touching off a conflagration below.[11] Thus, Sherman had his hands full until mid-morning.

Halsey's remaining task group, Davison's 38.4 off Samar, found targets of its own. *Franklin* searchers attacked destroyers off Panay, and coincidently with the Kurita detection, an *Enterprise* scout found Vice Admiral Nishimura Shoji's two battleships in the Sulu Sea. At 0905, the rest of the *Enterprise*'s armed searchers massed and attacked Nishimura with bombs and rockets.[12] Though the battleship *Fuso* sustained a hit, Nishimura continued to his destiny at Surigao Strait.[13] At 0940, Davison launched a follow-up strike on the destroyers off Panay while hustling to join Bogan.[14]

Thus, with Sherman's and Davison's full-sized task groups occupied, Halsey had only Bogan's bantam force, comprised of just the *Intrepid*'s and *Cabot*'s air groups, to attack Kurita's ships. Another disadvantage was the sheer distance to Mindoro, which required additional fuel tanks that cut into the bomb load of the strike's twelve Helldivers. However, the seven *Intrepid* and five *Cabot* TBM Avengers bore the improved Mark XIII torpedo tipped with the new Torpex explosive.[15] At 0910 the first strike lifted off, escorted by thirteen *Intrepid* F6F Hellcats and eight from the *Cabot*.[16]

The strike flew directly across the island-studded Sibuyan Sea, but a cloud bank obscured the expected Japanese position inside the Tablas Strait off Mindoro. The formation passed directly overhead at 1025 when the clouds thinned and revealed two circular formations.[17] Beholding the impressive bulk of the *Yamato* and *Musashi* for the first time, the fliers initiated a pattern to target these behemoths that recurred through the day. Kurita's ships increased speed to twenty-four knots, and at 1026, they commenced firing.[18] A riot of colorful midair blasts erupted around the U.S. aircraft, displaying red, yellow, and black bursts with occasional pink and violet streamers. The Helldivers split to attack the *Yamato* and *Musashi* with six aircraft each, while the *Intrepid* Avengers dove to make their runs on the *Musashi* near the edge of the ring and the cruiser *Myoko* just ahead of her. The *Cabot* TBMs pressed on toward the center against

Kurita's flagship *Yamato*. With no defending fighters present, the Hellcats dove as well to strafe gun positions.[19]

Antiaircraft fire buffeted the dive-bombers as they crossed directly over the eastern formation before they performed a wingover and nosed into vertical dives. As three thousand feet shot by on the altimeters, the pilots released their bombs before they and their rear seat gunners endured 10.5g pullouts.[20] Meanwhile, the torpedo planes, fifteen miles out, accelerated in a shallower dive. Two *Intrepid* Avengers split off to make runs against the *Myoko* while the remaining six turned southwest into the cloudbank over Tablas Island to screen their maneuver, but the clouds bottomed out at five thousand feet. The torpedo pilots could see the Helldiver attack already in full swing, forcing the *Musashi* to turn.

Three Avengers slid northwest to cross the *Musashi*'s bow and attack from the port side while the other three sped down her starboard flank. As they dipped below one thousand feet, they were abeam the target and banked right to line up their drops. With the dive-bombing attack finished, the *Musashi*'s gunners gave their full attention to the oncoming Avengers. Bursts exploded around one TBM, shearing off both wings. At two thousand yards, the remaining torpedoes dropped. Another Avenger took fire and passed over the formation to crash into the water beyond.[21]

As the *Musashi* twisted during the dive-bombing, two misses bracketed the bow, flooding tanks, and then another pair erupted on either side amidships. A fifth bomb detonated atop the thick armored roof of the forward turret. Two minutes later, the torpedo attack yielded a hit amidships on the starboard side not far from a near miss that opened voids opposite a boiler room. The concurrent attack on the *Myoko* produced a torpedo hit next to the number four engine room, flooding it and the aft generator room. Both starboard shafts stopped, causing the cruiser to drop out of formation. This would be the only torpedo hit of the day not made on the *Musashi*. The *Yamato* dodged the bombs, taking one close off the bow, while both *Cabot* torpedoes missed, for the loss of one TBM.[22]

At 1045 a follow-on attack consisting of ten Hellcats, twelve Helldivers, and nine Avengers from the *Intrepid*, and four fighters from the *Cabot*, lifted off and winged westward.[23] As this formation passed the first strike heading home, the returning air group commander radioed the outbound strike coordinator to concentrate on the same *Yamato*-type battleship his planes just struck.[24] The second strike found Kurita's formations north of Baton Island. Pushing over at 1138, this attack concentrated on the *Musashi* with much closer coordination than the preceding effort. Despite a reduced speed of twenty-two knots, the *Musashi* managed to dodge ten bombs, although five were close. Two struck, however, one into the bow, while the other passed through the superstructure, detonating above the port inboard engine room. Fires erupted in the engine room and two nearby boiler rooms. Severed steam lines bellowed, adding to the cacophony of the attack.[25]

The Avengers divided to attack from opposite sides. The injured *Musashi* managed to evade one torpedo forward, and two off the stern, but three hit across her port side. One struck opposite the forward turret, another below the bridge tower, while the third hit near the havoc raised by the amidships' bomb detonation, ruining the damaged engine room and depriving the ship use of its propeller shaft. With the *Musashi*'s speed further impaired, Kurita ordered an eighteen-knot formation speed, permitting her to regain station, but she soon lagged behind, elongating the formation.[26] The battleship's casualties mounted, particularly among the exposed gun crews, and with the ammunition handlers below decks where the amidships bomb exploded.[27] Despite the diminution in firepower, two Helldivers and a single Avenger crashed.[28] For the morning's loss of four TBMs and two SB2Cs, Bogan's fliers had knocked a cruiser off Kurita's order of battle, and created a liability with the *Musashi*. Now it was Sherman's turn.

By mid-morning, the worst of the Japanese raids trailed off, and it was time for Task Group 38.3 to switch to the offensive. Despite the *Princeton*'s ordeal, Sherman could commit two full-sized air groups to strike at Kurita. The *Essex* spotted on the flight deck eight Hellcats fitted with one 500-pound bomb apiece, ten Helldivers with 1,000-pound bombs, and sixteen Avengers with torpedoes.[29] Over on the neighboring *Lexington*, however, tempers flared. Cdr. Hugh Winters, the newly promoted air group commander, expected to lead the combined strike with aircraft armed appropriately for capital ship targets. However, his *Lexington* aircraft, including the TBMs, were still loaded with lighter bombs for work against airfields and shipping in the Manila region.

Winters locked horns with the ship's air officer, Cdr. Andrew Ahroon, who refused to open the magazines for the lengthy process of returning the original armament and then breaking out the armor-piercing bombs and torpedoes. With the sporadic air attacks that morning, one only had to witness the spectacle of the blazing *Princeton* to see what even a single hit could do with fueled planes and ordnance set out. The argument went up to the *Lexington*'s Capt. Ernest Litch, who firmly sided with Ahroon. Winters considered bumping the issue up the chain of command, but there was no time to send a message to Sherman on the *Essex*, or even have an audience with Vice Adm. Marc Mitscher in flag plot. Instead, a frustrated Winters stomped down from the carrier's island to lead his men "on a bear hunt loaded for quail."[30]

At 1050, the *Essex* sent aloft her strike, along with the *Lexington*'s lightly armed eight F6Fs, ten SB2Cs, and sixteen TBMs.[31] However, the bad luck dogging Sherman's men continued. The cloud cover intensified and became turbulent, separating the air groups.[32] The *Essex* formation skirted the cloud front around its southern face. Eventually, the planes banked north over the Tablas Strait and found only the *Myoko* limping southwestward. Escorting fighters sent ahead found two circular formations moving east at the northern end of the strait.[33] The destroyer *Shimakaze* also spotted the intruders, and Kurita ordered twenty-four knots despite the *Musashi*'s handicap.[34] The *Essex* bombers travelled up the coast of Mindoro and orbited above its eastern extremity at Dumali Point to await the *Lexington* group.[35] However, when Winters' strike arrived, he had only five Helldivers and eleven Avengers remaining with his fighters.[36] With the *Musashi* straining to attain twenty-two knots, Kurita reluctantly slowed.[37] At 1217, as antiaircraft fire burst around his aircraft, Winters directed the *Essex* men to attack the trailing group while he went straight against the *Yamato* in the leading formation.[38]

Winters suggested his bombers use the intervening cloud cover and strike at the nearest battleships. He then led his bomb-armed fighters into dives spread across the rest of the ships to distract the antiaircraft fire.[39] The *Lexington* fliers received an unexpected reinforcement when five *Essex* Helldivers continued over to their targeted formation. The *Yamato* took a bomb forward, causing substantial flooding and a minor fire. Plummeting Helldivers over the *Musashi* managed two near misses alongside the aft turret and a close miss right aft that wrecked the aircraft catapult. The five remaining *Essex* SB2Cs dove on the other Japanese formation, producing a near miss on the light cruiser *Yahagi*.

The sixteen torpedo-armed *Essex* Avengers split their attack, with half making individual runs against two battleships and the escorting cruisers. Another five tipped against the *Musashi* while the remaining trio attacked a *Kongo*-class battleship. The *Musashi* sustained a torpedo hit on the starboard bow, flooding storerooms and further eroding her reserve buoyancy forward. In exchange, one Helldiver sustained damage and ditched upon return to Task Group 38.3, and two *Essex* TBMs were shot down.[40] The *Lexington* lost a TBM downed over Kurita's ships, while a Japanese fighter pounced on a returning SB2C within sight of the U.S. carriers.[41]

As the American fliers found their way to the northeast, and Japanese sailors dealt with mounting casualties and flooding, U.S. plane handlers spotted a fresh strike on the *Essex,* as well as on the flight decks of the *Enterprise* and *Franklin* in Davison's task group. At 1259 the *Essex* initiated the afternoon's strikes with eight 500-pound bomb-armed Hellcats and a dozen Helldivers. The *Lexington* sent aloft twelve SB2Cs, this time with 1,000-pound armor-piercing bombs.[42] Off Samar, the *Enterprise* launched fourteen rocket-armed Hellcats, nine Helldivers, and eight Avengers at 1313.[43] The *Franklin* followed suit fifteen minutes later with twelve F6Fs, eight sporting underwing rockets, twelve SB2Cs with their side-by-side bomb crutches carrying a pair of 500-pound bombs, and ten TBMs with torpedoes.[44] *Enterprise* armorers modified the trunnion bands for 500-pound bombs to permit the loading of two 1,000-pound bombs on the parallel crutches for their SB2Cs.[45] At 1350 Bogan's diminutive task group sent eight fighters, twelve dive-bombers, and three torpedo planes off the *Intrepid,* as well as another eight Hellcats and three Avengers from the *Cabot*.[46] The Battle of the Sibuyan Sea approached its crescendo.

As the four American flights started out, the *Musashi* struggled. She had absorbed hits that would have ruined other capital ships, but the accumulated damage was beginning to tell. Her stem settled two meters deeper, and the accumulated mass of floodwater elsewhere and counter-flooding seawater made her sluggish.[47] Unfortunately for the ship and her beleaguered crew, the wounded giant appeared outwardly as formidable as ever. Furthermore, the recent evasive maneuvers scattered both Japanese formations. Reducing speed to eighteen knots, Kurita set about restoring order.

The pilots of the second *Essex* strike encountered the same weather that bedeviled their shipmates in the morning attack. Over the Sibuyan Sea, though, the flight found the clouds thinning, and a break in the cover revealed their target twenty-five miles ahead on a northeasterly heading. Lookouts on the *Nagato* reported the aircraft as well, prompting Kurita to raise speed to twenty-two knots. When the attackers nosed over at 1440, the Japanese swung to port in unison, putting the ships broadside to the dive-bombers. This time the *Yamato* became the center of attention. As tracers arched up past their windscreens, the Helldivers plummeted toward two thousand feet before releasing their payloads. One SB2C took hits on a wing and struck the sea inverted. The rest of the *Essex* attackers sped away to the southeast. The *Yamato* took a bomb forward, wrecking her anchoring machinery and inducing a 5-degree list.[48]

Meanwhile, the *Enterprise* planes approached from the south to find Kurita at 1430 beyond the Tablas Strait in two formations heading east. To dive out of the sun, the fliers edged past over the southern fringe of the Sibuyan Sea. With his exposed antiaircraft gunners depleted from strafing and bomb detonations, the *Musashi*'s gunnery officer asked to employ the main battery's *sanshikidan* shells on the distant American aircraft, but Captain Inoguchi Toshihira refused. Nevertheless, at fifteen miles out, the *Enterprise* fliers came under fire from the other ships. When the aircraft banked north once past the western formation, the ships turned to parallel their track, except for the *Musashi*, a cruiser, and a destroyer toward the rear that turned to the west. This separated the two groups of vessels, so the *Enterprise* strike leader selected the standout battleship.

Once more, the pilots encountered intense fire in their dives, and once more, the SB2Cs completed their attacks before the TBMs could get into position. Helldiver pilots claimed seven hits and two near misses. They also noted an oil slick emanating from the *Musashi* before they pulled away and sped northward over open water.[49] The Avengers benefitted from the battleship's isolation and the day's diminution of antiaircraft fire as both divisions of four made their runs from either bow.[50] The *Enterprise* crews reported two, and possibly three, hit geysers. To the fliers' relief, everyone arrived at the rally point, another sign of the toll taken on the Japanese gunners. As the formation headed home, two *Essex* stragglers happily joined up, only to realize their mistake halfway to the *Enterprise*.[51]

Four bombs struck the staggering *Musashi*. One punched through the forecastle, detonating in a berthing compartment below. Another crashed alongside the funnel, wreaking havoc among the remaining antiaircraft positions. One Helldiver delivered both its bombs just forward of turret one, wiping out Sick Bay. The *Musashi* sluggishly dodged two torpedoes to starboard that missed ahead and astern, and another that crossed behind from port, while crewmen reported that two passed right under the hull amidships. Yet, four others struck in rapid succession, a pair practically on opposite sides of the forward turret barbette, and two more against the starboard amidships citadel. Although the list stabilized at one degree, the bow was now four meters lower, threatening to submerge the foredeck.[52]

The *Franklin*'s strike found Kurita's ships five miles north of Sibuyan Island. Flying closer, they discerned an orderly formation to their right comprising the *Nagato* and two *Yamato*-class battleships. With no Japanese fighter cover, the *Franklin* Hellcats split to cover both the Helldivers and Avengers in their respective attacks. Resulting rocket hits damaged the screening destroyers *Kiyoshimo* and *Hamakaze*.

For once, the attacking aircraft this day extended considerable attention to ships other than the *Musashi*. Seven Helldivers selected the *Nagato* as she swung to port to spoil the aim of her attackers from astern. However, she sustained hits on four casemated secondary guns, and damage to her uptakes that brought her speed down to twenty-one knots; but within thirty minutes, her engineers restored power and the *Nagato* regained two knots. Fragments also shredded her communications suite and claimed fourteen lives. Two Helldivers attacked the cruiser *Tone*, but her helm came over at the right instant to cause both pilots to miss. Or so they thought. Captain Mayazumi Haruo's hard turn did not prevent a pair of bombs from demolishing his sea cabin and starting a short-lived fire near the shell room for the high-angle guns.

However, the *Musashi* was not neglected by the *Franklin* Helldivers. The remaining trio rolled onto the stricken battleship and a bomber's twin 500-pounders landed just forward of the bridge tower. These went on to wreck a 25-mm gun, destroy the captain's elevator shaft, and demolish the entrance to the number seven fireroom. Another pair hit forward, one to gouge a slight depression on the armored roof of the first turret, the other to punch through the deck alongside to wreck officer quarters below.[53] Meanwhile, four Avengers swept around ahead of the *Nagato* and *Musashi* to approach the *Musashi* from the south, and five more charged in from the opposite side. The antiaircraft fire concentrated on this latter threat, holing three TBMs and knocking the other two into the sea. The surviving Avenger pilots admitted to making their drops from four thousand to six thousand yards out, another indication of the stiff resistance they faced.[54]

Scarcely had the *Franklin* pilots started their runs when the combined *Intrepid* and *Cabot* strike drew in from the east. As the *Franklin*'s attack ended, half of the *Intrepid*'s Helldivers dove on a second battleship, while the other four tipped above the staggering *Musashi*. The accumulated bomb and torpedo hits had by now overcome the ship's agility, so she made a much easier target than from the morning's first raid. In rapid succession, the first bomb crashed near the top of the bridge tower and detonated within the pilothouse, wrecking it and sending steel shards through Captain Inoguchi's right shoulder. Seventy-eight other casualties fell from this hit. The next destroyed a 25-mm mount to port before plunging through storerooms to damage the uptakes. The third pierced the lower bridge tower from behind, ravaging the interior immediately below the flag level. The last hit on the forward deck and shattered the remnants of the eviscerated Sick Bay.

The torpedo planes concentrated on the *Musashi* as well, the *Intrepid* flight passing astern to make runs on her starboard side. As before, the SB2Cs completed their dives before the TBMs could attack, but most of the Avengers approached to within two thousand yards before dropping. The Japanese observed eleven hits from the tandem *Franklin* and *Intrepid-Cabot* attacks. Three torpedoes struck the port bow, and another soon after to starboard alongside the forward turret. A fifth barreled into port amidships, flooding a fireroom.

Damage from a close trio of torpedoes broke through the armored citadel to open a magazine to the sea, erasing more reserve buoyancy. Several feet aft, yet another torpedo struck and collapsed the outer bulkhead of the port outer engine room, which filled in four minutes. A hit occurred on the port quarter, flooding the after turret's magazine and a shaft alley. A final hit to starboard added little to the *Musashi*'s woes. As this final attack drew away, the pilots noticed a wholesale turnabout by the rest of Kurita's ships.[55] The Japanese were retreating.

While the afternoon waned, aircraft returned to their respective task groups. The *Lexington* and *Essex* completed recovery of their combined strike by 1527, and the solo *Essex* follow-up at 1616.[56] At 1703 the *Intrepid* and *Cabot* planes returned, and thirteen minutes later, the *Enterprise* and *Franklin* took their fliers back on board.[57] Inside the ready rooms on the six carriers, tired but exultant young men recounted their missions to intelligence officers. The antiaircraft fire was universally credited as intense and accurate, if ineffective.[58] However, as for damage inflicted on the enemy, the tally was bewildering. By sunset, the preliminary results traveled up the Task Force 38 chain of command, revealing that four, and possibly all five, battleships were torpedoed and bombed, one likely sunk. Torpedoes reportedly struck three heavy cruisers, and others took bombs. A light cruiser and destroyer apiece were confirmed sunk, and another destroyer likely driven under.[59] By any measure, Kurita's force had certainly been walloped.

However, the combined efforts of six air groups actually managed to cripple the *Myoko*, moderately impair the *Yamato*, *Nagato*, *Tone*, *Yahagi*, *Kiyoshimo*, and *Hamakaze*, and fatally damage the *Musashi*. As Kurita's other ships drew away, the *Musashi* gradually succumbed to the extensive flooding. An attempt to beach her came to naught with the loss of her remaining engine room.[60] With water lapping over the fore deck, and a mounting list, Captain Inoguchi directed destroyers to take off the crew. The great ship settled by the head, until at 1935, she suddenly rolled and disappeared beneath the sea with a rumbling roar, taking Inoguchi and 1,178 men with her.[61]

The damage assessments, and word of Kurita's withdrawal, arrived in the midst of discussion on Halsey's flagship about the sighting of enemy carriers off northern Luzon. For Halsey, the belated discovery of the carriers completed the picture of Japanese intentions. Three major forces were in motion: heavy surface forces in the southern and central Philippines, both attacked that day, and a supporting carrier task force closing from the north, all timing their actions for 25 October.[62] The southern force was out of effective range with Halsey's ships now north of Samar, but the larger force in the Sibuyan Sea was still within range. At 1715, the night carrier *Independence* launched a pair of radar-equipped TBMs to track the remnants of Kurita's battered force.[63]

At 1935, the Avengers' radars detected ships not far from where they had turned about, but on a *southeasterly* course. The trackers reported at 2040 that the formation was moving east, exiting the Sibuyan Sea. At midnight, a relief team of Avengers detected the Japanese ships lining up for the run through the San Bernardino Strait. One of them was a *Yamato*-type.[64] Not long after, however, the TBMs were recalled.[65] Thus, the close of 24 October proved a fitting coda for the Battle of the Sibuyan Sea, not only because of Kurita's transit into the open Philippine Sea, but because Halsey lost all interest in those ships.

Over the next twenty-four hours, Nishimura's force sailed to near annihilation before the Seventh Fleet's entire battle line while Halsey dashed north, and Kurita and Taffy Three's escort carriers startled one another off

Samar hours later. Frantic calls from the Seventh Fleet's commander, Vice Adm. Thomas Kinkaid, and unintended goading from Admiral Nimitz, forced Halsey to come about, but Kurita relented and withdrew.[66] What role did the Sibuyan Sea action play in Halsey's profound decision to leave the San Bernardino Strait open, despite knowledge that Kurita was forcing it?

In the days and years after the Battle of Leyte Gulf, Halsey took account of the reported degradation in Kurita's "Center Force": "[F]lash reports indicated beyond doubt that the Center Force had been badly mauled with all of its [battleships] and most of its [heavy cruisers] tremendously reduced in fighting power and life."[67] In 1952, he penned, "The Central Force, according to our pilots, had suffered so much topside damage, especially to its guns and fire-control instruments, that it could not win a decision.... (The pilots' reports proved dangerously optimistic, but we had little reason to discredit them at the time.)"[68] Yet, until the electrifying discovery of the carriers north of Luzon at 1650, Halsey was taking nothing for granted. As the four afternoon strikes set out, at 1415 he directed that the *Independence*'s shadowing missions be ready before sunset. At 1512, Halsey informed his subordinate commanders, and Nimitz, that he had a plan to have his fast battleships and cruisers stand off San Bernardino Strait for a night surface action.[69] The sighting to the north changed his calculus completely.

Years later, Halsey wrote, "[N]ot only was the Northern Force fresh and undamaged ... its carriers gave it a scope several hundred miles wider than the others. Moreover, if we destroyed those carriers, *future operations need fear no major threat from the sea* [emphasis added]."[70] Perhaps this refers to a tasking Nimitz sent him on 7 October 1944: "Warning Order. On the assumption that the situation will permit the withdrawal of Task Force 38 from the vicinity of CENTRAL PHILIPPINES, be prepared to execute the following task ... with target dated about 10 November if so directed by later dispatch. This operation is called HOTFOOT (Carrier raid on JAPAN)."[71]

Hotfoot was intended to be the naval portion of a joint raid with Army Air Force B-29's newly based in the Marianas, a plan known as San Antonio I.[72] Furthermore, Halsey certainly witnessed the vitriol directed by senior aviators at Adm. Raymond Spruance's failure to sink the enemy carrier force off the Marianas when he visited Hawaii the preceding summer.[73] At any rate, Kurita's surface menace was eclipsed by a carrier-borne threat; yet, by October 1944, ample operational evidence suggested that the best days for Japan's carrier aviators were well past.[74] Still, a fraternal showdown with carrier foemen became paramount for Halsey. The untouched Japanese carriers now warranted the attention of the entire Third Fleet.[75]

Even when night scouting reports confirmed Kurita's resumed heading for Leyte, Halsey contrived an explanation for the latest turnabout. The Third Fleet after-action report baldly declared:

> Although the Center Force continued to move forward, the Commander THIRD Fleet decided that this enemy force must be blindly obeying an Imperial command to do or die, but with battle efficiency

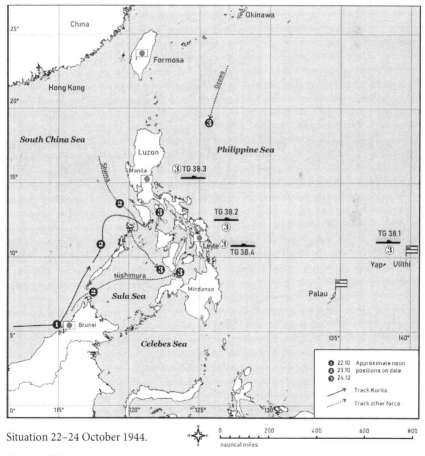

Situation 22–24 October 1944.

Vincent O'Hara.

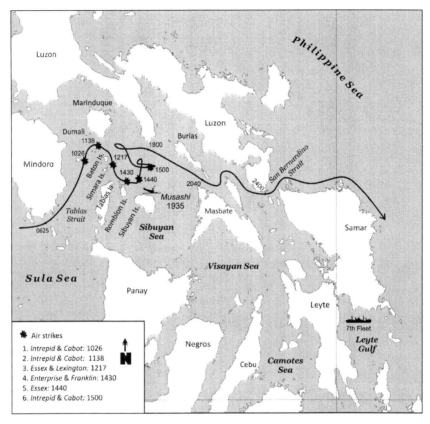

Kurita's Passage through the Sibuyan Sea. *Vincent O'Hara.*

greatly impaired by torpedo hits, bomb hits, topside damage, fires, and casualties. From long experience with the Japs, their blind adherence to plan, and their inability to readjust disturbed plans, the commander THIRD Fleet recognized the possibility that the Center Force might plod through the San Bernardino Straits and on to attack Leyte forces, a la Guadalcanal, but commander THIRD Fleet was convinced that the Center Force was so heavily damaged that it could not win a decision.[76]

In 1952, Halsey reiterated, "Furthermore I was confident from the reports of my aviators that Kurita's Force in the Sibuyan Sea had been damaged to such an extent that even if they sortied through San

Bernardino Strait, Kinkaid had adequate strength to defend against them. ... Even if the Central Force meanwhile passed through San Bernardino and headed for Leyte Gulf, it could only hope to harry the landing operation. It could not consolidate any advantage, because of its reported damage."[77] Even with years of hindsight, Halsey reasoned that the nuisance of a surface raid on one amphibious campaign was outweighed by the elimination of a carrier threat to future operations.

More than any other action in the Battle of Leyte Gulf, the Battle of the Sibuyan Sea best illustrates the consequences of the American way of war in the Pacific conflict's final year. The battles at Surigao Strait and off Cape Engano the following day were set pieces where the U.S. Navy ensured it held all the advantages. The drama off Samar was a testament to valor, improvisation, and luck. The Sibuyan Sea effort, however, was hamstrung by operational overreach in campaigning beyond optimal land-based air support, prebattle fatigue, and pending commitments elsewhere. These illustrate the drastic risks accepted to attain worthwhile goals. These risks, though, did not pay off so handsomely that day. On 24 October 1944, the Sibuyan Sea exacted the price of daring.

About the Author

Karl Zingheim is the staff historian for the USS *Midway* Museum in San Diego. A long-time resident of San Diego, he is a graduate of the U.S. Naval Academy and earned a master's degree in military history from Norwich University. He qualified as a surface warfare officer while serving in the commissioning crew of the USS *Fort McHenry* (LSD 43). He then became an instructor for foreign naval officers at the International Training Department of the Naval Amphibious School, Coronado. An early advocate for the creation of the Midway Museum, his enthusiasm for military history and scale modeling found unique application after the *Midway* arrived. He has contributed to numerous documentary features, particularly the *Dogfights!* series on cable television's History Channel. He is a frequent lecturer on war studies for the Midway Institute for Teachers program, specializing in both the World Wars and Cold War topics. For the 2019 academic year, he helped establish the new military history curriculum at San Diego State University.

Notes

1. See S. E. Morison, *Leyte* (Boston: Little, Brown, 1958), 13–17; and Thomas J. Cutler, *The Battle of Leyte Gulf* (New York: Harper Collins, 1994), 41–42. Richard W. Bates et al., *The Battle for Leyte Gulf, October 1944: Strategical and Tactical Analysis*, vol. 1 (Newport: U.S. Naval War College, 1952–1957), 34.
2. This was in addition to efforts of the Seventh Fleet's escort carrier aircraft. Bates et al., *Battle for Leyte Gulf*, 3:110–11.
3. War Diaries for Task Groups 38.2, 7; 38.3, 29; and 38.4, 14. Remarkably, aircraft from the Seventh Fleet's escort carriers were not considered for such reconnaissance.
4. Carl Solberg, *Decision and Dissent: With Halsey at Leyte Gulf* (Annapolis: Naval Institute Press, 1995), 81–83.
5. Figures from Bates et al., *Leyte Gulf*, 5:46.
6. Carrier Air Group Eighteen History. A battleship and cruiser were missed in the counting.
7. Bates et al., *Leyte Gulf*, 5:164–65.
8. Bates et al., *Leyte Gulf*, 2:49. This was Halsey's Operation Order No. 11-44 of 1 October.
9. U.S. Strategic Bombing Survey Interrogations, Vol. 1, No. 115, 503.
10. Task Group 38.3 War Diary.
11. Bureau of Ships, "USS *Princeton* (CVL 23) Loss in Action, Battle for Leyte Gulf, 24 October 1944, War Damage Report No. 62," 30 October 1947, 1.
12. Task Group 38.4 War Diary.
13. Bates et al., *Leyte Gulf*, 5:69.
14. Task Group 38.4 Action Report. Had Kurita opted to take this southern route, he would have contended with just Davison's and Bogan's truncated air groups that day.
15. Torpex offered 50 percent more power by weight than TNT. John Campbell, *Naval Weapons of World War II* (Annapolis: Naval Institute Press, 1985), 159.
16. Task Group 38.2 War Diary. USS *Cabot* CVL 28 After Action Report. The other "day" light carriers provided combat air patrols and antisubmarine sweeps for their task groups.
17. Gregory G. Fletcher, *Intrepid Aviators* (New York: New American Library, 2012), 49.

18. Boeichoboei Kenshusho, *Senshi Sosho, Kaigun Sho Go Sakusen 2: Fuiripin Oki Kaisan* (Tokyo: Asagumo Shinbusha, 1970), 165. Hereafter: *Sho Go Sakusen.*
19. Fletcher, *Intrepid Aviators*, 51, taken from Carrier Air Group 18 After Action Report.
20. John F. Forsyth, *Hell Divers: U.S. Navy Dive-Bombers at War* (Osceola, WI: Motorbooks International, 1991), 13–15.
21. Fletcher, *Intrepid Aviators*, 240–50.
22. Boeichoboei, *Sho Go Sakusen*, 166–67.
23. Task Group 38.2 War Diary. Fletcher, *Intrepid Aviators*, 260.
24. Fletcher, *Intrepid Aviators*, 260. Fletcher, however, does not provide a specific source for this directive.
25. Boeichoboei, *Sho Go Sakusen*, 167.
26. Boeichoboei, *Sho Go Sakusen*, 131, 167, 168, 170.
27. Akira Yoshimura, *Battleship* Musashi: *The Making and Sinking of the World's Biggest Battleship*, trans. Vincent Murphy (Tokyo: Kodansha International, 1991), 163.
28. Carrier Air Group 18 War Diary.
29. Carrier Air Group 15 After Action Report.
30. Hugh T. Winters, *Skipper: Confessions of a Fighter Squadron Commander* (Mesa, AZ: Champlin Fighter Museum Press, 1985), 124.
31. USS *Lexington* After Action Report.
32. Winters, *Skipper*, 125. Some *Essex* fighters separated and stayed with the *Lexington* formation.
33. Carrier Air Group 15 After Action Report.
34. Boeichoboei, *Sho Go Sakusen*, 172.
35. Carrier Air Group 15 After Action Report.
36. USS *Lexington* After Action Report.
37. Boeichoboei, *Sho Go Sakusen*, 172–73.
38. USS *Lexington* After Action Report.
39. Winters, *Skipper*, 126.
40. Action details from Carrier Air Group 15 After Action Report, and Boeichoboei, *Sho Go Sakusen*, 172–74.
41. USS *Lexington* After Action Report.
42. Carrier Air Group 15 After Action Report.
43. Task Group 38.4 War Diary.
44. Carrier Air Group 13 After Action Report.
45. USS *Enterprise* After Action Report.

46. Task Group 38.2 War Diary; USS *Cabot* After Action Report.
47. William H. Garzke Jr. and Robert O. Dulin Jr., *Battleships: Axis and Neutral Battleships in World War II* (Annapolis: Naval Institute Press, 1985), 68.
48. Action details from Boeichoboei, *Sho Go Sakusen*, 175, 177; and Carrier Air Group 15 After Action Report.
49. Action details from Carrier Air Group 20 After Action Report; and Boeichoboei, *Sho Go Sakusen*, 177–78.
50. Edward P. Stafford, *The Big E: The Story of the U.S.S.* Enterprise (New York: Random House, 1962), 465.
51. Carrier Air Group 20 After Action Report.
52. Boeichoboei, *Sho Go Sakusen*, 175–76.
53. Action details from Carrier Air Group 13 After Action Report; and Boeichoboei, *Sho Go Sakusen*, 179–82.
54. Carrier Air Group 13 After Action Report. The timings of the *Franklin* and *Intrepid* strikes were so close together, the Japanese did not discriminate between them in their damage account for the *Musashi*.
55. Action details from Task Group 38.2 War Diary; and Boeichoboei, *Sho Go Sakusen,* 181–82.
56. Carrier Air Group 15 After Action Report; USS *Lexington* After Action Report.
57. Carrier Air Group 13 After Action Report; USS *Enterprise* After Action Report.
58. This is a common refrain among the reports from the various groups.
59. Third Fleet After Action Report. The individual strike coordinators inexplicably tolerated the wild overclaiming.
60. Yoshimura, *Battleship* Musashi, 168.
61. Boeichoboei, *Sho Go Sakusen*, 196. The casualties include 117 survivors from the cruiser *Maya* sunk the day before. Another 1,329 men were saved.
62. Third Fleet After Action Report.
63. USS *Independence* After Action Report.
64. Third Fleet After Action Report.
65. USS *Independence* After Action Report.
66. This is the infamous encoding faux pas in the "Where is Task Force 34?" message debacle.
67. Third Fleet After Action Report.

68. William F. Halsey Jr., "The Battle for Leyte Gulf," U.S. Naval Institute *Proceedings* 78 (1952): 490.
69. Bates et al., *Leyte Gulf*, 5:165, 169–70. Though not an addressee, Kinkaid intercepted this message. Reference Commander Third Fleet Dispatch DTG 240612 October 1944.
70. Halsey, "The Battle for Leyte Gulf," 490.
71. Commander in Chief, Pacific Fleet, "Running Estimate and Summary," 7 October 1944.
72. Wesley F. Craven and James L. Cate, *The Army Air Forces in World War II*, vol. 5, *The Pacific: Matterhorn to Nagasaki, June 1944 to August 1945* (Washington, D.C.: U.S. Government Printing Office, 1953), 141.
73. E. B. Potter, *Bull Halsey: A Biography* (Annapolis: Naval Institute Press, 1985), 271.
74. This disconnection between perception and reality about Japanese carrier aviation is preserved in the Third Fleet's After Action Report's puzzlement over the paucity of aircraft with Ozawa's carriers.
75. Solberg contends that a translated copy of captured Japanese plans was available. The employment of carriers as decoys was deduced, at least among junior intelligence staffers, but the problem lay in persuading the senior staff and Halsey *after* orders to leave the San Bernardino Straits were given. Solberg, *Decision and Dissent*, 120–25.
76. Third Fleet After Action Report.
77. Halsey, "Battle for Leyte Gulf," 490.

8

SYRACUSE IN THE PACIFIC?
——— *Kevin J. Delamer* ———

O N 25 OCTOBER 1944, a line of Japanese cruisers and battleships bore down on the defenseless mass of transport ships in Leyte Gulf. Only a thin screen of escort carriers, destroyers, and destroyer escorts barred the path of the Japanese armada. Ultimately, the incredible bravery of the "tin can sailors" turned back the threat of the invasion force.[1] The narrow escape of the transports raises an interesting strategic question that rests on a counterfactual proposition: what would have happened if Kurita had pressed on, sweeping aside the remnants of the escort carrier-based task groups, and had fallen on the defenseless transports? The resulting slaughter would likely have been enormous. A Japanese "Ride of the Valkyries" might have done incalculable damage.[2] But while the impact of that damage would have been extremely damaging to the campaign in the Pacific, would success at Leyte Gulf have provided Japan with a turning point in the course of the war?

A New Paradigm

In the late summer of 1972, having recently assumed duties as president of the U.S. Naval War College, Rear Adm. Stansfield Turner donned his academic regalia over his uniform in preparation for that year's convocation. In doing so, he signaled the introduction of a new curriculum that would rely on classic scholarship. The signature case study in the new strategy course would be the Peloponnesian War. A critical campaign of that long-ago conflict would serve as a focal point in the course.[3] It would also serve as a point of dramatic comparison for the great historian Samuel Eliot Morison. "One need only think of what would have happened had Operation SHO-GO worked. General MacArthur's Army would have been cut off, like that of Athens at Syracuse in 413 BC. Third Fleet alone could not have maintained its communications."[4] Would MacArthur have been left, abandoned? Would America have been forced from the Western Pacific?

With all deference to Morison, the official historian of U.S. naval operations in World War II, it would seem highly unlikely that a successful blow against the American transports at Leyte Gulf would have altered the war's outcome. As the U.S. Army's historian of the campaign, Louis Morton, concluded in his review of Morison's volume, "Even if Japan had won the battle she would still have lost the war."[5] Comparing the material impact of the counterfactual, the political impact, and the global strategic environment at the time, it would appear that Morison overstated the potential impact of a Japanese victory. Leyte was never comparable to Syracuse.

The Athenian Example

The first order of business in comparing the ancient battle in the Hellenic world and the contest in the waters around Leyte Gulf is to understand the scope and impact of the Athenian expedition to the island of Sicily. The Sicilian expedition did have similarities to the invasion of the Philippine Islands. In each case, a dominant naval power sent a large body of troops to attack a target that was located a great distance from the home country. Those troops relied almost entirely upon the fleet for support. In the case of the Sicilian campaign, Athens committed an overwhelming proportion of its military might to the endeavor.

Originally proposed as a disposal force, the Sicilian expedition was intended to influence events ashore more by threat and perception than by combat. It was "a force of 60 ships and no hoplites,[6] a low-risk operation that depended more on surprise, psychology, and diplomacy than on the fortunes of battle."[7] However, the operation grew well beyond the original scope, largely due to the political machinations of Nicias, the most prominent Athenian statesman of the day. The Athenian assembly met twice to consider a request for military assistance from Egesta, a Greek colony in Sicily. Nicias had opposed sending an expedition in the first assembly held to discuss the matter: "The Hellenes in Sicily would fear us most if we never went there at all, and next to this, if after displaying our power we went away again as soon as possible."[8] In the second assembly, after his preference for foregoing the entire expedition had been rejected, Nicias instead asserted, in what amounted to a bluff, that a massive force would be required, hoping that the enormous cost and the risk would bring about a reconsideration. Instead, the assembly unexpectedly acceded to his new requirements and named him as one of the three commanders.

Sixty Athenian triremes were accompanied by forty troopships.[9] Thirty-four additional vessels from subject allies were included in the fleet as well. The Sicilian expedition deployed the largest force of hoplites fielded by Athens during the war, save for the army sent briefly to neighboring Megara early in the conflict.[10] The Athenian assembly reinforced failure a year later, devoting even more troops, ships, and money, none of which Athens could afford to lose.

The relief force was sent to Sicily just as the Spartan army prepared to invade the Athenian homeland of Attica. The fiscal, material, and manpower strain imposed by this expeditionary operation left Athens only one option at home, retreat behind the long walls of Athens and Piraeus. Worse, the Spartan king and general Agis built a fort in Attica that was continuously manned by the Peloponnesian allies in rotation. The war in Sicily deprived Athens of troops at precisely the time these forces were most needed at home. Of equal importance, the presence of Peloponnesian troops in Attica, combined with the absence of 20,000 slaves sent with the expedition, denied Athens the ability to excavate silver from the mines at Laurium, the source of much of the wealth of Athens.[11] The large force sent to Sicily thus also denied Athens the fiscal resources necessary to continue the war. Naval forces were, and remain, extremely expensive. The magnitude of the naval losses represented a particularly onerous burden.

The size of the fleet that Athens risked in Sicily is thus an important consideration. A force of 134 vessels might seem relatively small when compared to the vast armadas that fought World War II.[12] For context, let us compare contemporaneous fleets. Following the end of the First Peloponnesian War (460–445 BCE),[13] Cimon of Athens, the most influential citizen of that city-state, deemed that "it was necessary even in peace to keep a large fleet distributed at various bases.... In the course of time 100 ships were held in commission for eight months every year."[14] By this standard, Athens sent a force roughly equal to the entire strength of the navy maintained in active service before the war. This naval force was accompanied by an army that included about one third of the Athenian hoplites, including contingents from allied powers.[15] These statistics provide a stark contrast to the American resources allocated to the Philippine campaign in October 1944.

The Material Dimension

In assessing the impact of a potential victory by the Imperial Japanese Navy at Leyte Gulf, the possible scope of that success must be the first consideration. A complete triumph of the type won by Admiral Togo Heihachiro at Tsushima during the Russo-Japanese War (1904–5) was not possible.[16] What might a Japanese victory look like? More importantly, what objectives were beyond the reach of Japanese naval power in October of 1944? Japanese victory would probably have been limited to the action off Samar and would have entailed heavy damage to the transport fleet and most of MacArthur's heavy equipment. The most decisive version of the victory might have entailed a defeat of Adm. Jesse Oldendorf's battleships rushing to rescue the transports.[17] By no stretch of the imagination could Kurita's force have contended with Adm. William "Bull" Halsey's Third Fleet. The Japanese decision to sacrifice the force of aircraft carriers commanded by Vice Admiral Ozawa Jisaburo as a diversion bears out that assessment. Halsey had to be removed from the scene of action for Kurita to achieve any measure of success. A thorough and effective attack on the transports of the U.S. Seventh Fleet would have forced Kurita to loiter in the area long enough for a final showdown with Halsey. The only possible outcome of that collision would have been the destruction of the remnants of the Imperial Japanese Navy, in that case without the ignominy of being destroyed in port, either without fuel, unable to repair the Leyte Gulf battle damage, or both.

The material superiority of the U.S. Navy was almost inconceivable. The overwhelming industrial might of the United States allowed for the commissioning of seventeen fleet aircraft carriers, nine light aircraft carriers, seventy-seven escort carriers, eight battleships, twelve heavy cruisers, fifteen light cruisers, and eight antiaircraft cruisers. Shipyards around the country churned out an incredible number of lighter warships, including 175 *Fletcher*-class destroyers and more than one hundred of the newer *Gearing*-class and *Sumner*-class destroyers. An additional 355 destroyer escorts were produced concurrently, as well as thousands of merchant ships and thousands more landing craft and landing ships. Japan, by comparison, produced five fleet aircraft carriers, two light aircraft carriers, nine escort carriers, two battleships, one light cruiser, and sixty-two destroyers. Many of these vessels were laid down before the war began. The contrast is disturbing. Considering the fact that the light carriers were converted ocean liners and the escort carriers all converted merchant vessels, the inability of Japan to replace combat losses is stunning.[18] Aircraft production is another indicator of America's material advantage. In the first year of full wartime mobilization, 1943, the United States produced 85,989 military aircraft with an even greater number produced the following year. Japan produced only 76,320 aircraft between 1939 and 1945. Japan could not compete industrially.[19]

The loss of the transport and merchant shipping in Leyte Gulf would have significantly impeded Allied operations planned over the succeeding year. The critical shortage of landing ships and beaching craft slowed the pace of operations for the Allied powers throughout the last two years of the war, even without potential dramatic losses at Leyte Gulf. Amphibious ships and the landing craft were shuttled from between theaters in the Pacific as operational demands dictated.[20] The thirty-seven attack ships, 151 tank landing ships, and hundreds of cargo ships and smaller vessels were a shared asset across the two Pacific theaters. The complete loss of these assets would have precluded further amphibious operations until the ships were replaced.

In context, however, the potential losses must be balanced against American productive capacity. More than 2,700 Liberty ships were produced during the war, concurrently with more than five hundred Victory ships. Together, these two classes of cargo ship constituted the majority of the ships in the amphibious task groups and fleet train at anchor in Leyte Gulf. The problem for Japan was the limited number of targets in the invasion fleet. The tank landing ships (LSTs) were the most critical commodity. Their loss would have slowed the advance, but these vessels could have been replaced as well. In late 1942, American shipyards were launching three Liberty ships a day with an average construction time of 105 days. By 1944, the average length of time to build a Liberty ship was forty-two days. Seventeen shipyards were producing these vessels, with sixteen more producing other oceangoing cargo and passenger ships.[21] The losses could have been made up in months. In contrast, the Athenians required years to rebuild the triremes lost at Syracuse. Athens would not be capable of deploying a similar sized fleet again until the Battle of Arginusae seven years after the defeat in Sicily.[22]

The manpower that the United States applied to the Leyte Gulf operation must also be considered. While Athens sent roughly one-third of its warriors to Sicily, the American order of battle for the initial invasion of the Philippine Islands amounted to four divisions organized into two corps with a ranger battalion attached. Even with the two divisions that were held in reserve on board the transports, the entire force represented a small portion of the overall U.S. military establishment. The Sixth Army amounted to 202,500 ground troops.[23] When compared to the 8 million men serving in the U.S. Army at the time, the number of troops was insignificant.[24] As a percentage of the available manpower, this number pales in comparison to the commitment made by Athens to the Sicilian expedition. Materially, whether in terms of armaments or manpower, the outcome at Leyte could not possibly change the balance of forces between the United States and Japan. The loss of all the exposed shipping, an unlikely outcome, would not have diminished American power sufficiently to change the course of the war.

The Political Impact

The only path for avoiding defeat that remained open to Japan in late 1944 was to inflict enough casualties to convince the governments of the Allied powers that a negotiated peace was the best option. War weariness among Japan's adversaries was Tokyo's sole lifeline. A degree of logic informed this perception. Army Chief of Staff Gen. George Marshall, credited as the architect of the force that emerged victorious in the war, allegedly asserted that a democracy could not fight a seven-year war.[25] While Marshall was supposedly offering advice on concluding the war with Japan, the depth of American rage at the manner in which the war had begun remained deep. A negotiated settlement was not in the offing.[26]

The United States did not seek a negotiated settlement after the bloody battles that followed Leyte. Okinawa and Iwo Jima were the bloodiest battles of the Pacific campaign, yet neither led to a negotiated settlement. Had the majority of the force in Leyte Gulf been destroyed, it might well have been the bloodiest battle of the entire Pacific War, but it remains unlikely that it would have led to negotiations any more than the subsequent battles had. The magnitude of the casualties was not, however, preordained. The massive bombardment endured by the Marines on Guadalcanal on 14 October 1942 consisted of more than an hour of uninterrupted shelling by two battleships. While forever enshrined in Marine Corps lore as "the night," the barrage of over 950 14-inch shells failed to dislodge the defenders of Henderson Field and only forty-one men were killed in action, including casualties among the aircrew.[27] On several occasions, warships had managed to break through to groups of helpless transports and yet failed to inflict the damage that was expected and, in some instances, claimed.[28]

At Leyte, the Japanese naval vessels would have been forced to divide their attention between the shipping anchored offshore and MacArthur's army ashore. Success for Operation Sho-Go would not necessarily have produced the casualty levels seen in the later battles. With nine ships sunk and almost four hundred damaged off Okinawa, the naval casualties might have been more severe at Leyte. It was unlikely, however, that the casualties would have reached a level that would have swayed the American public to turn against the war. Unlike the Athenian expedition to Sicily, American public support for the war in the Pacific never wavered.

This commitment by the American public was remarkably stable regardless of the difficulties encountered. So firm was the backing for continuing the conflict, in spite of the high number of casualties, that researchers studying the relationship between losses and public opinion during the Korean and Vietnam wars concluded that the sustained level of support for prosecuting World War II "would constrain the significance of any casualty-opinion relationship."[29] Political support for continuing military operations in the Pacific remained extremely strong throughout the conflict. In November 1944, after the public release of information on casualties and on Japanese atrocities, a plurality of American adults surveyed during a National Opinion Research Center poll were in favor of continuing the war and imposing harsh measures on Japan. One in eight was in favor of the complete extermination of the Japanese people. Rather than shrink in the face of the vagaries of war, the American public had grown more committed to the complete defeat of Japan.[30]

While sources for the Peloponnesian War are far scarcer, the communications attributed to Nicias reveal a lack of faith on the part of the principal commander in theater. Against the commander's wish to abandon the effort, the assembly chose to reinforce the expedition with more troops, ships, and silver. The troops in the reinforcement, however, had a smaller proportion of Athenian hoplites and more men from the subject allies.[31] The composition of the force may have represented a need for specific military skills outside those typical of the Athenian warrior class, but the increase in participation by subject city-states implies a diminishing level of support in Athens. Whereas the original contingent was composed largely of Athenians, only 1,200 Athenian hoplites were included in the relief force out of a total of five thousand troops. When measured against the late-war increase in the willingness of Americans to inflict harsh punishment upon Japan at the conclusion of World War II, it is clear that the Athenian support for the war against Syracuse paled in comparison to the growing American dedication to continuing the conflict in the Pacific.[32] This effect was part of a broader strategic environment in 1944 that differed greatly from the strategic conditions in which the Sicilian expedition took place during the Peloponnesian War.

The Strategic Environment

The broad contours of the international environment in late 1944 also suggested that Japan's bid to regain the initiative, or at least forestall further advances by the Allies, was fruitless. Where the Athenians had embarked on the Sicilian expedition in a period of high tension but nominal peace, the invasion of the Philippines was part of a global, coalition war.[33] The strategic imperatives that drove the United States involved both alliance considerations and international developments. Each set of requirements was driven by unique factors but, taken together, the circumstances favored the Allies and dictated that Japan surrender unconditionally.

In late 1944, the global situation of the Axis alliance reached a desperate point. Italy had been driven from the war a year earlier and the artificial rump state that Germany created in the north was a drain on German resources rather than a strategic asset.[34] Germany was reeling. While the high-risk, Allied attempt to cross the Rhine in the Netherlands—Operation Market Garden (17–27 September 1944)—had been thwarted, mounting losses, combined with the loss of critical resources from the Balkans, rendered the German position precarious. Soviet armies were in Poland, Romania and its oilfields were overrun, and the Baltic republics were under pressure. Germany, which had never effectively coordinated policy and strategy with its Pacific ally, was losing the ability to defend itself, much less aid Japan.

The collapse of Germany was rapidly leaving Japan to face the Allies alone. The eventual loss of the Baltic coastal regions would deny the Kriegsmarine its only effective training area for new submariners and, given the appalling casualty rates in the U-boat arm, helped bring the war in the Atlantic to an end.[35] The majority of the Allied naval force supporting the campaign in Europe was then available for transfer to the Pacific. Whatever losses Japan might inflict at Leyte, the warships would be replaced not only by the enormous productive capacity of the United States but also by the transfer of Allied assets from the Atlantic. Regardless of the outcome at Leyte Gulf, the correlation of forces was turning dramatically against Japan as a result of the collapse of the Axis and the shift in the international sphere.

The stability of the alliance opposing Japan also represented a very different situation than the conditions that existed at the time of the Athenian operations in Sicily. The defeat suffered by Athens at Syracuse resulted in a political shift. The alliance opposing Sparta in the Peloponnesian War began as the Delian League, a group of Hellenic city-states that banded together for protection against the Persian Empire after the battles of Salamis and Plataea (480–479 BCE). It evolved into an empire ruled by Athens, an empire consisting of restive "allies." As a consequence of the defeat, "the subjects of the Athenians showed a readiness to revolt, even beyond their ability, judging the circumstances with passion and refusing even to hear of the Athenians being able to last out the coming summer."[36] It was the position of Athens that was desperate, not that of Sparta. The Allied cause in World War II never suffered from any such defections.

By contrast, Australia, Britain, and New Zealand would not have been provoked to rebel against the hegemony of the United States following a defeat. The United States had not coerced any of the Allied powers into providing forces for the invasion of Leyte. The nature of the alliance was voluntary and, while the United States played the dominant role in deciding the course of action in the Pacific theaters, it did so in consultation with the other Allies. The Allies were not about to abandon the United States, much less oppose American objectives militarily. The position of the United States as the dominant Western power did meet with some political resistance from declining powers like France and Britain,[37] but the general confluence of interest meant that any differences were over operational and strategic issues and not the guiding policy.

Alliance dynamics were also affected by the nature of the forces engaged. Part of the Athenian problem had been the fact that almost half of the available hoplite class had been placed at risk in Sicily. The Spartans placed in jeopardy a single, full-blooded Spartiate, and even he was the son of a disgraced father. The Spartan assistance to Syracuse was a disposal force. No Spartiate hoplites (full citizens of Sparta) and no Spartan ships were sent to Sicily. The military and naval force sent by Sparta was, in fact, expendable.[38] While Athens lost thousands of irreplaceable citizens and 160 triremes, Sparta's military power was never in danger. The comparison to the Pacific War is instructive.

The Japanese force in the Philippines was substantial. It would grow to more than half a million troops later in the campaign, although a far smaller number contested the landings at Leyte.[39] While substantial, the contribution of the Imperial Japanese Army paled as a percentage of the entire force when compared to the naval forces risked by Japan. Virtually the entire remaining combat power of the Imperial Japanese Navy was thrown into the breach at Leyte. Only one sortie by a major combat unit occurred after the October battle. The *Yamato* was sent to intervene in events at Okinawa in April 1945 with fuel sufficient only to sail to the embattled island. It was never intended to return.[40] The units that survived and retired to the Dutch East Indies were unable to repair battle damage. The ships that retired to the Home Islands were left without fuel. Regardless of the outcome of the engagements around the Philippine Islands, the Imperial Japanese Navy was a spent force. It would never intervene in events again in a meaningful way.

The underlying reason for the degraded condition of the Japanese navy had as much do to with the American war on Japanese commerce as with major naval battles. Japanese naval assets were largely relegated to bases in the Dutch East Indies. This disposition was the result of the strategic impact of petroleum resources, in particular the location of the supplies and the inability of Japan to transport those supplies to the Home Islands. The Japanese tanker fleet declined in total tonnage during the first nine and a half months of 1944.[41] Japan could not move fuel oil to the fleet. The fleet had to come to the sources of supply. This constraint made the movements of that fleet predictable, both preceding the battles around Leyte Gulf and in whatever operations followed. In order to refuel, the Japanese warships had to return to the East Indies, where no repair facilities were available. The inability to permanently repair battle damage suffered by those vessels further hampered any future utility for the fleet. Whatever the outcome in Leyte Gulf, the range and operational options available to the Imperial Japanese Navy were reduced to a crippling degree by the destruction of merchant tanker capacity.

This conundrum regarding the impact of American unrestricted submarine warfare raises a further difference in the strategic circumstances when compared to the Athenian operations in Sicily. The United States was effectively self-sufficient in 1944. While it had to import some critical raw materials, particularly rare earths and bauxite, the basic sinews of military power—steel and petroleum—were available domestically. Japan, on the other hand, had to import virtually all these commodities. This situation was very different from the circumstances that prevailed during the Peloponnesian War. In that case, the invader was effectively an island power that required the importation of everything necessary to sustain not only combat power, but life itself. Driven behind the long walls, Athens was highly dependent on imports, just as was Japan. Sparta, more like the United States of 1944, could produce everything it needed to satisfy domestic demand and continue the conflict. The economic and logistic circumstances in the two cases were reversed. A defeat at Leyte Gulf would do nothing to alter this strategic reality and the continuing submarine offensive would further degrade Japanese logistics, regardless of the fate of MacArthur's troops or the amphibious force supporting them.

The nature of the target of each invasion was also vastly different. Athens placed at risk a substantial portion of its military power in order to secure an island that was larger in area than the aggregate of all the land in the Athenian Empire. While some city-states in Sicily were friendly and the campaign was initiated at the invitation of one such city, much of the population was predisposed to resist intervention. The American forces, on the other hand, were welcomed in the Philippines as liberators. It was the army on the defensive, that of Japan, that faced a hostile population that supported guerilla warfare against the occupiers.[42] Athens was fighting in hostile territory and as the fortunes turned against the invading army, so, too, did the few allies in the region. Athens, however, had more significant problems than the defection of a few Sicilian city-states.

Greek city-states that had refrained from taking sides in the contest between Athens and Sparta began to climb on the Spartan bandwagon. "Neutrals now felt that even if uninvited they no longer ought to stand aloof from the war."[43] The defeat in Sicily, and particularly the loss of more than half of the Athenian navy, not only spurred rebellion, but drew new enemies into the fight. The formerly neutral states of the Peloponnesus were one problem. A new and far more dangerous enemy was also drawn into the game, not directly, but decisively nonetheless.

It was not a new enemy in any real sense. It was an old enemy that had withdrawn from Hellenic affairs decades earlier. Sparta could never hope to match Athens at sea without outside assistance, particularly financial support, which only the Persian Empire could provide.[44] While absent from the affairs of the Greeks for half a century, Persia remained the nearest thing in the ancient world to a superpower. Athens had relied on economic might and sea power to dominate the period between the Persian Wars (490–479 BCE) and the Peloponnesian War. With the destruction of the fleet, Athens' ability to extract tribute waned and so did Athenian economic power. This fiscal-maritime disaster had no analog in World War II.

American economic might was organic. It was a function of industrial and resource wealth beyond anything Japan, or in fact the entire Axis, could match. Paul Kennedy, in his landmark *The Rise and Fall of the Great Powers*, quotes an assessment of the "Relative War Potential of the Powers in 1937." If the aggregate war potential of the world was valued at 100, the United States, in 1937, possessed 41.7 percent of that global aggregate. This feat was accomplished while American defense spending represented the smallest percentage of national income of any of the powers.[45] That year was perhaps the worst year of the Great Depression, economically speaking. This was also a time before the conversion of civilian industry to military production. Between that point and the battles around Leyte Gulf, the American share of military might had increased substantially. While other powers were overrun (France), defeated (Italy), or had production facilities disrupted or destroyed (Germany, the Soviet Union, Britain), the United States alone remained inviolate. As a result of defeat at Syracuse, Athens faced adversaries fueled by the influx of money from the greatest economic power of the time. In 1944, that economic behemoth was the United States. A Japanese victory at Leyte Gulf would have done nothing to change this calculus.

Internationally, shifting priorities among the Allied powers also ensured that the pressure would continue to build against Japan. The impending defeat of Germany meant that Josef Stalin and the other

Allied leaders had begun to contemplate the postwar world. While Roosevelt conceived of a global system dominated by his four policemen,[46] Stalin inhabited a much darker psychological realm. This fact ensured that the two Allies would be competing for influence in a postwar world. East Asia would be one of the primary venues, as competition in Europe quickly became too dangerous. No such imperative drove the Athenian partners to remain in the fight. Where postwar rivalries were not even on the horizon at the time of the Sicilian debacle, the specter of a Soviet quest for security through spheres of influence made a decisive end to the Pacific War an imperative. Leyte Gulf, whatever the outcome, was not going to alter that trajectory either.

Conclusion

Looking back on the events of October 1944 across the intervening seventy-five years, a few striking facts are worth noting. The battles around Leyte Gulf forever broke the power of the Imperial Japanese Navy. The irony of the composition of Admiral Oldendorf's battle line, predominantly ships sunk or damaged at Pearl Harbor, offers an insight into why Japanese success at Leyte Gulf would have been irrelevant in the long run. Any state that could raise these ships and restore them to service while concurrently producing hundreds of new warships was indomitable. By October of 1944, Japan was backed into a strategic and economic corner from which it could not emerge. A part of this was due to the American submarine force, whose role at Leyte Gulf was peripheral, but whose effect was strategic. Entire books have been devoted to the economic strangulation inflicted upon Japan by the campaign waged by the fleet boats.[47] Even if Japan had been a match for the United States industrially at the outset, unrestricted submarine warfare and the ineffective Japanese response would have made the outcome at Leyte Gulf moot.

None of these observations, by any stretch of the imagination, diminishes the sacrifices and incredible bravery of what became known as the "Last Stand of the Tin Can Sailors," which turned back the Japanese battle line and saved the invasion fleet.[48] These sailors and the fliers from the jeep carriers saved, potentially, tens of thousands of lives and hundreds of thousands of tons of shipping. The broader point, however, was that this battle never possessed the capacity to change the course of the war in the manner the Japanese planners hoped.

Campaigns are planned to achieve strategic effects. These effects, however, must be realistically understood. Historical analogies can be useful tools for historians and strategists. One of the basic methods of the "Strategy & War" course offered by the Naval War College is the use of historical case studies to inform future strategic planning. The lessons derived, however, must be based on accurate parallels. Japan embarked on the Pearl Harbor operation attempting to replicate the strategic script that brought victory in the Russo-Japanese War.[49] It did so without fully considering the broader strategic and international context of 1941. At Leyte Gulf, it cast the dice once again, unaware that those dice were loaded against it. Even a victory of the magnitude of Tsushima would not have saved Japan in October 1944. When engaged in historical analysis, whether to inform policy and strategy or for its own sake, the wise course would avoid the hyperbole that crept into Morison's otherwise superb description of the largest naval battle in history. With all due respect to Morison, Leyte Gulf could never have become an American Syracuse.

About the Author

Kevin J. Delamer is a retired naval aviator. A graduate of the United States Naval Academy, he holds an undergraduate degree in naval architecture and a master's degree in national security and strategic studies from the Naval War College, where he graduated with highest distinction. He has also completed graduate studies in aeronautical engineering, aviation safety, and history. He is currently an adjunct professor of strategy for the College of Distance Education of the Naval War College, teaching both classroom and web-enabled courses.

During his naval career, he served in a number of operational assignments with helicopter squadrons, flying a variety of aircraft models and earning distinction as the Helicopter Antisubmarine Squadron 12 Pilot of the Year in 1990. A graduate of the U.S. Naval Test Pilot School, he has accumulated time in dozens of helicopter models and served as the lead test pilot for the Presidential Helicopter Program and as a test pilot with the NASA-Army Experimental Rotorcraft Program. In nonflying billets, he served as the director of political-military affairs at Naval Forces Central Command and subsequently as executive assistant to the commander. He retired from active duty after five years teaching in residence at the Naval War College where, in addition to resident faculty duties, he also lectured for the College of Distance Education on a number of subjects, including World War II.

Delamer is the author of a chapter in the Naval Institute-published centennial history of naval aviation, *One Hundred Years of U.S. Navy Air Power*, as well as various technical papers and encyclopedia articles, and is an occasional contributor to the Naval Institute's news blog and *Proceedings* magazine. He resides in Owings, Maryland, with his wife, the former Lora Marie Sutherland, where he is the senior naval science instructor at Northern High School. They have four grown children.

Notes

1. "Tin can sailor" is a term used to refer to the crews of World War II destroyers.
2. In Norse mythology, the Valkyries were female figures who chose which warriors would die in battle, carrying a portion off to Valhalla, the hall of slain heroes, where they would prepare for the climactic battle that marked the end of the world. The phrase "Ride of the Valkyries" has come to mean a heroic, if likely suicidal, charge.
3. The attire of Stansfield Admiral Turner can be seen in the photo in the *Naval War College Review* as well as the official portrait on display in Conolly Hall at the Naval War College. On the curriculum, see "Challenge: A New Approach to Professional Education," *Naval War College Review* 25, no. 8 (1972): 4–5.
4. Samuel Eliot Morison, *History of United States Naval Operations in World War II*, vol. 12, *Leyte: June 1944–January 1945* (Boston: Little, Brown, 1958), 337.
5. Louis Morton, review of *History of United States Naval Operations in World War II*, vol. 12, *Leyte: June 1944–January 1945*, by Samuel Eliot Morison, *Pacific Historical Review* 28, no. 2 (1959): 203.
6. A hoplite was a citizen-soldier of the ancient Greek city-states. See Victor Davis Hanson, *The Western Way of War: Infantry Battle in Classical Greece* (New York: Alfred A. Knopf, 1989), 27–35.
7. Donald Kagan, *The Peace of Nicias and the Sicilian Expedition* (Ithaca and London: Cornell University Press, 1981), 185; For a discussion of the concept of a disposal force, see Julian S. Corbett, *Some Principles of Maritime Strategy* (London: Longmans, Green, 1911; reprint, Annapolis: Naval Institute Press, 1988), 60–61.

8. Thucydides, *The History of the Peloponnesian War*, 6.11[4], quotes are from the Richard Crawley translation and are taken from *The Landmark Thucydides: A Comprehensive Guide to the Peloponnesian War*, trans. Richard Crawley, ed. Robert B. Strassler (New York: The Free Press, 1996). Citations are given in book, chapter, sentence format to facilitate using any of the numerous translations.
9. A trireme (literally "three-rower") was the standard warship in the Hellenic world in the late fifth century BCE. See John R. Hale, *Lords of the Sea: The Epic Story of the Athenian Navy and the Birth of Democracy* (New York: Viking, 2009).
10. Kagan, *The Peace of Nicias and the Sicilian Expedition*, 185–87; Hale, *Lords of the Sea*, 187; Donald Kagan, *The Outbreak of the Peloponnesian War* (Ithaca and London: Cornell University Press, 1969), 246–48.
11. Donald Kagan, *The Fall of the Athenian Empire* (Ithaca and London: Cornell University Press, 1987), 4–5.
12. By contrast, the Normandy invasion force consisted of 138 warships of destroyer-escort size and larger, as well as an additional 221 escort vessels and thousands of amphibious assault ships and craft. Williamson Murray and Allan R. Millett, *A War to Be Won: Fighting the Second World War* (Cambridge, MA: Harvard University Press, 2000), 420.
13. The First Peloponnesian War, fought between 460 and 445 BCE, was an inconclusive conflict that set the stage for the Second Peloponnesian War or, as Thucydides described it, "the [great] war between Peloponnesians and the Athenians," Thucydides, 1.1[1]. See Donald Kagan, *The Peloponnesian War* (New York: Viking, 2003), 14–18.
14. William Ledyard Rodgers, *Greek and Roman Naval Warfare* (Annapolis: Naval Institute Press, 1937), 120.
15. Kagan, *The Fall of the Athenian Empire*, 2.
16. The entire Russian Second and Third Pacific Squadrons, effectively the Russian Baltic Fleet, were completely destroyed by the Imperial Japanese Navy off the Island of Tsushima on 27 May 1905. For descriptions of the battle, see Julian S. Corbett, *Maritime Operations in the Russo-Japanese War* (Annapolis: Naval Institute Press, 1994), 2:240–94.
17. The U.S. battleships that fought at Surigao Strait early in the morning still had sufficient stocks of armor-piercing ammunition. The accompanying cruisers and destroyers were largely depleted, particularly

the destroyers, which had expended all their torpedoes. See James D. Hornfischer, *The Last Stand of the Tin Can Sailors: The Extraordinary World War II Story of the U.S. Navy's Finest Hour* (New York: Bantam, 2004), 345–46.

18. For U.S. ships, see Samuel Eliot Morison, *History of United States Naval Operations in World War II*, vol. 15, *Supplement and General Index* (Boston: Little, Brown, 1947; reprint, Edison, NJ: Castle Books, 2001), 30–111. For Japanese ships, see Paul S. Dull, *A Battle History of the Imperial Japanese Navy: 1941–1945* (Annapolis: Naval Institute Press, 1978), 357–67.
19. Murray and Millett, *A War to Be Won*, 535.
20. The Pacific was split into several theaters but was effectively divided between Nimitz and MacArthur for overall responsibility. It was between MacArthur's Southwest Pacific Area and Nimitz's Pacific Ocean Area that the resources were shuttled.
21. Murray and Millett contend that the average time to build a Liberty or Victory ship was reduced from 105 to 56 days. Other sources contend that Liberty ships were built, on average, in 42 days in 1944. The difference may result from the inclusion of the slightly more complex Victory ships in the former assessment or from differences in accounting for fitting out. In either case, production time dropped dramatically. See Murray and Millet, *A War to Be Won*, 536; Colton Company, "WWII Construction Records: Private-Sector Shipyards that Built Ships for the U.S. Maritime Commission," http://www.shipbuildinghistory.com/index.htm (accessed 17 August 2018).
22. Rodgers, *Greek and Roman Naval Warfare*, 173–85.
23. Charles R. Anderson, *Leyte* (Washington, D.C.: U.S. Army Center of Military History, 1994), 10–11.
24. The National World War II Museum, "Research Starters: US Military by the Numbers," https://www.nationalww2museum.org/students-teachers/student-resources/research-starters/research-starters-us-military-numbers (accessed 30 July 2018).
25. Somewhat ironic, as Britain, a democratic government, was the victor in the Seven Years' War over autocratic France. For the quote, see Andrew J. Bacevich, "Endless war, a recipe for four-star arrogance," *Washington Post*, 27 June 2010, http://www.washingtonpost.com/wp-dyn/content/article/2010/06/25/AR2010062502160.html?noredirect=on&sid=ST2010062703373 (accessed 8 August 2018).

26. David C. Evans and Mark R. Peattie, *Kaigun: Strategy, Tactics, and Technology in the Imperial Japanese Navy, 1887–1941* (Annapolis: Naval Institute Press, 1997), 493.
27. Richard B. Frank, *Guadalcanal* (New York: Random House, 1990), 315–19.
28. As an example, USS *Houston* and HMAS *Perth* chanced upon a 56-ship Japanese troopship convoy anchored in Banten Bay while trying to escape the fall of Java. The two cruisers were only able to sink one enemy transport while forcing three more to beach. Samuel Eliot Morison, *History of United States Naval Operations in World War II*, vol. 3, *The Rising Sun in the Pacific, 1931–April 1942* (Boston: Little, Brown, 1948; reprint, Edison, NJ: Castle Books, 2001), 365–66.
29. Hadley Cantril, "Opinion Trends in World War II: Some Guides to Interpretation," *Public Opinion Quarterly* 12, no. 1 (1948): 38–39, http://www.jstor.org/stable/2745585 (accessed 11 August 2018); quote, Scott Sigmund Gartner and Gary M. Segura. "War, Casualties, and Public Opinion," *Journal of Conflict Resolution* 42, no. 3 (1998): 297, http://www.jstor.org/stable/174515 (accessed 11 August 2018).
30. National Opinion Research Center, *Japan and the Post-War World* (NORC Report No. 32) (Denver: University of Denver, 1946), 20.
31. Thucydides, 7.20[2], 7.42[1] detail the 1,200 Athenian hoplites sent out of 5,000 that arrived with Demosthenes and the relief force as opposed to the original force sent to Sicily in which 4,000 of the 5,000 hoplites were Athenian, Thucydides, 6.25, 6.31[2].
32. A survey was taken during February 1944 in which the largest segment of respondents favored a lenient approach to postwar Japan. In the intervening ten months, the increasing casualties appear to have combined with the revelations regarding Japanese atrocities to harden American attitudes. National Opinion Research Center, *Japan and the Post-War World*, 18–20.
33. The Sicilian expedition was undertaken during the Peace of Nicias, an armistice agreed to by Athens and Sparta in 421 BCE, largely out of exhaustion. Tensions were elevated, in no small part due to the Athenian participation in the Battle of Mantinea between Sparta and the Argive alliance in 418 BCE. See Kagan, *The Peace of Nicias and the Sicilian Expedition*, 19–20, 107–37.
34. Italian dictator Benito Mussolini was imprisoned by the Italian government following his ouster from power in July 1943. After

his rescue by German paratroops, Adolf Hitler allowed Mussolini to establish the Italian Socialist Republic or RSI (Republica Sociale Italiana) in Northern Italy. This state, nominally an ally of Nazi Germany, seriously hampered German operations in Italy. See Santi Corvaja, *Hitler & Mussolini: The Secret Meetings*, trans. R. L. Miller (New York: Enigma, 2001), 314–55.

35. Gerhard L. Weinberg, *A World at Arms: A Global History of World War II* (New York: Cambridge University Press, 1994), 781.
36. Thucydides, 8.2[2].
37. President Franklin Roosevelt and some of his lieutenants did not take the Free French General Charles de Gaulle seriously. Also, de Gaulle, in his postwar capacity as the Chairman of the Provisional Government of France, needed an international opponent after the war for domestic political reasons, and the United States was it. See Michael H. Creswell, review of Charles L. Robertson, *When Roosevelt Planned to Govern France* (Amherst and Boston: University of Massachusetts Press, 2011), https://www.h-france.net/vol12reviews/vol12no129creswell.pdf.
38. Kagan, *The Peace of Nicias and the Sicilian Expedition*, 258–59.
39. The Japanese 16th Division, with attached units totaling 20,000 troops, initially opposed the landings on Leyte. By December 1944, the number deployed to the island rose to 65,000. See Ronald Spector, *Eagle Against the Sun: The American War with Japan* (New York: The Free Press, 1985), 511.
40. Samuel Eliot Morison, *History of United States Naval Operations in World War II*, vol. 14, *Victory in the Pacific, 1945* (Boston: Little, Brown, 1947; reprint, Edison, NJ: Castle Books, 2001), 205–9.
41. Japanese tanker tonnage at the outset of 1944 was 863,000 dwt, Dan van der Vat, *The Pacific Campaign: World War II, the U.S.-Japanese Naval War, 1941–1945* (New York: Simon & Schuster, 1991), 333; Japanese tanker losses in 1944 up to 20 October were approximately 576,000 dwt, Joint Army-Navy Assessment Committee, *Japanese Naval and Merchant Shipping Losses During World War II by All Causes* (Washington, D.C.: Department of the Navy, 1947), 49–67; Japanese tanker production for the entire 1944 fiscal year amounted to 555,000 dwt, a peak year for production, and there were no further tankers produced in 1945, United States Strategic Bombing Survey, *Japanese Merchant Shipbuilding* (Washington, D.C.: Military Supply

Division, 1947), 44; Mark P. Parillo, *The Japanese Merchant Marine in World War II* (Annapolis: Naval Institute Press, 1993), 167.
42. Milan Vego, *The Battle for Leyte, 1944: Allied and Japanese Plans, Preparations, and Execution* (Annapolis: Naval Institute Press, 2006), 62–63.
43. Thucydides, 8.2[1].
44. Kagan, *The Fall of the Athenian Empire*, 16.
45. In 1937, the United States spent 1.5 percent of national income on defense while Germany and Japan devoted well over 20 percent of national income to defense expenditures. Paul M. Kennedy, *The Rise and Fall of the Great Powers: Economic Change and Military Conflict from 1500 to 2000* (New York: Random House, 1987), 332.
46. Roosevelt envisaged Britain, the USSR, China, and the United States as cooperating to support an international organization ensuring order. Each power was to have spheres of influence that overlapped those of the others. See Robert H. McNeal, "Roosevelt through Stalin's Spectacles," *International Journal* 18, no. 2 (1963): 201.
47. See, for example, Clay Blair Jr., *Silent Victory: The U.S. Submarine War against Japan* (Philadelphia and New York: J. B. Lippincott, 1975); Charles A. Lockwood, *Sink 'Em All: Submarine Warfare in the Pacific* (New York: E. P. Dutton, 1951); James F. DeRose, *Unrestricted Warfare: How a New Breed of Officers Led the Submarine Force to Victory in World War II* (Hoboken, NJ: John Wiley, 2000; reprint, Edison, NJ: Castle Books, 2006).
48. Perhaps the most vivid account of this aspect of the battle is Hornfischer's *The Last Stand of the Tin Can Sailors*.
49. Japan initiated the Russo-Japanese War with a surprise attack on Port Arthur, which initially immobilized the squadron of capital ships based there. The attack was conducted in advance of the declaration of war. It set the conditions for a successful, limited war that ended in a negotiated settlement. Such a settlement was never an option in the global coalition war into which Japan drew the United States in December of 1941. For a more complete analysis, see Yoji Koda, "The Russo-Japanese War: Primary Causes of Japanese Success," *Naval War College Review* 58, no. 2 (Spring 2005): 11–44, in particular 39–43.

9

AFTER THE BATTLE
Sea Power and the Ormoc Campaign
Vincent P. O'Hara

IN A COMMUNIQUÉ RELEASED ON 29 October 1944 the Pacific Fleet informed the nation that a great naval battle had been fought in Philippine waters; it had resulted in "an overwhelming victory for the Third and Seventh United States Fleets." It asserted, "The Japanese Fleet has been decisively defeated and routed."[1] In short, the United States was claiming decisive victory in a great naval battle. According to the script, "Decisive victory in a naval battle was supposed to enable the victor to 'control the seas,' to cut off the enemy's seaborne supplies and reinforcements, and ensure the arrival of one's own. That was what strategists in both the U.S. and Japan had long believed."[2]

The Battle of Leyte Gulf certainly seemed decisive, but after the battle the Americans did not assert control of the seas around Leyte. The Japanese took this as confirmation that they had severely damaged the enemy in the air battle of Formosa, which took place a week before the Leyte landings, in the surface action off Samar, and with kamikaze attacks. Shortly after the battle the Japanese navy's chief of staff reported to the Imperial Throne that the Americans had lost five or six carriers, three cruisers, and one destroyer was sunk, and four carriers, two battleships, and one cruiser were damaged. As for Formosa, "twelve enemy ships—cruisers and above—had been sunk and another twenty-three enemy ships had been otherwise destroyed."[3] Of course, by this point, many Japanese doubted such pronouncements. The architect of the A-Go plan and commander of the Combined Fleet, Admiral Soemu Toyoda, "automatically cut claims by half."[4] According to Commander Moriyoshi Yamaguchi, a staff officer who transferred to Luzon on 20 October 1944, "The published number

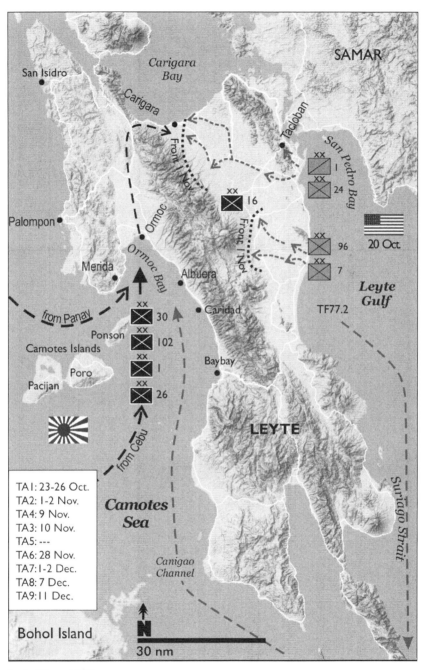

Leyte. *Vincent O'Hara.*

[of enemy ships sunk in the Formosa battle] was about 30, the actual number I thought was one-third of that or about ten including the five carriers."[5] In short, by the end of October, even Japanese skeptics up and down the chain of command believed that the Imperial Navy had sunk at least ten carriers and dealt the U.S. Navy a staggering blow. Through a dazzling exercise in creative reality, the Japanese simply ignored their decisive defeat in the Battle of Leyte Gulf and proceeded to control the waters off the island's west coast, assisted by a defensive posture adopted by U.S. naval forces stationed in the gulf, American ignorance of Japanese intentions, the ability to assert periodic air superiority, and bad weather.

Gen. Douglas MacArthur, commander in chief, South West Pacific area (CinCSWPA), had anticipated a swift conquest of Leyte, thinking the Japanese would conserve their forces for the fight on Luzon. However, the Japanese area command resolved to reinforce the island even before the naval battles of 25 October. The 16th Cruiser Division and destroyer-transports (APDs) *T6*, *T9*, and *T10*, and landing ships (LSTs) *T101* and *T102* conducted Operation TA1 on 23 October. Applying costly lessons learned in the Solomons, the troops arrived in recently constructed vessels designed for counter-landings on disputed islands. The APDs displaced 1,800 tons. They could be loaded with landing craft and nearly five hundred troops, and were capable of 22 knots. The T100-type LSTs were 950-ton, 13-knot amphibious assault ships. Both classes had a strong anti-aircraft armament. Over eight days the Japanese navy delivered, without loss, 6,150 troops of the 30th and 102nd Divisions to Ormoc, a port on Leyte's west coast.[6] Naturally, such success bolstered the conclusion that Leyte was the place to fight, and the Japanese scheduled more convoys. The Pacific Command's war diary did not note that the enemy was reinforcing Leyte via Ormoc Bay until November 1.[7]

Adm. Thomas Kinkaid, commander of the Seventh Fleet, and Adm. Chester Nimitz, Commander in Chief Pacific (CinCPac), perhaps a little dazzled by the magnitude of the battle they had just won, perhaps a little complacent after the apparent completeness of their victory, neglected the U.S. Navy's own painful lessons from the Solomons and failed to blockade Leyte with warships, trusting MacArthur's assurances that Army air could do the job. But Leyte's "mud and grass" airfields proved inadequate, and atrocious weather—thirty-five inches of rain between 17 October and 25 November—turned the airstrips into quagmires.[8] After their extended operations, the fast carriers needed to resupply and rest their pilots. A stream of air reinforcements from Formosa allowed the Japanese to periodically assert local air superiority, and kamikaze attacks gave the U.S. Navy a new sense of peril. On 29 October the Seventh Fleet redeployed back to Ulithi Atoll. Kinkaid retained only three battleships, four cruisers, and thirteen destroyers (TG 77.1) in Leyte Gulf. Fearing mines and feeling pinched for resources, Rear Adm. R. G. Weyler, ComTG 77.1, concentrated on defensive operations. His mission was "to cover, protect, and defend Leyte gulf and the invasion forces and ships engaged in the Leyte operation against attack by enemy surface forces."[9]

Japan's second Leyte reinforcement operation, TA2, included APDs *T6*, *T9*, and *T10*. It departed Manila at 0700 on 31 October and arrived at Ormoc on 1 November, bringing a thousand men of the 26th Division. A follow-up convoy of four transports, equipped with extra derricks and barges for amphibious operations, *Kashii Maru* (8,407 GRT [gross register tonnage]), *Kinka Maru* (9,305 GRT), *Takatsu Maru* (5,350 GRT), and *Noto Maru* (7,191 GRT), and a powerful escort followed closely behind.[10] Sailing under rainy skies and with strong air cover, the convoy entered Ormoc Bay at 1830 on 1 November and immediately began disembarking ten thousand troops of the elite 1st Division fresh from Manchuria.[11] U.S. Army air P-38s from Tacloban attacked and caused some casualties but scored no hits. That afternoon B-24s sank *Noto Maru*, but she had already unloaded 90 percent of her cargo.

On the other side of Leyte, Japanese aircraft harassed TG 77.1 to ensure it did not intervene. Attacks started at 0950 and lasted nine hours. Kamikazes sank the destroyer *Abner Read* and damaged *Claxton* and *Ammen*. Conventional strikes damaged destroyers *Killen*, *Anderson*, and *Bush*. That evening Kinkaid reported his losses to MacArthur and requested assistance from Task Force 38, the fast carriers of Adm. William F. Halsey, "if Army Air could not provide more fighter coverage."[12]

On 2 November *T9*, which had sprinted over to Cebu, brought to Ormoc the headquarters of the 35th Army. The assignment of an army headquarters to Leyte reflected the extent of Japanese ambitions. Confidence was so high, one high staff officer "enthusiastically discussed plans to seize MacArthur and demand the surrender of the entire American army."[13] MacArthur did not help the Navy understand how bad the situation was becoming. For example, Nimitz's war diary for 2 November notes: "CinCSWPA reports enemy has been driven into the small and confined Ormoc area. . . . Enemy losses are estimated as 30,000. Completion of the Leyte-Samar operation believed by CinCSWPA to be near."[14]

On 5 November TF 38 returned and launched massive strikes against enemy airfields on Luzon. These claimed 439 Japanese planes, but this temporary infusion of air power was intended to disrupt kamikaze operations, not shut down the Ormoc pipeline. In fact, only two weeks after the greatest naval victory in history, the Japanese had nearly doubled their forces on Leyte and the U.S. Army faced a protracted slog through mud and jungle, in part because the Navy had failed to assert sea control.

On 9 November in Operation TA4, *T6*, *T9*, and *T10* dashed in from Manila with a thousand men of the 1st Division and unloaded at Ormoc without a problem. The follow-up convoy, TA2's three surviving transports with a ten-ship escort, carried ten thousand men of the 26th Division and 6,600 tons of supplies.[15] This convoy likewise enjoyed an untroubled passage, but as it approached Ormoc, B-25s and P-38s attacked at low altitude. A Japanese history described the damage they inflicted as, "The *Kashii Maru* had all loading tackle destroyed and landing barges on deck destroyed. The *Kinka Maru* suffered slight damage to engines and also suffered some damage to deck equipment. The [*Takatsu*] *Maru* also suffered temporary engine trouble and deck damage. No important damage was done to escorts." CinCSWPA claimed that "medium bombers and fighters based at Leyte attacked a convoy of 15 DD's and 4 large AP's in Ormoc Bay. Report indicates that 7 DD's and 3 of the AP's were sunk."[16]

The convoy entered the bay at 1830 on 9 November. Several PT Boats intervened that night. *PT525* and *PT524* fired torpedoes shortly after midnight before a destroyer chased them off. (A Japanese account tells of repelling an attack by "10 enemy torpedo boats.") The ships were supposed to depart at dawn, but air raids and accidents had disabled nearly all the four dozen *daihatsu* (landing craft) left at Ormoc. Improvised rafts and the smaller escorts, pressed into ferry service, got the troops ashore within three hours after sunrise, but most of the equipment remained on board. Expecting a day of air attacks, the freighters weighed at 1030 on 10 November. An hour later, B-25s attacked north of the Camotes Islands. They sank *Kashii Maru* and *Takatsu Maru*, and forced *Escort 11* ashore.[17]

As TA4 was outbound, it passed TA3 inbound. This consisted of *Celebes Maru* (5,863 GRT), *Taizan Maru* (3,528 GRT), *Mikasa Maru* (3,142 GRT), *Saiho Maru* (4,639 GRT), and *Tensho Maru* (5,013 GRT), carrying two thousand men of the 26th Division and most of the division's equipment. The escort included destroyers *Shimakaze*, *Hamanami*, *Take*, and *Hatsuharu*, with minesweeper *W30*, and subchaser *Ch46*. Destroyers *Naganami*, *Asashimo*, and *Wakatsuki* from TA4 peeled off and joined TA3, while *Take* and *Hatsuharu* replaced them in TA4. The convoy arrived after 1000 and had begun unloading when carrier aircraft appeared overhead.[18] In fact, Task Force 38 had broken off refueling operations and rushed back to Philippine waters in response to a report that Vice Admiral Takeo Kurita had sortied from Brunei on 9 November with *Yamato*, *Nagato*, *Haruna*, a cruiser, and four destroyers. At 0827 that morning a scout aircraft also reported the convoy heading south from Manila. This followed word that Kurita had turned back. With the escape of their main prey, the ten carriers of TGs 38.1, 38.3, and 38.4 began launching full-deck strikes at 0900, sending 347 aircraft against the convoy. Reportedly the skies over Ormoc became so crowded, some squadrons had to orbit for twenty minutes before the attack coordinator could assign them a target. The aviators delivered 141.7 tons of bombs, 28 torpedoes, and 194 rockets, and sank every ship except *Asahimo* and *Ch46*. The Americans lost nine aircraft, eight to the "extremely intense and accurate AA fire from enemy destroyers." Many of the Japanese soldiers made shore, but most of the equipment and munitions did not.[19]

Despite this setback the Japanese persisted. Small craft delivered units of the 102nd Division on 17 November, and other elements from Cebu ferried into Palompon. The next TA operation, TA5, was delayed by TF38 strikes against Manila on 13, 14, and 19 November. The first focused on the harbor and sank seventeen cargo ships, displacing 93,572 GRT, four destroyers, and a light cruiser. Still, the Japanese high command continued to reinforce Leyte. TA5's first echelon, consisting of *T111*, *T141*, and *T160*, escorted by the submarine chaser *Ch46*, departed Manila on 23 November. Air strikes caught the transports sheltering off Masbate Island on 24 November and destroyed all three. The second echelon—*T6*, *T9*, and *T10*, escorted by *Take*—left Manila on the 24th. Aircraft from TF38 found them on the 25th at Marinduque Island and sank *T6* and *T10*; the others returned to Manila. This was the first operation completely frustrated by air power.

Rear Adm. T. D. Ruddock (ComTG 77.2) took over defense of Leyte Gulf on 16 November. By the 25th he had four battleships, five cruisers, and sixteen destroyers. Ruddock finally initiated offensive action, sending a pair of minesweepers to sweep the Canigao Channel into the Camotes

Sea on 27 November. The Americans were surprised to find the passage had never been mined. Mines or no mines, U.S. Navy warships finally had access to Leyte's west coast and destroyer divisions finally began patrolling the approaches to Ormoc Bay on a regular basis.[20]

On the night of 27–28 November Destroyer Division (DesDiv) 43, *Waller*, *Saufley*, *Renshaw*, and *Pringle*, appeared off Ormoc. The division made a surface contact—evaluated as a small barge—and dusted it with a few salvos; it then bombarded shore targets. At 0040 on 28 November it turned south and at 0129 picked up another contact off Ponson Island. This was the army transport submarine *Yu2*. In a twelve-minute engagement at ranges that dropped to several hundred yards, the destroyers blasted *Yu2*. *Pringle* illuminated with star shell and as she passed, she observed, "submarine was dead in water, sinking and being abandoned by the crew." *Renshaw* reported passing through survivors in the water. The division then headed home.[21]

TA6 departed Manila on 27 November, hard on the heels of TA5. It included *Shinetsu Maru* (2,212 GRT) and *Shinsho Maru* (2,880 GRT), escorted by *Ch45* and *Ch53* and *Patrol Boat 105*. They reached Ormoc on the evening of the 28th. That night four U.S. PT boats were on patrol. *PT127* accompanied by *PT331* fired four torpedoes from 900 yards and claimed a hit on a vessel "showing a pyramid superstructure amidships giving it the appearance of a Destroyer Escort." There was an explosion followed by "a large column of black billowing smoke which appeared to come from the amidships section of the target." *PT128* and *PT191* followed. They "commenced torpedo run on targets now visible at Ormoc City. . . . There were three ships in a staggered formation." The boats attracted "accurate 40-mm, 37-mm and some 75-mm fire." Then, two minutes after launching four torpedoes from 1,900 yards they saw an explosion "with great billow of black smoke rising after impact." The boats retired at 30 knots. These attacks accounted for the 442-ton *Ch53* and *P105*.[22] The next morning Army aircraft bombed *Shinsho Maru* and forced her ashore in flames. *Shinetsu Maru* and *Ch45* departed having landed most of their supplies. Aircraft caught them en route and sank both.

TA7 included three echelons. The first group consisted of three army landing craft, *SS5*, *SS11*, and *SS12*, 750-ton, 14-knot vessels that could accommodate nearly two hundred troops, escorted by *Ch20*. *SS5* ran aground on Masbate Island, but the others arrived at Ipil on the 30th. They unloaded two hundred troops and supplies and all returned to

Manila on 1 December. The second group, *SS10* and *SS14*, unloaded near Palompon on the 1st. Afterward, they vanished. That night DesDiv 44 (*Conway*, *Cony*, *Eaton*, and *Sigourney*) had departed Leyte Gulf at 1720 at 30 knots to "conduct Anti-shipping sweep of Camotes Sea, and destroy enemy." The weather was heavily overcast and squally.[23]

The division found Ormoc Bay empty. Then, shortly after midnight on the 2nd they overheard on the radio that *PT 491* was stalking a column of three Japanese ships. DesDiv 44 headed in that direction and at 0224 on 2 December scoped a single contact. After five minutes of gunfire starting at five thousand yards, and several hundred shells from all four destroyers, the target burst into flames. After that the destroyers visited Palompon and fired two hundred rounds into the area. They returned to Ormoc at 0445 and pounded the beaches with a thousand rounds. The force rejoined TG 77.2 at 0945. PT boats reported the destruction of another vessel. The missing transports *SS10* and *SS14* were the likely victims.

On the afternoon of 2 December American flyers reported another Ormoc convoy, in fact, the third echelon of TA7—destroyers *Kuwa* and *Take* and *T9*, *T140*, and *T159*. Rear Adm. Russell S. Berkey, Commander, Cruiser Division 15, who took command of naval forces in Leyte Gulf on 2 December, dispatched DesDiv 120 commanded by Cdr. John C. Zahm—*Sumner*-class "super" destroyers *Allen M. Sumner*, *Cooper*, and *Moale*—to intercept.

A bright moon, calm seas, and foaming wakes made Zahm's ships easily visible from the sky during their five-hour run into the Camotes Sea, but the first air attack did not come until 2308 when a bomb near-missed *Sumner*, spraying the ship with fragments and wounding eleven men. From that time on, bogies continuously haunted her radar, and over the next hour *Sumner* engaged aircraft seven times.

The ships approached the bay from the south, fifteen hundred yards apart in line abreast, from left to right, *Sumner*, *Cooper*, and *Moale*. Zahm wanted to maximize the class' heavy forward armament, present a smaller target, and cover more area. The racket of antiaircraft gunfire heralded their approach.[24]

At 2355, as Division 120 was passing Ponson Island, *Sumner*'s radar registered a contact 20,000 yards off the starboard bow in the Albuera area "close against the beach." Perhaps barges, more likely false. Meanwhile, at 0002, *Moale* scoped another contact off her port bow near Ormoc. The

Americans turned north-northwest at 0003, and two minutes later Zahm ordered his ships to open fire to starboard.

Take was at Ormoc's pier boarding survivors from pervious sinkings, while *Kuwa* was patrolling at slow speed two miles offshore. When *Sumner*'s guns erupted, *Kuwa* immediately turned south while *Take* cast off and followed. These escort-type destroyers had half the size and armament of the *Sumner* class, but were equipped with the renowned Type 93 "Long Lance" torpedo.[25]

For the first three minutes *Sumner* fired toward Albuera on what she described as a "small transport." The division leader was having other problems. "During protracted periods the main battery director was actually spinning from target to target in order to attempt to cover the threatened sectors as plane after plane made runs on the ship." *Cooper*'s report indicated she engaged at 0003 (her captain having noted that times might be off as much as five minutes) at a target off her starboard bow in the direction of Ormoc, distance 12,200 yards. This was *Kuwa*. *Cooper*'s first salvo fell short, but she claimed hits on a "large destroyer" with the second. *Moale*, according to her report, did not engage until 0009.[26] Her initial target was also *Kuwa*. As ranges rapidly closed, the Japanese replied with 5-inch volleys supplemented by streams of bullets from the 3-inch and 25-mm guns arming the landing ships, and from strafing aircraft. The Americans also reported motor-torpedo boats and shore batteries on both the east and west coasts of Ormoc Bay. A *Sumner* sailor wrote, "The night began to light up like a huge fireworks display from the red and green tracers going in all directions, from ships and shore installations burning and exploding in multi-colored fireballs, and from winks of fire coming from the many guns firing at us."[27]

Sumner turned west at 0008 and three minutes later due north. Meanwhile, "*Moale* had commenced emergency maneuvers to avoid torpedoes that might have been fired and to confuse reported bogies." She reported her first target burning. *Cooper* concurred. "The enemy ship was in flames, thoroughly wrecked and sinking when fire was ceased [0011] to get another ship."[28] At around 0010 *Cooper* shifted her guns to *Take* and claimed more hits. However, the Japanese had torpedoes swimming, and at 0013 a Long Lance clobbered *Cooper* amidships. The force of the explosion knocked the large destroyer 45 degrees to starboard. Her last salvo ricocheted off the water. *Cooper* then jackknifed and sank in thirty seconds; 191 of her men perished. By this time *Kuwa*, her upperworks

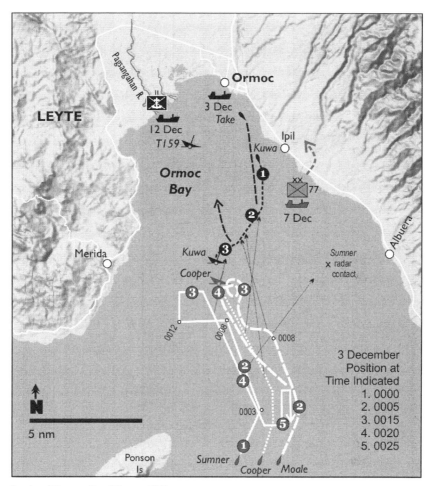

Battle of Ormoc Bay. *Vincent O'Hara.*

shredded by 5-inch shells, was hors de combat. She would eventually join *Cooper* at the bottom of Ormoc Bay. American shells also slammed into *Take* and disabled an engine.[29]

Having lost track of *Cooper*, Zahm turned southeast at 0016 to clarify the situation. At 0022 Zahm learned that *Cooper* had been torpedoed. He swung back to help at 0025, but when *Moale* radioed that she had seen *Cooper* sink, Zahm judged a rescue attempt too risky and at 0032 turned toward home. As *Moale*'s captain explained, "The strike was designed as an offensive; however, there was a strong feeling of being on the defensive throughout."[30]

During this half-hour battle, *Cooper* fired 300–400 shells, *Sumner* 842 (including air engagements), and *Moale* 550. One small shell hit *Sumner*. Three rounds struck *Moale* and damaged her after torpedo mount and holed her hull above the waterline. Near misses peppered both American ships with splinters. *Sumner* welded more than forty patches over holes in the ship's bow that ranged from "the size of a dime to that of a bowling ball."[31]

Three hours after the Americans departed, having completed unloading, the Japanese convoy weighed anchor. Drifting in the bay, *Cooper*'s survivors observed their exit. Seaplanes subsequently rescued 104 of *Cooper*'s men, and they described the landing vessels as submarines. These reports led to the belief that a submarine had ambushed *Cooper*; in fact, she was the last of the thirty-two U.S. warships sunk by the Japanese in a surface action.

Continuing Japanese resistance on Leyte and contested air superiority caused postponement of the campaign's next step: the invasion of Mindoro. On 7 December American forces exploited the delay by transporting the newly arrived 77th Division directly into Ormoc Bay between Ipil and Albuera, using a force of fifty-one transports ranging from APDs to LSTs, and supported by a dozen destroyers, seventeen minesweepers, and other craft. The objective was to slam shut the "enemy's back door."[32] The Japanese reacted violently, with massive kamikaze and conventional air strikes that crashed three destroyers, a destroyer transport, and a landing ship, sinking *Mahan* and *Ward*. It was a terrible cost, but the division landed successfully and quickly closed on Ormoc.

That night, in Operation TA8, the Japanese attempted to insert four thousand men of the 68th Brigade into Palompon. The convoy consisted of *Hakuba Maru* (2,858 GRT), *Akagisan Maru* (4,634 GRT), *Shinsei Maru No. 5* (2,599 GRT), and *Nichiyo Maru* (6,300 GRT), and the APD *T11*. The small destroyers *Ume*, *Momo*, and *Sugi*; and subchasers *Cha18* and *Cha38* provided the escort. Marine squadrons flying out of Tacloban began attacking as the force neared Leyte, and the convoy commander decided to send the transports to San Isidro near Leyte's northwestern tip while the escort returned to Manila. Continuing air attacks eventually sank all five transports. Most troops reached shore but nearly all equipment and supplies went down with the ships.[33]

TA9 left Manila on 9 December with "great expectations," carrying three thousand troops in three transports, and a special naval landing force equipped with amphibious tanks embarked on *T140* and *T159*.[34]

The convoy's escort force included the old destroyers *Yuzuki*, flagship of Captain Seiji Sawamura, and *Uzuki*, the *Matsu*-class destroyer *Kiri*, and *subchasers Cha17* and *Cha37*. U.S. Army aircraft jumped the transports off Palompon on the afternoon of 11 December, sinking *Mino Maru* (4,667 GRT) and *Tasmania Maru* (4,106 GRT) and causing Sawamura to send *Sorachi Maru* (4,107 GRT), accompanied by the subchasers, into Palompon. While *Uzuki* rescued survivors, Sawamura continued to Ormoc Bay with *Yuzuki*, *Kiri*, *T140*, and *T159*. He intended to bombard American positions after the troops were ashore.

At the same time, thirteen medium landing ships (LSMs) and infantry landing craft (LCIs) carrying supplies for the 77th, escorted by Capt. J. F. Newman's DesRon 14—*Caldwell*, *Reid*, *Conyngham*, *Smith*, *Coghlan*, and *Edwards*, steamed for the same destination. At 1703, still in Surigao Strait, two kamikazes crashed *Reid* and secondary explosions detonated her after magazine. She sank with heavy loss of life. After sending two LSMs shepherded by *Conyngham* to deliver supplies south of Ormoc, the balance of the American force headed for Ipil, arriving at 2330 on 11 December.

Sawamura had just arrived himself. Under the impression that the town was still in Japanese hands, a barge attempted to dock at Ormoc's pier. When it encountered a storm of gunfire, the Japanese moved west to the mouth of the Pagsangahan River, where the landing ships disgorged the naval troops and their four tanks under the fire of U.S. tank destroyers and artillery, which destroyed many of the supplies just unloaded.[35]

Meanwhile, when shells straddled *Caldwell*, Newman assumed that shore batteries had him under fire. He ordered his destroyers south, seeking maneuvering room. At 0155 on 12 December, as the Japanese ships began to depart, *Coghlan*'s radar registered three pips. She turned toward the contacts and opened fire from 14,000 yards, closing to 6,000. She ceased fire at 0217, claiming one ship sunk. This was probably *T159*, which foundered off the beach. *T140* suffered heavy damage but managed to pull away and, with the two destroyers, flee the bay. Sawamura believed he was facing cruisers. *Coghlan* fired a total of 221 five-inch rounds and eight star shells, and did not notice any return fire.[36]

Sawamura rounded the peninsula and *Kiri* landed more troops at Palompon. There, *PT490* and *PT492* ambushed *Uzuki*. The American boats spotted the enemy destroyers, idled into within a thousand yards from target, and released six torpedoes. One exploded beneath *Uzuki*'s bridge and a second amidships, "sending oil, water, and debris hundreds of feet in the air."³⁷ Nor did *Yuzuki* survive the night; Marine aircraft caught and sank her in the Visayan Sea.

DesRon 14 suffered more air attacks during the return and two kamikazes crashed *Caldwell*. Another barely missed *Conyngham*. Her skipper felt compelled to comment, "The destroyers are not serving as an A.A. screen. They are serving as bait for suicide pilots, an effective means of diverting the attack from the LCI and LSM component of the echelon, but it is questionable as to whether the cost in destroyers justified the protection offered."³⁸

After this episode, the hard-pressed Japanese defenders of Leyte received no more help. On Christmas Day 1944, MacArthur declared the island secured except for "minor mopping up," adding that it was "perhaps the greatest defeat in [the] military annals of the Japanese Army."³⁹ Resistance, however, persisted until 8 May 1945.

Two conclusions follow from this brief study of events after the Battle of Leyte Gulf. The first is that a "decisive naval battle" in and of itself does not establish sea control. It creates conditions in which sea control may be asserted if the victorious power so elects. In this case, the U.S. Navy retained major warships in Leyte Gulf as a static defensive force for an entire month after the battle and did not use these powerful surface assets to interfere with Japanese traffic in the Camotes Sea. The second conclusion is that air power alone—even overwhelming air power as exercised by the carriers of TF 38—could not isolate Leyte. Air attacks devastated individual convoys, but shipping was safe at night and in bad weather, of which this campaign had plenty, and the fast carriers had to rest and refuel, and had other tasks that required their attention. Nightly patrols by surface warships, employed in conjunction with air power, proved the recipe for ending Japanese traffic into Ormoc.

Some have argued, from the American point of view, that it was better for the Japanese to throw troops into Leyte, having thousands drown in the process, than seeing the Imperial Army hoard them on Luzon for a final battle. But this smacks of rationalization. In fact, the defense of Leyte delayed the conquest of the Philippines, and 3,500 Americans died on Leyte, more than twice as many as on Guadalcanal. As Samuel Eliot Morison expressed it, "All this sort of thing is anticlimax after the great naval battle, but it must be told. In spite of the victories of 25 October, soldiers, sailors and aviators were dying daily for the liberation of Leyte."⁴⁰

About the Author

Vincent P. O'Hara is an independent historian and the author of twelve books or edited volumes, most recently, *Six Victories: North Africa, Malta, and the Mediterranean Convoy War, November 1941–March 1942* (Naval Institute Press, 2019). He has written extensively about naval warfare in World War II, and his work *The U.S. Navy against the Axis* (Naval Institute Press, 2007) also covered the battles of Leyte Gulf. He was assistant editor of *World War II at Sea: An Encyclopedia* (ABC-CLIO, 2012) and has published in magazines and journals, including *Naval War College Review*, *Naval History*, *Warship*, *MHQ*, *Storia Militare*, and others.

O'Hara was the Naval Institute Press Author of the Year for 2015. He represented the United States at 75th anniversary ceremonies for Operation Torch held in Algiers and Oran, Algeria, in November 2017. He has presented papers or spoken at the Harold C. Deutsch WWII Round Table, Minneapolis; the USS *Midway* Museum, San Diego; the U.S. Navy Hampton Roads Museum, Norfolk; the Institut National d'Etudes Strategiques, Algiers; the U.S. Navy Surface Warfare Association, San Diego; and other venues.

Notes

1. U.S. Naval War College, *Command Summary of Fleet Admiral Chester W. Nimitz* ("Graybook"), Vol. 5, *1 January 1944–December 1944*, 2276.
2. Ronald H. Spector, *Eagle Against the Sun: The American War with Japan* (New York: The Free Press, 1985), 511.
3. Damage from *Reports of General MacArthur* (Tokyo: Department of the Army, General Headquarters Far East Command, 1950), 2:401n; and Shigeru Fukudome, "The Battle off Formosa," U.S. Naval Institute *Proceedings* 78 (21 December 1952): 598.
4. John Prados, *Combined Fleet Decoded: The Secret History of American Intelligence and the Japanese Navy in World War II* (New York: Random House, 1995), 610.
5. United States Strategic Bombing Survey (Pacific), *Interrogations of Japanese Officers*, Nav-44, 179.
6. *Reports of General MacArthur*, 2:405–6. On 26 October aircraft from Rear Adm. T. L. Sprague's escort carriers, while searching for

remnants of the Second Strike Group, found the convoy as it was returning from Ormoc and sank light cruiser *Kinu*, destroyer *Uranami*, and transport *T102*.

7. Graybook, 5:2122.
8. Samuel Eliot Morison, *Leyte: June 1944–January 1945*. (Annapolis: Naval Institute Press, 2011), 350.
9. United States Navy World War II Action and Operational Reports (Action Report), CTG 77.1 "Engagement with Japanese Air Forces in Leyte Gulf, Philippine Islands on 1 November 1944," 7 November 1944, 2.
10. Destroyers: *Kasumi, Okinami, Akebono, Hatsuharu, Ushio*, and *Hatsushimo*; frigates: *Okinawa, Shimushu, Escort 11*, and *Escort 13*.
11. U.S. Armed Forces Far East, History Division, Japanese Monographs Series 84, *Philippines Area Naval Operations, Part II, October–December 1944* (Washington, D.C.: U.S. Army, 1947), 100–101.
12. Action Report CTG 77.1, 1 November 1944, 2–20. Quote: Morison, *Leyte*, 346.
13. Spector, *Eagle*, 513.
14. Graybook, 5:2124.
15. Escorting destroyers included *Kasumi, Nagamani, Asashimo, Wakatsuki, Ushio*, and *Akishimo*. Otherwise, the escort's composition was as in TA2.
16. Quotes: Interrogations, 163; Graybook, 5:2134.
17. Monograph 84, 103.
18. Allyn Nevitt, "The TA Operations to Leyte," www.combinedfleet.com/taops2.htm. *Celebes Maru* ran aground en route.
19. Monograph 84, 104. Action Report, TG 38.3, "Ormoc Bay Strike 11," November 1944, 6 December 1944.
20. Action Report, CTU 78.3.6, "Minesweeping Operations Invasion of Ormoc Bay," 22 December 1944, 3.
21. Action Reports, USS *Pringle* and USS *Renshaw*, 27–28 November 1944.
22. Action Reports, *PT127* and *128*, Night of 28/29 Nov. 1944. Monograph 84, 106.
23. Action Report, ComDesDiv 44, "Camotes Sea 102 December 1944," 8 December 1944, 1.
24. The U.S. actions are synthesized from the action reports of *Sumner* (4 December), *Cooper* (7 December), *Moale* (5 December), and

ComDesDiv 120 (6 December), which are not referenced except for direct quotations.
25. Nevitt, "Long Lancers," *Kuwa* TROM.
26. Action Report, ComDesDiv 120, 2.
27. Quotes: *Sumner*, 4; Eugene George Anderson, "Nightmare in Ormoc Bay," USS *Allen M. Sumner* (DD 692), http://www.dd-692.com/nightmare.htm.
28. Quotes: Action reports of *Moale*, 4, and *Cooper*, 7.
29. Generally, *Take* is credited for sinking *Cooper*, but a recent dive on *Kuwa*'s wreck shows her torpedo tubes empty and trained to port, and she might have delivered the deadly blow. See Nevitt, "Long Lancers," *Kuwa* TROM.
30. Nevitt, "Long Lancers," *Kuwa* TROM.
31. Anderson, "Nightmare in Ormoc Bay."
32. *Reports of General MacArthur*, 1:234. See Morison, *Leyte*, 377–85.
33. Marine air groups were staged up from the Solomons to augment MacArthur's antishipping capabilities. See Graybook, 5:2409.
34. Monograph 84, 109.
35. M. Hamlin Cannon, *United States Army in World War II: The War in the Pacific. Leyte: The Return to the Philippines* (Washington, D.C.: Office of the Chief of Military History, Department of the Army, 1993), 317–18.
36. Action Report, USS *Coghlan*, 12 December 1944, 7.
37. Robert J. Bulkley Jr., *At Close Quarters: PT Boats in the United States Navy* (Annapolis: Naval Institute Press, 2003), 400.
38. ComDesRon 14, Action Report, 18 December 1944, 19–20.
39. *Reports of General MacArthur*, 1:236–37.
40. Morison, *Leyte*, 364.

10

JACK & JIM

David F. Winkler

THIS IS THE TALE OF TWO AMERICANS from totally different backgrounds who would both serve as commissioned officers in the United States Navy during one of the most epic battles in naval history. Both were born within two months of each other in 1922. Jim was born in Charleston, South Carolina, to a naval officer and a mother who had grown up in an Army household. Little Jimmy followed his parents to the Far East when his father served with the Asiatic Fleet. Unfortunately, he contracted rickets and dysentery, which set him back physically, but he grew up sharing his father's passion for reading. The young lad subscribed to *Time* and *New Yorker* to remain current on world events. To ensure Jim had an adequate education as his father jumped from one assignment to another, his parents scrapped together funds to send him to a boarding school at Saint James, located near the Antietam battlefield in rural Maryland.[1]

Jack came into the world in St. Louis. His father was a stockbroker. In contrast to Jim, Jack was more interested in cars and mechanics. While Jim attended the boarding school, Jack worked his way through the public school system in St. Louis County, eventually graduating Clayton High school and applying for and getting admitted into Washington University.

Jim also decided to pursue higher education, following in his father's footsteps by applying to the U.S. Naval Academy. Appointed to enter Annapolis in the fall of 1939, Jim was slated to graduate with the class of 1943. However, the onset of World War II in Europe compressed Jim's time at Annapolis. He was now slated to receive his naval commission in 1942. In contrast, having met a young lass who would be his first wife, Jack planned to continue his education.[2]

The Japanese attack on Pearl Harbor changed that. Jack decided he wanted to fly, and he applied to the Army Air Corps, passed the tests, took his physical, and was asked if he suffered from hay fever. His honest response eliminated him from consideration. When he returned home, a friend suggested he try the Navy. Perhaps because he lived in the heartland, it had never dawned on Jack that the Navy flew planes. Passing all of the Navy's tests, he also passed the physical as it seems the Navy didn't inquire about hay fever.[3]

In Annapolis, Jim graduated and initially received orders to Harvard to assist in setting up a naval reserve officer commissioning program. In December he then received orders to the USS *Ringgold*, a new *Fletcher*-class destroyer that was being completed at Federal Shipbuilding and Drydock Company yard in Kearny, New Jersey.[4]

As Jim arrived at his ship in New Jersey, Jack received instructions to report for flight training. Initially, he didn't have to go far: there was a ground school established on Grand Avenue in St. Louis, and then he flew Piper Cubs out at Kratz Field, located across the Missouri River at St. Charles. Jack recalled: "We went up once or twice ... then one day we flew, and he [the instructor] got out and said, 'Okay, take her up.' I said, 'By myself?' He said, 'Yeah.' So I went up and flew around the field a couple of times, and landed."

With that, Cadet Jack progressed through the pipeline that had been established to train naval aviators. After attending preflight in Iowa, Jack was sent to Naval Air Station (NAS) Glenview outside of Chicago and trained with the N3N biplane. He then traveled down to Corpus Christi, where he learned to fly Vultee Vindicators at one field and then moved on to fly SNJs (Scout Trainers, North American made) at another.[5]

Meanwhile Ensign Jim experienced a different type of pipeline. Following the commissioning of *Ringgold* on 30 December 1942, the new destroyer fitted out at the Brooklyn Navy Yard and then headed south to Guantanamo Bay, Cuba, for a shakedown cruise and workups. Jim worked hard and qualified on paper to be a gunnery department head or "gun boss." Following a return to Brooklyn, the destroyer again headed south into the Caribbean to operate with the recently commissioned aircraft carrier *Lexington* in a protected sanctuary that had been established in the vicinity of Trinidad. By mid-year *Ringgold* had received orders to transit the Panama Canal and report for duty with the Pacific Fleet. However, Jim's hopes for action against the Japanese were dashed as orders awaited him at Pearl Harbor. Since he had diligently qualified to be a gun boss, he had orders to be one on yet another newly constructed destroyer. Returning from Hawaii, Jim reported to the Boston Navy Yard where *Bennion* was under construction.[6]

Bennion's commissioning on 14 December 1943 nearly coincided with that of Jack, who earned his gold bars as well as wings of gold. Ensign Jack received orders to Vero Beach, Florida, the training base for F6F Hellcats, to undergo operational training. Upon completion, Jack found himself at the Grumman aircraft plant on Long Island, where he was given a new plane to fly to the West Coast. From San Diego, he boarded the jeep carrier *White Plains* for a trip to Oahu. After a short stay in Hawaii, Jack received orders to the carrier *Essex* and was flown to Majuro, to arrive shortly after the carrier and much of the rest of the Fifth Fleet had departed for the Marianas campaign. His tardiness would cost him the opportunity to participate in an air battle that would become known as the Marianas Turkey Shoot.[7]

By the time Jack finally arrived, the carrier had established a reputation with her Air Group 15, "the Fabled Fifteen," under the command of Cdr. David McCampbell. For Jim, the effort to capture the Japanese-held islands of Saipan, Guam, and Tinian proved to be his first experience in combat. In addition to performing shore-bombardment missions, the destroyer, which had left the East Coast in March, served as a radar picket ship and directed fighters to engage incoming enemy aircraft. Both *Essex*, with Jack now embarked, and *Bennion* participated in the Palau operation in early September.[8]

For Jack, his first combat mission was made more memorable in that McCampbell assigned him to be his wingman. In retrospect, Jack understood McCampbell wanted to test his skills. He met the air group commander's expectations.

Following the effort to capture Palau, the two warships separated with their respective task force organizations. As part of Task Force 38, *Essex*'s air group participated in airstrikes against Japanese airfields on Formosa. During one raid on 12 October, a melee ensued in which Jack received credit for shooting down two Japanese aircraft. Jack's fellow pilots also had outstanding success. During the three-day air offense against Japanese land-based aircraft, they eliminated more than five hundred airplanes, which would not be able to join in the fight in the Philippines.[9] As Jack and his fellow naval aviators battled over the skies of Formosa, Jim and

Bennion made preparations off Manus Island for the forthcoming invasion of the Philippines.

Bennion was now part of the Seventh Fleet under the command of Vice Adm. Thomas C. Kinkaid, who divided his fleet into a Northern Attack Force (Task Force 78) and a Southern Attack Force (Task Force 79). Within the Southern Attack Force were two task groups, 79.1 and 79.2, each made up of more than sixty Navy transports carrying the troops. *Bennion*, a component of the Southern Attack Force, served with Fire Support Unit South, commanded by Rear Adm. Jesse B. Oldendorf, which included refurbished battleships that had been at Pearl Harbor on 7 December 1941 and a number of heavy and light cruisers. Destroyer Squadron Fifty-Six (DesRon 56), which included *Bennion*, provided the screen for these major surface combatants. On 18 and 19 October, Jim was kept busy as these gun-bearing ships used their main batteries in shore fire operations to support the beach and landing preparations being conducted by UDT (underwater demolition team) frogmen and accompanying minesweepers. *Bennion*'s experienced CIC team handled the Fighter Direction Air Control of the Combat Air Patrols (CAP) that were being provided by the Taffy groups of escort carriers operating off the island of Samar.[10]

In contrast, *Essex* served under Third Fleet commander Adm. William F. Halsey with Task Force 38—that included the Navy's other large carriers as well as its most modern battleships. Halsey's impressive forces stood ready to drive off an anticipated naval reaction. Aircraft from Carrier Air Group 15 flew off *Essex* to scout for enemy forces.

D-day was on 20 October. *Bennion*, with the amphibious force, entered Leyte Gulf on schedule near dawn. In addition to the major combatants pounding the beaches with shells of various sizes, converted landing craft equipped with rocket batteries approached the beach to fire rocket attacks at point-blank range. With *Bennion* in the first row of fire support ships out from the beach, Jim had a spectacular view of the largest mass landing in the Pacific theater to date. Fortunately, the Army troops storming ashore met only light opposition.

Unfortunately for *Bennion*, a Japanese shore battery decided to target the destroyer. A round hit the forward part of the vessel, with shrapnel taking a toll elsewhere. Jim's assistant gunnery officer, standing next to him, had his right arm amputated by one flying shard. Flying metal wounded two enlisted fire controlmen who were also standing near Jim. Four other sailors were wounded by the fragments. Despite the casualties, Jim's gun crews kept up their barrage.[11]

With the arrival of the American invasion force, the Imperial Japanese Navy reacted by ordering the implementation of a complex contingency plan involving four major fleet elements. The scheme involved using Japan's remaining carriers, which lacked trained aircrews—the "Northern Force" under Vice Admiral Jisaburo Ozawa—to lure Halsey's covering force away from Leyte in order to enable three surface groups to approach the landing area to wreak havoc on the invasion force. The largest of the three surface groups—the "Center Force" under Vice Admiral Takeo Kurita—would pass through the San Bernardino Strait and approach the landing forces from the north. Two other surface groups under the command of Vice Admirals Shoji Nishimura and Kiyohide Shima would pass through Surigao Strait located to the southwest of the landing areas.[12]

Departing from Brunei, Kurita's force included the super battleships *Yamato* and *Musashi*, battleships *Nagato*, *Kongo*, and *Haruna*, heavy cruisers *Atago*, *Maya*, *Takao*, *Chokai*, *Myoko*, *Haguro*, *Kumano*, *Suzuya*, *Tone*, and *Chikuma*, light cruisers *Noshiro* and *Yahagi*, and fifteen destroyers.

This force came under the surveillance of the submarines *Darter* and *Dace* as the force steamed past Palawan Island early on 23 October. After reporting the position of the Japanese formation, the two submarines raced ahead to conduct a submerged attack at first light. Spreads of torpedoes sank the heavy cruisers *Atago* and *Maya* and damaged *Takao*, forcing that cruiser to turn back with two destroyer escorts. The two submarines combined to remove five warships from Kurita's order of battle.[13]

The setback did not deter Kurita. Next, he would have to endure air attacks from Task Force 38 on 24 October while his Central Force transited the Sibuyan Sea en route to San Bernardino Strait. However, before Task Force 38 could go on the offense, it had to take defensive actions against three waves of attacking Japanese aircraft that were based in Luzon. For the veteran Hellcat fighter pilots of VF-15, flying from *Essex*, the oncoming swarms of airplanes flown by inexperienced air crews proved to be easy targets. Commander McCampbell alone added nine planes to his growing tally. Unfortunately, one aircraft did penetrate the American defenses and placed an armor-piercing bomb into the light carrier *Princeton*, leading not only to the eventual loss of that ship, but heavy damage to the light cruiser *Birmingham*, which was alongside assisting when flames touched off one of *Princeton*'s magazines.[14]

Having taken part in the defensive efforts in the morning, Jack would now take part in the effort to cripple Kurita's Central Force. Earlier attacks that day from *Intrepid* and *Cabot* scored hits on the super battleships *Yamato* and *Musashi*, the battleship *Nagato*, and the heavy cruiser *Myoko*, forcing that warship to detach and retire to Borneo.[15]

Jack recalled heading to the Sibuyan Sea on a flight with "at least 20 or 24 fighters, probably 15 or so dive bombers, and 10 to 12 torpedo planes." He remembered the formation was at 17,000 or 18,000 feet when they spotted Kurita's Central Force. As they prepared for what would be Jack's first attack on an enemy ship formation, the young pilot was startled that the Japanese antiaircraft fire emitted puffs of differing smoke colors as the shells went off. "There was a blue burst, there were red bursts, there were orange bursts." Jack later learned that the different colored bursts enabled gun crews to track their firing from that of other ships in the formation. As a Hellcat pilot, Jack's job would be to fly down first to strafe and divert the antiaircraft fire on the bombers and torpedo planes. Seeing how much antiaircraft fire they were drawing, Jack decided to fly down as vertically as possible and chose to attack the largest ship in their fleet, which happened to be the *Musashi*. "When you strafe, the more vertical you are, the safer it is because it is harder for the anti-aircraft gunners to raise their guns up in a vertical position." Reflecting decades later, Jack seemed to remember that every time he triggered his guns, it seemed that the antiaircraft fire stopped—admitting it was likely a figment of his imagination. Jack kept firing and came in so low that he felt as if he was going to fly down the smoke stack of the super battleship before pulling out. After pulling out and getting out of range of the enemy gunnery Jack joined up with his section leader, Lt. George Carr, and they circled and gained altitude. They then noted that the torpedo planes below had not cleared Kurita's ships on their run and were taking a lot of antiaircraft fire. George signaled to Jack, "Let's go back in." That directive "frankly scared the hell out of me," but Jack executed the dive and provided relief to the torpedo planes. After completing that run, the air group joined together in formation for the return flight to *Essex*. Landing on the *Essex*, neither George nor Jack had a scratch on their airplanes but noted several of the returning torpedo planes had obvious damage.[16]

Essex's air group would be credited with ten scored hits on *Musashi*, which caused the super battleship to list to port. Ordnance dropped from a third wave of attacking aircraft off *Enterprise* and *Franklin* sealed the fate of the mammoth warship. Kurita reversed his flotilla to evade further attacks; however, in the late afternoon he again reversed course to make a run at San Bernardino Strait the next day to confront weaker American forces off Samar and be driven off. Overall it was a good day for Jack's squadron VF-15. Besides supporting the dive-bombing and torpedo attacks, Jack and his colleagues claimed forty-three of the more than two hundred Japanese aircraft destroyed that day.[17]

As Jack's squadron was fending off a Japanese air attack on the morning of 24 October, *Bennion* was on picket station in the eastern approaches to Leyte Gulf. There Jim learned that the two groups that composed the Japanese Southern Force were en route to Surigao Strait when the CO showed him an intelligence report. Upon seeing that a night action was anticipated for that evening, Jim took stock of what was available in the magazines and the five upper handling rooms to assure appropriate rounds for a night surface action were available for each gun. Whereas *Bennion* had fired thousands of 5-inch rounds in anger since arriving in the Western Pacific, the same could not be said for the torpedoes. They were made ready for a war shot. While standing the noon-to-four officer of the deck watch on the bridge that afternoon, Jim followed the distribution of plans that laid out the disposition of the available forces needed to meet the threat. Rear Admiral Oldendorf had six old battleships, eight cruisers, and twenty-six destroyers available to block the oncoming forces. He also had PT boats.

Jim watched those small torpedo boats speed past his bridge wing late that afternoon. "Their engines were unbelievably noisy. We could hear the PTs five miles away and see them even further because they were engulfed in a cloud of their own exhaust fumes." Jim was not impressed.

Bennion received orders to join with her eight sister destroyers of DesRon 56 to attack the column of Japanese battleships and cruisers after they had emerged from Surigao Strait. Steaming from its eastern picket station, *Bennion* came under sporadic air attack as Japanese planes popped in and out of the cumulus clouds in search of targets. One of Jim's 5-inch guns brought down a "Val," and smaller caliber AA guns combined to destroy a "Zeke."[18]

Positioned with two other destroyers on the right side of the mouth of the strait, Jim and his gunners and torpedomen waited.

Shortly after 0300 Jim felt a tug on his trouser leg as a sailor motioned him to look into the gun director's optics. Jim's eyes locked in on the jumbo pagoda superstructure of a Japanese battleship. With his fire control radar operator reporting that he had good ranges on the enemy combatants, Jim contacted the bridge to report they were locked on to a Japanese battleship. The captain responded that two battleships, a cruiser, and at least three destroyers had been reported and that *Bennion* would target the second battleship with five torpedoes. Looking out once again, Jim now saw the second battleship and directed the plotting room below to get a firing solution. Once obtained, Jim reported this down to the bridge, and the captain responded: "Very well. Train out the tubes but don't launch or shoot until I give the order."[19]

Moments passed. Suddenly Jim heard the purr of the fireroom blowers rise to a high-pitched whine and felt vibration due to sudden acceleration. Over the ship's general announcing system and sound-powered phone networks the phrase "Starting run-in for the attack" was passed.

Bennion would be the tail end of a three-destroyer section rushing at the Japanese with a relative closing speed of fifty knots. Spotting the oncoming destroyers, the Japanese warships opened fire. Towering splashes rained water down on the American destroyer. As the Japanese steamed forward they came into range of Rear Admiral Oldendorf's battleships and cruisers that were positioned to rake the oncoming Japanese column with their main batteries. Jim gazed at enormous billows of flame from 16- and 14-inch guns, followed tracer shells that seemed to arc slowly toward their targets, and watched as they tore into topside turrets and peeled aside heavy armor plate.[20]

With *Bennion* coming to within six thousand yards, the Japanese battleship seemed a stone's throw away as Jim squinted into the rangefinder optics. The plot room reported, "We have a good solution." With the commanding officer's permission, Jim pushed the "fire" button on the torpedo console and then stood up in the hatch to watch the five fish leap off the port beam and splash into the water.

After firing, the American tin cans maneuvered independently to avoid enemy gunfire. As Japanese ships fell out of their column it became difficult to distinguish friend from foe. Jim peered into the darkness from his perch atop the Mark 37 Director and saw a large warship looming on the port bow. Reporting his sighting to the captain, Jim observed the warship ripple-fire salvos at the destroyer *Albert W. Grant*. The ripple fire, a Japanese technique, confirmed to Jim that this was an enemy warship.

Though Oldendorf had rationed each destroyer to expend five fish each to have a reserve for future contingencies, Jim and *Bennion*'s CO were of like mind given the circumstances. With the torpedoes set to run at a deeper depth, Jim responded to the report from the plot room, "We have a solution," and pressed the red torpedo-firing buttons to launch the remaining five torpedoes at the target that stood a mere three thousand yards distant.[21]

Bennion then heeled sharply to clear the area. Postwar analysis would credit a hit from this salvo on the battleship *Yamashiro*.[22] Ninety minutes after the start of the battle, DesRon 56 regrouped and headed south into the strait to catch up to any escaping stragglers. At first light *Bennion* caught sight of the crippled Japanese destroyer *Asagumo*. If armed with torpedoes, the wounded warship still posed a danger. Jim directed his forward 5-inch guns to commence firing salvos at a range of ten thousand yards and then ordered rapid continuous fire when the range fell to six thousand yards. Repeating hits punished the Japanese tin can. *Asagumo*'s hull could stand no more. As *Bennion* continued to close, the Japanese destroyer began to slide under the surface, bow first.

Turning back, *Bennion* suddenly came into the gunsights of a descending Zero. Jim quickly reacted, swinging *Bennion*'s 5-inch battery onto the approaching plane. A head-on 5-inch round penetrated the engine cowling and blew the Zero to pieces.[23]

Bennion was located too far to the south to participate in the next segment of the Battle of Leyte Gulf—the Battle off Samar—a struggle that would one day be dubbed "The Last Stand of the Tin Can Sailors."[24]

Kurita, who had reversed course and made an unchallenged dash through the San Bernardino Strait that evening, was able to do so because Admiral Halsey believed Kurita had withdrawn, enabling him to pursue Ozawa's carrier force, which had been located on the afternoon of 24 October. Thus, Jack would also not be able to reengage Kurita's column. Jack reflected: "We went on Bull's Run."[25]

Halsey, believing the enemy carrier force to be the main threat, steamed north and detached his six fast battleships of Task Force 34, under Vice Adm. Willis Lee, at 0240 to forge ahead, with the objective of eventually finishing off the enemy fleet after the carrier planes of Task Force 38 had taken their licks during the morning and afternoon. The first strike was in the air after 0500, arrived over Ozawa's carriers after 0700, and scored hits on the *Chitose* and *Zuiho*. *Essex* pilots launched a second strike that morning and damaged the last surviving carrier from the attack on Pearl Harbor—*Zuikaku*.²⁶

Two more air assaults in the afternoon further depleted Ozawa's Northern Force. Two of the *Essex* dive-bombers planted 2,000-pounders that penetrated deep into *Zuikaku*, expediting that carrier's plunge to the ocean floor. Other attackers scored hits on the hybrid battleship/carrier *Ise*. Jack recalled there was a request for volunteers to go on a fifth attack mission, understanding that they would likely return after dark. Jack recalled the call for volunteers received a tepid response: "We didn't like after dark. We were not trained for night landings, and night landings scared the hell out of a carrier pilot." So instead, pilots, including Jack, were assigned to the mission. Jack recalled: "I remember we had a rendezvous and were heading out to attack this fleet. McCampbell was leading. As we were climbing out, somebody picked up his mike and said, 'Rebel 99, this is Rebel 43. My engine is running rough, and I request permission to return to the carrier.' McCampbell picked up his mike and said, 'This is Rebel 99. Stay in formation. All of our engines are running rough.'" The fifth raid targeted the hybrid battleship/carrier *Hyuga* and scored seven near hits. Jack and his fellow fliers did manage to get back to the fleet before dark as Task Force 38 continued to steam north to close on the enemy.²⁷

Had Task Force 34's battleships reached Ozawa's force, they would have been left to conduct target practice on burning hulks. As it was, three American cruisers and nine destroyers continued the pursuit, catching and sinking the crippled Japanese carrier *Chiyoda*, the destroyer *Hatsuyuki*, as well as possibly the light cruiser *Tama*. Halsey, having pulled his battleships in an effort to intercept Kurita's escaping Central Force, failed to reach San Bernardino in time.²⁸

Following Jack and Jim's involvement in the Battle of Leyte Gulf, both would be heading stateside. Jim was first to go. It turns out he wanted to be like Jack—a naval aviator. About a week after the battle, Jim stepped onto a whaleboat for a short ride to a departing cargo ship bound east. Before stepping off *Bennion*, Jim said farewell to his skipper, who lamented his departure from the surface navy. Jim recalled thinking and then responding with: "Captain, this past week, in a single twenty-four-hour period, we shot down three Zeros, sank an enemy destroyer with gunfire and made a torpedo hit at point blank range to help sink a Japanese battleship. I think I am ready to try something new."²⁹

Jim Holloway would eventually earn his wings of gold, fly combat missions during the Korean War, command the carrier *Enterprise* during her first combat tour to Vietnam, and go on to become the twentieth Chief of Naval Operations.

Jack's air group was relieved in November. Rather than head back to the States he transferred to Air Group 20 and flew additional missions off *Enterprise* before heading stateside. Looking back, he recalled he had a total of eighty-two carrier landings and thirty-five combat flights. Jack did not include combat air patrols in the tally. After some leave back in St. Louis, Jack rejoined his old squadron, which was reconstituted at Los Alamitos. With the end of the war, Jack left active duty and served in the reserves for a few years before resigning his reserve commission. Eventually he got into the car leasing business with a small start-up company named Executive Car Leasing. However, when the company looked to expand beyond St. Louis, he found the name existed elsewhere. So Jack Taylor recounted the quest for a new name influenced by his time in the service: "All right. We had an 'E' logo.... Because we have the 'E' logo, we want it to start with an 'E.' We were thinking about '*Essex*.' But '*Essex*' is kind of a ponderous name. So then we thought: I was on the *Enterprise*; let's think about '*Enterprise*.'"[30]

Though Jack and Jim had served on two different ships named *Enterprise*, the lineage gave the two successful men a common bond that would foster a strong friendship in later years.[31]

About the Author

David F. Winkler earned his PhD in 1998 from American University in Washington, D.C. His dissertation, *Cold War at Sea: High Seas Confrontation between the United States and the Soviet Union*, was published by the Naval Institute Press in 2000, and was republished under the title *Incidents at Sea: American Confrontation and Cooperation with Russia and China, 1945–2016* in December 2017.

The Class of 1957 Distinguished Chair at the U.S. Naval Academy for the 2019–20 academic year, Winkler has been a historian with the nonprofit Naval Historical Foundation for over two decades. He wrote *Amirs, Admirals, and Desert Sailors: The U.S. Navy, Bahrain, and the Gulf*, which also was published by Naval Institute Press in 2007, and was managing editor of *The Navy*, an illustrated coffee table book published by the Naval Historical Foundation. His 2014 book, *Ready Then, Ready Now,*

Ready Always, covers the history of the U.S. Navy Reserve and was published by the Navy Reserve Centennial Book Committee. In addition, he writes a monthly naval history column in the Navy League of the United States *Sea Power* magazine. Winkler received his commission as a Navy ensign in 1980 through the NROTC unit at Pennsylvania State University. In addition to a BA in Political Science, he has an MA in International Affairs from Washington University. He is a retired Navy Reserve commander. Dr. Winkler currently resides in northern Virginia with his wife Mary and two daughters Katherine and Carolyn.

Notes

1. David F. Winkler, "Operational: James Lemuel Holloway III (1922–)," in *Nineteen-Gun Salute: Case Studies of Operational, Strategic, and Diplomatic Naval Leadership during the 20th and Early 21st Centuries*, ed. John B. Hattendorf and Bruce A. Elleman (Newport, RI: Naval War College Press, 2010), 194–95.
2. Jack Taylor oral history conducted by David F. Winkler, 9 July 2001, Naval Historical Foundation.
3. Thomas McKelvey Cleaver, *Fabled Fifteen: The Pacific War Saga of Carrier Air Group 15* (Philadelphia, PA, and Oxford, UK: Casemate, 2014), 49–50.
4. James L. Holloway III, unpublished memoir, Naval Historical Foundation.
5. Taylor oral history.
6. Holloway memoir.
7. Cleaver, *Fabled Fifteen*, 121–22.
8. See *Bennion* and *Essex* entries, *Dictionary of American Naval Fighting Ships* at www.history.navy.mil.
9. Taylor oral history; Cleaver, *Fabled Fifteen*, 152; Samuel Elliot Morison, *The Two-Ocean War: A Short History of the United States Navy in the Second World War* (Boston: Little, Brown, 1963), 429.
10. Morison, *Two-Ocean War*, 432–35; Holloway memoir.
11. Holloway memoir.
12. Morison, *Two-Ocean War*, 436–38.
13. John Prados, *Combined Fleet Decoded: The Secret History of American Intelligence and the Japanese Navy of World War II* (Annapolis, MD: Naval Institute Press, 1995), 637–38.

14. Morison, *Two-Ocean War*, 441.
15. Prados, *Combined Fleet Decoded*, 639.
16. Taylor oral history.
17. Cleaver, *Fabled Fifteen*, 180.
18. Holloway memoir.
19. James L. Holloway III, *Aircraft Carriers at War: A Personal Retrospective of Korea, Vietnam, and the Soviet Confrontation* (Annapolis, MD: Naval Institute Press, 2007), 1–2.
20. Holloway, *Aircraft Carriers at War*, 4; Holloway memoir.
21. Holloway memoir.
22. "The Battle for Leyte Gulf, October 1944: Strategical and Tactical Analysis, Vol. V, Battle of Surigao Strait," (Newport, RI: Naval War College, 1958).
23. Holloway memoir.
24. See James D. Hornfischer, *The Last Stand of the Tin Can Sailors: The Extraordinary World War II Story of the U.S. Navy's Finest Hour* (New York: Bantam, 2003).
25. Cleaver, *Fabled Fifteen*, 178; Taylor oral history.
26. Cleaver, *Fabled Fifteen*, 186–87; Morison, *Two-Ocean War*, 465.
27. Taylor oral history; Cleaver, *Fabled Fifteen*, 188–89; Prados, *Combined Fleet Decoded*, 652.
28. Prados, *Combined Fleet Decoded*, 652–53.
29. Holloway, *Aircraft Carriers at War*, 9.
30. Taylor oral history; Cleaver, *Fabled Fifteen*, 211.
31. In 2000, the two men would team up on a unique project to build a museum room in Holloway's former command *Enterprise* (CVN 65) that depicted the history of the eight U.S. Navy ships to bear that name.

THE TIN CAN SAILORS ARE GONE

What Naval History Loses with the Passing of the World War II Generation

——— *James D. Hornfischer* ———

I AM NOT SURE A CIVILIAN CAN TESTIFY credibly on the subject of sailors at war. I've never been shot at except with a paintball gun. Never had to memorize *Reef Points* or recite on demand the number of days left until the Navy-Army football game. Certainly, I've never had the experience of facing down a ship twenty times the size of my own in a broad-daylight surface action.

Of course, no one who has served since 25 October 1944 knows that ordeal either. And so, when the veterans of the Battle off Samar are gone, civilian testimony to their experience may be the last word standing. I came to know them rather well in the window of time before the whole World War II generation steamed toward sunset at taps.

When I was growing up in western Massachusetts in the mid-1970s, my interest in naval history was the product of watching the great documentary *Victory at Sea* and *Baa Baa Black Sheep*, the fun but ludicrous drama about a Marine fighter squadron in the South Pacific, playing Avalon Hill wargames, and building Monogram and Revell plastic models. As a thirteen-year-old subscriber to Naval Institute *Proceedings* and a reader of *Jane's Fighting Ships*, I went with my parents to see the carrier *John F. Kennedy* and the missile cruiser *Richmond K. Turner* when they visited Boston. I had a reasonably clear idea of what I was looking at.

But reading was a gateway to exploring naval history in ever greater depth. I read a good account of the Battle off Samar in a Bantam paperback called *Tin Cans* by Edward Roscoe—a condensation of his larger book about destroyer operations during World War II. He told the story well of Taffy 3's exploits in the Battle off Samar. The names of the ships that were lost in that battle—USS *Hoel*, *Samuel B. Roberts*, *Gambier Bay*, *Johnston*, and *St. Lo*—were emblems of a certain kind of gallantry, the indelible heroism of the hopelessly outgunned.

Years later, a dinner in New York with a colleague from my days at HarperCollins, Bantam Books editor Tracy Devine, set me on the path to writing *The Last Stand of the Tin Can Sailors*. (Jim: "Who can we get to write such a book?" Tracy: "Maybe you should do it.") Soon I would begin the work of exposing old men's worst nightmares to the light of day.

The victors in the Good War were not always eager to talk about it. The reasons are diverse, and always highly individual. One of the most memorable interviews I ever did ended three hours after the man said he was not going to be able to speak with me at all. James F. "Bud" Comet of the *Samuel B. Roberts*, a destroyer escort sunk in the battle, had some hard feelings about what had happened in a life raft after the fighting was over. He felt that the ugly things he had seen while adrift had never been acknowledged by his shipmates. Going to the reunions bothered him, tore at his scabs. After the old seaman second class had unburdened himself to me, I had a perspective on the human experience of battle that resonated strongly. Bud wistfully expressed the hope that his father, looking down upon him from the hereafter, was "pleased with the way I've conducted myself." His comment, I thought, stood for everyone who fought in the battle. It made for a fine final line in my book.

Eyewitness testimony gives narrative history a heartbeat, enables it to rise above the cleansing chronology of an after-action report or other written accounts. When it's possible for a writer to engage with participants directly, he can register the tone of the speaker's voice and the direction and mood of his glance, and thereby reach further into the experience itself.

As gunnery officer in the USS *Johnston*, Lt. Robert C. Hagen abandoned his battered destroyer and floated in shark-infested waters as it began to sink. The war crystallized as a hard-to-discuss horror when he was riding on the swells. Looking back at his sinking ship, he saw the ship's doctor, Robert Browne, still on board. Refusing to leave the ship until all the wounded had been evacuated from the wardroom medical triage to the deck, Dr. Browne had just entered the wardroom again when a large shell from a Japanese warship followed him inside. He never came out again. Browne was Hagen's best friend. Bob Hagen was a hard man, and proud. Recounting this moment to me, the man who had spent two hours slewing the crosshairs of his gun director across the broad front of the overwhelming flotilla pursuing him, was compelled to humble himself and swallow back his sadness. That momentary look in his eye and break in his voice got me past the veneer of bravado that suffused the ghostwritten account he produced for the *Saturday Evening Post* in 1945.

Hagen's published reminiscence was a rarity. For too many years, in fact, the Navy seemed to avoid celebrating the heroism shown by our sailors on that day. The heroism was made necessary by larger embarrassments: inexcusable communication lapses and errors in judgment. The recrimination was quiet and festered hidden for years, and so the story was never properly celebrated. What a shame. As the novelist Herman Wouk wrote in *War and Remembrance*, "The vision of Sprague's three destroyers—the *Johnston*, the *Hoel*, the *Heermann*—charging out of the smoke and the rain straight toward the main batteries of Kurita's battleships and cruisers, can endure as a picture of the way Americans fight when they don't have superiority. Our schoolchildren should know about that incident, and our enemies should ponder it." For too many years they were denied the chance. A nation rises to the level of the stories it tells about itself. The stories are told best when writers have access to the participants themselves.

※ ※ ※

The story of the Battle off Samar starts, as so many epics do, with an entirely unpromising absence of excitement. It begins with a task unit of six escort carriers idling in a rear area as larger, mightier fleets engage. Known as "Taffy 3," the task unit has the mission of providing air support for Douglas MacArthur's troops on Leyte. Though the Japanese fleet had scarcely appeared in nearly four months, the U.S. move against the Philippines has provoked Japan to unleash a massive and complex campaign to stop us, a climactic counterstroke, a Pacific naval version of the Ardennes offensive. With major elements of the Third and Seventh Fleets on the prowl, Taffy 3 is poorly situated to see much of the action.

By the fall of 1944, little is left of Japan's naval air arm, so the hopes of the Sho Plan, the Imperial Japanese Navy's plan to resist invasion of the Philippines, rest on the stout hulls of six battleships. Two of these are the largest ever built, the *Yamato* and the *Musashi*. In two converging groups, amply supported by cruisers and destroyers, they will try to slip through the archipelago's waters and attack the U.S. beachhead from the north and south. But their success will depend on deception, namely on the ability of a northern aircraft carrier force to lure Adm. William F. Halsey's fast carrier task force out of its position covering and supporting the landings.

The men on the thirteen ships of Taffy 3 don't know any of this. And they certainly cannot know that this extravagantly optimistic Japanese plan will very nearly succeed to a T. They cannot know that it will fall to them, these escort carriers, destroyers, and destroyer escorts, to turn back the greatest surface force Imperial Japan had ever sent to sea.

Before dawn on 25 October, the jeep carriers launch TBM Avengers on a routine antisubmarine patrol. As the men of Taffy 3 run through morning general quarters, there is no immediate cause for concern when one pilot reports a large fleet to the north. Taffy 3's commander, Rear Adm. Clifton A. F. "Ziggy" Sprague, chews out the pilot for breaking radio silence to report the presence of what are surely American ships. "No, sir," reports Ens. William C. Brooks of VC-65, based on USS *St. Lo*. The masts he sees moving between gaps in the clouds are distinctive Japanese pagodas.

Puffs of flak appear in the sky as the American pilot makes a report and starts taking fire. Then the northern horizon is lit by the flashes of still heavier guns. The realization dawns on Admiral Sprague that something has gone disastrously wrong. Steaming in a circular formation, his CVEs are contained within a circular screen of seven destroyers and destroyer escorts. Against these thirteen ships come twenty-three ships of Vice Admiral Takeo Kurita's Center Force. The largest of them, the 72,000-ton *Yamato*, matches in displacement all thirteen of the U.S. ships combined.

Sprague turns his carriers into the wind so they can launch planes. Fortunately for the Americans, the eastward flight-operations heading is also a retirement heading, but his slow jeep carriers will need luck to escape. He orders all his ships to make smoke, his carriers to launch planes, and soberly calculates that he has perhaps fifteen minutes before he will be enjoying a swim in the warm Philippine Sea. The jeeps have twenty minutes to get their planes aloft. At that point Sprague will have to turn them out of the wind in favor of a southward retirement course.

On the trailing western edge of Taffy 3's screen is the destroyer USS *Johnston*. Her captain, Cdr. Ernest E. Evans, has been around the fleet for a while. Early in the war, he had been an officer on an old four-stack destroyer during the disastrous Battle of the Java Sea. He remembers, too well, the sting of having to retreat, routed in battle. When the *Johnston* was commissioned in Seattle-Tacoma in October 1943, he evoked that memory, telling his crew that he would not again retreat in the face of the enemy. He invited anyone who wanted off such a ship to take the opportunity. It seems no one did. Probably it struck them as the kind of bold rhetoric that new captains are prone to indulge in on commissioning day.

Confronted with an overwhelming force, Evans seizes the chance to demonstrate the meaning of his promise. He comes out of his sea cabin and coolly issues a series of orders. "All hands to general quarters, prepare to attack a major portion of the Japanese fleet. All engines ahead flank, make smoke, stand by for a torpedo attack. Left full rudder." The screen commander, riding in USS *Hoel*, has yet to issue any orders to his tin cans. Captain Evans is acting on his own.

Launched within naval gun range of their targets, the U.S. pilots are on top of their enemy within minutes, with little time to gain altitude before attacking. Avenger pilots armed for an antisubmarine patrol drop their depth charges ahead of Japanese cruisers, hoping to damage hull plates with a well-placed underwater explosion. Diving Wildcats strafe bridges and gun emplacements, doing what they can with what little they have.

Meanwhile the *Johnston*, bone in teeth at thirty-two knots, charges the Japanese alone. She has to cross several miles of shell-torn ocean before her 5-inch guns can fire effectively. The range of her guns is 18,000 yards, but to fire torpedoes, the *Johnston* will need to get within 10,000. Her gunnery officer, Lt. Bob Hagen, stationed high in the gun director, says to himself, *Please, Captain, let's not go down without firing our torpedoes.*

Captain Evans has the ship dashing through open water as splashes from shells of every size—5-inch, 6, 8, 14—rise up around him. At 18,000 yards, Hagen opens fire on the leading cruiser. The range closes: 10,000 yards, 9,000. Still they're unhit. Now Evans orders all ten of his torpedoes fired. As they run in hot, straight, and normal, the skipper throws the helm hard over to port, reversing course to rejoin Taffy 3.

It's at this point, around 7:30 a.m., that our first blood is drawn. The *Johnston* walks into two Japanese salvoes, one 6-inch, the other 14-inch. The smaller salvo strikes the bridge, killing several men and wounding Captain Evans. The blast blows the cap from his head and tears the shirt from his chest and two fingers from his left hand. The 14-inch shells penetrate down into the machine shop and the after engine room. The *Johnston*'s speed drops to seventeen knots. Declining offers of medical assistance, Evans regroups as fires rage below.

The *Johnston*'s torpedoes, speeding in the other direction, find the mark. They blow the bow off the leading Japanese cruiser, *Kumano*. A second cruiser quits the pursuit in order to stand by her. Thanks to Evans' initiative, the force of six Japanese heavy cruisers is down to four, right off the bat.

The other destroyers by now are forming up into a column to make their own torpedo attack. The destroyer *Heermann* nearly collides with at least four other U.S. ships while racing through the carrier formation to join the screen flagship, *Hoel*. The destroyer escort *Samuel B. Roberts* follows along. Within a few short minutes, the three ships spy the *Johnston* up ahead on an opposite course. Her mainmast has fallen across the pilot house, gun shields are buckled, blackened and torn. With all her torpedoes expended, she should be well entitled to call it a day.

But Ernest Evans has a different view of his obligations. As the other captains watch, dumbstruck, the damaged *Johnston* falls in astern them, going back in. Evans figures he can provide gunfire support to the torpedo attack.

The battle is forty-five minutes along. From the first moment he heard Ziggy Sprague's messages, Vice Adm. Thomas Kinkaid, commander of the Seventh Fleet, had been issuing plain-language pleas to Admiral Halsey: *"Fast battleships needed urgently off Samar. Request Lee proceed to speed to cover Leyte. My situation is critical. Support by air strike may be able to prevent enemy from destroying CVEs and entering Leyte."*

The audience for these messages goes far beyond Admiral Halsey's flag on the battleship *New Jersey*. Admiral Nimitz hears them at CINCPAC HQ. He has never been one to second-guess his theater commanders, but events appear to be spiraling out of control. His standing orders to Halsey are unfortunately ambiguous, giving the Third Fleet a covering role but making offensive action against the Japanese fleet its "primary task" if the opportunity arises or "*can be created*" (emphasis added). He knew Halsey was going north, but he also thought, as did most everybody that day, that Halsey had detached his battle line, Task Force 34, to watch the exit of San Bernardino Strait.

As that clearly isn't the case, Nimitz composes a query to Halsey: "*Where is TF 34?*" To confuse any Japanese radio intelligence groups that manage to intercept and decrypt their encoded messages, CINCPAC staff follows the practice of adding meaningless phrases to the beginning and end of all messages. The actual message sent to Halsey reads: Turkey trots to water GG Where is rpt where is TF 34 RR the world wonders.

Halsey's staff is supposed to delete the first and last clauses. But since the context of the situation seems to make "the world wonders" apropos, though perhaps out of character for the gentlemanly Nimitz, that language was retained. Halsey reads the dispatch, "Where is, repeat, where is TF 34? The world wonders," and loses his composure. As he whips his cap to the deck, his chief of staff, Mick Carney, barks, "What the hell's the matter with you? Pull yourself together." Halsey does. Orders fly, and finally, all too slowly, the battleships pull out of line and turn south. Bare miles from engaging the Japanese carriers, they will be far too late to save Admiral Sprague's jeeps.

By the time the *Hoel*, *Heermann*, and *Roberts* reach torpedo-firing range, the battle has become a ship-to-ship free-for-all. The *Johnston* is caught between a column of Japanese heavy cruisers and a squadron of destroyers to its west. The *Hoel* fires half her torpedoes, then gets hit hard, and is left circling helplessly as cruisers and battleships close her in on three sides. The *Samuel B. Roberts* fires her three fish then engages the heavy cruiser *Chikuma*, ten times her displacement, in a gunnery duel at point-blank range. The Japanese cruiser can't depress her guns sufficiently to hit the small ship so close off her starboard beam, and the *Roberts*' two 5-inch guns can't penetrate the cruiser's belt armor, but they make a fiery mess of her upper works.

The *Hoel*, battered by some forty shells, is the first American ship to sink. She goes down around 8:40 a.m. Of her 325 men, 267 are lost. A salvo of battleship shells finds the *Roberts*, blasting a fifty-foot hole in her side and leaving her dead in the water and sinking. The Japanese cruisers finally get the range on the carriers, two hitting the *Gambier Bay* and knocking out an engine. She falls out of formation, to be surrounded and sunk by Japanese cruisers.

Captain Evans' *Johnston*, the first ship into the fight, is the last to sink, around 10:10 a.m. Burning fiercely, she goes down with 184 of her 329 men, Captain Evans among them. His exact fate is unclear. But his example, and his heroism, are apparent to all. He will receive a posthumous Medal of Honor for his actions on this day.

But despite these terrible losses, something extraordinary happens. As time goes on, the air attacks intensify. U.S. planes from Taffy 2, farther to the south, are able to load with bombs and torpedoes, and bring real heat against Kurita's force. Taffy 3's own pilots, including Eugene Seitz, make run after run against Kurita's ships, even after their machine-gun ammunition is spent. The dummy runs by the U.S. fighter pilots constantly force the Japanese cruiser skippers to turn away to avoid attacks.

Admiral Kurita, meanwhile, is fighting this battle in a deep fatigue. He has been in combat for nearly seventy-two hours straight. His flagship, the cruiser *Atago*, had been blown out from under him by a submarine torpedo a few days before. Fished from the sea, he was transferred to *Yamato* in time to face five waves of airstrikes from Halsey the following afternoon. When he encounters Taffy 3 on the morning of the 25th, his first thought is that he's found Halsey's Third Fleet.

This may be the key to everything: he has misperceived his opponent. Throughout the battle, Taffy 3, its surface ships and aviators alike, never do anything to allow that illusion to fade.

The pilots of Taffy 3 press home their bluffing attacks, forcing the Japanese cruisers to turn away from pursuit. And the Americans hit them hard. By the start of the second hour of the uncommonly long engagement, two of Kurita's cruisers, *Chikuma* and *Chokai*, struck by aerial torpedoes and surface gunfire, are dead in the water and sinking. His destroyers are holed by relentless strafing. And his commanders are consistently exaggerating the size of the American ships. *Fletcher*-class DDs become *Baltimore*-class CAs; *Casablanca*-class CVEs are *Essex*-class fleet carriers.

As a result, Kurita comes to doubt his ability to reach Leyte Gulf and do meaningful damage to the enemy. Though his rationales for his decision will be many and conflicting, he ultimately concludes that the prudent course is withdrawal.

With the *Hoel* and *Gambier Bay* sunk, and the *Samuel B. Roberts* and *Johnston* dead in the water, Admiral Kurita issues to his far-flung squadron this order: "*Rendezvous, my course north, speed 20.*" Routed by pygmies, the mighty Center Force turns away and heads for home. On Sprague's flagship, the escort carrier *Fanshaw Bay*, a signalman sees the silhouettes of enemy ships getting smaller and exclaims, "Goddamn it, boys, they're getting away!"

The Battle off Samar has two separate and equally tragic endgames. As the men on Taffy 3's surviving ships are taking in the enormity of the near disaster all around them, Japanese aircraft approach. To the horror of one and all, the planes begin diving down and crashing into the four surviving carriers. All of the ships take some damage. But the unlucky

U.S. Third Fleet arrives at Leyte.

"DAWN OF LIBERATION—Sun breaks through clouds in fitting symbolism as invasion armada arrives off Leyte to open Philippines campaign on October 20, 1944." [*original caption*]

Troops on the beach at Leyte.

LSTs disgorge their contents through their maws.

Order amid apparent chaos in preparation for the coming campaign.

Adm. William F. Halsey Jr. and Vice Adm. Marc A. Mitscher just prior to the Battle of Leyte Gulf.

USS *White Plains* (CVE 66) under attack off Samar. "Near misses by Jap[anese] shells during attack." [*original caption*]

Near misses by Japanese gunfire as seen from the deck of USS *Kalinin Bay* (CVE 68).

U.S. destroyers charge into the fray while making smoke to reduce the enemy's visibility during the battle off Samar.

"USS *Gambier Bay* (CVE 73) straddled by Japanese shells and falling behind the rest of her task group, during the battle off Samar, 25 October 1944. Photographed from USS *Kitkun Bay* (CVE 71). A Japanese cruiser is faintly visible on the horizon at right." [*original caption*]

"BATTLE OFF SAMAR, 25 October 1944. Ships of Carrier Division 25 under shell attack by the Japanese Fleet. Photo taken from USS *White Plains* (CVE 66)." [*original caption*]

"SUWANEE HIT—BUT COMES BACK FIGHTING—A tremendous billow of smoke rises from the escort carrier USS SUWANEE as it is set afire by enemy action.... Severely damaged, the fighting ship made her way to Puget Navy Yard ... was repaired—and is now back in action, seeking revenge." [*original caption*]

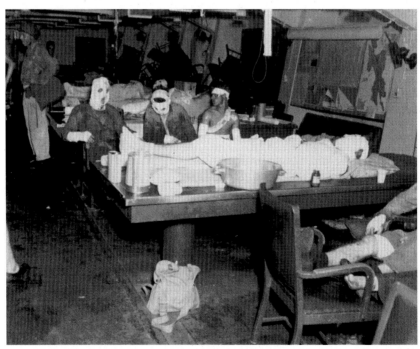

"Wardroom of USS *Suwanee* (CVE 27) in use as an emergency sick bay following the kamikaze hit of 25 October." [*original caption*]

Photograph of a watercolor. "Following the surprise dawn landing of the 77th Division at Ormoc, the naval attack force ran a day-long gauntlet of Kamikaze attack by scores of Jap[anese] planes as it returned to Surigao Strait and Leyte Gulf. The screening destroyers, 'fishtailing' at thirty knots in the confined shoal waters, found their course unavoidably leading through flotillas of Filipino outriggers almost becalmed in the spotty airs of an incongruously lovely day. The *Mahan*-class destroyer *Flusser* is firing at a dive bomber coming out of the high sun, while machine guns have fallen silent after 'flaming' the suicide plane about to hit the *Fletcher*-class destroyer in the middle distance." [*original caption*]

USS *Bennion* (DD 662). Then-Lt. (and future Chief of Naval Operations) James L. Holloway III served in her during the Battle of Surigao Strait.

"USS IOWA—ONE OF NAVY'S MOST POWERFUL AT SEA—Bristling on all sides with guns ready for action, the USS *Iowa* symbolizes the might of the Navy as she plows ahead at full steam somewhere at sea." [*original caption*]

Japanese battleship *Yamato* (*center*) during the Battle of Leyte Gulf.

one is the USS *St. Lo*. A bomb-laden Zeke runs her down from astern, low on the water, rises up and plummets into her flight deck. A series of secondary explosions gut her, the last one being produced by her main bomb stowage. The ship is gone in twenty minutes. *St. Lo*'s survivors are picked up almost immediately by the screen, but a much longer ordeal awaits the survivors of the ships sunk during the running sea battle.

Though they are spotted by aircraft throughout the afternoon, it takes a full fifty hours for rescue ships to find them. Scattered across miles of ocean, they endure shark attacks, exposure, and hallucinations induced by salt-water ingestion. More than a hundred men die on the life rafts and floater nets. Despite a poorly organized search and rescue effort, the men are finally rescued through the initiative of a transport commander idling in Leyte Gulf.

It will go down as the greatest upset victory in the history of our Navy and also one of its most embarrassing moments. We can find reason to criticize the conduct of most of the high command in this battle, from Admiral Halsey, who failed to communicate clearly with his colleagues as he went north in pursuit of the Japanese carriers, to Admiral Kinkaid, who hung his fate on the unverified assumption that Halsey was watching his back, to Admiral Nimitz who gave Halsey in the first instance excessively flexible operational orders that permitted him to abandon his "cover and support" mission in favor of offensive action. Underlying all of this was the unfortunate divided command structure that placed the Seventh Fleet under General MacArthur, who required all messages to and from the Third Fleet be relayed through his headquarters at Manus, thousands of miles away, causing critical delays. But the final legacy of the Battle off Samar should be one of appreciation and inspiration, not recrimination.

Moving forward nearly half a century, the Navy, equipped with ships named after the legendary ships of the Leyte action, goes on to fight other battles in other oceans. In April 1988, the USS *Samuel B. Roberts* (FFG 58) is in the Persian Gulf escorting Kuwaiti tankers during the Iran-Iraq War. As tensions with the Iranian navy escalate, the ship gets caught in a minefield, and as she tries to get out, she detonates a mine. According to her skipper, Capt. Paul Rinn, the 4,000-ton ship becomes a 6,000-ton ship within just a matter of minutes. Her back is broken, and her flames rise high into the night as her compartments flood. It is only through multiple acts of resourcefulness and bravery that the crew is able to contain the flooding and save the ship.

When Captain Rinn told this story at a reunion of the first USS *Samuel B. Roberts* in 2001, he described his sailors running through the ship's main passageway while going to general quarters, reaching up and touching a bronze plaque that he had had made to commemorate the old *Samuel B. Roberts* (DE 413). It listed the names of her whole crew. The namesake ship's legacy was an important part of the sense of tradition he instilled in his men.

In the years since the book came out, I was privileged to have opportunities to see the continued engagement of these veterans with the active Navy. Captain Rinn helped host a wonderful historical reminiscence through the auspices of the Surface Navy Association in Washington, D.C. There were some marvelous reunion events in San Diego. The seventieth anniversary of the battle provide an occasion for Naval Academy midshipmen to meet with veterans at a hotel there. Their legacy touched the present then, as it continues to do today.

In November 2016 I visited the Pentagon to attend the dedication of a conference room in honor of two captains who fought at Samar, Ernest Evans and *Samuel B. Roberts* skipper Robert W. Copeland. The surface navy, eager to cultivate its fighting culture, wanted to honor these illustrious names. Vice Adm. Thomas S. Rowden, the commander of surface forces, had been touting the notion of "distributed lethality," which looked to vest more offensive capability in destroyers and cruisers, as opposed to just aircraft carriers and submarines. It's been a while since the surface fleet distributed much lethality since 25 October 1944. The experience of such a war has been unavailable for decades, except by way of a vicarious experience through books or the disappearing occasions to meet living witnesses. But what the surface forces are all about was crystallized in World War II, from Guadalcanal's epic surface actions to the Battle off Samar.

Active-duty naval personnel, hearing about the battle, tend to listen closely, often wondering, I sense, whether they have the same mettle as the tin can sailors and pilots of Taffy 3. The members of the World War II generation have generally denied any claim to special qualities of heroism. They see themselves as ordinary people, doing what ordinary people would do. To my eye that is exactly what inspires people today, be they naval officers or civilians.

"When great men blunder," a wise man once wrote, "they count their losses in pride and reputation and glory. The underlings count their losses in blood." Those who have experienced such loss went home to live humble, productive lives. If they were haunted by the pain of their war experience, they remained patient with me as they shared their memories of it, helpfully answering so many questions—"What happened? What happened next? What did you think? What did you do? What did it sound like? Did you think of your family? What prayers did you utter?" Now and then they talked about it, showing by direct testimony that ordinary people are capable of great things.

As historians of World War II content themselves with writing from records—including very many excellent oral histories, thanks to the U.S. Naval Institute and Columbia University in particular—we can continue to hold out hope that greatness may lie within our own ordinary selves, a potential awaiting the right circumstances to be unlocked and revealed. With the World War II generation gone, we won't have living and breathing examples of what that sort of humble courage looks like. But it remains their legacy as they pass, and it will enrich us to remember it as we prepare to face whatever the future has in store.

About the Author

James D. Hornfischer is the author of four books on the U.S. Navy during World War II. *The Last Stand of the Tin Can Sailors* (2004), about the Battle off Samar, received the Samuel Eliot Morison Award for Naval Literature from the Naval Order of the United States and was chosen by *Naval History* magazine as one of "a dozen Navy classics." Hornfischer's most recent book, *The Fleet at Flood Tide: America at Total War in the Pacific, 1944–1945* (2016), a *New York Times* bestseller, received the Commodore John Barry Book Award from the Navy League of the United States. Hornfischer is also the author of *Neptune's Inferno: The U.S. Navy at Guadalcanal* (2011); *Ship of Ghosts* (2006), about the cruiser USS *Houston* (CA 30) and the odyssey of its crew in captivity; and coauthor with Marcus Luttrell of *Service: A Navy SEAL at War* (2012). He serves on the board of the Naval Historical Foundation.

The trustees of the USS *Constitution* Museum presented Hornfischer in 2018 with the Samuel Eliot Morison Award for Distinguished Service for work that "reflects the best of Admiral Morison: artful scholarship, patriotic pride, and eclectic interest in the sea and things maritime and a desire to preserve the best of our past for future generations." A native of Massachusetts and a graduate of Colgate University and the University of Texas School of Law, he lives in Austin, Texas, with his family.

PART II
The Archives

As explained in the introduction, the Naval Institute's *Proceedings* and *Naval History* magazines have published many articles focused on the Battle of Leyte Gulf. This selection of articles provides an edifying and entertaining collection that both historians and buffs alike will find enlightening and enticing. Naval Institute members can find even more on the USNI website, where all the magazines' articles (dating back to 1874) reside in digital form. For example, there is a 13,000+ word article by the iconic Samuel Eliot Morison that should be included here, but its size runs the risk of turning this volume into a weightlifting challenge, so it has been regretfully omitted.

Readers are also reminded that the USNI archive also contains a vast library of oral histories, a sampling of which are offered in Denis Clift's original essay presented earlier.

Titles, bylines, citations, and the author bios that follow are reproduced as they appeared with the original articles, which in some cases offers some additional historical perspective.

The first two articles (Alan Rems' "Flawed Victory at Sea" and my own "Greatest of All Sea Battles") offer general views of the overall battle. Alan is a frequent contributor to *Naval History*, was named as the magazine's 2008 Author of the Year, and is the author of the acclaimed *South Pacific Cauldron: World War II's Great Forgotten Battlegrounds* (Naval Institute Press, 2014).

An obviously valuable piece in this collection is an article written for *Proceedings* by Fleet Admiral Halsey in 1952 in which he offers his version of the events along with explanations for some of the actions he took during the several days of the battle. Much of the rancor seen in the November 1947 *Life* article ("Bull's Run: Was Halsey Right at Leyte Gulf?") does not appear in this article, Halsey apparently having salved his wounds in the interim five years.

Another admiral, Vice Adm. Jesse Oldendorf, provides his views in an article that focuses on the Battle of Surigao Strait, where he was the on-scene U.S. commander. Taking advantage of the open forum that *Proceedings* provides, this is a Comment & Discussion piece written in response to the long article by Samuel Eliot Morison mentioned above, and which provides Admiral Oldendorf's perspective on that momentous night surface action.

The Japanese perspective is offered through two articles. James A. Field Jr. served as a member of the U.S. Strategic Bombing Survey that reviewed enemy records and interviewed top army and navy officers, government officials, industrialists, political leaders, and many hundreds of their subordinates throughout Japan after the war, resulting in 108 volumes and thousands of pages. He later wrote a book (*The Japanese at Leyte Gulf: The Sho Operation*) and subsequently provided a summary of that book for *Proceedings* ("Leyte Gulf: The First Uncensored Japanese Account") in March 1951. Rear Admiral Tomiji Koyanagi was Admiral Kurita's chief of staff during the battle and shared his thoughts in a February 1953 article appropriately titled, "With Kurita in the Battle of Leyte Gulf."

In "MacArthur, FDR, and the Politics of Leyte Gulf," I recount how politics was a major factor in the decision to divide the Pacific theater between Admiral Nimitz and General MacArthur, a decision that contributed to the mistakes made at Leyte Gulf.

Capt. Walter Karig, Lt. Cdr. Russell Harris, and Lt. Cdr. Frank Manson paint a vivid picture of the action off Samar, relying on first-person accounts as well as detailed research. This triumvirate wrote a series of six books called Battle Report that covered World War II and Korea. Captain Karig also ghost-wrote several of the Nancy Drew books under the pseudonym "Carolyn Keene" and published many novels, including *Zotz!*, which was eventually made into a 1962 movie of the same name. And Captain Manson is the co-author (with Malcom Cagle) of *The Sea War in Korea*, twice published by the Naval Institute (originally in 1957 and again for the fiftieth anniversary of that war) as well as the contributor of a 361-page oral history that is loaded with insights about many of the key figures of World War II, whom he knew personally.

The Battle off Samar occurred as it did largely because of Halsey's decision to go north leaving no assets behind, and Alan Rems provides a useful summation of that controversy—both then and subsequently—in his October 2017 *Naval History* article "Seven Decades of Debate."

Capt. Andrew Hamilton focuses on the famous message sent from Nimitz to Halsey when it appeared that all hell had broken loose (which it had) with Kurita's powerful surface force in pursuit of the vulnerable "Taffies," concluding (in 1960) that "the fateful double-blooper message ... proves that in the most technological of all worlds, the human link in the chain of battle is sometimes the weakest."

One of the more colorful accounts of the Battle of Surigao Strait appeared in *Naval History* magazine in 2010, written by then-Lt. James L. Holloway III, who later became the Navy's twentieth chief of naval operations.

The final two selections illustrate the value of *Proceedings* magazine as one component of the Naval Institute's open forum. One is a Professional Note (a regular *Proceedings* feature that focuses on topics relevant to the sea services professions) by Thomas Hone and Norman Friedman that hypothesizes a gunnery duel between the biggest battleships of the Japanese and American navies at the time of Leyte Gulf. The other is a Comment & Discussion piece (another regular *Proceedings* feature that allows readers to continue discussions proffered in preceding issues) that adds the professional opinion of retired Vice Adm. Lloyd Mustin to the discussion. Tom Hone's *Battle Line: The United States Navy 1919–1939* (co-authored with his son, Trent) and *The Battle of Midway: The Naval Institute Guide to the U.S. Navy's Greatest Victory* are both Naval Institute Press books that have received much well-deserved praise. Norman Friedman is a virtual institution himself, writing countless articles and books for the Naval Institute over many decades.

These thirteen articles stand as tangible testimony to the value of the Naval Institute's two magazines, which have captured a substantial amount of naval history for nearly a century and a half.

12

FLAWED VICTORY AT SEA
Alan Rems

Naval History, October 2017

On 23 October 1944, three days after General Douglas MacArthur's forces landed on Leyte Island in the Philippines, the Japanese navy emerged to fight. Awaiting them in the waters east of Luzon was Admiral William F. Halsey Jr.'s powerful U.S. Third Fleet. Operating with broad authority under an irrational command arrangement, Halsey would make critical decisions that would overshadow all else in his eventful career.

Few military maxims are more hallowed than the need for unity of command—the assignment of all forces in an operational area under a single command. Because U.S. Army and Navy leaders could not agree on a commander, command in the Pacific remained divided. Until the Philippines campaign, the operations of MacArthur in the Southwest Pacific and Admiral Chester W. Nimitz in the Central Pacific sharply diverged, so that few coordination problems resulted. With convergence of their operations in the Philippines, however, two U.S. fleets found themselves operating together under different lines of authority and with separate communication systems, a formula for confusion—and worse.

The U.S. Seventh Fleet, known as "MacArthur's Navy," functioned as the Leyte invasion force. Commanded by Vice Admiral Thomas C. Kinkaid, the relatively small Seventh Fleet was substantially reinforced by Nimitz.

Subordinate to Nimitz, Halsey's Third Fleet provided the covering force. Halsey was ordered to "cover and support" MacArthur's invasion forces and "destroy enemy and naval forces" that might threaten the operation. These were essentially defensive orders similar to those issued to covering forces for previous invasions. But Nimitz didn't stop there. Months earlier, during the Battle of the Philippine Sea, the Japanese fleet escaped because of the caution exercised by Admiral Raymond A. Spruance. Anxious not to lose such an opportunity again, and with considerable confidence in Halsey, Nimitz went further without consulting MacArthur, instructing Halsey, "In case opportunity for destruction of major portion of the enemy fleet offers or can be created, such destruction becomes the primary task."[1] As historian Samuel Eliot Morison wryly observed about that instruction, it would become "the tail that wagged the dog."[2]

Interpreting such conflicting orders, highly aggressive "Bull" Halsey believed he was given a broad mandate to engage and destroy the enemy. Halsey was frustrated at having missed the great carrier battles of the Coral Sea, Midway, and the Philippine Sea; his ultimate goal became eliminating Japan's carrier fleet. He had repeatedly played the odds and won, and would have no reluctance to do so again.

A Gambler at War

Perhaps no other U.S. World War II leader at Halsey's command level had, until then, risked so much so often with equal success.

When the nation was still reeling from the Pearl Harbor attack and needed a boost in morale, Halsey won the gratitude and trust of Nimitz by leading perilous carrier raids in the Central Pacific. These successful attacks turned Halsey into a national hero, his image further enhanced by safely transporting Lieutenant Colonel Jimmy Doolittle's airmen for their epic raid on Tokyo.

Afterward, Halsey left the sea for 20 months to command the war in the South Pacific from behind a desk in Noumea, New Caledonia. At the outset, when the issue at Guadalcanal was in doubt, his aggressive style ended in near disaster. At the Battle of the Santa Cruz Islands, Halsey ordered Kinkaid, then his subordinate, to attack a superior Japanese force, ending in the loss of one carrier and damage to the last remaining U.S. carrier in the Pacific. Yet even this action yielded a considerable benefit by inflicting heavy losses on the Japanese carrier aircraft, which severely limited the enemy's subsequent operations. Weeks later, fighting in the "Nelsonian spirit," Halsey won the Naval Battle of Guadalcanal, ending Japan's hope to reclaim the island.[3] Later in the Solomons campaign, when many still considered such a maneuver too hazardous, Halsey leapfrogged heavily defended Kolombangara to seize lightly occupied Vella Lavella.

And Halsey's capacity for risk was not limited to dealing with the Japanese. In close succession, he fired the two ranking Marine commanders in the Pacific, including highly respected Major General Charles D. Barrett, who committed suicide before his removal was announced. Barrett's death saved Halsey from needing to defend his action, about which Marine Corps Commandant Lieutenant General Thomas Holcomb remarked, "[F]ew people would have believed that Halsey was right."[4] While Barrett's suicide traded one crisis for an even greater one, Halsey authorized an audacious cover-up that made the cause of death appear accidental.

Afterward, in what he called his "most desperate emergency" in the South Pacific, Halsey ignored every rule against operating carriers near a major enemy base to repel a force of heavy cruisers that threatened the Bougainville beachhead. He risked two carriers and their precious air groups, but the Japanese vessels were caught in harbor and pummeled in a raid described as "a second Pearl Harbor in reverse."[5]

With the winning of the Solomons, Halsey returned to sea, alternating with Spruance in command of a fleet designated the Third Fleet when commanded by Halsey and the Fifth Fleet when Spruance led it. A surface admiral, Spruance depended on advice from gifted Vice Admiral Marc A. Mitscher in conducting carrier operations.

In the more than two years since Halsey commanded at sea, carrier forces had increased exponentially and tactics markedly evolved. When leading his successful carrier operations early in the war, Halsey relied heavily on his chief of staff, Captain Miles A. Browning, a brilliant though erratic airman with "a slide-rule mind."[6] Browning was now gone, replaced by non-aviator Rear Admiral Robert B. Carney. As observed by historian Clark G. Reynolds, although they shared a "fiery temperament," their relationship was not "conducive to stimulating disagreements."[7] Without an aviator such as Browning to challenge his thinking, Halsey followed his own instincts that had so far paid off handsomely.

The original Philippine invasion plan involved beginning with Mindanao, at the southern end of the archipelago. But, when Halsey's pilots encountered little opposition over the central Philippines, he was convinced enemy air strength had been severely depleted and urged skipping Mindanao to strike directly at Leyte. Halsey guessed wrong about enemy strength, but the accelerated invasion caught the Japanese off guard. During his final operation before Leyte, Halsey had further opportunity to exercise his gambler's instinct.

Raiding in the South China Sea to suppress Japanese ability to funnel aircraft into the Philippines, two of his cruisers sustained serious damage. Rather than sink the vessels and withdraw at high speed, Halsey had them taken under tow, the slow-moving cripples serving as lures while his other ships lurked at a distance. The Japanese didn't bite, but the force returned safely, burnishing Halsey's image as a consummate gambler.

Opening Moves

When the Japanese fleet did not respond immediately to the Leyte invasion, Halsey expected some respite. Since his ships and men had spent many months at sea and were in great need of refit and rest, he began rotating his four carrier groups to Ulithi. First to depart was Vice Admiral John S. McCain's group, the largest with approximately 400 of the fleet's 1,000 aircraft.

The Battle of Leyte Gulf began off Palawan on 23 October, when two submarines sighted and attacked a column of Japanese surface ships, sinking two cruisers and damaging another. Commanded by Vice Admiral Takeo Kurita and designated the Center Force by the Americans, the vessels were spotted the next morning in the Sibuyan Sea headed toward San Bernardino Strait. Flying from the three carrier groups posted east of Luzon and Samar, Halsey's aviators pounced, mortally wounding the giant battleship *Musashi* and heavily damaging one cruiser. Kurita temporarily withdrew, while Halsey, relying on extravagant aviator reports, convinced himself the Center Force was badly whipped.

As a precaution in case Kurita renewed his advance and penetrated San Bernardino Strait, Halsey issued a bulletin warning that, if he later so ordered, his battleships with supporting units were to form Task Force (TF) 34 and engage the enemy. Information copies were sent to Nimitz and the Commander-in-Chief of the U.S. fleet (as well as the Chief of Naval Operations), Admiral Ernest J. King. Although Kinkaid was not an addressee, the message was intercepted by his message center, the ambiguous wording providing Kinkaid unwarranted comfort that TF 34 was actually being formed. The enemy threat, meanwhile, remained very real. Far from being in the shattered condition Halsey assumed, Kurita's Center Force remained formidable with four battleships, six heavy cruisers, two light cruisers, and ten destroyers. In late afternoon, Kurita reversed course and again headed for San Bernardino Strait.

That morning, Halsey's aviators had spotted a smaller Japanese force in the Sulu Sea headed toward Surigao Strait. Designated the Southern Force, this was correctly interpreted as the other half of a pincer that was to converge with the Center Force at Leyte Gulf. After launching mostly unsuccessful air attacks, Halsey's carriers departed to join the attack on the Center Force. Kinkaid was alerted and prepared to engage the enemy that night in Surigao Strait.

All along, Halsey wondered where the Japanese carriers were. The answer came in late afternoon, when four carriers with their supports were observed approaching from the north. As a result of severe attrition suffered in opposing Halsey's South China Sea raid, this Northern Force, commanded by Vice Admiral Jisaburo Ozawa, mustered only 116 aircraft. It was a decoy intended to lure Halsey away while the Center and Southern forces converged at Leyte Gulf.

Several years later, Halsey described his three options.[8] If he stood fast at San Bernardino Strait, he would have yielded the initiative and invited attack from both land-based aircraft and Ozawa's carrier planes. The second choice was to form TF 34 and leave it behind to guard San Bernardino Strait, while his carriers attacked the Northern Force. Such separation, he believed, would violate the military principle not to divide one's forces, which might then be beaten in detail. For Halsey, his third option was obvious. To preserve fleet integrity and retain the initiative, he chose to pursue the Northern Force with his entire fleet.

"Bull's Run"

Late on the evening of 24 October, Halsey headed north with three carrier groups while McCain was ordered to refuel at sea and rejoin him. Halsey's movement was duly reported to Kinkaid, who assumed, from ambiguities in both the message intercepted earlier and this message, that TF 34 remained behind and was guarding his rear. Specifically, had Halsey simply reported that "all" his ships were headed north, rather than that he was departing with "three" carrier groups, Kinkaid's misconceptions would not have occurred. Soon afterward, Halsey's night fighters discovered that Kurita's ships were moving east again, which was reported to Kinkaid. Thereafter, the fighters were reassigned to search for the Northern Force. Near midnight, a much-relieved Kurita passed unhindered through San Bernardino Strait on his way to Leyte Gulf.

Halsey's bold decision did not go unquestioned. Carrier group commander Rear Admiral Gerald F. Bogan urged formation of TF 34 to confront Kurita. Brushed off by a Halsey aide who fielded the message, Bogan gave up. Elsewhere in the fleet, Mitscher's chief of staff, Captain Arleigh A. Burke, concluded that the Northern Force was a decoy. Up to then, Halsey essentially had ignored Mitscher, the nominal commander of the Third Fleet's fast carrier force, and directed carrier operations himself. The vice admiral told Burke, "If he wants my advice, he'll ask for it."[9]

At Surigao Strait that night, Kinkaid's Seventh Fleet crossed the enemy "T," essentially destroying the Southern Force and putting to flight an independent trailing force. In all, the Japanese lost two battleships, three cruisers, and four destroyers. Kinkaid's staff was savoring their victory in the predawn hours of 25 October when it occurred to them it was never verified that TF 34 was covering San Bernardino Strait. In a message advising Halsey of the action in Surigao Strait, Kinkaid asked if the northern strait was being covered. And here the problem of unlinked communication systems exacted its full price. That message took two-and-a-half hours to reach Halsey, too late for his response to alert Kinkaid to the impending danger.

After being spotted in the late afternoon of the 24th, the Northern Force's main body was not sighted again for nine hours and not accurately plotted until 0710 on the 25th. Mitscher, who had resumed tactical control of the carriers, had launched his aircraft an hour earlier, so they were airborne when the target was pinpointed. Meanwhile, shortly before 0700, Kinkaid's inquiry about San Bernardino Strait was finally delivered. Not yet grasping the dire implications, Halsey responded that his battleships were all operating with the carriers, and he returned to the business at hand.

But Kinkaid would not go away. While the results of the first strike were tensely awaited, Halsey received a plain language message, sent more than an hour earlier, with the alarming news that enemy ships were attacking Kinkaid's escort carriers. Further messages from Kinkaid followed, including at 0900 a plea for help received by radio. This prompted Halsey to order McCain to head for Leyte Gulf, which could be of only limited help since he was still very distant. Time still remained, though, for the fast battleships to form TF 34 and catch Kurita on his return trip before he slipped back through San Bernardino Strait. Intent on using his battleships to fully annihilate the enemy's carrier force, Halsey let pass an opportunity that might have gone far to redeem his performance.

While strike reports streamed in announcing great success against Ozawa's decoy force, Halsey attempted to quiet Kinkaid by reporting his position, making it obvious he was too far away to assist. But then there arrived a message that Halsey could not avoid. Though Nimitz learned early in the war not to interfere with his commander on the scene, the situation sounded so dire he could no longer stand aside. He signaled to Halsey: "WHERE IS REPEAT WHERE IS TASK FORCE THIRTY FOUR." Appended to the message was the required "padding" at the beginning and end to help prevent enemy decoding, which customarily was removed by the recipient message center before delivery. From the poem "The Charge of the Light Brigade," there was appended at the end of the message the phrase "THE WORLD WONDERS."[10] Because those words made sense when joined to the primary message, they were not removed, as they should have been, before the message was delivered.

Halsey was furious on receiving such a biting communication, which had also been sent as an information copy to King and Kinkaid. Breaking into tears and hurling his cap to the deck, Halsey needed to be brought to his senses by Carney. Had Nimitz's message not forced him to act, Halsey might have pressed on with all his forces to annihilate Ozawa.[11] Over the next hour, Halsey pondered his choices before deciding to detach all his battleships with supporting vessels as TF 34 along with Bogan's carrier group for air cover. Two carrier task groups were left behind to deal with the Northern Force. With Ozawa's ships then just 42 miles from the muzzles of the fast battleships, Halsey gave up his dream of using their guns to finish off the enemy carrier force.

After a delay of more than two-and-a-half hours to refuel the destroyers, TF 34 finally got off the mark. Halsey raced ahead with just two of the battleships and supporting vessels, arriving at San Bernardino Strait more than two hours too late to intercept Kurita.

Although Kinkaid had ordered nighttime air surveillance, for various reasons his airmen achieved nothing. Thus, it was a rude surprise when Kurita suddenly appeared off Samar after dawn on 25 October. During the following two-and-a-half hours, Kinkaid's unprepared vessels wrote a glorious page in U.S. naval history. Escort carrier pilots trained for ground support threw themselves into attacks from above while destroyers and destroyer escorts dashed from smokescreens to deliver suicidal charges. Believing from the ferocious defense that he was facing more formidable forces, expecting even more powerful forces would arrive, and not knowing if Ozawa had lured Halsey away, Kurita reorganized his forces and withdrew.

As for Ozawa, through a combination of air, surface, and submarine attacks, all four of his decoy carriers were lost, along with four other vessels. Two carrier-battleships, a light cruiser, and five destroyers made it away safely, thanks to Halsey's not leaving behind any fast battleships to finish them off.

Summing Up

When the results were tallied, it was clear that the Americans had scored a tremendous victory at the Battle of Leyte Gulf. At a cost of one light carrier lost by Halsey and two escort carriers, two destroyers, and a destroyer escort lost by Kinkaid, they sank three battleships, four carriers, ten cruisers, and nine destroyers.[12] Never again would the Japanese have the ability to fight a fleet action. Still, the Seventh Fleet had only narrowly escaped disaster, and enemy surface forces that should have been eliminated by Halsey's fast battleships returned home safely. When the complete story eventually emerged, "Bull's Run" became one of the best-known and hotly debated events in naval history.

About the Author

Mr. Rems is the author of *South Pacific Cauldron: World War II's Great Forgotten Battlegrounds* (Naval Institute Press, 2014). He has been a regular contributor to *Naval History* since his article titled "Halsey Knows the Straight Story" appeared in the August 2008 issue and earned him selection as the magazine's Author of the Year.

Notes

1. E. B. Potter, *Nimitz* (Annapolis, MD: Naval Institute Press, 1976), 325.
2. Samuel Eliot Morison, *History of Naval Operations in World War II*, vol. 12, *Leyte, June 1944–January 1945* (Boston: Little, Brown, 1958), 58.
3. Ibid., 175.
4. Alan P. Rems, "Halsey Knows the Straight Story," *Naval History*, August 2008, 40–46.

5. Clark G. Reynolds, *The Fast Carriers: The Forging of an Air Navy* (Annapolis, MD: Naval Institute Press, 1992), 99.
6. Samuel Eliot Morison, *The Two-Ocean War* (Boston: Little, Brown, 1963), 154.
7. Reynolds, *Fast Carriers*, 257.
8. FADM William F. Halsey Jr., USN (Ret.), "The Battle for Leyte Gulf," U.S. Naval Institute *Proceedings* 78, no. 5 (May 1952): 490.
9. Thomas J. Cutler, *The Battle of Leyte Gulf: 23–26 October 1944* (New York: Harper Collins, 1994), 213.
10. The ensign who couldn't "keep his thoughts out of operational dispatches" was transferred out by Nimitz. See E. B. Potter, *Bull Halsey* (Annapolis, MD: Naval Institute Press, 1985), 323.
11. Morison, *Leyte*, 329. Morison was told by Halsey that "the query from Nimitz . . . was the final factor that influenced his decision."
12. Halsey lost the light carrier USS *Princeton* (CVL 23) to bombing by a land-based aircraft during the attack on Kurita in the Sibuyan Sea; the other American losses were incurred during Kinkaid's desperate battle with Kurita off Samar.

13

GREATEST OF ALL SEA BATTLES
— Lt. Cdr. Thomas J. Cutler, U.S. Navy (Ret.) —

Naval History, October 1994

The Battle of Leyte Gulf was the biggest and most multifaceted naval battle in history. It involved hundreds of ships, nearly 200,000 participants, and spanned more than 100,000 square miles. Some of the largest and most powerful ships ever built were sunk, and thousands of men went to the bottom of the sea with them. Every facet of naval warfare—air, surface, subsurface, and amphibious—was involved in this great struggle, and the weapons used included bombs of every type, guns of every caliber, torpedoes, mines, rockets, and even a forerunner of the modern guided missile.

But more than mere size made this battle significant. The cast of characters included such names as Halsey, Nimitz, MacArthur, even Roosevelt. It introduced the largest guns ever used in a naval battle and a new Japanese tactic that would eventually kill more U.S. sailors and sink more U.S. ships than any other used in the war. It was the last clash of the dreadnoughts and the first and only time that gunfire sank a U.S. aircraft carrier. It was replete with awe-inspiring heroism, failed intelligence, sapient tactical planning and execution, flawed strategy, brilliant deception, incredible ironies, great controversies, and a plethora of lessons about strategy, tactics, and operations.

If all this is true, why is Leyte Gulf not a household word—like Pearl Harbor? Why have fewer Americans heard of it than the Battle of Midway or the Normandy invasion of Europe? The answer lies in timing. Leyte Gulf occurred late in the war, after several years of conflict, when great battles had become commonplace. Tales from such places as Midway, Stalingrad, Guadalcanal, and Normandy were by then frequent fare. More significant, however, was that the Battle of Leyte Gulf happened when most of the United States had accepted ultimate victory as merely a matter of time rather than as a debatable question. Midway was accepted widely as the turning point of the war in the Pacific, a dramatic reversal of what had been a losing trend. The D-Day invasion at Normandy was seen as the true beginning of the end of war in Europe. But many saw Leyte Gulf as the continuation of a normal and inevitable trend. Lacking the drama of earlier battles, Leyte Gulf was then eclipsed by later events—a near-reversal at the Battle of the Bulge, ferocious fighting at Iwo Jima and Okinawa, and the cataclysmic dropping of atomic bombs on Hiroshima and Nagasaki.

But the Battle of Leyte Gulf was indeed pivotal. It represented the last hope of the Japanese Empire and the last significant sortie of the Imperial Japanese Navy. It was vastly important to millions of Filipinos and thousands of Allied prisoners of war whose liberation from Japanese oppression depended upon it. And, while a U.S. victory in the battle may have been viewed as somewhat mundane by that stage of the war, a defeat would have been disastrous.

Prelude

On 11 March 1942, a U.S. Army general stood at the water's edge and surveyed his wilting domain. Where lush vegetation and vibrantly colored tropical flowers had flourished, all that remained was the shattered remnants of an army on the verge of capitulation. Trees had been reduced to mere jagged stumps. Buildings that had housed a proud garrison lay in ruin. General Douglas MacArthur, 25 pounds lighter than he had been three months earlier, removed his gold-encrusted khaki cap and raised it in a final salute to Corregidor, the island-fortress he had been ordered to abandon.

In the gathering darkness of those early days of the war, when defeat had followed defeat, the brave but futile stand that MacArthur's forces had made on the fortified peninsula of Bataan had been a welcome ray of light. MacArthur had been elevated to heroic proportions not equaled since Admiral George Dewey had defeated the Spanish Fleet in these same Philippine waters at the close of the last century. To allow him to fall into the hands of an enemy whose propagandists predicted that they would see him hanged publicly in the Imperial Plaza in Tokyo was simply unthinkable. So President Franklin D. Roosevelt had ordered the general to leave.

This was no simple order. First, there was the natural reluctance of the general to abandon his command. Then came the realization that escape from the Philippines was more easily ordered than carried out. Japanese forces virtually controlled the air and sea approaches such that only a bold and clandestine move had any hope of success. And finally, there were MacArthur's special ties to the Philippines. His father, General Arthur MacArthur, had been both war hero and military governor there, and young Douglas's first assignment after graduating from West Point had been a tour of duty in the Philippines as a second lieutenant in the elite Corps of Engineers. He returned there several more times during his career, and by the time the Japanese landed troops at Lingayen Gulf in December 1941, MacArthur had become a field marshal of the Philippine Army and commander of U.S. Army Forces in the Far East.

As evening darkness descended upon Manila Bay and rain-laden clouds erased the moon, Lieutenant John D. Bulkeley's PT-41 threaded its way through the defensive minefield and headed for the blackened waters of Mindoro Strait, where enemy ships were known to prowl. On board, General MacArthur vowed to recover from this ignominious moment, to avenge the inevitable defeat, to come back as soon as possible with the forces necessary to drive out the invading Japanese, and to restore the honor of the United States—and his own. In a few days he voiced this determination to the world, capturing the imagination of those Americans and Filipinos who had placed their faith in him with three small but powerful words: "I shall return."

The Return

The course of the war dictated that two years would pass before MacArthur could make good on his promise. By the time U.S. forces were poised to recapture the Philippines, the Battle of Midway had turned the tide of battle in the Pacific, amphibious assaults on Japanese island strongholds had become almost commonplace, and the most powerful fleet in U.S. history roamed the Pacific in search of a final showdown with the Imperial Japanese Navy.

But at last, in October 1944, MacArthur was able to make his promised return, bringing a huge invasion force to land on Leyte Island on the eastern side of the Philippine archipelago. In support of that momentous invasion, the Joint Chiefs of Staff had assigned Vice Admiral Thomas C.

Kinkaid to command the naval forces that would actually carry out the assault. Kinkaid's forces were designated the Seventh Fleet. Admiral William F. Halsey, in command of the awesome striking power of the Third fleet—consisting of four powerful task forces containing 14 aircraft carriers and more than 1,000 aircraft—lurked nearby in case the Japanese Navy showed up to contest the landing.

On 20 October, a landing craft crunched up onto the shore of Leyte Island, and the bow-door rattled down into the surf. The craft was still some distance from the dry sand of the beach, so General MacArthur and his entourage had to step off into knee-deep water and wade the rest of the way in. It was one of those moments that carved a graven image in the American heritage.

MacArthur strode across the sand to a waiting microphone and transmitter. He took the handset and held it close to his lips.

"People of the Philippines," MacArthur said in his resonant voice. "I have returned."

The gray skies above opened suddenly, and rain cascaded from the clouds like tears so fitting to this emotional moment.

"By the grace of Almighty God," MacArthur continued. "Our forces stand again on Philippine soil—soil consecrated in the blood of our two peoples."

With the sounds of mortal combat still thundering around him, soldiers of both sides dying not far away, this man, whom many characterized as an egotistical demagogue and others worshipped as a military saint, sent his words out over the Philippine archipelago to a people who had long awaited his return. "The hour of your redemption is here," he intoned, and countless numbers of Filipinos rejoiced. "Your patriots have demonstrated an unswerving and resolute devotion to the principles of freedom that challenge the best that is written on the pages of human history."

In the years that followed, MacArthur's detractors panned this moment. They accused him of "grandstanding," which is undeniable. They criticized his use of the first-person, which is certainly questionable. Some even characterized his speech as trite and overblown, which is arguable. But an objective observer would recognize that this was truly an important moment in history. Just as General Dwight D. Eisenhower had spoken on the shores of Normandy to a people long-suffering under the boot of Adolf Hitler's tyranny, so General MacArthur had given new hope to a people who had trusted in the United States to free them from Japanese domination.

"Rally to me," MacArthur challenged. And many did. In the months following the landing at Leyte, many Filipinos laid down their lives, fighting as guerrillas in the Japanese rear as U.S. troops pushed on inexorably through the islands. These people, at least, had listened when MacArthur said, "Let the indomitable spirit of Bataan and Corregidor lead on. As the lines of battle roll forward to bring you within the zone of operations, rise and strike."

The Response

Just after midnight on 18 October 1944, the sound of anchor chains rattling in hawsepipes drifted across the still waters of the Lingga Roads anchorage as seven battleships, 15 cruisers, and 20 destroyers of the Imperial Japanese Navy prepared to get under way. Deep in the bellies of these great steel whales, young sailors, firing their boilers, turned huge valvewheels to regulate the flow of the oil, which at the moment was more precious than gold to the Japanese Empire. Most of these vessels were combat-hardened veterans of the Pacific War, many still pocked with the scars of battle, some partially debilitated by the ravages of war and long ocean transits. The cruiser *Mogami* had endured a horrific pounding at Midway. Yet there she was, still afloat, still able to inflict great harm, under way for the Philippines and a chance for revenge. The battleship *Haruna*, which had struck a German mine in World War I and had been reported sunk time and again in this one, steamed out of the Lingga anchorage, her shadowy form hauntingly vague in the subdued light of the distant stars. The destroyer *Shigure*, veteran of the Coral Sea, Solomons, and New Guinea campaigns, had been the sole Japanese survivor at the battle in Vella Gulf. As her crew worked to bring her anchor into short stay, some of them surely wondered if their luck would continue through the coming engagement.

Of all the ships making up this powerful force, the most formidable were the gigantic battleships *Yamato* and *Musashi*. At the time, these two 862-foot-long, 70,000-ton behemoths were the largest surface warships ever built.

This formidable task force, under Vice Admiral Takeo Kurita, was the most powerful element in a multifaceted operation the Japanese had dubbed *Sho Go*, Operation Victory. This complex plan relied heavily upon both timing and surprise and called for Kurita to hit the U.S. forces from two different directions in what is traditionally called a pincer attack. After refueling in Brunei, the larger of the two elements, including the superbattleships *Yamato* and *Musashi*, would remain in Kurita's tactical command and proceed northward, then cut through the Philippine archipelago using the Sibuyan Sea as passage. Once across this rather narrow inland waterway, this force would pass through San Bernardino Strait, proceed south along the coast of the island of Samar and attack the U.S. landing forces at Leyte Gulf from the north.

Meanwhile, the other, smaller element, consisting of the battleships *Yamashiro* and *Fuso*, the heavy cruiser *Mogami*, and four destroyers, was placed under the command of Vice Admiral Shoji Nishimura. It would sortie from Brunei after Kurita's force and take the shorter but more hazardous route through the Philippines via the Sulu and Mindanao seas. With proper timing, Nishimura would pass through Surigao Strait and enter Leyte Gulf from the south at about the same time Kurita's force was attacking from the north.

Complexity and the need for near-perfect timing were obvious disadvantages to the plan, but the biggest problem facing the Japanese was that the United States had such an overwhelming advantage in available forces. Japanese intelligence reports, though not perfect, were providing a reasonably accurate assessment of what was waiting at Leyte. The Japanese were aware of the large amphibious fleet (Kinkaid's Seventh) that was spearheading the invasion. If this were the only force to contend with, Kurita thought his two-pronged attack would have an excellent chance for success. But the Japanese knew that Halsey's forces were also lurking about, spoiling for a fight, and they also knew that they had no hope of surviving a battle with such a gargantuan agglomeration of naval striking power. Halsey and Kinkaid together had more than enough forces available to take on any number of pincer elements, coming from any number of directions. How then could the Japanese hope to contend with such overwhelming odds?

The answer lay in an age-old weapon that served inferior forces for as long as there has been warfare. Deception was to be the offsetting element that might negate some of the preponderant U.S. advantage. Although the Japanese knew that their carrier striking forces had been rendered impotent by their lack of trained pilots, they reasoned that the U.S. forces might not fully appreciate this fact and might still consider the carriers a force to reckon with. So the Japanese command had decided that Admiral Jisaburo Ozawa's role in the forthcoming battle would be to serve as a decoy. His carrier striking forces had been rendered virtually useless by catastrophic losses of pilots and aircraft at the Battle of the Philippine Sea the previous June (known popularly as the "Marianas Turkey Shoot"). These carriers had been operating in Japanese home waters since the June battle, trying desperately but hopelessly to train new pilots and effect repairs.

Hoping that the United States was not fully cognizant of how limited these carriers were, the Japanese plan called for Ozawa to approach from the north in a straightforward manner, hoping to be detected in order to lure some portion of the U.S. forces away from Leyte Gulf. With luck, it would be the U.S. carrier striking forces that would be lured away, giving Kurita's powerful surface ships a fighting chance of carrying out their mission against the amphibious forces at Leyte. The success of the plan depended upon how much the Japanese could draw off the U.S. Navy's air power to chase Ozawa. Except for the support land-based air forces stationed in the Philippines could provide, Kurita would be very vulnerable to air attack once he moved within range of U.S. aircraft. Operation Victory was a long shot. But the plan was workable.

Sibuyan and Sulu Seas

On the morning of 24 October 1944, Admiral Halsey initiated the first phase of the Battle for Leyte Gulf when he picked up a radio handset and ordered the aircraft squadrons of his powerful Third Fleet: "Strike! Repeat: Strike!" Earlier that morning his reconnaissance aircraft had spotted Kurita's force on the western side of the Sibuyan Sea and had discovered Nishimura's force starting to cross the Sulu Sea. Hundreds of U.S. aircraft took to the skies to intercept these oncoming Japanese forces.

Aircraft from the USS *Enterprise* (CV 6) reached Nishimura's force in the Sulu Sea and launched a coordinated but largely ineffective attack that caused minor damage to the battleship *Fuso* and the destroyer *Shigure*. Undaunted, Nishimura's force continued to Surigao Strait.

In the Sibuyan Sea, lookouts in Kurita's force had spotted the earlier reconnaissance planes from Halsey's force. Kurita had increased speed immediately to 24 knots and prepared for battle. Tense minutes ticked by as the Japanese waited for the attack. The night before, Kurita's ships had been attacked by two U.S. submarines in the Palawan Passage west of the Philippines. Two cruisers had been sunk, one of them Kurita's flagship, and the admiral had been rescued from the sea by one of his destroyers and later transferred to the superbattleship *Yamato*.

Two hours passed before radar finally detected the anticipated U.S. aircraft, and at 1025 they roared in off the starboard beam. This first engagement lasted only 24 minutes, but it was intense and not without consequence to both sides. Extra antiaircraft guns had been added to Kurita's ships when it had become clear that Japanese air power would lend little support, making these ships very prickly prey. Battleships, cruisers, and even the destroyers bristled with hundreds more 25-mm guns than they had ever had before, and the effect was noticeable. Several of the torpedo bombers were splashed in the early moments of the attack and a Hellcat fighter soon joined them. But a number of the U.S. aircraft penetrated the wall of heavy fire, and great geysers leaped skyward from the water close aboard Kurita's flagship, *Yamato*. The heavy cruiser *Myoko* was damaged severely and began to limp, soon falling behind Kurita's formation.

Kurita's lookouts spotted the second wave of U.S. aircraft at a little past noon. The planes went for the Japanese force like angry bees out of the hive. In just minutes, three of the torpedo planes had left their stingers in the superbattleship *Musashi*, which set a pattern as subsequent attack waves began concentrating on the same ship.

All day the attacks continued. Wave after wave of U.S. aircraft descended upon Kurita's hapless force. With no air cover, Kurita's ships had no hope of victory and little for survival. Although U.S. aircraft were falling from the sky and airmen were dying, the virtually endless supply of planes and pilots pouring forth from Halsey's great fleet ensured the outcome. As the day wore on, the incoming strikes grew larger in number, and proportionately fewer aircraft succumbed as more and more Japanese antiaircraft batteries fell silent.

As the day wore on, the *Musashi*—a vessel once proclaimed unsinkable by her Japanese designers—began to list. The great battleship had absorbed 19 torpedo hits and nearly as many bombs. Most of her bow was under water.

Her crew had tried to run her aground rather than sink—at least that way her great guns could remain in service as a gigantic shore-battery—but damage to her steering equipment relegated her to slow circles in the

Sibuyan Sea, and it seemed only a matter of time before she would succumb. As evening approached, the *Musashi* began to roll slowly to port, gaining momentum as she went. Sailors ran along the rotating hull in the opposite direction like lumberjacks at a log-rolling contest, trying to stay on the upward side of the ship. Many of them were barefooted in preparation for the anticipated swim, and the barnacles encrusted along what had been her underwater hull lacerated their feet as they ran. Some dived into the sea only to be sucked back into the ship through gaping torpedo holes. Within minutes, the battleship was standing on end, her gigantic propellers high in the evening sky, her bow already deep in the dark sea. She paused there for a moment; then there was a convulsive underwater explosion, and the *Musashi* plunged into the deep, taking half of her 2,200-man crew with her.

Despite his serious losses and a temporary turn back to the west, Admiral Kurita's force had shown incredible stamina in the face of the aerial onslaught. The remainder of his force, still potent by any standard, continued on across the Sibuyan Sea toward San Bernardino Strait, the passage that would take him to Leyte Gulf.

Midwatch in Surigao Strait

As darkness descended over the Philippines and Kurita's force pressed on toward San Bernardino Strait, Rear Admiral Jesse B. Oldendorf, Kinkaid's subordinate in command of Seventh Fleet's Bombardment and Fire Support Group, prepared to meet Nishimura's force approaching Leyte Gulf from the south through Surigao Strait. Partly because of a geographical accident and partly because of sensible planning, Oldendorf had prepared quite a reception for Nishimura.

Approaching through the confined strait would force the Japanese to maintain a narrow formation. Oldendorf's disposition of forces would put the oncoming Japanese force into the jaws of several succeeding pincers, as PT boats and destroyers gnawed at his flanks along the way. This alone would have been a difficult gauntlet to run. But the array of battleships and cruisers across the northern end of the strait was something out of the oldest textbooks on naval tactics, known as "capping the 'T'" and giving the U.S. ships a tremendous advantage in firepower by placing Oldendorf at the advantageous cap and the unfortunate Nishimura forming the vulnerable base of the T.

With the moon and stars blanketed by clouds, ensuring total darkness in the strait, Nishimura headed for the southern end of the strait that Ferdinand Magellan had once sailed in his famed circumnavigation of the earth. The U.S. PT boats attacked valiantly but were driven off, suffering more damage than they were able to inflict. Although these diminutive craft had little effect on the oncoming Japanese, their radio reports provided Oldendorf with valuable information on the enemy's progress up the strait.

The next phase of the battle began when U.S. destroyers charged down the strait, sowing the blackened waters with torpedoes while withholding gunfire so as not to reveal their positions. This time the damage to Nishimura's ships was severe.

Toward the end of the midwatch in one of the U.S. destroyers retiring from the fray, a young torpedoman peered into the darkness and said, "Would you look at that?" His voice was full of wonder. "Over there. Off the starboard side. In the sky." Several crimson streaks of light flashed across the sky from north to south like meteors. Several more followed almost immediately. A throaty rumble like distant thunder, felt more than heard, rolled in from the north. "The heavies are shooting," someone said.

Oldendorf's cruisers and battleships had indeed begun their barrage. On board one of the destroyers still pressing the attack down in the strait, a squadron commodore heard a strange sound overhead and looked up. In the black sky above, he saw the tracer shells of the cruisers and battleships arcing their way southward, adding to the damage inflicted by the destroyers. "It was quite a sight," he later said. "It honestly looked like the Brooklyn Bridge at night—the tail lights of automobiles going across Brooklyn Bridge."

The Battle of Surigao Strait proved to be an epoch of history. In those brief and terrible minutes, surface ships fought surface ships without the intrusion of those interlopers from the sky that had stolen the show from the gunships in this war. Battleships at last unleashed the havoc they were designed for. Yet it was not the grand show long dreamed about. Despite their frightful destructive power, in this showdown in Surigao Strait their little brothers, the destroyers, outdid these leviathans. The torpedo that—for all of its early-war development problems and in spite of its inability to measure up to the pyrotechnic glamor of gunfire—had done the most damage in that last night surface action. The great guns spoke in anger that night, not merely at an enemy with whom they had a score to settle, but also in frustration at their own untimely impotence, in one final gasp of pent-up fury that would serve as a ceremonial salute to their own passing.

As the sun rose next morning, several columns of thick black smoke towered into the brightening sky like remnants of the black shroud that had engulfed Surigao Strait the night before. The morning light revealed clusters of men clinging to debris littering the waters of the strait, and large smears of oil stretched for miles. As U.S. destroyers moved in to pick up the Japanese survivors, most of them swam away or disappeared beneath the oily water, shunning rescue in one last great act of noble defiance.

Far to the north, in Leyte Gulf, U.S. sailors in the amphibious transports had spent the night watching with fascination and some dread as the flashes of gunfire had reflected off the clouds to the south. They need not have worried. The scorecard for this battle was an impressive one, and notably one-sided. All told, the Japanese had lost two battleships, three cruisers, and four destroyers as a result of this last of the great gun and torpedo battles. By comparison, one U.S. destroyer and several PT boats had been damaged in the action. One of the PTs was sunk, but no other U.S. ships had been lost. Exact personnel casualty figures for the Japanese are unknown, but they were in the thousands. The United States had lost but 39 men, with another 114 wounded.

As 25 October 1944 got under way, the U.S. Navy had dealt another devastating blow to its Imperial Japanese counterpart. But the Battle of Leyte Gulf was not yet over. What naval historian Samuel Eliot Morison later dubbed "the main action" had not yet occurred. Only a few more hours were left to this greatest of all sea battles, but before they were over, many more ships and men would perish.

"Charge of the Light Brigade"

Despite the one-sided victory in Surigao Strait, the potential for disaster loomed rather large on the morning of the 25th. The day before, Third Fleet reconnaissance aircraft had detected Ozawa's decoy force coming down from the north, and Halsey had taken the bait. Mistakenly believing that his earlier strikes in the Sibuyan Sea had eliminated Kurita's fleet, the aggressive Admiral Halsey took his entire fleet northward in pursuit of Ozawa's carrier forces, leaving the entrance to San Bernardino Strait unguarded. With Halsey's massive striking power lured northward and Kinkaid's Seventh Fleet punch drawn southward to cover Surigao Strait, the landing forces in the gulf were left virtually unprotected and would be easy pickings for a marauding force of gunships such as the one on its way through San Bernardino Strait. Confused communications caused by an awkward command structure and by some unwarranted assumptions on the part of both Halsey and Kinkaid had exacerbated the situation.

Thus, the only element left between Kurita and the vulnerable transports in the gulf were the Seventh Fleet escort carriers (CVEs) and their accompanying destroyers. Any tactician worth his salt could see that this was no great obstacle. They were ill prepared for a surface battle of any description, much less one with a force of Kurita's size and power.

So, by a combination of clever tactical deception and dogged determination on the part of the Japanese, and poor communications and some misjudgment on the part of the U.S. Navy, the greatly outclassed Japanese fleet had managed to set itself up for what just days before had seemed impossible. Despite the costly setbacks in Palawan Passage, the Sibuyan Sea, and Surigao Strait, the Japanese had achieved the main objective of their elaborate plan. The door was open to Leyte Gulf.

Admiral Kurita steamed through that open door during the night of 24–25 October, emerging from San Bernardino Strait into the Philippine Sea with the expectation of running headlong into waiting U.S. forces. All he found was an empty sea.

Expecting to be pounced on at any moment, Kurita headed south. For the next six-and-a half hours anxious Japanese eyes scanned the surface for ominous shadows, while weary ears listened to the strange chorus echoing in the ocean's depths, trying to discern manmade sounds from the natural ones residing there. As the sky brightened in the east, the tension level increased. Soon the skies, too, would be potentially hostile as U.S. war-birds left their nocturnal roosts to begin their diurnal search for prey.

Finally, just before 0630, lookouts spotted several masts piercing the horizon to the southeast. They were the telltale thin masts of U.S. ships, and as Kurita turned his formation toward them, more masts appeared on the horizon. It soon became clear that a sizable U.S. force lay ahead. Probably because the Japanese were expecting to encounter Halsey's powerful Third Fleet, the lookouts began mistakenly reporting the U.S. ships as full-size carriers, cruisers, and even battleships, instead of the Seventh Fleet CVEs and escorts that they actually were. By this error the

Japanese forfeited a great psychological advantage, entering the battle with a fatalistic feeling of sacrifice and little hope of victory rather than with the confidence that should have accompanied this tremendous tactical advantage.

Nevertheless, Kurita did not hesitate to attack, and he ordered his fleet to engage the enemy. Within minutes, the *Yamato*'s mighty 18.1-inch guns were firing for the first time at enemy shipping. The Battle off Samar was under way.

Ironically, this was the anniversary of the Crimean War's Battle of Balaclava, in which a much inferior British cavalry unit charged against the heavy artillery of the Russians, inspiring Alfred Lord Tennyson to write his immortal poem, "The Charge of the Light Brigade." In a similar act of suicidal courage, the U.S. destroyers and destroyer escorts of the vulnerable escort carriers came about and charged headlong at the giant Japanese attackers. Furthermore, although they were not equipped to fight heavily armored ships, the escort carriers' aircraft also attacked the oncoming Japanese battleships and cruisers.

What followed was one of the wildest melees in naval history, marked by errors of judgment, innovative tactics, terrible carnage, and selfless valor. The U.S. escort ships and aircraft had no hope of defeating, nor even inflicting serious damage upon their Japanese adversaries. Yet they attacked with a tenacity that rivals the awe-inspiring feats of John Paul Jones, Stephen Decatur, and David Farragut. By their sacrificial actions and the confusion that resulted among the Japanese forces, the day was saved. Kurita, still believing he was fighting far more powerful forces, broke off the engagement at the critical moment and retired. In his wake were the sunken remains of four U.S. ships and their noble crews: two destroyers, one destroyer escort, and one aircraft carrier—a terrible loss in human terms; an incredible achievement in terms of the cold calculus of war. By all rights, many more U.S. ships should have been at the bottom of the Philippine Sea.

> When can their glory fade?
> O the wild charge they made!
> All the world wondered.
> Honour the charge they made!
> Honour the Light Brigade,
> Noble six hundred!

Epitaph

Far to the north, Halsey's powerful Third Fleet was engaging Ozawa's force at about the same time the wild melee was proceeding off Samar. The magnitude of the battle of Leyte Gulf comes better into perspective when one considers that this northernmost engagement—in which four aircraft carriers, a cruiser, and two destroyers were sunk—can be reasonably described as anticlimactic. With no insult intended toward those who fought there, this Halsey-Ozawa showdown remembered as the Battle of Cape Engano was almost mundane in comparison to the other actions associated with Leyte Gulf. It was unquestionably one-sided, yet it was indecisive. It was fought by unquestionably brave men, yet there were no unusual feats of bravery recorded. It was the result of a successful diversion on the part of Ozawa, yet Kurita's failure to press his advantage at Samar robbed the diversion of its real impact.

Particularly frustrating was the missed chance for Halsey's battleships to get into the fray. In response to desperate calls for help in the south once Kurita had begun his attack, Halsey had broken off his battleships from the carrier force and headed south in a hopeless chase that served only to place those powerful gunships in a frustrating limbo between battles. Although Halsey would never admit his mistake in going north after Ozawa's decoy force, he would later lament his decision to take his battleships south, saying "I consider this the gravest error I committed during the Battle of Leyte Gulf."

In the final analysis, the battle was not decisive in the same sense that the Battle of Midway had been. What occurred there in Philippine waters did not alter the course of the war. But, perhaps just as significant, the result of the Leyte Gulf battle permitted the course of the war to continue. This has less dramatic appeal than a reversal, but from the U.S. point of view it was no less important. Had the Japanese prevailed in their fairly modest goal of disrupting the landings, the impact on the U.S. conduct of the war could have had some far-reaching consequences.

In trying to convince President Roosevelt of the importance of recapturing the Philippines, MacArthur had warned the president earlier about the postwar ramifications of by-passing this important archipelago, pointing out that U.S. prestige in the Far East would suffer a serious blow if the Philippines were not liberated. A similar loss of credibility could well have resulted from defeat.

This gargantuan sea battle, ensuring the recapture of the Philippines, cut Japan's oil supply lines once and for all. Without oil, it would only be a matter of time before the once-powerful Japanese war machine would grind to a halt.

At battle's end, Japan had lost four aircraft carriers, three battleships (including one of her super-dreadnoughts), nine cruisers, a dozen destroyers, hundreds of aircraft, and thousands of airmen and sailors. It was a tremendous defeat by any standard, and it ensured that the Imperial Japanese Navy had finally been eliminated as a meaningful threat in the Pacific.

About the Author

Commander Cutler is the author of *The Battle of Leyte Gulf: 23–26 October 1944* (New York: Harper Collins Publishers, 1994), the critically acclaimed 50th-anniversary account of the great battle. He also appeared on the Arts & Entertainment documentary "The Battle of Leyte Gulf," which was coproduced by Lou Reda Productions and the Naval Institute (VHS cassette copies are available by calling 800-234-USNI). The former associate chairman of the U.S. Naval Academy's Department of History and 25-year veteran of the U.S. Navy is currently a consulting editor for the U.S. Naval Institute *Proceedings* and this publication. For his book *Brown Water, Black Berets* (Annapolis, MD: Naval Institute Press, 1988) Cutler won the Alfred Thayer Mahan Award for Naval Literature.

THE BATTLE FOR LEYTE GULF

Fleet Admiral William F. Halsey Jr.,
U.S. Navy

Proceedings, May 1952

October 1944 marked the return of General MacArthur to the Philippines. Rangers had gone ashore on some of the islets in the mouth of Leyte Gulf on October 17th. Three days later, General MacArthur ordered his forces ashore on Leyte. They encountered light opposition. And just three days after that, on October 23rd, the battle for Leyte Gulf began. I shall describe this battle as, aboard the USS *New Jersey*, I saw it develop. This description is based on my log and war diaries.

There were two U.S. Fleets in the waters off the Philippines. The *Seventh* Fleet was under command of Vice Admiral Thomas Kinkaid. His superior was General MacArthur. Kinkaid had under his command at Leyte, exclusive of the amphibious forces, six old battleships, sixteen escort carriers, four heavy cruisers, four light cruisers, thirty destroyers, and twelve destroyer escorts, which in itself was a powerful force. Its mission was defensive. It had bombarded the beaches, convoyed the transports to the landing area, and stood by to guard them while they unloaded, and it was to protect them during their retirement.

The *Third* Fleet was under my command. My superior was Admiral Nimitz. My mission was offensive. When I received orders to cover the Leyte landings my mission did not change. It was still offensive. The tasks assigned my force were to gain air supremacy over the Philippines, to protect the landings and to maintain unremitting pressure against Japan, and to apply maximum attrition by all possible means in all areas. Finally, should opportunity for destruction of a major portion of the enemy fleet offer, such destruction would become the primary task of my forces.

If the two fleets had been under the same command, with a single system of operational control and intelligence, the Battle for Leyte Gulf might have been fought differently and with better coordination.

My Fleet was composed of Task Force 38 under Vice Admiral Pete Mitscher. It was divided into four Task Groups. Task Group 38.1 commanded by Vice Admiral McCain, Task Group 38.2 commanded by Rear Admiral Bogan, Task Group 38.3 commanded by Rear Admiral Ted Sherman, and Task Group 38.4 commanded by Rear Admiral Davidson. These Groups were not uniform in strength but averaged a total of 23 ships per group, divided approximately as follows: two large carriers, two light carriers, two new battleships, three cruisers, and fourteen destroyers.

On October 23 we learned from one of our submarines, USS *Darter*, that a sizeable portion of the Japanese Navy was proceeding northwestward in the China Sea and would undoubtedly attempt passage through one of the Straits to reach the Leyte Gulf Area. We had been at sea since October 6 and during the entire time had repeatedly struck air fields and enemy installations on Formosa, Okinawa, and Luzon. We had been under severe enemy air attacks and had been most active throughout this period at sea. We planned to send each of the Groups in rotation into Ulithi for repairs and replenishment, and Task Group 38.1, on October 23rd, was en route to Ulithi for this purpose. The other three Task Groups were standing eastward on the Philippines, awaiting their turn to retire, and meanwhile preparing further offensive strikes in support of MacArthur. On the basis of the *Darter*'s report, I ordered them to close the islands and to launch search teams next morning in a fan that would cover the western sea approaches for the entire length of the chain.

Accordingly, by daylight on October 24, the three carrier groups were disposed off the east coast of the Philippines from Central Luzon to just north of Surigao Strait, from which points they could search and attack any shipping that entered either San Bernardino or Surigao Straits, or the waters immediately to the westward thereof.

Our early searches on the 24th of October found two Japanese Forces: one apparently headed for Surigao Straits (this Force will be hereafter referred to as the Southern Force) and a second and stronger Force in the Sibuyan Sea (hereafter called the Central Force).

The Group on its way to Ulithi was ordered to reverse course and prepare to fuel at sea.

Our planes hit the Central Force repeatedly throughout the day and reported sinking the battleship *Musashi*, three cruisers, and a destroyer, and inflicting severe damage on many other units. These seemed to mill around aimlessly, then withdraw to the west. They were still in the Sibuyan Sea at 1600 on course 290, but later turned east again.

That they might attempt to transit San Bernardino Strait, despite their fearful mauling, was a possibility I had to recognize. Accordingly, at 1512 I sent a preparatory dispatch to all Task Force Commanders in the *Third* Fleet and all Task Group Commanders in Task Group 38, designating four of their fast battleships, with supporting units, and stating that these ships will be formed at Task Force 34 under Vice Admiral Lee, Commander Battle Line, with the mission of engaging decisively at long ranges.

This dispatch, which played a critical part in next day's battle, I intended merely as a warning to the ships concerned that, if a surface engagement offered, I would detach them from Task Force 38, form them in Task Force 34, and send them ahead as a battle line. It was definitely not an executive dispatch, but a battle plan, and was so marked. To make certain that none of my subordinate commanders misconstrued it, I told them later by voice radio: "IF THE ENEMY SORTIES, TASK FORCE 34 WILL BE FORMED WHEN DIRECTED BY ME."

Meanwhile, at 0943, we had intercepted a message from one of Task Group 38.4's search teams, reporting that it had sighted the enemy's Southern Force—two old battleships, three heavy cruisers, one light cruiser, and eight destroyers, southwest of Negros Island, course 060, speed 15 knots—and had scored several damaging hits with bombs and rockets. We did not send a strike against this comparatively weak force.

It was headed for Surigao Strait, where Kinkaid was waiting with approximately three times its weight of metal—six old battleships, four heavy cruisers, four light cruisers, and twenty-one destroyers, plus thirty-nine PTs. Our estimate, at the time, was that this Force would be soundly defeated by Oldendorf's group of the 7th Fleet.

Task Group 38.3, the northernmost Group off Luzon, was under continuing violent attack by carrier planes. The Group shot down 110 of them, but they succeeded in bombing the light carrier *Princeton*, which later had to be abandoned and sunk. The *Birmingham* and three destroyers were damaged by the explosion of the *Princeton*'s magazines and were sent to Ulithi with the *Princeton* survivors.

The discovery of the Southern Force buttressed my conviction that the Japs were committed to a supreme effort, but the final proof was still lacking. There was no naval carrier strength (CVs or CVLs) involved in these known forces converging on the Philippines. It did not seem probable that the Japanese would commit such a large portion of their naval strength without providing some measure of naval air support. The location of their carriers up to this point was a mystery. We believed that a strong carrier Task Force was probably also converging on the Leyte Gulf area from the north, probably having sailed directly from Empire ports. On this basis, orders were issued to the Northern Task Group to conduct an intensive air search to the north and east of their positions to attempt to locate the suspected enemy carrier force.

During the late afternoon reports were received from our Northern Carrier Group 38.3 and from land based air searches that the suspected Japanese Northern Force had actually been located. We had also received information indicating that Commander *Seventh* Fleet was prepared to meet any enemy force which might attempt the passage of Surigao Strait. The enemy force to the north, as reported from our air searches, was shown to consist of practically all the remaining operative Japanese carrier strength plus supporting surface ships, and was thought at the time to be the most formidable threat to our present and future operations in the Western Pacific.

We had all the pieces of the puzzle, and fitting them together, we noticed that the three Forces had a common factor: A speed of advance so leisurely—never more than 15 knots—that it implied a focus of time and place. The crippled Central Force's second approach to San Bernardino against overwhelming strength, after being heavily mauled, was comprehensible only if they were under adamant orders to rendezvous with the other forces off Samar next day, the 24th, for a combined attack on the transports at Leyte.

Three battles offered. The Southern Force I could afford to ignore: it was well within Kinkaid's compass. The Central Force, according to our pilots, had suffered so much topside damage, especially to its guns and fire-control instruments, that it could not win a decision. I believed it, too, could be left to Kinkaid. (The pilots' reports proved dangerously optimistic, but we had little reason to discredit them at the time.) On the other hand, not only was the Northern Force fresh and undamaged, but its carriers gave it a scope several hundred miles wider than the others.

Moreover, if we destroyed those carriers, future operations need fear no major threat from the sea.

We had chosen our antagonist. It remained only to choose the best way to meet him. I had three alternatives:

1. I could guard San Bernardino with my whole fleet and wait for the Northern Force to strike me. Rejected. It yielded to the enemy the double initiative of his carriers and his fields on Luzon that would allow him to use them unmolested.
2. I could guard San Bernardino with Task Force 34 while I struck the Northern Force with my carriers. Rejected. The heavy air attacks on Task Group 38.3 which had resulted in the loss of the *Princeton* indicated that the enemy still had powerful air forces and forbade exposing our battleships without adequate air protection. It is a cardinal principle of naval warfare not to divide one's force to such extent as will permit it to be beaten in detail. If enemy shore based planes joined with his carrier planes, together they might inflict far more damage on my half-fleets separately than they could inflict upon my fleet intact. Furthermore I was confident from the reports of my aviators that Kurita's Force in the Sibuyan Sea had been damaged to such an extent that even if they sortied through San Bernardino Strait, Kinkaid had adequate strength to defend against them.
3. I could leave San Bernardino unguarded and strike the Northern Force with my whole fleet. Accepted. It preserved my Fleet's integrity, it left the initiative with me, and it promised the greatest possibility of surprise. Even if the Central Force meanwhile passed through San Bernardino and headed for Leyte Gulf, it could only hope to harry the landing operation. It could not consolidate any advantage, because of its reported damage. It could merely hit-and-run. I felt Kinkaid was amply strong to handle this situation if it should develop.

My decision was to strike the Northern Force. Given the same circumstances and the same information as I had then, I would make it again.

About 1950 on the 24th, I informed Commander *Seventh* fleet: CENTRAL FORCE HEAVILY DAMAGED ACCORDING TO STRIKE REPORTS. AM PROCEEDING NORTH WITH THREE GROUPS TO

ATTACK CARRIER FORCE AT DAWN. At 2330, I ordered Mitscher: SLOW DOWN TO 16 KNOTS. HOLD PRESENT COURSE UNTIL 2400, THEN PROCEED TOWARD LAT 16 LONG 127 (northeastward). The purpose of this was to permit the three Groups to close up and to avoid over-running the Northern Force's "Daylight Circle," the limit which it could reach by dawn from its last known position. If the enemy slipped past my left flank, between me and Luzon, he would have a free crack at the transports. If he slipped past my right flank, he would be able to shuttle-bomb me—fly from his carriers, attack me, continue on to his fields on Luzon for more bombs and fuel, and attack me again on the way back. I had to meet him head-on. It was also essential to bring him under attack at dawn. Otherwise I would, at least partially, lose the advantage of initiative and surprise. I was trusting the *Independence*'s night search planes to set my course.

They began to report and by daylight the composition of the Northern Force was established as one large carrier, three light carriers, two hermaphrodite battleships with flight deck afts, three light cruisers, and at least eight destroyers.

I ordered Task Force 34 to form and take station 10 miles in advance, and my Task Group Commanders to arm their first deck-load strike and launch it at earliest dawn, and launch a second strike as soon afterwards as possible.

The first strike took off at 0630. At 0850, a flash report reaches me: ONE CARRIER SUNK AFTER TREMENDOUS EXPLOSION. TWO CARRIERS, ONE LIGHT CRUISER HIT BADLY, OTHER CARRIER UNTOUCHED. FORCE COURSE 150 SPEED 17.

We had already increased our speed to 25 knots. If the enemy held his course and speed, he would be under our guns before noon.

At 0648, I had received a dispatch from Kinkaid: AM NOW ENGAGING ENEMY SURFACE FORCES SURIGAO STRAIT. QUESTION IS TASK FORCE 34 GUARDING SAN BERNARDINO STRAIT. To this I replied in some bewilderment: NEGATIVE. IT IS WITH OUR CARRIERS NOW ENGAGING ENEMY CARRIERS. Here was my first intimation that Kinkaid had intercepted and misconstrued the preparatory dispatch I had sent to my Fleet the preceding day. I say "intercepted" because it was not addressed to him, which fact alone should have prevented his confusion. I was not alarmed, because at 0802 I learned from him: ENEMY VESSELS RETIRING SURIGAO STRAIT. OUR LIGHT FORCES IN PURSUIT.

When the Southern Force pushed into Surigao soon after midnight of the 24th, it pushed into one of the prettiest ambushes in naval history. Rear Admiral Jesse B. Oldendorf, Kinkaid's tactical commander, waited until the enemy line was well committed into the narrow waters, then struck from both flanks with his PTs and destroyers, and from dead ahead with his battleships and cruisers. Almost before the Japs could open fire, they lost both their battleships and three destroyers. The rest fled, but the heavy cruiser *Mogami* was badly damaged, later collided with the heavy cruiser *Nachi*, and was sunk by Japanese destroyers about noon. About 1000 on the 25th, Army B-24s sank the light cruiser *Abukuma*, which had been previously torpedoed by our PTs. One of Oldendorf's PTs was sunk, and one destroyer was damaged.

At 0822, twenty minutes after Kinkaid's second dispatch, I received his third: ENEMY BATTLESHIPS AND CRUISERS REPORTED FIRING ON TASK UNIT 77.4.3, FROM 15 MILES ASTERN. Task Unit 77.4.3, commanded by Rear Admiral Clifton A. F. Sprague and comprising six escort carriers, three destroyers, and four destroyer escorts, was the northernmost of three similar Task Units in the *Seventh* Fleet's Task Force 77.4, assigned to guard the eastern approaches to Leyte. The enemy ships were evidently part of the Central Force, which had steamed through San Bernardino during the night. I wondered why search planes had not given warning of the enemy's approach, but I still was not alarmed. I figured that the sixteen little carriers had enough planes to protect themselves until Oldendorf could bring up his heavy ships.

Eight minutes later, at 0830, Kinkaid's fourth dispatch reached me: URGENTLY NEED FAST BATTLESHIPS LEYTE GULF AT ONCE. That surprised me. I was not previously committed to protect the *Seventh* Fleet. My job was offensive, to strike with the *Third* Fleet, and we were even then rushing to intercept a force which gravely threatened not only Kinkaid and myself, but the whole Pacific strategy. However, I ordered McCain, who was fueling to the east: STRIKE VICINITY 11-20 N 127-00 E AT BEST POSSIBLE SPEED,—and so notified Kinkaid.

At 0900 I received his fifth dispatch: OUR LIGHT CARRIERS BEING ATTACKED BY FOUR BATTLESHIPS, EIGHT CRUISERS PLUS OTHERS. REQUEST LEE (Commanding Task Force 34, and Battle Line) COVER LEYTE AT TOP SPEED. REQUEST FAST CARRIERS MAKE IMMEDIATE STRIKE. I had already sent McCain. There was nothing else I could do.

Then came the sixth dispatch, at 0922: COMMANDER TASK UNIT 77.4.3 (Rear Admiral "Ziggy" Sprague's Unit) UNDER ATTACK BY CRUISERS AND BATTLESHIPS 0700 11-40 N 126-25 E. REQUEST IMMEDIATE AIR STRIKE. ALSO REQUEST SUPPORT BY HEAVY SHIPS. MY OLD BATTLESHIPS LOW IN AMMUNITION.

This was a new factor, so astonishing that I could hardly accept it. Why hadn't Kinkaid let me know before? I looked at the date-time group of his dispatch. It was "242225" or 0725 local time, one hour and fifty-seven minutes ago, and when I compared it with the date-time groups of the others, I realized that this was actually his third dispatch, sent eighteen minutes after he had first informed me that Task Unit 77.4.3 was under attack.

My message was on its way to him in five minutes: I AM STILL ENGAGING ENEMY CARRIERS. MCCAIN WITH FIVE CARRIERS FOUR HEAVY CRUISERS HAS BEEN ORDERED ASSIST YOU IMMEDIATELY—and I gave him my position, to show him the impossibility of the fast battleships reaching him.

The next two dispatches arrived close to 1000, almost simultaneously. The first was from Kinkaid again: WHERE IS LEE. SEND LEE. I was impressed by the fact that it had been sent in plain language, not code. I was speculating on its effect. The second dispatch was from CinCPac and asked the location of Task Force 34.

At that moment the Northern Force, with its two remaining carriers crippled and dead in the water, was exactly 42 miles away. However, in view of the urgent request for assistance from Commander *Seventh* Fleet, I directed Task Force 34 and Task Group 38.2 to proceed south toward San Bernardino Strait, and directed Commander Task Force 38 with Task Groups 38.3 and 38.4 to continue attacks against the enemy carrier force.

I notified Kinkaid: TASK GROUP 38.2 PLUS SIX FAST BATTLESHIPS PROCEEDING LEYTE BUT UNABLE TO ARRIVE BEFORE 0800 TOMORROW.

While I rushed south, Task Groups 38.3 and 38.4 repeatedly struck the Northern Force and late that afternoon it retired in straggling disorder. When it was over the score for the Northern Force was:

Sunk—four carriers, one light cruiser, and two destroyers.

Slightly damaged—two battleships, one light cruiser, and two destroyers.

A curious feature of this engagement is that the air duel never came off. Our strikes found scarcely a handful of planes on the enemy carriers' decks and only fifteen on the wing. We assumed that the rest had ferried into

Luzon, and that our attack had caught them by surprise, because during the morning our radars picked up large groups of bogeys approaching from the westward, but they presently reversed course and disappeared.

Meanwhile, Kinkaid had been sending me another series of dispatches: ENEMY RETIRING TO NORTHEASTWARD. Later: LIGHT CARRIERS AGAIN THREATENED BY ENEMY SURFACE FORCES. Still later: SITUATION AGAIN VERY SERIOUS. YOUR ASSISTANCE BADLY NEEDED. LIGHT CARRIERS RETIRING LEYTE GULF. Finally, at 1145: ENEMY FORCE OF THREE BATTLESHIPS, TWO HEAVY CRUISERS, NINE DESTROYERS, 11–43 N. 126–12 E., COURSE 225, SPEED 20.

This position was 55 miles northeast of Leyte Gulf, but the course was not toward the entrance. Moreover, the dispatch had been filed two hours before I received it, and I had no clue as to what had happened since then. The strongest probability was that the enemy would eventually retrace his course through San Bernardino Strait, and my best hope of intercepting him was to send my fastest ships in advance.

I threw a screen of light cruisers and destroyers around the battleships *New Jersey* and *Iowa* as Task Group 34.5, and told them on TBS: PREPARE FOR 30 KNOTS AND BE READY FOR NIGHT ACTION. I also notified Kinkaid that we would arrive off San Bernardino at 0100 next morning, seven hours earlier than my original schedule.

I was puzzled by the Central Force's hit-and-run tactics and still more puzzled when I learned the complete story. Four battleships, six heavy cruisers, two light cruisers, and eleven destroyers which had survived our air attacks on October 24th had transited San Bernardino that night, while two destroyers remained until the sinking of *Musashi* and the damaged *Myoko*. When they were sighted next, at 0631 on the 25th, they were only 20 miles northwest of Sprague's Task Unit.

The enemy continued to close, and presently his fire began to take toll. Sprague's losses to the guns were three ships from the screen, and one escort carrier.

At 1050 the enemy's shore-based air struck, but at 1310 planes from Task Group 38.1 arrived. In the emergency, McCain had launched them from far outside their range of return. After their attack, they had to land and rearm at Tacloban and Dulag fields on Leyte, which had fallen to MacArthur only a few days before. Together with planes from Task Group 77.4, they sank a light cruiser and a destroyer and damaged most of the other ships. Task Group 77.4 had lost 105 planes.

The Central Force was in full retreat by late afternoon, and by 2200 it was reentering San Bernardino, with my force still two hours away. However, shortly after midnight one of my van destroyers made contact with a straggler, and sank it. This was our last surface action.

Thus ended the major action of the threefold Battle for Leyte Gulf. Six of our ships had been sunk and thirteen damaged. In my official report, I was able to write with conviction that the results of the battle were: "(1) The utter failure of the Japanese plan to prevent the reoccupation of the Philippines; (2) the crushing defeat of the Japanese Fleet; and (3) the elimination of serious naval threat to our operations for many months, if not forever." The Japanese had lost one large carrier, three light carriers, three battleships, six heavy cruisers, and nine destroyers.

In all of the foregoing I have attempted to describe the battle as it unfolded before my eyes at the time, using only the information which was available then. No battle of such magnitude can be fought without someone getting hurt. The later established facts that no Japanese air attacks developed from Luzon on the 25th; that the Central Force suffered less damage due to air attacks on the 24th than originally reported; and that this force did finally make its sortie from San Bernardino Strait to surprise the *Seventh* Fleet. Units could not be determined in advance. Only "Monday Morning Quarterbacks" can speak of such items with certainty. As seen on the afternoon of the 24th and as viewed in retrospect, a Japanese Carrier Force to the north, particularly if allowed the initiative, was the most urgent and serious threat to the final success of our forces.

After the surrender, the U.S. Strategic Bombing Survey learned, from the study of Japanese documents and the interrogation of Japanese naval officers, the Japanese plans for the Battle of Leyte Gulf.

The Japanese were divided into three forces, the Northern, designated Mobile Attack Force; the Central, designated Second Diversionary Attack Force; and the Southern, divided into two forces designated the First Diversionary Attack Force and "C" Force.

The plan called for two segments of the Southern Force to enter Leyte Gulf via Surigao Strait and attack the transports and supporting units off the Leyte beach-head. The Central Force was to arrive in Leyte Gulf via San Bernardino Strait two hours later and attack what remained of our forces after their engagement by the Southern Force. The planes from the carriers in the Northern Force had been launched on October 24, and had attacked Task Force 38.3 and then landed on Luzon, from which point they were to continue to attack our forces within range. Few planes remained aboard these carriers. The carriers were to permit themselves to be attacked by my Task Forces so that my Fleet would be pulled north and brought under attack by land based planes in Formosa and Luzon. The Japanese northern forces were expendable so long as they gave the southern forces the opportunity to destroy our forces lying off the beaches at Leyte.

The plan failed because the Southern Force never passed Admiral Oldendorf's Force and the Central Force was so badly damaged by air strikes on October 24 that it was retiring and had so advised CinC Combined Fleet. However, CinC Combined Fleet on receipt of this message sent the following dispatch: "With confidence in heavenly guidance the entire force will attack." The Central Force again changed its course toward San Bernardino Strait. The attack on Sprague's Forces were broken off and the enemy withdrew without pressing into the Gulf because the air and torpedo attack launched by Kinkaid's Forces had further damaged his communication and fire-control facilities, had resulted in severe damage to four of his cruisers, and had caused his force to fall into disorder. Furthermore, he was far behind schedule and he was afraid of our air attacks. When he heard that the Northern Force was attacking my fleet he decided to join this attack, but when no engagement offered in daylight he retired through San Bernardino. The Northern Force was disposed of by my Task Forces.

In conclusion I would like to emphasize certain principles and lessons which were illustrated by this action.

It had always been a cardinal principle of our naval tactics to bring all force of the opposing enemy under effective attack. In modern naval warfare there is no greater threat than that offered by an enemy carrier force. To leave such a force untouched and to attack it with anything less than overwhelming destructive force would not only violate this proven principle but in this instance would have been foolhardy in the extreme.

The battle also illustrates the necessity for a single naval command in a combat area responsible for and in full control of all combat units involved. Division of operational control in a combat area leads at the least to confusion, lack of coordination, and overloaded communications, and could result in disaster.

For two and a half days during the progress of this battle my communication officers decoded no dispatch on the circuit linking me with Commander *Seventh* Fleet that had a precedence lower than urgent. Much of this traffic consisted of intelligence summaries of previous unrelated action and other matters not directly related to the tactical situation of the battle. I am certain there should always be a command circuit linking all commanders in a combat area which is kept clear of all traffic except that of an urgent tactical nature.

The Battle for Leyte Gulf stands as a tribute to the effective employment of seapower and sea-air-power and of close mutual support. There was glory in it for all.

The credit for our overwhelming victory belongs in full measure to all who participated in its many phases and most particularly to those pilots and sailors who made the supreme sacrifice in order that our cause might prevail.

About the Author

Graduating from the Naval Academy in the Class of 1904, **Admiral Halsey** was a destroyer skipper in World War I. Progressing through higher commands, taking Naval War College and Army War College courses, and qualifying as a naval aviator in 1934, he became first commanding officer of the *Saratoga*, then Commandant, Naval Air Station, Pensacola, and, in 1940, Commander Aircraft Battle Force with the rank of Vice Admiral. During World War II, as a leader of the greatest naval force ever assembled, he opened up the road to Tokyo.

At Admiral Halsey's request, the Naval Institute has sent payment for this article to the Naval Historical Foundation's Endowment Trust Fund.

ADMIRAL OLDENDORF COMMENTS ON THE BATTLE OF SURIGAO STRAIT

Vice Adm. Jesse B. Oldendorf, USN (Ret.)

Proceedings, April 1959

This article appeared in the Comment & Discussion section of the magazine and is Admiral Oldendorf's response to an article published in the December 1958 *Proceedings*, which was an excerpt from Samuel Eliot Morison's book *Leyte: June 1944–January 1945* (Volume XII of his monumental series *History of United States Naval Operations in World War II*).

※ ※ ※

Since the account of the operations during the Battle of Surigao Strait was written from available records which are not always complete or which contain information gleaned from many sources many months or years after the event, it might be of interest to future historians to know how the picture looked to the officer in command from information available to him at the time.

Radio contact reports from our aircraft and submarines had definitely alerted me to the possible intentions and to the composition of the Central and Southern Forces of Admirals Kurita and Nishimura, so that Admiral Kinkaid's order to prepare for night action came as no surprise. Admiral Kinkaid's order stated that a force of approximately two battleships, three heavy cruisers, three light cruisers and ten destroyers could be at the northern end of Surigao Strait by midnight. (I did not know until several months later that there were actually two separate commands in this Southern Force.) It was obvious that the objective of the Japanese Forces was the destruction of our transports and that my mission was to protect them at all costs. In order to accomplish my mission, the force under my command must be interposed between the enemy and the transports. I realized that I must not lose sight of my mission no matter how much I might be tempted to engage in a gunnery duel with him.

I selected the position of the battle line off Hingatungan Point because it gave me the maximum sea room available and restricted the enemy's movements. This position also permitted me to swing my battle line to cover the eastern entrance to the Gulf should the Central Force under Admiral Kurita arrive ahead of the Southern Force. I selected the battle plan from the General Tactical Instructions and modified it to meet the conditions existing, i.e., lack of sea room to maneuver and possible enemy action. I was quite sure that the Japanese commander knew the size and composition of my force as enemy planes had been present over the area since shortly after our arrival. With this knowledge, I supposed that he had a plan to circumvent me.

I thought that quite possibly he planned to slip some of his light forces into the Gulf by passing them to the eastward of Hibuson Island after the battle line was engaged. For that reason I stationed the preponderance of my light forces on the left flank. One duty which was never delegated to my staff was the drafting of battle plans.

When the dispositions and functions of the various types had been determined, it would be necessary to make the maximum use of my destroyers' major weapon—torpedoes—because of the shortage of major caliber service ammunition and for that reason the gun battle should be fought at short ranges in order to obtain the maximum number of hits. I sent for Admirals Weyler and Berkey and explained my plan in detail and asked for their comment. I met with their unqualified approval. I then turned the plan over to my staff to be put into despatch form to be sent out by visual signal as there was insufficient time to code and decode if sent by radio. The various units of my force were in position by shortly after sundown and the patrol of the twelve and a half mile east-west line at five knots commenced. This very low speed was selected to avoid more frequent reversals of course by simultaneous ship turns. The problem of handling this large force in these narrow waters with its swift and changing currents and ships keeping in position could not have been accomplished without excellent radar (SG) and high frequency radio telephone (TBS). The navigation problem was expertly handled by Commander John Sylvester, USN, of my staff—now Vice Admiral Sylvester.

To the best of my recollection, after I had informed Admirals Kinkaid and Wilkinson of my intentions, Admiral Wilkinson placed Desron 54 (Captain Coward) under my command and so informed him. I then directed Captain Coward to patrol an east-west line about 40,000 yards south of the battle line and upon the approach of the Japanese force to report its formation, course, and speed. Captain Coward then informed me that he expected to attack with torpedoes after getting off his report. He was directed to submit his battle plan, which was to attack in two sections, one from the east and one from the west. I approved his plan, but directed that each section retire to its own side of the Strait after delivering its attack and then proceed north. There were two reasons for these instructions: first, I did not believe that the Japanese radar could follow his ships against the high background of the Strait and, second, I did not want his ships to foul the range for other attacks. In a night action the movements of the various components of a command must be accurately known or the action will develop into a melee with individual units unable to determine friend from foe. How capably Captain Coward, his commanding officers, and men performed their tasks is too well known to require from me more than a very "well done."

At about the same time as Admiral Wilkinson's message to Captain Coward and me, Admiral Kinkaid informed me that he had sent all of the Seventh Fleet Motor Torpedo Squadrons, under Commander S. S. Bowling, down the Strait. They were to remain south of a line latitude 10 degrees 10 minutes, to report enemy progress, and to attack if opportunity presented. Intermingled with contact reports from the MTBs was one reporting that his boat had hit something hard, which he believed to be a submarine. His position as given was near the head of the Japanese column. This report led me to consider the possibility that the enemy had submarines in advance of his column. I now think it quite possible that the young skipper did not know his position accurately and that he hit either a rock or some other obstruction.

In the version of the battle as printed in the *Proceedings* is this sentence: "Admiral Oldendorf still had another destroyer squadron to throw at Nishimura before opening gun fire. This was Captain Smoot's Destroyer Squadron 56, which had *the duty of screening* the left flank cruisers" (italics supplied). This squadron was concentrated in an approach formation stationed between the left flank cruisers and the battle line so as to be out of gun range and available to the OTC for a torpedo attack when ordered. If this squadron had been intended as a screen, it would hardly have been concentrated and only on one side (the wrong one from where a possible attack would come).

My one anxiety during the early stages of the battle was that the enemy would not keep coming toward me. If his radar located the position of my battle line, he might reverse course before coming within gun range. If he did so, I knew that I would be strongly tempted to go after him. By doing so, I would give up the advantage of my position and might uncover the Strait for one or more of his ships to slip through.

After ordering Desron 56 to attack, but before the division under Captain Smoot's personal command (*Newcomb*, *Leary* and *Grant*) could reach its firing point, which was directly ahead of the enemy column, it was taken under very heavy fire by the leading ship in that column. To cover Smoot's attack, I gave the order to commence firing. The gunnery officers must have been riding the triggers of their guns, because hardly had the words left my lips to be repeated over the telephone by my flag lieutenant, than the *Louisville* (my flagship) let fly with her first salvo without waiting to give the usual warning buzzer. The gun fire phase of the battle was on, and quite a pyrotechnic display it was. By increasing speed to fifteen knots the leading battleship, *West Virginia*, had reached a position so that her first salvo passed directly over the *Louisville*. It sounded like a train of box cars passing over a high trestle. Following this salvo with my binoculars, I had the satisfaction of seeing it land squarely on the forecastle of the leading ship (*Tamashiro*) of the enemy's column. The six-inch cruisers, using flashless powder, were firing so rapidly that the whole sky surrounding them was one incandescent glow.

I gave the order to cease firing at 0409 when I learned that some of our own ships were firing on the *A. W. Grant* and as we were rapidly running out of enemy ships within range. I did not like the idea of using our own ships as substitute targets. Consulting the radar screen, I determined that the enemy force, made up mostly of cripples, was retiring. I ordered Division Xray to assemble, then to proceed down the Strait and attack with torpedoes. Before proceeding down the Strait with the left flank cruisers, I directed the battle line (Admiral Weyler) to remain in position. Division Xray could not be located on my radar screen and I did not know whether it was ahead or astern of me. I could see gunfire ahead at each side of the Strait which I thought was destroyers firing. If friendly, I did not want to fire on them; if enemy, I was running into a perfect torpedo set-up. My staff was keeping a running check to warn me when my ships were getting into torpedo areas. When so informed, I ordered column right to course 250 and after firing on the *Mogami* and a destroyer which was standing by at 0537, I ordered ships right 18 to dodge torpedoes if they had been fired and to wait for daylight.

It might not be out of place to remark at this point that I could never understand how the *Nachi* managed to collide with the *Mogami*. The *Mogami* was on fire and burning like a gigantic torch. That collision was worse than running ashore in clear weather at the base of a lighthouse.

Shortly before or just after I turned south with my left flank force in pursuit of the retiring enemy remnants, I learned that Kurita's Central Force had passed out of San Bernardino Strait about midnight. Whether this information came from a patrol plane (Black Cat) or a submarine, I do not remember. It is not mentioned in Admiral Morison's book *Leyte* and I suppose not in the War College Analysis, although I have never seen that paper. I feel sure that I had this information from some source because it influenced my actions. I did not want to expose my ships needlessly to torpedo attacks or to proceed too far from the eastern entrance to the Gulf.

At 0732, when I received the report that battle had been joined off Samar between Kurita's Central Force and Admiral Sprague's escort carriers, I was ordered to concentrate my force as soon as possible at the northern end of Surigao Strait, to report when concentrated and the amount of ammunition remaining by ships. My staff was put to work assembling this much needed information. When it had been reported, I received orders to go to the relief or assistance of Sprague. I was to divide my force and to take only the ships with the greatest amount of ammunition augmented by destroyers from the amphibious command (they had their full quota of torpedoes) plus the light cruiser *Nashville*. After a couple of false starts, my force proceeded out of the eastern entrance for quite some distance when it was recalled by Admiral Kinkaid because Kurita's Central Force had had enough from Admiral Sprague and was retiring north. I then took station with my force patrolling the eastern entrance (inside) where I had intended to be before the diversion in support of the escort carriers.

When, despite the vocal dissent of my chief of staff, I proceeded out of the Strait in obedience to Admiral Kinkaid's order, I felt that the Commander of the Seventh Fleet knew as well as I that we were committing a strategical error. There was no choice on my part, nor on his. An important segment of his command was being badly mauled by a greatly superior force. Though I have never discussed this point with Admiral Kinkaid, I believe that he was in much the same position as a gentleman who comes upon a thug beating a woman. He may be reluctant to become involved in a brawl, but he cannot stand idly by and see a woman beaten.

I agree with Admiral Morison's comment that the most intelligent act of any Japanese commander in the entire battle was Admiral Shima's retirement. Departing from what did happen to what might have happened: Supposing that Admiral Sprague had intercepted the messages (or hunch) which I did that Admiral Kurita's Central Force had passed out of San Bernardino Strait at midnight, he would undoubtedly have withdrawn his command of escort carriers from the direct line between San Bernardino and Surigao Straits. Kurita, then encountering no opposition, might have continued on south until he met my force with its greatly depleted ammunition supply at or near the eastern entrance to the Gulf of Leyte. I had planned to greet him in much the same manner as I had Nishimura, use the torpedoes of my light forces covering them with gun fire while the service ammunition lasted, then to shift to H.E. and hope for the best. While thus occupied, it would have been a comparatively simple matter for Shima to return for a go at the transports. Needless to say, I was very glad that this situation did not develop.

LEYTE GULF
The First Uncensored Japanese Account
——— James A. Field Jr. ———

Proceedings, March 1951

Throughout the war the Japanese government pursued a systematic policy of falsifying news from the fighting fronts in order to bolster its own position and to maintain home front morale. No matter what their outcome, all battles—Midway, the Marianas, Leyte Gulf—were reported as famous victories. Americans who followed the Japanese communiques will remember the series of disasters that the United States there suffered, being reduced first to a sixth-rate naval power, then to fifth-rate status, then to fourth, third, and second-rate positions as the result of repeated "defeats."

Following the arrival of American occupation forces in Japan, restrictions on accurate reporting of the course of the war were removed. It was obviously important to set the record straight and to explain to the Japanese public how such an unsurpassed series of victories had led to such utter defeat. It was important not alone for academic reasons of historical accuracy, but also as a vital step in the re-education of the Japanese, and as an object lesson in what happens when a people permits totalitarian control of all sources of information.

Probably the most important early step in this direction was the notable series of articles dealing with the events of the Pacific War which appeared shortly after the surrender in *Asahi Shimbun*, a leading Tokyo newspaper. The narrative here given is a translation of the fifth and last article of this series, which appeared in the issue of October 18, 1945. It is of historical interest not only as the first uncensored account of the Battle for Leyte Gulf to be given the Japanese people, but also because it helps to clarify certain obscure and important aspects of the operation. Where the article is in error, footnotes have been added. Some of its implications are discussed in the commentary which follows.

HOW THE COMBINED FLEET PERISHED

Rush into Leyte Fails—Tragedy off the Philippines

Air Fight off Formosa

After MacArthur's Army and Nimitz's Marines, advancing simultaneously, landed on Morotai and Peleliu Islands on September 15, 1944, their intention of charging into the Philippines from these island bases became apparent. Since the Philippines provided the best theater for our air force to maneuver from its shore bases, we had long been preparing for decisive battle there in the hope of arresting the advance of the U.S. forces and of turning the tide of the war in our favor.

The First Air Fleet (under the command first of Vice Admiral Kempei Teraoka and, from October, of Vice Admiral Takajiro Onishi), which had retreated from Yap in the Central Pacific to Davao and thence to Clark, was to cooperate with the Army Air Forces in the Philippines. The Second Air Fleet (under the command of Vice Admiral Shigeru Fukudome) was to send part of its strength to Formosa, its headquarters remaining in Kajima Prefecture, Kyushu. The latter Fleet created from its best trained pilots a special "T" Attack Force, ready to dash to the Philippines. "T" Attack Force was composed of approximately 600 planes, and was named for "Typhoon." In view of the painful experience of Yahata Squadron which, owing to the bad weather, had been unable to fly to Iwo Jima and cooperate with the fleet in the Battle of the Marianas, thus contributing to that defeat, "T" Attack Force had undergone the most rigorous training so that it could overcome even a typhoon.

In advance of the landings in the Philippines, the U.S. Third Fleet staged a full-scale attack on Formosa on October 12, 1944. Our Base Air Forces, with "T" Attack Force from Kajima as the key unit, met the enemy off the shore of Formosa. However, we were obliged to rely chiefly on night operations so that the results were difficult to ascertain and were consequently considerably exaggerated, with fires often being counted as sinking ships. Consequently, despite the announcement of a tremendous victory, the U.S. Fleet was far from annihilated. Furthermore, as a result of the distance and bad weather, the First Air Fleet in the Philippines had only been able to play a small part in the battle.

Formation of the Kamikaze Force

While our Base Air Forces were diverted by the battle off Formosa, the U.S. Seventh Fleet forced its way into Leyte Gulf on October 17, and the intentions of the U.S. Marines [sic] of landing on Leyte became plain. Our air forces hastily broke off the battle off Formosa, and the Second Air Fleet was hurried to the Philippines to join the forces there. However, our operational strength had suffered seriously owing to the heavy attrition of the best-trained elements in the battle off Formosa. Additionally, there was a very serious shortage of fighter planes, and we were far from confident of victory over the U.S. Fleet. Therefore Commander-in-Chief Onishi decided that there was no way of destroying the aircraft carriers other than by striking them with loaded planes, and on the 19th he ordered the establishment of the Kamikaze force. The Shikishima Squadron was the first Kamikaze unit to reach the front in the battle off the coast of the Philippines.

Prior to the battle off Formosa, the First Mobile Fleet had undergone very arduous training in the neighborhood of Bungo Strait. The Second Fleet with its battleships was based at Lingga, south of Singapore, close to the source of oil supply. The Fifth Fleet, which since the beginning of the war had been stationed in the North Pacific, was in home waters.

The First Mobile Fleet, after the loss of three aircraft carriers and a great number of pilots in the Battle of the Marianas, had been reinforced by the battleships *Ise* and *Hyuga*, remodeled into semi-aircraft carriers. During the battle off Formosa, however, it had been obliged to yield its 200 best planes to the newly formed "T" Attack Force without receiving replacements; consequently it was compelled to reinforce with less well-trained pilots from anti-submarine units, and the carriers were forced to embark such outdated models as Type 97 fighter planes. The result was that by the time of the battle off the Philippines the military skill of the carrier squadrons had greatly deteriorated.

It was nevertheless evident that with the Philippines under the control of the U.S. Army the transportation of fuel from the South Sea oilfields to the homeland would be suspended completely, thus consigning our fleets, which consumed a great deal of oil, to the same fate as the Italian Navy. Therefore it was finally decided that we should take the offensive and force a final decisive battle rather than sit back and wait to be annihilated. Thus a dash of the entire fleet had been worked out, and on October 18 Sho 1 Operation was ordered.

The organization of the fleet was as follows. Main Body of the Mobile Fleet under Vice Admiral Jisaburo Ozawa: Carrier Division 3, carriers *Zuikaku, Zuiho, Chitose, Chiyoda*; Carrier Division 4, *Ise, Hyuga*; Cruiser Division 10, *Oyodo, Tama, Kiso, Isuzu*; plus destroyers *Akitsuki, Hatsuzuki, Wakatsuki, Shimotsuki*, and four *Maki*-type destroyers.

First Diversion Attack Force under Vice Admiral Takeo Kurita (Commander Second Fleet): Battleship Division 1, *Yamato, Musashi, Nagato*; Battleship Division 3, *Kongo, Haruna*; Cruiser Division 4, *Atago, Takao, Chokai, Maya*; Cruiser Division 5, *Myoko, Haguro*; Cruiser Division 7, *Suzuya, Kumano, Tone, Chikuma*; Destroyer Squadron 2, *Noshiro* and destroyers; from Destroyer Squadron 10, *Yahagi* and *Tsuki*-type destroyers. Second Diversion Attack Force under Vice Admiral Kiyohide Shima (Commander Fifth Fleet): *Nachi, Ashigara, Abukuma*. Scheduled to join en route from the First Diversion Attack Force were Battleship Division 2, *Fuso, Yamashiro*, plus *Mogami* and four destroyers including *Shigure*.

Immediately following the order for Sho 1 Operation, the First Diversion Attack Force sortied from Lingga and the Second Diversion Attack Force from Amami Oshima. On the 20th the First Diversion Attack Force was at Brunei and the Second Diversion Attack Force at Bako, and on the same day the Main Body left Bungo Strait for the south. On the 21st the Second Diversion Attack Force was south of Bako, and on the following day the First Diversion Attack Force sailed northeastward from Brunei. Thus we were advancing toward Leyte Gulf from three directions.

The plan of the operation was as follows. The First Diversion Attack Force was to dash into Leyte Gulf from the north before daybreak of the 25th via the Sulu Sea and San Bernardino Strait. The Second Diversion Attack Force was to join the second detachment composed of *Yamashiro, Fuso, Mogami*, and others in the Sulu Sea, and dash into Leyte Gulf via Surigao Strait; thus the Gulf was to be attacked from both north and south at the same time. With the cooperation of the Base Air Forces, the fleets were to destroy the shipping in the Gulf, thus cutting off the retreat of the American forces ashore. The Main Body of the Mobile Fleet was to attract the U.S. Task Force east of Luzon and create a diversion. It was thus intended to assist the two Diversion Attack Forces from the rear and, so to speak, it was a kind of decoy bird sacrificed to make a trap.

Battle of Leyte

Shortly after the First Diversion Attack Force had left Brunei, *Myoko* was hit by a torpedo from a submarine and forced to leave the squadron. Near

Palawan Strait, First Diversion Attack Force was subjected to a concentrated torpedo attack by several submarines: *Atago* was sunk and *Takao* disabled and forced to turn back while making emergency repairs. On the 24th First Diversion Attack Force was subjected to six air raids in the course of the day and many warships, including *Musashi* and *Nagato*, were damaged. A dispatch was therefore sent to Combined Fleet Headquarters requesting permission to stop the advance and retire. Headquarters, however, ordered the advance to continue, and in the evening of the same day Admiral Toyoda, Commander-in-Chief of the Combined Fleet, sent a dispatch of encouragement to the entire Fleet, saying that it should advance in confidence of divine assistance. First Diversion Attack Force therefore continued eastward and before daybreak of the 25th passed through San Bernardino Strait. East of Samar, however, it encountered a group of U.S. aircraft carriers.

The U.S. fleet did not seem to have expected us at this point, as they were aware of our having turned back from their reconnaissance flights of the evening before. It was also beyond our expectations, and it was a very sudden event to both sides. The time was 0700. Our battleships opened fire simultaneously, *Yamato* firing her main battery at a range of some 20,000 meters.

After three or four salvoes from *Yamato* and *Musashi* [sic], one enemy aircraft carrier was instantly sunk, and another carrier listed heavily and began to sink. The rest of the enemy fleet was put to flight and disappeared into a squall. We pressed the enemy very hard and observed a huge hole on the damaged aircraft carrier which stretched from the port side to the starboard. The main battery of *Yamato*, which had a bore of 45 centimeters, struck right hard! The Tenth Destroyer Squadron sank two aircraft carriers by torpedo attack. Thus we achieved the unusual result of sinking carriers by gun and torpedoes.

First Diversion Attack Force turned southward again to carry out the original mission. However, a dispatch was received with the news that Second Diversion Attack Force had been annihilated, and the advance toward Leyte was broken off. First Diversion Attack Force headed toward the north in search of the U.S. Task Force but without results, and it then had to head homeward on account of shortage of fuel in the destroyers. During the retirement, *Musashi* capsized as the result of flooding, and at 2100 finally sank to the bottom of the sea near the Philippine Islands. *Kongo* also sank in mid-November, while returning to the home islands from Formosa after this battle.

As for the Second Diversion Attack Force, after joining *Fuso*, *Yamashiro*, *Mogami*, and others, it approached Leyte Gulf via Surigao Strait with *Nachi* and *Ashigara* in the rear. Second Diversion Attack Force had, however, been subject to constant attacks from torpedo boats. When we approached the entrance to Leyte Gulf at 0300 of the 25th, *Fuso*, *Yamashiro*, and *Mogami* were sunk instantly under the concentrated fire of the U.S. fleet which had been awaiting us behind islands on both sides of the Strait. The U.S. fleet was hiding itself behind the islands and thus our radar was of no use for the moment, a matter of the greatest disadvantage.

On sighting the sinking vanguard ships, *Nachi* and *Ashigara* turned around after firing torpedoes and headed toward home. During the retirement they were damaged by air raids. *Abukuma* was sunk by an attack from torpedo boats. Shortly afterward, *Nachi* was sunk by air attack at Manila Bay. Thus both First and Second Diversion Attack Forces were unable to achieve the first objective of the operation—to dash into Leyte Gulf and destroy the shipping.

Four Carriers and Three Battleships Lost

The Main Body of the Mobile Fleet, for its part, was discovered by a U.S. submarine shortly after leaving Bungo Strait. While moving southward it discovered, on the morning of the 24th, the U.S. Task Force, including three aircraft carriers, east of Luzon. At 0800 the Zed flag was hoisted to the top of the mainmast. In spite of bad weather, two groups of fighter planes attacked the enemy fleet at noon, sinking one carrier and badly damaging a second. Almost all these fighter planes had to land at the bases in Formosa [sic] or the Philippines, thus almost emptying the parent carriers.

In the evening of the same day, the aforementioned dispatch of encouragement from the Commander-in-Chief was received. Pursuant to the original objective of diverting the U.S. Fleet, Carrier Division 4, *Ise* and *Hyuga*, and four destroyers, led the advance. In the morning of the 25th, when Carrier Division 4 turned back and rejoined the Main Body, the first great American air raid began.

Twenty to thirty enemy carrier planes attacked each aircraft carrier, either by dive bombing or by launching torpedoes. Every ship was surrounded by columns of water, and after a while *Chitose* listed heavily to starboard, slowed down, moved on for a while, and then suddenly capsized and disappeared from the surface. From that time on the fleet was subjected to air attacks every thirty to fifty minutes throughout the day. *Zuikaku*, the flagship, lost her radio antennae in the first attack and, owing to her inability to communicate, the headquarters including Commander-in-Chief Ozawa had to transfer to the cruiser *Oyodo*.

Most tragic of all was *Chiyoda*, whose commander was Captain Hideichiro Shiro, a former naval aide to the Imperial Family. In the second attack *Chiyoda* was hit aft and received many near misses, with resultant fire and flooding. She listed heavily, unable to advance. During the attacks the whole crew stuck to the guns and discharged a tremendous antiaircraft fire. In the intervals between attacks, the entire crew concentrated on fighting the fire and the flooding. Once the fire was extinguished and the list almost removed, but the next attack came too soon. On the disappearance of the American planes, the entire crew again resumed the pumping operation. The efforts of a destroyer to take *Chiyoda* in tow were hindered by air raids, so it was decided to abandon her, and the entire crew assembled on deck in order to move to a destroyer. Then another attack forced the men back to the gun positions. Unable to rescue the crew, the Main Body fled northward, and after a while when *Isuzu* came back, *Chiyoda* was no longer there. Probably *Chiyoda* sank to the bottom of the sea, unable to move but continuing to fight back.

In the meantime the two aircraft carriers *Zuikaku* and *Zuiho* also sank as a result of flooding caused by torpedo hits. *Tama*, *Kiso*, and destroyers *Akitsuki* and *Hatsuzuki* all sank. The only survivor ships, *Ise*, *Hyuga*, *Oyodo*, and a few others, returned to their base at Amami O. Shima.

Despite the considerable results achieved by First Diversion Attack Force, the Battle of the Philippine Islands ended with the tragic result of the loss of four aircraft carriers and three battleships. Unable to achieve the final objective of destroying the enemy ships in Leyte Gulf, our Mobile Fleet perished at this battle, not to be reestablished again.

The End of Naval Forces

The organization of our naval forces at the battle of Okinawa last spring was as follows:

Third Air Fleet under the command of Vice Admiral Kempei Teraoka, Fifth Air Fleet under the command of Vice Admiral Matome Ugaki, Tenth Air Fleet under the Command of Vice Admiral Minoru Maeda, at the bases in southern Honshu; plus the First Air Fleet under the command of Vice Admiral Takajiro Onishi, including all remaining air strength, for cooperation from Formosa. Kikusui Operation was decided on, and it was characterized by the use of Kamikaze planes.

In the execution of Kikusui No. 1 Operation, battleship *Yamato*, cruiser *Yahagi*, and three destroyers were formed into a separate Diversion Attack Force under the command of Vice Admiral Seichi Ito, on board the flagship *Yamato*. This force departed Bungo Strait on April 6, in order to join the Okinawa front. However, on the next day, the 7th, all of the vessels were sunk by concentrated bombing and torpedo attack from U.S. planes on the sea south of Kyushu. This was the last spark, marking the end of our naval forces.

From that time the air raids on the main islands increased in intensity, and the remaining ships, unable to move, became good targets for American planes at Kure and Yokosuka naval bases. *Nagata* was considerably damaged at Yokosuka, while only the masts of *Haruna*, *Ise*, and *Hyuga* now appear above the surface at Kure naval base. Thus when the war ended, we had no battleships which were able to move, and only two lesser type aircraft carriers remained afloat.

Thus the people, confident of the preservation of the Combined Fleet and awaiting its activities, were surprised at the truth and driven to a nostalgia for the glorious days of our naval forces.

Commentary

In assessing an account of this sort, information regarding the source is of course of first importance. But, since *Asahi Shimbun* does not identify the author, it is necessary to fall back on internal evidence.

In this connection four attributes of the narrative are noteworthy. There is a general emphasis on aviation matters; the operations of the northern carrier force are stressed; access to naval dispatch files seems indicated by the story of the Surigao Strait action in which the report of the U.S. fleet "hiding itself behind the islands" is a close paraphrase of *Shigure*'s dispatch report of the battle; finally, the summary of the planning phase is a good one and the table of organization of the surface fleets is, with minor exceptions, accurate.

From these observations several tentative conclusions can be drawn. The presumption of access to naval dispatch files and the whole tone of the account indicate that the author was in all probability a naval aviator, and one in a position to know the overall situation. The scanty and inaccurate treatment of the actions of the southern forces make it clear that he was not a member of one of these. The erroneous listing of *Kinu* in Ozawa's command suggests that the circumstantial detail in the account of the Battle off Cape Engano was derived from discussion with the survivors of that action rather than from personal participation.

There is obviously nothing conclusive about this type of reasoning but, accepting it for the sake of argument, it is clear that all conditions can be satisfied if the author is identified as an aviation officer attached to a major staff in the homeland, quite possibly to that of Commander-in-Chief, Combined Fleet. Tentative acceptance of such identification gives the account real historical importance, an importance, oddly enough, greater with respect to its errors than with regard to its statements of fact. Two erroneous statements, at least, serve to shed a little light on questions hitherto obscure.

The first of these is the statement that Kurita was to advance on Leyte Gulf via the Sulu Sea. For although Combined Fleet Headquarters did not specify the route in any of its operation orders, this account indicates that employment of the Sulu Sea route was assumed. Such an assumption is natural, as a glance at the chart will show this to be the most direct of all possible approaches from Brunei Bay to San Bernardino Strait. Nevertheless the First Diversion Attack Force advanced by passing west of Palawan and thence south of Mindoro. Why was this longer approach adopted?

Discussing this question in his action report, Admiral Kurita listed three alternative routes: through the Sulu Sea, via Palawan Passage (the route actually taken), and a course still further to the westward over the Dangerous Ground. In the report the reason for the choice made is stated to have been the difficulty of deploying tankers on the alternative routes within the time available, overall pressure of time in meeting the prescribed schedule, and danger of "large type planes." Consequently, although "submarine hazards were greatest on this route," that along the west side of Palawan was taken.

Of these reasons, that pertaining to tankers seems pointless, as these would be needed only on the return from Leyte and would thus have ample time for deployment. The argument from general shortage of time was presumably decisive in the rejection of an approach via the Dangerous Ground, but as between the other routes acted to strengthen the advantages of the Sulu Sea passage which is 150 miles shorter than that actually taken.

Thus it seems that fear of "enemy large type planes," i.e., of PB4Y air search from Morotai, was the governing consideration, outweighing the disadvantages of greater distance and increased submarine hazards.

It is interesting to note that Kurita makes no mention of the danger to be feared from carrier plane attacks. In any choice of route this factor was an important one since, owing to the geography of the Philippines, carrier search and attack radii varied considerably in their coverage of the various approaches. Assuming task force launching points sixty miles off the eastern shore of the Philippines, maximum search coverage is assured by three forces, one off Lamon Bay, one off San Bernardino Strait, and one off Leyte Gulf. Three-hundred-mile arcs from these positions give a line running roughly southeast-northwest and including the waters immediately southwest of Negros, the Cuyo and Calamian Islands, and the China Sea west of Luzon. This searched area covers far more of the approach actually taken than it does of the alternative via the Sulu Sea. Intending to arrive off Leyte Gulf before dawn of the 25th, Kurita was within this 300-mile radius from about midnight of October 23–24, and was sighted by the dawn search shortly after 0800. The result was that he was subjected to a five-hour attack at a distance of only 130 miles from the Lamon Bay launching point, and of 190 to 160 miles from that off San Bernardino Strait.

The Sulu Sea route promised better things. Here the approach was in along the radii of carrier search and attack rather than one following a close circumference. The advantages of such a direct in and out procedure are not esoteric—that they were recognized, if tardily, by the Japanese is shown by Kurita's retirement track on the morning of the 26th, when he detoured for a time to the southward in order to increase his distance from the carrier launching points. And what was good for the retirement would have been good for the approach.

Accepting an 0600 arrival at Leyte Gulf, a 24-knot run-in from a point X in 10–10N 120E would have permitted a minimum of exposure. This would have meant a faster approach than that planned, but the shorter overall distance to be run would have balanced the increased fuel expenditure. Passing through point X at 0800 on the 24th, Kurita would have been some 360 miles from the nearest carrier group at about the time the dawn search could be expected to reach its limiting distance. There would consequently have been a good chance of avoiding discovery prior to the afternoon search, and thus either avoiding or greatly minimizing the attacks to be expected before sunset; furthermore, avoidance of early discovery would have increased the chances that Ozawa's luring operation would succeed. And even if the First Diversion Attack Force had been sighted by the dawn search, exposure to subsequent attack would have been predictably less than on the route actually chosen.

Measured against this greater freedom from attack by the "Task Force," the most feared enemy, as well as from known submarine hazards in Palawan Passage, the threat of detection by the Morotai search does not seem significant. For one thing, Balabac Strait would have been passed during late afternoon and first daylight inside the Sulu Sea would have found the force far to the northward; as things turned out Admiral Nishimura followed a similar route to Surigao Strait and was undetected by these planes. Kurita, however, having made his choice, lost three cruisers to the anticipated submarine hazards and a battleship, another cruiser, and two destroyers to Third Fleet air attack in the Sibuyan Sea. The extent to which these dangers were predictable, and consequently could either have been avoided or minimized, would seem to demonstrate that in the question of the approach route the First Diversion Attack Force staff work was faulty.

The second important error in *Asahi Shimbun*'s narrative is the statement that the two groups sent to force the Surigao entrance to the Gulf, Shima's Second Diversion Attack Force and Nishimura's slow battleships, "joined" before the battle. This they did not do, but the misapprehension raises again the vexed question of the intended command relationship of these two forces. The appearance of two independent groups at the same place and time and charged with the same mission has always been one of the most puzzling features of the operation. The sending of Shima's fleet to Surigao was a last-minute decision, but this fact would hardly have precluded dispatch orders to rendezvous under a designated commander.

So far as it is known, no such orders were issued. But the statements in this account, that the Second Diversion Attack Force "was to join" Nishimura's group, and that "after joining" they then entered Leyte Gulf, afford evidence that such was the intent or understanding at Headquarters.

If this is true, it is important. It adds credibility to the astounding statement of Commander Nishino, the senior survivor of Nishimura's force, that his Admiral deliberately advanced the time of arrival because he "did not want to be under the command of Shima." In retrospect, Nishimura's speedup, which not only exposed his force to sighting early in the approach but also prevented effective coordination with Kurita, seems more and more the decisive factor in the Japanese failure to penetrate the Gulf. To the extent, then, that one can place reliance on *Asahi Shimbun*'s statements about "joining," one must emphasize the key role of Nishimura in ensuring, for the most unworthy reasons, the failure of his country's last chance.

For the design of the whole operation was based on an attack on the Gulf from two directions at the same time. To accomplish this end, Kurita having been delayed by air attacks, Nishimura should have entered Surigao no earlier than 0700; instead, he arrived and engaged at 0330, two hours earlier than the "dawn" prescribed in the original operation order. Some blame here attaches to Kurita for not sending a positive revision of his plan, but this error pales beside the enormity of Nishimura's behavior.

The *Asahi* account emphasizes the importance of the failure in Surigao Strait as being the main cause of Kurita's decision to abandon his attempt to break into Leyte Gulf. This emphasis appears to be justified.

Kurita originally had thought that his larger force, coming from the north, would draw the covering forces out of the Gulf and thus leave Nishimura free to enter. At the time the question was academic: simultaneous arrival would in all probability let one force enter unopposed, and it did not much matter which. Arrivals widely separated in time would, of course, expose both groups to the risk of being defeated in detail, and this above all was to be avoided.

As Kurita moved forward through the Sibuyan Sea it appeared to some of the Japanese that his estimate was being borne out. In the absence of good information of U.S. dispositions, the scale of carrier attack against his force indicated that the enemy was already concentrating against the stronger Japanese fleet and that it would indeed be Nishimura who would get in among the transports. Such apparently was the interpretation of the events of the 24th that was made at Combined Fleet Headquarters, as shown by the following extract from a dispatch originated shortly before midnight of the 24th and received by Kurita about 0100 of the 25th, shortly after he had succeeded in passing San Bernardino Strait:

> ... BY FIRST DIVERSION ATTACK FORCE'S PENETRATION ATTACK BATDIY 2 AND SECOND DIVERSION ATTACK FORCE SHOULD AT THE MINIMUM OBTAIN THE OPPORTUNITY TO MAKE A PENETRATION ATTACK X EVEN IF FIRST DIVERSION ATTACK FORCE'S NEGOTIATION OF SAN

BERNARDINO STRAIT IS SOMEWHAT BEHIND SCHEDULE IT SHOULD BE ABLE TO GET IN POSITION TO ENGAGE ENEMY SURFACE FORCES WHICH MAY ATTEMPT TO INTERFERE WITH US IN A DECISIVE ENGAGEMENT X

Here Kurita's original appreciation of probabilities reappears: with luck Ozawa will draw off the "Task Force," Kurita will draw off the covering forces, and Nishimura will get into the Gulf. Here also, perhaps, in the final sentence of the dispatch, can be seen the germ of Kurita's decision to break off and turn northward the next day.

Various reasons for this decision are listed in the action report; others were put forward by various participants when interrogated after the war. Insofar, however, as it is possible to rank them in order of importance, the crucial factor seems to have been what had happened in Surigao Strait. The time at which it had happened made it obvious that the victorious American forces inside could reach the northern entrance to the Gulf long before Kurita, and this and other factors, coupled with the reduced strength of the First Diversion Attack Force, raised the fear of a trap. Furthermore, the conditions in the Combined Fleet dispatch quoted above had been fulfilled insofar as Kurita could fulfill them—the Surigao forces had had their chance. What remained was to fulfill the implications of the dispatch, to seek decisive engagement with enemy surface forces. These had been reported, falsely, as lying to the northward off San Bernardino Strait; northward, in consequence, Kurita turned.

In this connection, one may perhaps wonder whether much would have been accomplished had Kurita continued on toward Leyte. The Battle for Leyte Gulf was fought on Saint Crispin's day, and the outnumbered participants in the troubles off Samar, together with those who waited within the Gulf for whatever might be coming, have always felt a little like the veterans of Agincourt. American comments on this aspect of the battle have consequently been governed more by the profound shock of Kurita's astonishing appearance within striking distance than by reasoned analysis.

But it must be remembered that, impressive though the Japanese squadron seemed to those who engaged it, Kurita no longer had the potent force with which he had sortied from Brunei Bay. When he started his last approach toward Leyte, he had with him only four battleships, two heavy and two light cruisers, and seven destroyers; this was a force considerably inferior to the Seventh Fleet. It is of course true that American ships were short of fuel and ammunition; so far as fuel went, so was Kurita. Many American destroyers had expended their torpedoes in Surigao Strait, but there were many others in the transport screen to draw on and, of Kurita's seven destroyers, three had also expended theirs. American fire control gear was superior. The U.S. forces controlled the air. Fatigue in the American ships was in no way comparable to that of the Japanese. And once again the attacking force would have had to force a strait, once again it would have had to form the shaft of a "T." Had Kurita gone on there might have been a good fight, but hardly a certain Japanese triumph. There was no assurance of his wreaking "incredible carnage," as some have thought. Kurita did not abandon a sure thing.

One other point which emerges from a consideration of Leyte Gulf is the extent to which any commander is at the mercy of his subordinates, of his supporting forces, and of his sources of information—the fact that the exercise of command is at best a marginal function. The effects of Nishimura's adventures in initiative were of the greatest magnitude in governing Kurita's chances of success. Again, when Kurita turned north, he thought he had won a victory off Samar despite the heavy damage he had suffered, a feeling which remains evident in *Asahi Shimbun*'s report of "considerable success." Like Toyoda when he decided to commit his carrier pilots to the battle off Formosa, Kurita thought this because his subordinates told him so. He had lost three heavy cruisers; he had reported sinking three or four carriers, two heavy cruisers, and some destroyers. This was not unprofitable, and consequently the prospect of another such engagement with the force reported to the northward seemed promising.

That it was necessary for those on board the flagship to accept such reports, most notably that from the mendacious Commander Tenth Destroyer Squadron, was in part owing to the dispersion of the fleet during the battle. For this Kurita was certainly to some extent responsible. But some of the blame can be attributed to inadequate radar exploiting gear on board the Japanese ships—smoke blocked off vision, and the radar screen was so cluttered that morning, especially after the American torpedo attack, that a PPI picture meant little and even first-class plotting crews had difficulty telling which pips were which. And, again, some of the responsibility falls on a subordinate.

At 0755 a torpedo attack by American screening ships caused Batdiv 1 to turn away and run north for ten minutes. The moment was critical and the attack well timed: when the turn was made the range to the escort carriers was about ten miles; at 0810 after pursuit had been resumed the distance was 15 miles; had the decision been to turn toward rather than away from the torpedoes it would have been of the order of seven or eight miles and the issue, assuming no major torpedo damage, would in all probability have been very different. Once before, in another war, a turn away from torpedoes by the stronger fleet permitted a weaker antagonist to extricate himself from seemingly inevitable destruction, and so it happened here. We do not know whose decision this was, whether that of Admiral Ugaki, Combatdiv 1, or whether of the captain of *Yamato*, with *Nagato* conforming without signal. In any case it was important. Credit for having forced the maneuver goes, of course, to the attacking ships, but it must be recognized that the Japanese could have reacted differently. As they did not, Kurita's task was further complicated and, as the action report states, "our battleship force was unable to establish visual contact with the enemy except for those units which were forced to drop out of formation."

Kurita was not fortunate in his subordinates. Throughout the operation it is hard to find an occasion where, given a choice, they took the right alternative or where, with a chance to exercise initiative, it was intelligently done.

Finally, the *Asahi Shimbun* article acts to reinforce the argument of all the responsible Japanese officers regarding the crucial weakness in naval air strength, not only for attack but for search. Because of this lack the striking power of their principal fleets was limited to gun range; because of it the commanders were blind. With the single exception of Ozawa's strike on the 24th, only when the enemy was within sight from the bridge did the Japanese know where he was; except for the target of this strike, only the American ships in Surigao Strait and off Samar were ever located. In this article, written a year after the event, the uncertainty that beset Ozawa and Kurita remains. The strength, the movements of the "Task Force" are unknown; its location is never mentioned; its attacks come from the void. The Japanese were fighting a disembodied fleet. The wonder still is that they did so well.

About the Author

Educated at Harvard University and Trinity College, Cambridge University, **Mr. Field** saw active duty in the U.S. Naval Reserve from 1942 through 1946. Attaining the rank of lieutenant commander, he served as gunnery officer of CarDiv 26 and subsequently as a member of the Naval Analysis Division of the U.S. Strategic Bombing Survey. Now a member of the Department of History at Swarthmore College, Mr. Field is best known for his book *The Japanese at Leyte Gulf*.

17

WITH KURITA IN THE BATTLE OF LEYTE GULF

Rear Admiral Tomiji Koyanagi, former Imperial Japanese Navy

Proceedings, February 1953

In 1944 I was chief of staff to Vice Admiral Takeo Kurita, Commander in Chief of the Second Fleet of the Japanese Navy. Built around powerful battleships and cruisers, this fleet constituted the First Striking Force (sometimes translated, First Diversionary Attack Force), which was the main attack force in the Battle for Leyte Gulf. Many critical accounts of this battle have been written, and I do not mean to challenge them. I wish only to recall and review the course of events and describe the battle as I saw it. Although wounded twice within two days, I was with Admiral Kurita throughout the battle, always in good position to see what transpired. It is my hope that this essay may be of some value in clarifying the Battle for Leyte Gulf.

In June, 1944, the Japanese Navy suffered a devastating defeat in the fateful Battle of the Philippine Sea. We had to give up our hoped-for decisive battle and withdraw to Okinawa for fuel before returning to Kure. There the operations staff was called to Tokyo to report on the battle and confer regarding future operations. We had counted so heavily on a great victory to swing the tide of war in our favor that no plans had been prepared for the next move. Now Combined Fleet and Imperial General Headquarters were both at a loss as to what to do. It was certain, however, that the Second Fleet must go to Lingga Anchorage because fuel necessary for training was not available in Japan.

At Lingga Anchorage, on the eastern coast of central Sumatra, we had trained in early 1944, only to lose three aircraft carriers and most of our carrier planes in the June battle. Now what remained of that fleet was at Kure where all ships were being prepared to depart from the homeland, all, that is, except Vice Admiral Jisaburo Ozawa's Mobile Fleet, whose carriers were offensively useless until planes and trained pilots became available. Meanwhile the fall of the Marianas was imminent as American attacks were increasing in intensity. It was estimated that the next big enemy offensive would come within three or four months, and it was hopeless to think that our carriers could be restored to fighting strength in that time.

Under these circumstances, only our Second Fleet and land-based air forces would be available for the next operation. But considering the low combat efficiency and reduced strength of our air force and the difficulty of cooperation between it and the fleet, it was clear that the latter would have to bear most of the burden. It also appeared that our next sea battle was likely to be our last.

We spent two busy weeks at Kure before starting for Lingga. For the first time, radar was installed in all battleships and cruisers. Anti-aircraft guns were mounted on every available deck space. The work was carried out in grim determination with the knowledge that there would be no friendly air patrol for the next battle.

The First Striking Force arrived at Lingga in mid-July. On August 10 the operations officer and I flew to Manila for a conference. A member of the Naval General Staff predicted, in a situation estimate, that the next big enemy operation would be in the Philippines in late October. The senior staff officer of Combined Fleet Headquarters presented the *SHO* [Victory] Operation order, which was, in outline, as follows:

> Make every effort to discover enemy invasion forces at maximum distance (approximately 700 miles) by means of land-based air searches, and determine the enemy's landing place and time as early as possible so as to permit our forces to get into position for battle. The First Striking Force should be moved up to Brunei, North Borneo, in sufficient time to rush forward and destroy the enemy transports on the water before they disembark their troops. If this fails and the transports begin landing operations, the Attack Force will engage and destroy the enemy in their anchorage within at least two days of the landing, thus crippling the invasion effort.

The First and Second Air Fleets will first surprise attack the enemy carriers with a view to reducing their strength, then, two days before the arrival of our surface force, will launch all-out attacks on the carriers and transports and thus open the way for the First Striking Force to approach and engage the enemy.

Questions, answers, deliberations, and discussions followed. Disturbed at the idea of hurling our Attack Force in wherever the enemy attempted to land, instead of using it in a decisive engagement, I asked: "According to this order the primary targets of the First Striking Force are enemy transports, but if by chance carriers come within range of our force, may we, in cooperation with shore-based air, engage the carriers and then return to annihilate the transports?" This question was answered affirmatively by Combined Fleet Headquarters.

Once the plans were clear, fleet training began at Lingga; with emphasis on the following points:

1. Anti-aircraft action. Enemy air attacks must be repelled solely by our shipboard fire power. Every weapon, down to and including rifles, must be used at maximum efficiency for this purpose.
2. Evasive maneuvers against air attack. We practiced fleet ring formations and mass maneuvering as well as individual ship movements to evade bombs and torpedoes.
3. Night battle training was stressed as a possible opening to a decisive fleet engagement. Special emphasis was placed on night firing of main batteries with effective use of star shell and radar. Aggressive torpedo attacks were also worked out and tested.
4. Battle within the enemy anchorage. There were many problems to be worked out on this point, such as how to break into the anchorage where enemy shipping would be massed; how to destroy the enemy screening force; and how to attack the transports.

During our three months' stay at Lingga the training progressed most satisfactorily. We were fortunate in having unlimited fuel available from Palembang, Sumatra. Our radar sets were the best available. And thanks to the guidance and assistance of electronics experts from the homeland, who worked night and day in training radar operators, the sets were dependable and accurate in locating targets, and valuable in increasing the accuracy of our heavy caliber gunfire.

While training continued, high ranking officers made studies of various locales and tactics. There were three likely landing points in the Philippines: Lamon Bay in the North, Leyte Gulf in the middle, and Davao Gulf in the south. Passages and pertinent topographical data were carefully analyzed. Fleet instructions and methods of approaching these areas were diligently studied and deliberated, and there were frequent conferences.

Such large-scale penetration tactics as confronted us had never been practiced in peacetime. As the studies progressed, the difficulties of our task became more apparent. But training gave us confidence that we would be able to withstand enemy air attack, and the idea developed that we could put up a good fight. We felt sure that the problem of penetrating the anchorage could be solved.

The Combined Fleet policy that our force should destroy enemy transports at anchor, and not engage his carrier task force in decisive battle, was opposed by all of our officers. The United States fleet, built around powerful carrier forces, had won battle after battle ever since attacking the Gilbert Islands. Our one big goal was to strike the United States fleet and destroy it. Kurita's staff felt that the primary objective of our force should be the annihilation of the enemy carrier force and that the destruction of enemy convoys should be but a side issue. Even though all enemy convoys in the theater should be destroyed, if the powerful enemy carrier striking force was left intact, other landings would be attempted, and in the long run our bloodshed would achieve only a delay in the enemy's advance. On the other hand, a severe blow at the enemy carriers would cut off their advance toward Tokyo and might be a turning point in the war. If the Kurita Force was to be expended, it should be for enemy carriers. At least that would be an adornment for the record of our surface fleet, and a source of pride to every man.

Our greatest fear was that our planes might not locate the enemy at maximum search radius, in which case our force would be unable to reach the transports before they began unloading. If our attack should be delayed until several days after the enemy invasion, then judging from past experience, his transports would be emptied by the time of our arrival. It would be foolish to sink emptied transports at the cost of our great surface force!

While we tried to break into the anchorage, the enemy carrier forces would rain incessant air attacks upon us, and probably force us to a decisive engagement before we could even reach the transports. Thus top priority should be given to engaging the carrier striking force of the enemy.

Our officers were of the opinion that the Commander in Chief, Combined Fleet should come from the homeland and personally command his fleet at this crucial phase of the war. Many officers also complained about Combined Fleet's basic policy and expressed the hope that the operation order would be modified. But since it was an order, there must be no talk of changing it, and we should comply without hesitation or question. Outwardly I rejected all complaints of this nature, but inwardly I understood and sometimes even agreed with my officers.

In short, our understanding was that we were to make every effort to break into the enemy's anchorage, but if the enemy striking force came within range, then we would carry on a fleet engagement.

I still believe that Combined Fleet understood this to be our operational policy, because it had been fully explained in Manila and was later submitted in writing. But our whole force was uneasy, and this feeling was reflected in our leadership during the battle.

In the early morning of October 21, 1944, we received a Combined Fleet order to break into Tacloban Anchorage at dawn on October 25 and there destroy enemy ships. There were three routes from Brunei to Leyte Gulf.

1. Through Balabac Strait, east into the Sulu Sea, and into Tacloban Anchorage through Surigao Strait.
2. North through the Sulu Sea, transit San Bernardino Strait, turn south along the east coast of Samar, and approach Tacloban from the east.
3. North through Palawan Passage, into the Sibuyan Sea, pass through San Bernardino Strait, and head south along Samar to Tacloban.

Analyzing these, we found number one was the shortest course to our objective, but it was within range of Morotai-based enemy search planes and would expose us to attack for the longest time. Number three was beyond enemy search plane range and offered less chance of encountering carrier air patrols, but it was the longest route and it passed through the narrow Palawan Passage, a favorite hangout of enemy submarines. Number two was a compromise between one and three.

Combined Fleet suggested that we approach in two groups, from the north and south, and it was accordingly decided that Admiral Kurita would take most of the ships via the third route, while a detachment of two old battleships and four destroyers under Vice Admiral Nishimura took route number one. These groups were both to reach Leyte Gulf at dawn of the 25th, a difficult achievement in itself considering the treacherous currents in narrow straits which each had to navigate. Timing was complicated by the great distances between the routes. And then there were the dangers of lurking enemy submarines and powerful enemy surface fleets. If concerted action was impossible, each force would carry out its attack alone.

The Kurita force sortied from Brunei on October 22 and was attacked next dawn in Palawan Passage by two submarines, with the result that the cruisers *Atago* and *Maya* were sunk and *Takao* was seriously damaged.

The submarine hazard in Palawan Passage had been expected, and our force was keeping a strict alert and zigzagging at 18 knots. But this submarine attack was a complete surprise, for we had sighted neither torpedo wake nor periscope and had no chance to evade. The main causes of our failure here were that a shortage of fuel restricted our speed and that we had no planes for antisubmarine patrol. All ship-based seaplanes had been transferred to San Jose, Mondoro, because the submarine threat had made it impossible to plan on recovering them. We tended to deprecate American submarines and torpedoes during the early part of the war, but by late 1944 they were our greatest menace, and our anti-submarine measures were totally inadequate.

When flagship *Atago* was sunk, Kurita's staff transferred to a destroyer. Nine hours passed before we cleared submarine-infested waters and could transfer to *Yamato*, flagship of the First Battleship Division. During this time Vice Admiral Ugaki in *Yamato* had assumed temporary command of the entire force.

We had thought from the beginning that a *Yamato*-class battleship, the most powerful in the world, should have been flagship for the SHO Operation. Combined Fleet, expecting a night action, rejected this idea because the commanding officer should always be in a heavy cruiser, the key ship of night actions. Combined Fleet had never given up this traditional principle of fleet engagements, but the sacrifice of *Atago* proved them wrong.

On October 24 Kurita's force in the Sibuyan Sea was the target of fierce raids by carrier-based planes from 1030 until 1530. The *Yamato*-class battleship *Musashi* was sunk, a heavy cruiser had to drop out of formation, and other ships were damaged. We had expected air attacks, but this day's were almost enough to discourage us.

Nothing was heard from Ozawa's Mobile Fleet which was supposed to be maneuvering northeast of Luzon. We estimated that the enemy carrier force was just east of Lamon Bay, Luzon, but we had no indication that our air forces had been attacking it. Like a magnet, Kurita's force seemed to be drawing all of the enemy's air attacks, as we approached San Bernardino Strait. If we pushed on into the narrow strait and the air raids continued, our force would be wiped out.

We reversed course at 1530 to remain in the Sibuyan Sea where we could maneuver until our situation improved and at 1600 despatched a summary report to Combined Fleet; it concluded with our opinion that:

> Were we to have forced our way through as scheduled under these circumstances, we would merely make of ourselves meat for the enemy, with very little chance of success to us. It was therefore concluded that our best course was to retire temporarily beyond range of hostile planes until friendly planes could strike a decisive blow against the enemy force.

At the same time we sent a message urging land-based air forces to attack the enemy. When, by 1715, the enemy air raids had ceased, we turned east again, without waiting for Combined Fleet's reply, and headed for San Bernardino Strait. We had expected the air attacks to be maintained at least until sundown, but the enemy must have wanted to recover his planes before dark. By continuing aerial contact with us he would have known that our retreat was only temporary. Then the enemy carrier force commander could have ignored Ozawa's Mobile Fleet and concentrated his ships outside San Bernardino Strait to ambush us. If he had done so, a night engagement against our exhausted force would undoubtedly have been disastrous for us.

Thus the enemy missed an opportunity to annihilate the Japanese fleet through his failure to maintain contact in the evening of the 24th. On the Japanese side, of course, Admiral Kurita should have notified Nishimura of our temporary retreat and ordered him to slow his advance. At 1915, a message was received from Commander in Chief Toyoda which read: "With confidence in heavenly guidance, all forces will attack!"

Another message received from his chief of staff said: "Since the start of this operation, all forces have performed in remarkable coordination, but the First Striking Force's change in schedule could mean failure for the whole operation. It is ardently desired that this force continue its action as prearranged."

These messages clarified the decision of Combined Fleet, so we responded: "Braving any loss and damage we may suffer, First Striking Force will break into Leyte Gulf and fight to the last man." And another message was sent to air bases requesting attacks coordinated with the surface fleet.

Six hours behind schedule, we finally passed through San Bernardino Strait at midnight of the 24th, and turned southward, hugging the east coast of Samar and planning to reach Leyte Gulf around 1000.

In the afternoon of the 24th, enemy search planes to the north located Ozawa's ships and judged them to be the main Japanese force, and a threat to the amphibious operation in Leyte Gulf. Erroneously thinking that Kurita had withdrawn in the Sibuyan Sea, the enemy left his position at San Bernardino Strait during the night and proceeded northward to strike Ozawa's fleet, making this the one part of our plan which worked perfectly.

I still cannot understand how the enemy, with his highly developed intelligence system, so badly overestimated Ozawa's force of two old battleships, one regular carrier, three light carriers, three light cruisers, and ten destroyers.

Just as day broke at 0640 on the 25th, and we were changing from night search disposition to anti-aircraft alert cruising disposition (ring formation) enemy carriers were sighted on the horizon. Several masts came in sight about 30 kilometers to the southeast, and presently we could see planes being launched.

This was indeed a miracle. Think of a surface fleet coming up on an enemy carrier group! We moved to take advantage of this heaven-sent opportunity. *Yamato* increased speed instantly and opened fire at a range of 31 kilometers. The enemy was estimated to be four or five fast carriers guarded by one or two battleships and at least ten heavy cruisers. Nothing is more vulnerable than an aircraft carrier in a surface engagement, so the enemy lost no time in retiring.

In a pursuit the only essential is to close the gap as rapidly as possible and concentrate fire upon the enemy. Admiral Kurita did not therefore adopt the usual deployment procedures but instantly ordered: "General attack." Destroyer squadrons were ordered to follow the main body. The enemy withdrew, first to the east, next to the south, and then to the southwest, on an arc-like track. In retreat he darted into the cover of local squalls and destroyer smoke screens, while attacking us continuously with destroyer torpedoes and attack planes.

Our fast cruisers, in the van, were followed by the battleships, and little heed was paid to coordination. Because of the enemy's efficient use of squalls and smoke screens for cover, his ships were visible to us in *Yamato* only at short intervals. The enemy destroyers were multi-funneled, with high freeboard. Their appearance and torpedo firing method convinced us that they were cruisers. We pursued at top speed for over two hours but could not close the gap, in fact it actually appeared to be lengthening. We estimated that the enemy's speed was nearly 30 knots, that his carriers were of the regular large type, that pursuit would be an endless seesaw, and that we would be unable to strike a decisive blow. And running at top speed, we were consuming fuel at an alarming rate. Admiral Kurita accordingly suspended the pursuit at 0910 and ordered all units to close. After the war I was astonished to learn that our quarry had been only six escort carriers, three destroyers, and four destroyer escorts, and that the maximum speed of these carriers was only 18 knots.

Giving up pursuit when we did amounted to losing a prize already in hand. If we had known the types and number of enemy ships, and their speed, Admiral Kurita would never have suspended the pursuit, and we would have annihilated the enemy. Lacking this vital information, we concluded that the enemy had already made good his escape. In the light of circumstances I still believe that there was no alternative to what we did. Reports from our ships indicated that we had sunk two carriers, two heavy cruisers, and several destroyers. (We learned later that these statistics were exaggerated.) Our only damage was that three heavy cruisers had to drop out of formation.

Our task had been to proceed south, regardless of opposition encountered or damage sustained on the way, and break into Leyte Gulf. But for our unexpected encounter with the enemy carrier group, it would have been simple. We estimated that the enemy carrier task force which was east of San Bernardino Strait on the 24th, had steamed south during the night and taken new dispositions next day, separating into at least three groups so as to surround us; and that we had encountered the southernmost group.

We did not know on the morning of the 25th that Ozawa's Mobile Fleet had succeeded in luring the main enemy carrier task force northward. Admiral Kurita's main force consisted of four battleships, two heavy cruisers, two light cruisers, and seven destroyers. Our only report of enemy-strength (transports and escorts) in Leyte Gulf was from Admiral Nishimura, who had the report of a *Mogami* seaplane reconnaissance at dawn on the 24th. We had to estimate that there would be a change in the enemy situation as a result of intervening events. We waited eagerly, but in vain, for reconnaissance reports from our shore-based air force.

The enemy situation was confused. Intercepted fragments of plain text radio messages indicated that a hastily constructed air strip on Leyte was ready to launch planes in an attack on us, that Admiral Kinkaid was requesting the early despatch of a powerful striking unit, and that the United States Seventh Fleet was operating nearby. At the same time we heard from Southwest Area Fleet Headquarters that a "U.S. Carrier Striking Task Force was located in position bearing 5° distant 130 miles from Suluan light at 0945." (This report was later found groundless.)

Under these circumstances, it was presumed that if our force did succeed in entering Leyte Gulf, we would find that the transports had already withdrawn under escort of the Seventh Fleet. And even if they still remained, they would have completed unloading in the five days since making port, and any success we might achieve would be very minor at best. On the other hand, if we proceeded into the narrow gulf we would be the target of attacks by the enemy's carrier- and Leyte-based planes. We were prepared to fight to the last man, but we wanted to die gloriously.

We were convinced that several enemy carrier groups were disposed nearby and that we were surrounded. Our shore-based air force had been rather inactive, but now the two Air Fleets would surely fight all-out in coordination with the First Striking Force. If they could only strike a successful blow, we might still achieve a decisive fleet engagement, and even if we were destroyed in such a battle, death would be glorious.

It was these considerations which made us abandon our plan to break into Leyte Gulf. We proceeded northward in search of the enemy carrier groups.

Looking back today, when all events have been made clear, we should have continued to Leyte Gulf. And even under the circumstances and with our estimate of the enemy situation at that time, we should have gone into the gulf.

Kurita and his staff had intended to take the enemy task force as the primary objective if a choice of targets developed. Naturally, our encounter with the enemy off Leyte on the 25th was judged to be the occasion for such choice.

On the other hand, there was considerable risk in changing our primary objective when we did not know the location of the other enemy task forces or how effective our land-based air forces would be. We should have chosen the single, definite objective, stuck to it, and pushed on. Leyte Gulf lay close at hand and could not run away.

Enemy air raids of October 24th had been fierce, and next morning three of our heavy cruisers were damaged by air attacks. That afternoon we were pounded by carrier planes with no fatal damage, but near-misses caused most of our ships to trail oil. On the morning of the third day, we were again attacked from the air, and light cruiser *Noshiro* was sunk. Around 1100, flagship *Yamato* was the target of about thirty B-24s. The flagship suffered no direct bomb hits, but near-misses around her bow raised gigantic columns of water. In this raid I was wounded in the waist by splinters from a bomb blast.

In three consecutive days the enemy sent some 1,000 aerial sorties against us. Never was a fleet so heavily pounded by air attack.

To a surface fleet there is no engagement so disadvantageous and ineffective as an antiaircraft action. It does not pay off. We had no air cover to repel the enemy, for whom it was a pure offensive.

Yamato, being the largest ship and flying an admiral's flag, was a constant target of attack. It was only through the maneuvering skill of her captain that she came out of the action virtually unscathed.

During these three long days of one-sided air poundings, our consorts were being sunk or damaged all around, but the men never faltered. They remained full of fighting spirit and did their very best. Their gallant attitude made them worthy of praise as the last elite of the Japanese Combined Fleet.

The enemy's high-speed battleships and carriers had headed south again upon learning that the situation at Leyte had become serious and that Ozawa had suddenly turned northward in the morning of the 25th. If the enemy carrier task force had seen that Ozawa's fleet was merely a decoy and had started south a few hours earlier, it could have caught Kurita.

In fact, after suspending our southward drive in pursuit of the enemy off Samar Island on the morning of the 25th, we fully expected to encounter the Americans before we could reach San Bernardino Strait. We were still ready for a last decisive battle under any condition.

Early in the morning of the 24th, the Americans had sighted Kurita's main force in the Sibuyan Sea as well as the Nishimura detachment to the south of Los Negros Island. Both forces could have been tracked thereafter to show our movements and destination. We had anticipated that, and we expected the Americans to take every measure to intercept us.

Our most serious problem on the 24th was getting through and out of San Bernardino Strait. Just the navigation of the strait was difficult enough with its eight-knot current, and transiting it by day with a single ship required considerable skill; one can imagine the increased difficulty of doing it with a large formation of ships at night.

In the strait we had to maneuver in a single column which extended over ten miles; once through, our formation had to be changed to a night-search disposition which spread over a score of miles. At the time of shifting formation our force was extremely vulnerable to attack.

We anticipated enemy submarines at the exit of the strait to intercept us, and a concentration of surface craft to force a night engagement upon us. We were, therefore, greatly surprised when neither of these situations materialized.

We passed through the strait safely and headed southward, sure that the Americans were well aware of our movements. We also thought that the enemy's excellent radar must be tracking our force and plotting its every move. Thus we certainly never expected to encounter enemy carriers as we did so suddenly at daybreak of the 25th. I still wonder why those carriers came so unguardedly within range of our ships' gunfire.

On land or sea, retirement is the most difficult of all tactics to execute successfully. But the retiring tactics of the American carriers in the battle off Samar in the morning of the 25th were valiant and skillful. The enemy destroyers coordinated perfectly to cover the low speed of the escort carriers, bravely launched torpedoes to intercept us, and embarrassed us with their dense smoke screens. Several of them closed our force at 0750 and launched some ten torpedoes. Battleships *Yamato* and *Nagato* sighted them in time to evade but had to comb their tracks for five miles or more before resuming pursuit of the enemy.

The escort carriers maneuvered in tight combination. They made good their escape on interior lines, causing us to think that they were regular high-speed carriers. I must admit admiration for the skill of their commanders.

On October 26th, the air raids against Kurita's force ended around 1100. As on the day before, we expected to be attacked all day long. We had not the least expectation that the enemy would suspend his raids an hour before noon. Perhaps it was because we had pulled out of combat range of the enemy carrier task force.

Our greatest concern was that the enemy, following up his successes, might pursue us westward through San Bernardino Strait, into the Sibuyan or Sulu Seas, and launch annihilating air strikes. If this threat had materialized, the American victory would have been complete.

Some may say that this would have been risky for the Americans. But what Japanese strength could have opposed United States carriers in pursuit of Kurita's retreating force?

Our shore-based air force, judging from its inactivity, must have been pretty well knocked out, and Ozawa's battered fleet had been almost destroyed. We might have inflicted some damage, but there was no Japanese force strong enough to give serious opposition.

American reluctance to give all-out pursuit is perhaps justified by some strategic concept which advocates prudence and step-by-step procedure; but from the Japanese point of view, the Americans gave up pursuit all too soon and missed chances of inflicting much greater losses upon us.

Analyzing the whole course of events of this battle, we see that chance played a definite role in each part of the action and thus influenced the whole.

As in all things, so in the field of battle, none can tell when or where the breaks will come. Thus events and their consequences are often determined by some hair-breadth chance in which the human factor has no control at all. Chance can make the victor of one moment into the vanquished of the next.

The Japanese Navy's total of combatant vessels in this great battle theater was: nine battleships, four aircraft carriers, thirteen heavy cruisers, six light cruisers, and thirty-one destroyers. Of these we lost three battleships, all four carriers, six heavy cruisers, four light cruisers, and seven destroyers. These losses, most of which were caused by air attacks, spelled the collapse of our Navy as an effective fighting machine.

I would hardly say, however, that our losses were greater than we anticipated. Nor do I feel either that the Japanese lost because their strategy and tactics were wrong, or that the Americans won because their strategy and tactics were particularly good.

The physical fighting strengths of both parties were too greatly divergent. On logical analysis, the *SHO* Operation plan formulated by Combined Fleet Headquarters was unreasonable. Both carrier and land-based air forces had been weakened to a point where they could not be effectively coordinated with the surface fleet, which was thus subjected to concentrated enemy attack without any air protection.

In modern sea warfare, the main striking force should be a carrier group, with other warships as auxiliaries. Only when the carrier force has collapsed, should the surface ships become the main striking force. However majestic a fleet may look, without a carrier force it is no more than a fleet of tin.

A decisive fleet engagement determines conclusively which contending party shall have sea and air supremacy. By October, 1944, the Japanese fleet no longer actually had strength enough to carry on a decisive engagement. Its strength and ability had been so reduced that it had to resort to the makeshift plan of attacking transports. Just think of sending a great mass of surface craft, without air cover, nearly 1,000 miles, exposed to enemy submarines and air forces, with a mission of breaking into a hostile anchorage to engage. This was a completely desperate, reckless, and unprecedented plan which ignored the basic concepts of war. I still cannot but interpret it as a suicide order for Kurita's fleet.

When Kurita suspended chase of the escort carriers off Samar on the 25th, we had four battleships, two heavy cruisers, two light cruisers, and seven destroyers. Let us suppose that he had continued south, broken into Leyte Gulf as scheduled, destroyed all the transports and their escorts, and succeeded in withdrawing unscathed. Our initial operational objective would have been attained, but two facts remained. First, it was five days since the enemy convoy had started unloading. Hence, the transports would have discharged most of their cargo, making them practically worthless as strategic targets. Secondly, the convoy escorts were old ships and their destruction would have impaired but slightly the overall fighting efficiency of the enemy. If any of our ships had actually remained afloat after such an attack, they would still have been without carrier support, a tin fleet, existing only to be destroyed by the enemy. Their existence or non-existence could not have affected the tide of war, and Japan was waning toward her final defeat. It is clear that our *SHO* Operation could not have influenced the outcome of the war.

During the Pacific War there were two decisive naval battles in which the whole outcome of war hung in the balance. First was the Battle of Midway in early June, 1942. At that time the fighting power of the Japanese Navy was at its zenith, and everyone in Combined Fleet was firmly convinced of victory. But our defeat in the carrier duel at the outset of the battle cancelled our hope for a decisive engagement and we had to withdraw.

The second was in mid-June, 1944, the Battle of the Philippine Sea. There were many defects still to be remedied in our carrier striking force, but Combined Fleet was able to engage in battle with a fair degree of self-confidence. Once again we suffered an aerial defeat in the opening phase of the battle which drove us to a general retreat.

Until the Battle for Leyte, our battleship force was relatively immune from loss or damage and did maintain its fighting efficiency. To the uninitiated these ships must have appeared as great floating forts, and as the key by which Japan might recover from her hopeless situation. But a fleet of super-dreadnaughts alone, however powerful their guns, could no longer qualify as the main striking force in a decisive fleet engagement.

I have nothing but respect and praise for the excellence of weapons, thoroughness of training, tactical skill, and bravery of the enemy in this battle.

There is an old maxim: "Battle is a series of blunders and errors. The side which makes the least will win and the side which makes the most will lose."

The truth of this maxim was never more apparent than in the Battle for Leyte Gulf. Anyone who has experienced combat knows that errors in judgment made under fire are not always culpable. The ever-changing tide of battle subjects us to Fate and Chance, which are beyond our control.

Captain Toshikazu Ohmae has been kind enough to translate my essay on the Battle for Leyte Gulf. After completing the task, he asked me two questions concerning the action which, because they may also occur to American readers of this article, I have tried to answer as fully as possible. The questions and my answers, which have been reviewed and approved by Admiral Kurita, follow:

 (Q.) You (Vice Admiral Koyanagi) believe that the First Striking Force should have been committed to decisive battle with the enemy task force and should not have been expended on the enemy convoy. How did you estimate that the First Striking Force might have deployed to encounter and destroy the enemy task force?

(A). It was obvious that without air support we had no chance of defeating the elite enemy task force of crack battleships and high-speed regular aircraft carriers. It was indispensable that we have the cooperation of friendly air forces. Analyzing Japanese air strength, however, we could see that with Ozawa's Mobile Fleet still recovering from its losses in the Battle of the Philippine Sea, there remained only our land-based air forces—the First and Second Air Fleets.

As it turned out, these two air fleets achieved practically nothing during the battle, whereas in planning the *SHO* Operation we had counted heavily on them. They should have conducted all-out attacks on the enemy fleet to support our surface force in this battle. If they had damaged enemy battleships and carriers, the First Striking Force could have carried out a decisive sea engagement.

We knew full well that the combat effectiveness of our air force was limited and should not be over-estimated. It was the surface fleet that would have to bear the brunt of battle.

Despite all this we were of the opinion that the First Striking Force should be committed to the destruction of the enemy task force, his strongest fighting unit, because this would be our last chance against it. This was the desire of all our senior officers and we were happy with our assignment.

(Q). You have said that the message giving the position of the enemy task force at 0945 was one of the main reasons for suspending our penetration into Leyte Gulf. This dispatch is not recorded in any document, but granting its existence, it pertained to the enemy task force approximately three hours before, and nothing had been reported since. Hence our chances of catching this enemy were slim, while the stationary ships in Leyte Gulf could be hit with almost 100 percent certainty.

I assume then that the First Striking Force gave up entering the gulf to seek the new enemy task force because of its belief that it should have been committed to the destruction of the task force in the first place. But the target of your attack was changed three times. Pursuit of the escort carrier group was abandoned after two hours' chase, and forces were concentrated for breaking into Leyte Gulf, but this objective was soon given up, and you proceeded northward in search of the newly reported task force. What caused you to change target so often, and how did you plan to contact this enemy to the north?

(A). Though I have already written about giving up the pursuit of the enemy escort carriers in the morning of the 25th, I can easily imagine that everybody wonders why we did not continue the pursuit of the vulnerable escort carriers and attempt their complete annihilation.

But as a matter of fact, we had concluded that these were regular carriers. (It was only after the surrender that I learned it was an escort carrier group, when I was interrogated by members of the United States Strategic Bombing Survey in Tokyo.)

We judged that the enemy carrier group was steaming at a speed equal to or greater than ours because we did not close the distance to the enemy in two hours' pursuit. We could not observe the enemy situation because of local squalls and enemy smoke screens. Our intra-fleet communication was so congested that we received no information of the enemy from our van cruisers, and we concluded that the cruisers had also lost contact with the enemy.

Another factor was that we could not be indifferent toward our fuel situation. Endless pursuit would mean fruitless consumption of valuable fuel, and the consumption of fuel in two hours' top speed pursuits could not be overlooked. Our decision was to give up pursuit of the enemy carrier group.

The reason we then chose a northerly heading was that we wanted to separate from the enemy as much as possible. Critics may say that a southwesterly course would have quickened our regrouping, but there were local squalls to the southwest, and remnants of the enemy smoke screen still limited visibility. Moreover we had to consider the offensive possibilities of the group we had just been chasing. Proceeding southward, we would be exposed to possible counterattacks by the enemy task group which was thought to include high-speed battleships and large cruisers.

It was 1100 before we had regrouped, and by then not an enemy ship was in sight. The enemy force being driven away, we determined to return to the initial strategical objective, the breaking into Leyte Gulf, the operation set forth by the Commander in Chief, Combined Fleet, and we accordingly changed our course toward the Gulf.

Since our surprise encounter with the enemy task group early that morning, we had been so busily engaged in combat that there had been no time for cool analysis. Now that we were not engaged, the staff met for discussions of our next move. All available information was gathered and analyzed. It was concluded that the First Striking Force should give up the scheduled plan of breaking into Leyte Gulf and try for decisive battle with the enemy task force in the open sea. Admiral Kurita gave his consent to this new plan. The circumstances which led to this decision have been noted in my essay in detail.

It was certainly not a powerful enemy force in Leyte Gulf which repelled us from the Gulf. In fact we believed the force in Leyte Gulf to be rather weak. We seem to have been obsessed with the idea of the task force being our most important target.

After the war Admiral Kurita recalled:

> My force was attacked by an enemy bomber group which disrupted our formation as each ship evaded independently. I do not remember the exact time of that attack but it was just after we altered course toward Leyte Gulf. It was at a point where many men from a sunken enemy carrier were floating. Unlike the sporadic attacks we had experienced that morning, this bombing was of a far larger scale and appeared to be more systematic. I concluded that fresh enemy carrier task groups had commenced all-out attacks upon us. Shortly before that we had known through enemy radio interception that the force in Leyte Gulf was requesting reinforcements and that it would be two hours before they could reach Leyte Gulf. From Manila had come a message giving us the 0945 position of an enemy task force. On the basis of these pieces of information we concluded that the powerful enemy task force was approaching. As it would be disadvantageous for us to be subjected to severe air raids in narrow Leyte Gulf, I thought we should seek battle in the open sea, if possible, where maneuvering room would be unlimited. The systematic air raid came just after I had reached this decision, so I immediately consented to the suggestion of my staff that we should seek the enemy task force instead of going after the ships in Leyte Gulf. We had estimated that the enemy would not be far away, but we had not been able to confirm his exact position. We had no search planes, but we still believed that the Philippines-based air forces would conduct all-out attacks in the afternoon, delivering a serious blow to the enemy task force and revealing its position to us. We would then have a chance for a decisive sea engagement either by day or night.
>
> We anticipated no difficulty in making contact with the enemy task force, because we estimated that the enemy with all his power was already pursuing Kurita's force and would contact and challenge us by sunset at the latest.*

*Editor's Note [1953]

The reader should observe that Admiral Koyanagi's account of what happened in the Japanese Second Fleet on the morning of October 25, 1944, off Samar is more coherent than that to be found in interviews with Japanese naval leaders immediately after the war. Battle fatigue, poor communications, and a total lack of air reconnaissance influenced the Japanese decisions. In the eight years that have passed since the Battle for Leyte Gulf, it is inevitable that a certain amount of rationalizing should creep into most accounts of the battle.

About the Author

Koyanagi graduated from the Imperial Japanese Naval Academy in 1914. Captain of the battleship *Kongo* at the time of the attack on Pearl Harbor and commander of Destroyer Squadron 10 during the Guadalcanal campaign, he was Admiral Takeo Kurita's chief of staff during the battle of Leyte Gulf.

18

MacARTHUR, FDR, AND THE POLITICS OF LEYTE GULF

Lt. Cdr. Thomas J. Cutler, U.S. Navy (Ret.)

Naval History, October 2009

The Battle of Leyte Gulf was the largest and most multi-faceted naval battle in history, was replete with awe-inspiring heroism, and ended the viability of the Japanese Navy in the Pacific War. Yet this important American victory is forever tainted by a number of costly errors that have long been the source of much controversy. While the arguments have understandably been focused on the naval commanders involved, a review of the events leading up to this momentous battle reveals that the ultimate responsibility actually lies at a higher level and has its roots very early in the war.

Genesis

In early March 1942, Lieutenant John D. Bulkeley's PT-41 shoved off from the wooden pier at Corregidor and threaded its way through a defensive minefield, headed for the darkening waters of Mindoro Strait where enemy ships were known to prowl. Behind him was the bleak aftermath of battle, the shattered remnants of an army on the verge of capitulation. Trees whose fronds had once brushed majestically against the beautiful Philippine sky had been reduced to mere jagged stumps. Buildings that had housed a proud garrison now lay in ruins, their ragged remnants protruding from a pall of acrid smoke that further subdued the already fading twilight.

The tiny warship had been given a mission out of all proportion to its size—to extricate the legendary General Douglas MacArthur from the

Philippines before they capitulated to the Japanese. Bulkeley succeeded in that harrowing mission, a feat that earned him a Medal of Honor and changed the course of the entire Pacific War.

Dilemma

Six days later, on the other side of the world, one of the guests at a White House dinner asked the President to reveal how General MacArthur had escaped from the Philippines. Franklin Roosevelt, with a mischievous glint in his eye, replied in a conspiratorial tone, "General MacArthur took a rowboat and, disguised as a Filipino fisherman, rowed to Australia—right past the Japs."

Not everyone laughed at the President's outlandish explanation, and it appears that at least some of the guests were quite willing to believe it. In retrospect this seems rather naive, but when viewed in the context of the times, such a feat did not seem beyond the capabilities of Douglas MacArthur. Parents christened their newborn children with his name, mothers reportedly invoked his name to entice their children to eat spinach, colleges heaped honorary degrees upon him, the Blackfeet Indian tribe had conferred upon him the title of "Chief Wise Eagle," and a widely publicized news story reported that when an Atlanta junior high school teacher asked his class to name an American possession in the Far East, a pupil proudly answered "General MacArthur."

But there were many who felt quite differently about Douglas MacArthur. His many achievements—including heroic leadership in the Great War and a meteoric rise through the ranks of the Army—were offset by a towering ego that frequently manifested itself in Olympian declarations and pompous passages of purple prose. He rarely willingly shared the limelight, and his use of the first-person was legendary. His leadership during the Japanese invasion of the Philippines had been flawed, and his strong will and single-mindedness often took him to the very brink of insubordination.

Roosevelt was very aware of these antipodal reactions to MacArthur. He was being pressured by MacArthur's advocates to give him command of the entire Pacific war, while the general's enemies were violently opposed. From a purely military viewpoint, there seemed no logical place for MacArthur in the Pacific War. American naval leaders convincingly argued that the aqueous expanses of the Pacific dictated that the war there would primarily be a naval one and should therefore be led by an admiral rather than a general, yet MacArthur's larger-than-life persona and extreme seniority prevented his being subordinated to any naval commander. But viewed politically, MacArthur's considerable following posed a potential threat in future elections, perhaps even a presidential candidate to rival Roosevelt himself. There is an old political axiom that says "Keep your friends close and your enemies closer," and Roosevelt was nothing if not a savvy politician.

Roosevelt ultimately handled the sticky problem of what to do with MacArthur as most political dilemmas are handled: by compromise. MacArthur was not given command of the entire Pacific War, nor was he shelved. The Pacific was carved into theaters, with MacArthur named as Supreme Commander of the Southwest Pacific Area, which encompassed Australia, the Solomon Islands, the Bismarck Archipelago, New Guinea, the Netherlands East Indies (except Sumatra), and the Philippines, and the rest of the Pacific assigned to Admiral Chester Nimitz, with the title of Commander in Chief Pacific Ocean Areas. The seniority (and ego) aspects were handled by considering each as an independent command with neither the general nor the admiral answering to the other. This may have seemed a good solution but for one glaring problem. To find their common superior, one had to go to the other side of the world. Nimitz's immediate superior was the Chief of Naval Operations, Admiral Ernest King, and MacArthur answered to Chief of Staff of the Army, General George C. Marshall. Although King and Marshall deferred to a degree to Admiral William Leahy, the Chairman of the Joint Chiefs, it was Franklin Roosevelt who had the final word on matters concerning the conduct of the war, so the common commander in the Pacific was, effectively, the President himself. Initially this posed no major problem, but it would have severe consequences later.

Three Words

The course to the Battle of Leyte Gulf was set shortly after MacArthur's escape when he held a press conference in Australia. MacArthur was determined to recover from the ignominy of having been driven from the Philippines, to avenge the defeat by going back as soon as possible with the forces necessary to drive out the invading Japanese, to restore America's—and his own—honor. Voicing this determination to the world, MacArthur captured the imagination of those Americans and

Filipinos who had placed their faith in him with three small, but powerful, words: "I shall return."

So, in the summer of 1942, the newly-appointed Commander in Chief of the Southwest Pacific Area began planning to make good on his promise to the Philippines. But Douglas MacArthur's prophecy of return was not destined for fulfillment in any short order. The course of the war dictated that it would be more than two years before that return would even be considered feasible. And even then, one man's promise was not necessarily his government's policy.

Strategic Arbiter

Driven by the natural engine of the Northeast Trade winds, slowly undulating swells swept across the unbroken surface of the Pacific as far as the eye could see. From the gently heeling deck of the heavy cruiser, USS *Baltimore*, a fifty-one-year-old man peered through his *pince-nez* spectacles at the blue waters sparkling in the sunlight. He had long had a love-affair with ships and the sea, and now he appeared to be inhaling the warm salt air as though it were an elixir that could restore the color to his sallow cheeks and erase the deeply etched shadows beneath his intelligent but weary eyes. Although he could not have known at that moment, he would be dead within a year.

But before death could claim him, Franklin Roosevelt had much work to do. Important work. And that was why this wartime president was on his way to Pearl Harbor in July of 1944.

Whether that work was strategic or political, only Roosevelt knew for certain. The official purpose of the journey was for the Commander in Chief of the Army and Navy to meet with the two men running the war in the Pacific. But there were some who claimed that this trip was more politically motivated than strategically necessary, that Roosevelt had no need to confer directly with Nimitz and MacArthur; that he was jumping the chain of command by conferring with these two subordinate theater commanders; that his real motivation was to be seen (and photographed) with General MacArthur. 1944 was, after all, an election year, and just the day before his embarkation in *Baltimore*, Roosevelt had been nominated for an unprecedented fourth term as president.

Roosevelt may indeed have wanted to be photographed with his theatre commanders so that the voters might see him in his role as Commander in Chief, as potential rival Douglas MacArthur's boss. Or he may have come merely to resolve the differences among his principal advisors, to decide where American forces should go next in the Pacific. He had been getting conflicting advice from those who had his ear in Washington and perhaps it was time to hear what the on-scene commanders had to say without the filters and dilutions of the chain of command. Both MacArthur and Nimitz had moved steadily across the Pacific in their respective theaters, but now the time was approaching when they would converge, and each had a different view of where that convergence should occur.

Whatever his primary reasons, Franklin Roosevelt was about to arbitrate between these two Pacific theater commanders, and the future course of the war depended upon who would prove more convincing.

Showdown

After the President's arrival at Pearl Harbor and the formal inspections and other military rituals had been attended to, MacArthur, Nimitz, and Roosevelt sat down for a private dinner in a cream stucco mansion overlooking Waikiki's rolling surf that had been lent to Roosevelt by a local millionaire. The only other participant was Admiral William Leahy, Roosevelt's military aide and Chairman of the Joint Chiefs of Staff. The conversation at dinner was either highly classified or utterly mundane, because no record of it exists. But what was said *after* dinner *was* recorded, is no longer classified, and was far from mundane.

The four men left the table and moved into the mansion's large living room where huge wall maps of the Pacific had been hung. Nimitz and MacArthur alternately stood before the President, occasionally pointing at the maps with a long bamboo pointer, and presented their ideas for the future strategy in the Pacific. Nimitz, supported by King back in Washington, advocated bypassing the Philippines in favor of an invasion of Formosa, while MacArthur, to no one's surprise, steadfastly defended the imperatives of a Philippine invasion. Leahy, who was more observer of the proceedings than participant, later wrote: "After so much loose talk in Washington, where the mention of the name MacArthur seemed to generate more heat than light, it was both pleasant and very informative to have these two men who had been pictured as antagonists calmly present their differing views to the Commander-in-Chief." Noting that both Nimitz and MacArthur had told the President that they could carry out their respective plans with the forces then available in the Pacific, Leahy added that it was "highly pleasing and unusual to find two commanders who were not demanding reinforcements."

Nimitz's arguments made good strategic sense. Formosa was well situated geographically to block the flow of oil to Japan, and it was close to China where American planners had long hoped to establish airbases for the strategic bombing of the home islands. It would also serve well as a marshalling point for an invasion of Japan when the time came.

Whereas Nimitz's arguments had been pragmatic and almost purely operational in scope, MacArthur's were more poignant and strategic. He pointed out that the Chinese population on Formosa could not be counted upon to lend willing support to American forces and might in fact be openly hostile, whereas the Filipinos were, almost to a man, loyal to America. He cited the constant flow of information he had received from guerillas in the Philippines since the Japanese occupation, communications that were maintained at no small risk to the Filipinos involved. He further insisted that the United States had a moral obligation to the people of the Philippines to free them from Japanese oppression as soon as it was possible. He resorted to opening the old wounds of Bataan and Corregidor, pointing out that America had abandoned not only the loyal Filipinos there, but thousands of Americans as well. He added that there were, at that very moment, American men, women, and children languishing in Japanese concentration camps in the Philippines, suffering terrible privations as the numbered days of their wretched lives passed inexorably on. He warned that the Filipinos could forgive us for failing to protect them from the Japanese in the first place, that they would even forgive our failing in an attempt to rescue them, but what they would *not* forgive was our not even trying to free them. And if the Philippines alone were not incentive enough, MacArthur admonished that the eyes of all Asia would be watching what we did in the Philippines, that our post-war image in that part of the world was at stake.

MacArthur was at his best that evening. He had no notes, no prepared maps of his own, and absolutely no doubt that he was right. He used his considerable powers of persuasion with consummate skill, and by midnight it seemed that he was winning the day. Not only did Roosevelt appear to be accepting MacArthur's reasoning, but Nimitz's counter-arguments were coming forth less frequently, and Leahy seemed to have sided with MacArthur as well. The meeting adjourned just after midnight, however, without a decision, except that the four would reconvene in the morning.

The next day MacArthur took advantage of a private moment with Roosevelt to say that if the Philippines were bypassed, "I daresay the American people would be so aroused that they would register most complete resentment against you at the polls this fall." Never to miss the opportunity to bring all weapons to bear, General MacArthur had fired a silver bullet with this remark. At the very least he was prodding the political animal inside of Roosevelt, haunting him with the politician's nightmare, the specter of lost votes. Some historians have gone a step further, reading into MacArthur's admonition an implied threat that he would bring his influence among politicians back home to bear against Roosevelt in the coming election if the President did not give him what he wanted. Whether MacArthur did indeed intend that threat, and whether he had the political strength back in the United States to make good on it, are debatable issues. But what is certain is that Roosevelt had decided in MacArthur's favor. A little more than a week later, MacArthur received a letter from Roosevelt that read, in part, "As soon as I get back I will push on that plan for I am convinced that it is logical and can be done." The President also added (perhaps tellingly) that he wished "that you and I could swap places, and personally, I have a hunch that you would make more of a go of it as President than I would as General in the retaking of the Philippines."

More hurdles lay ahead, but MacArthur had won an important victory in Hawaii, one which virtually assured that his promised return to the Philippines would come to pass.

Strike!

A little after noon on 20 October 1944, a landing craft made its way toward the Leyte shore. Ahead, American dive bombers swooped out of the clouds, peppering the hillsides in back of the beach. Palm trees that fringed the far side of the beach burned like giant candles and the pungent smell of cordite hung heavily in the smoke-filled air. Standing on the deck of that diminutive naval craft, Douglas MacArthur, his gold-encrusted cap glinting in the tropical sunlight, scanned the approaching shore for familiar landmarks. Forty-one years before, young Lieutenant MacArthur had stood on that very shore, fresh from West Point, embarking on a long and glorious career. Now, his naval forces (the Seventh Fleet commanded by Thomas C. Kinkaid) and the heart of Nimitz's power (the Third Fleet commanded by William F. Halsey) were converging on the Philippines at Leyte to fulfill a promise, to avenge an ignominious moment, to regain lost honor.

The landing craft crunched up onto the shore and the bow-door rattled down into the surf. Still some distance from the dry sand of the beach, the General and his entourage had to step off into knee-deep water and wade the rest of the way in. It was one of those moments that would become a graven image in the American heritage, photos of which would flash around the world in newspapers and then settle indelibly into thousands of history books as icons of restored national honor.

MacArthur mounted the sandy shore and proceeded to a waiting microphone that had been prepared for the occasion. "People of the Philippines," he said in his resonant voice. "I have returned." The gray skies above suddenly opened and rain cascaded from the clouds like tears so fitting to this emotional moment. "By the grace of Almighty God," MacArthur continued, "our forces stand again on Philippine soil—soil consecrated in the blood of our two peoples."

With the sounds of mortal combat still thundering around him, soldiers of both sides dying not far away, this man, that many characterized as an egotistical demagogue and others worshipped as a military saint, sent his words out over the Philippine archipelago to a people who had long awaited his return. "The hour of your redemption is here," he intoned, and countless numbers of Filipinos rejoiced. "Your patriots have demonstrated an unswerving and resolute devotion to the principles of freedom that challenge the best that is written on the pages of human history."

In the years that would follow, MacArthur's detractors would pan this moment. They would accuse him of "grandstanding," which is undeniable. They would criticize his use of the first-person, which is certainly questionable. Some would even characterize his speech as trite and overblown, which is arguable. But an objective observer would most certainly be compelled to recognize that this was truly an important moment in history. Just as General Eisenhower had spoken on the shores of Normandy to a people long-suffering under the boot of Hitler's tyranny, so General MacArthur had given new hope to a people who had trusted in the United States of America to free them from the oppression of Japanese domination. His words symbolized the beginning of the end of a long nightmare of fear and privation. A truly objective observer could hardly deny the deep emotions that America's return had stimulated in many of the Filipino people.

"Rally to me," MacArthur challenged. And many did. In the months following the landing at Leyte, many Filipinos laid down their lives, fighting as guerillas in the Japanese rear as the Americans pushed inexorably on through the islands. These people had listened when MacArthur said, "Let the indomitable spirit of Bataan and Corregidor lead on. As the lines of battle roll forward to bring you within the zone of operations, rise and strike. Strike at every favorable opportunity. For your homes and hearths, strike! For future generations of your sons and daughters, strike! In the name of your sacred dead, strike!"

Consequences

Douglas MacArthur had changed the course of the war, directly by steering the American forces to the Philippines and indirectly by his mere existence, which had led to the creation of a second theater in the Pacific. That second front had actually proved beneficial as the war progressed, because it had often kept the Japanese off balance, causing them to shuttle assets from one theater to the other as MacArthur and Nimitz thrust forward, sometimes alternately, sometimes simultaneously.

But all of that was nearly forfeited when MacArthur's and Nimitz's forces converged on the Philippines. When the Japanese responded to the landings at Leyte with a last-ditch commitment of their remaining naval assets, it was clearly a desperate gamble that by all rights should not have come close to success. Yet it turned out to be a very near thing!

The complex events that led to this near disaster are well known. With Japanese forces coming from several directions, various elements of the two American fleets responded with devastating consequences for the Japanese. Halsey's Third Fleet wreaked havoc on the forces crossing the Sibuyan and Sulu Seas, and Kinkaid's Seventh Fleet all but annihilated the enemy forces coming up through Surigao Strait. But with the bulk of Kinkaid's firepower engaged to the south and Halsey taking the entire Third Fleet northward to chase a carrier decoy force, confused communications and a lack of coordination left the door wide open for a powerful Japanese surface force to steam in from San Bernardino Strait and attack the vulnerable remnants of the Seventh Fleet in the waters off Samar. Disaster was averted only by the incredible courage of the

American Sailors who sacrificed themselves by standing up to their gargantuan attackers and by the attacking Japanese commander's failure to adequately press his advantage at the critical moment.

Most analyses of this battle focus on the tactical decisions made by the various commanders—Halsey in particular—but by doing so, they are chasing a chimera with little hope of lasting lessons. We cannot change Halsey's impetuous bellicosity and we cannot count on an enemy admiral to make a crucial mistake. What we can do—and should—is look for the strategic decisions that determined the conditions in which those tactical decisions were made, and learn the lessons such scrutiny permits.

From the foregoing narrative, it should be apparent that among the preventable errors in this instance, one has its roots in the earliest days of the war, when Roosevelt decided to handle the MacArthur dilemma by creating two independent theaters in the Pacific. Despite any benefits that may have accrued, this decision suffered from a very significant flaw, one that violated a sacrosanct principal of war: *unity of command*. For most of the war, when Nimitz and MacArthur were virtually fighting independent wars in the Pacific, there was little need for coordination, other than at the logistical level. But once those two campaigns merged at Leyte Gulf, this problem should have been rectified. No wonder the two fleet commanders—Kinkaid who answered to MacArthur and Halsey who answered to Nimitz—had difficulty communicating and utterly failed at coordination. The absence of a unified commander set the stage for a series of blunders that cost many lives and narrowly averted a much greater disaster.

So, in the end, MacArthur and Roosevelt were central figures in the Battle of Leyte Gulf. MacArthur bears much of the responsibility for its very occurrence, and Roosevelt is accountable for the milieu that allowed costly errors to occur. These conclusions are drawn, not for the sake of recrimination, but for the potential lessons to be learned.

If there is one essential lesson in all of this, one might find it in semantics by differentiating between the words *policy* and *politics*. While both words have common roots, there is a significant difference in the two. Carl von Clausewitz, when making his most significant utterance in his classic work *On War*, used the German word *politik*, which has been variously translated as "War is a continuation of 'policy'—or of 'politics'—by other means." Judging from the experience of U.S. forces at Leyte Gulf, it becomes clear which should be the preferred translation. Strategic decision making that incorporates *policy* is sound and justified—actually essential. But when such decisions are made on the basis of *politics*, a Pandora's box is cracked open. Had Roosevelt been thinking solely as commander in chief and not as a politician, there might never have been a Battle of Leyte Gulf, or at the very least, it would have been fought without the embarrassing errors that taint this otherwise important U.S. victory in the Pacific War.

About the Author

Lieutenant Commander Cutler, the senior acquisitions editor for the Naval Institute Press, is the author of *The Battle of Leyte Gulf* (1994) and *A Sailor's History of the U.S. Navy* (2004), both published by the Naval Institute Press, as well as other books.

19

JEEPS VERSUS GIANTS

*Capt. Walter Karig, USNR,
Lt. Cdr. Russell L. Harris, USNR, and
Lt. Cdr. Frank A. Manson, U.S. Navy*

Proceedings, December 1947

"Enemy surface force of 4 battleships, 7 cruisers, and 11 destroyers sighted 20 miles northwest of your task group and closing at 30 knots!" The pilot's voice sounded thin and frantic over the radio.

Combat Information Center on the U.S. escort carrier *Fanshaw Bay* quickly relayed the message to the bridge, where Rear Admiral C. A. F. Sprague watched the planes from his carriers take off for another day of long, hard work—anti-submarine patrols, photographic missions, searches, combat air patrol, support to the troops on Leyte: enough to keep everyone on the jump till sundown.

"Air Plot, tell that pilot to check his identification," shouted the Admiral into the "squawk box." He felt annoyed. He had enough to worry about without having some screwy aviator report some of Halsey's fast battleships as enemy.

"Identification confirmed," the pilot snapped back. "Ships have pagoda masts."

Pagoda masts! The Admiral looked to the northwest. The sky beyond the squall was speckled by anti-aircraft bursts. That was enough for him.

"Come to course 090. Flank speed. Launch all aircraft!"

The lone search plane's pilot looked around him and saw the sky begin to blossom with thick puffs of anti-aircraft. He had expected to find submarines when he took off shortly before sunrise this fateful October 25, 1944. Instead he had found a whole damn Jap fleet.

Nosing his plane over, he headed down for the nearest cruiser to paste her with what he had been saving for a Nip sub—two depth charges.

A minute after the launching of planes had started, at two minutes before seven, the foretops of a large force of ships were sighted from the escort carrier's bridge.

Kurita had arrived, and the second phase of the great battle for Leyte Gulf had begun.

To defend the Philippines, the Japanese had developed the intricate "Sho Plan No. 1." An acute shortage of fuel in the Home Islands had divided the Japanese Imperial Fleet. Most of the heavy surface units had to be based in the Singapore area, near the oil, while the carriers remained in the Inland Sea, near the source of planes and pilots. The plan that resulted from this unbalanced division of the fleet, and which also was greatly shaped by the geography of the Philippine Archipelago, called for a three-pronged thrust against the American landings in Leyte Gulf.

The main object of the Japanese plan was to enter Leyte Gulf with heavy gunnery ships and disrupt the landing by sinking the "soft" invasion shipping. With the part of their fleet that was based in southern waters, the Japanese planned to clamp a salt water pincer on Leyte Gulf by splitting the battleships, cruisers, and destroyers into two groups, and sending the larger group under Admiral Kurita through San Bernardino Strait and the smaller one under Admiral Nishimura through Surigao Strait. The plan called for a rendezvous in Leyte Gulf and then a wild rampage, like the proverbial bull in the china shop.

But the Japanese knew that Halsey's Third Fleet stood on the alert near-by, waiting for any sign of action from the Japanese. If the Sho plan was to succeed, Halsey would have to be gotten out of the way. That job fell to Admiral Ozawa's carrier force, the third prong of the operation. His carriers, lacking trained air groups, were carriers in name only. They could not be expected to fight in the usual way.

So the role they were given to play in the complicated drama was one of lure and sacrifice. They would sortie from the Inland Sea, be discovered by the Third Fleet, and then maneuver in such a way as to lure the Americans north, away from Leyte Gulf, while the Japanese heavy surface units had a field day among the transports and landing craft off Leyte.

The lure worked. After a full day of all-out aerial attacks on the force heading for San Bernardino, Admiral Halsey turned north to attack what gave the appearance of being a fully manned, powerful carrier force. His too optimistic fliers had reported that the Jap central force west of San Bernardino Strait was heavily damaged and probably in no condition to do much fighting. With San Bernardino unguarded, however, it slipped through the Straits undetected and headed south, for Leyte Gulf.

In the meantime the Seventh Fleet, unaware of the fact that San Bernardino Strait had been left open, concentrated on chewing up the third, or southern, Japanese force, in Surigao Strait.

Admiral Cliff Sprague's escort carrier group, that so unexpectedly found itself blocking the path of Kurita's charge for Leyte Gulf, consisted of six escort carriers, three destroyers, and four destroyer escorts.

These escort carriers (CVEs) were known by a number of unflattering names: "Baby flat-tops," "jeep carriers," "Kaiser coffins," "tomato cans," "bucket of bolts," "wind wagon." Green sailors coming aboard for the first time were told by the old hands that CVE stood for "Combustible, Vulnerable, Expendable."

The "jeeps" were a type ship turned out en masse by slapping a runway on a hull designed for a tanker or a merchantman. The resulting ship was short (about half the length of a big carrier), slow ("What makes that thing run—squirrels?"), and thin-skinned (a "grease monkey" in the engine room could touch the hull and be only a half-inch from salt water). In a calm sea and with a following breeze these little ships might make 18 knots—provided the engineering officer had been leading a good life.

The destroyer escorts, too, were thin-skinned, and were designed for anti-submarine work. Never in their wildest dreams had the designers thought that either of these types would have to fight a battle with the heaviest units of the Japanese Navy.

Admiral Sprague's group was one of three similar groups. At the time of first contact his group was 50 miles off the southern half of Samar; Rear Admiral Felix Stump's group was about thirty miles southeast, off Homonohon Island; and Rear Admiral Thomas L. Sprague (no kin), who was in overall command of the eighteen carriers, had his group 120 miles away and roughly east of Dinagat Island. The operation plans for the Leyte landing directed the escort carriers to furnish combat and anti-submarine patrols, as well as air support and spotting services for the troops ashore. The three groups had arrived on October 18 and had been busy ever since.

The first indication that the Japanese had broken through San Bernardino came at 6:37 a.m. when the Combat Information Center on the *Fanshaw Bay* heard excited Japanese jabbering on the inter-fighter director net, but this was regarded as no more than an attempt at jamming.

At 6:45—18 minutes after sunrise—anti-aircraft fire was observed to the northwest, and three minutes later one of our patrol planes made that startling announcement to unbelieving ears.

"Five minutes after the sighting of the Jap force," said the commanding officer of the *Kitkun Bay*, "we were taken under heavy major caliber gunfire. We started scrambling our deck loads. There wasn't time to give them any instructions as to how they were to make or how they were to coordinate their attacks. We simply had to rely on training to insure that they would carry on and carry through.

"The wind was out of the northeast that morning, what little there was of it—which meant that, as we launched our deck loads, we continued to close this big task force very rapidly, since they were on a southerly course, headed for the entrance to the Gulf."

From the bridge of the Japanese flagship *Yamato*, Kurita sighted the Americans at almost the same time he was spotted; first he saw two carrier planes, and then the masts of Sprague's ships, hull down over the horizon. Groping blindly without search planes, it was the first he knew of the presence of American carriers.

At that moment his ships were shifting from night to day cruising disposition, which resulted in his formation being somewhat straggly. The battleships *Yamato* and *Nagato* were in column on a southeasterly course with the other two battleships, *Kongo* and *Haruna*, on the port quarter, maneuvering independently. Also to port of the flagship were six heavy cruisers, attempting to form up. Screening on the starboard beam were the light cruiser *Noshiro* and her seven destroyers. Ahead and a bit to port of the *Yamato* was the light cruiser *Yahagi* with her four destroyers. Leyte Gulf was sixty miles away, to the south-southwest.

When the American carriers were sighted, the range was about 38,000 yards, or 19 miles. Kurita immediately changed the course of his formation more to the east with the intention of getting up-wind from the carriers and at the same time closing the range. When the range had closed to 18 miles, Kurita gave the order for *Yamato* to open fire. For the first time her 18-inch guns, whose size had been one of the most closely guarded secrets of the Japanese Navy, were fired in anger. The time was 6:59 a.m.

Almost immediately the Japanese salvoes started falling less than 2,000 yards away from the little escort carriers who were rapidly launching all available planes. One by one, as the salvoes crept closer, the fighters and torpedo planes ran the length of the deck and took to the air. Most of them, in anticipation of a day of routine support work, were loaded with small, general purpose bombs or depth charges—not powerful enough to make a battleship even flinch. But there was no time to reload.

The first destroyer to leap at the Japanese was the *Johnston*. Without orders, like a mother lion who instinctively protects her young, the *Johnston* started making smoke ten minutes before the other escorts. Then when the shells began to drop so close that it seemed as if the *Johnston* would soon be hit, the commanding officer decided to launch a torpedo attack alone, before his ship was incapacitated.

Unaided, the *Johnston* dashed in toward a heavy cruiser, and at 7:20 a.m. launched a spread of torpedoes from a range of 8,000 yards. Her five-inch guns fired continuously. The *Johnston* was not hit until she started to retire. Then three 14-inch shells and three-inch shells smashed into her fragile hull, slowing her speed to 16 knots.

As the Japanese rapidly drew closer, their fire became more intense and more accurate. Admiral Sprague ordered his destroyers and destroyer escorts to spread a curtain of smoke between the carriers and the on-rushing enemy.

After launching planes on an easterly course, the carriers eased, in small increments, towards the south, giving their sterns to the Japanese. Smoke, pouring from the sterns of the galloping destroyers and DEs, spread thick and woolly over the sea; and at 7:20, when the carriers jumped into a seagoing foxhole (a heavy rain squall), the Japanese fire slackened and became less accurate.

Meanwhile Admiral Sprague ordered his escorts to form up for two torpedo attacks—the first by the destroyers *Hoel*, *Heermann*, and *Johnston*; the second by the slower, lighter destroyer escorts, *Butler*, *Dennis*, *Raymond*, and *Roberts*.

The *Johnston* was badly hurt by this time, and had expended all her torpedoes, but she turned and followed the *Hoel* and *Heermann* in as best she could to provide fire support while they launched their attacks.

The Japanese were pouring on steam. Kurita ordered all ships to make their best speed. The heavy cruisers, faster than the battleships, started a flanking movement to the left at 30 knots. The *Kongo* bolted formation and headed eastward with the enthusiasm of an unleashed puppy. The *Yamato* and *Nagato* closed from astern while the *Haruna* cut corners across their wakes. The *Yahagi* and her destroyer squadron remained to port of the flagship, while the *Noshiro* and her destroyers remained to the rear on the starboard flank. The attack was on.

"We were the southernmost destroyer of the three," related the captain of the *Heermann*, "and had to thread our way through the formation to join on the *Hoel*. I didn't know exactly where the enemy was. We had no radar contact; and as the visibility was very bad, I had not seen the enemy, nor had anyone in my ship. . . .

"It was rather difficult threading through the carriers, as the shell splashes were rather heavy in some spots. . . .

"About this time, I realized that we were on our way to make a daylight torpedo attack. The progress of the war and the natural instinct of the Japs to seem to want to fight at night had made me believe that I would never have such an opportunity. But I was on my way. I turned to the Officer of the Deck, and said, 'What we need is a bugler to sound the charge!' He looked at me like I was a little crazy and said, 'What do you mean, Captain?' I said, 'We are going to make a torpedo attack.' He gulped and went about his job.

"After that we had little more opportunity for such conversations, as things started to happen rather rapidly. First, we had to maneuver violently to avoid the *Samuel B. Roberts*, one of the destroyer escorts that was laying a smoke screen.

"About this time I think I had better say a little bit about the weather. The visibility was anything from 100 yards up to about 13 miles. There were many squalls. The rain was dense and heavy at any time you were in a squall. You came out and you might see a short distance to another squall, or maybe several miles. Most of the time the visibility was very bad.

"All the destroyers and destroyer escorts were continuing to lay smoke. The whole area was beginning to be covered with a dense black and white smoke screen.

"We avoided the *Dennis* and proceeded at full power to join the *Hoel*. A few minutes later I had to back emergency to miss the *Hoel*. I did not realize it at the time, but she had already been damaged. I thought she had slowed down to wait for me.

"We followed the *Hoel* in on a coordinated torpedo attack led by the Screen Commander, using *Hoel* as flagship. There were no orders issued, as none were necessary. It was made according to doctrine, in the manner in which we had planned such an attack during the many conversations and conferences we had held in port.

"The *Johnston*, which had already made a torpedo attack, joined and followed some place astern of the *Hoel* and *Heermann* to aid with her battery in supporting the attack. After the *Hoel* cut loose with her fish, an enemy heavy cruiser took us under fire. We fired torpedoes at him.

"By this time, we were under heavy fire and could hear the express train roar of the 14-inchers going over.

"The gunnery officer said that he watched with fatal fascination as they fired. First they fired two turrets. Then they fired two more turrets. Then all four. All the shells went on over. We took our five-inch director and moved our fire up and down their superstructure. Much to our surprise this must have done something to their fire control system, or at least to their morale, because they quit shooting at us and for about four minutes we were able to shoot at them without any interference.

"We fired our last torpedoes at the battleship at about 4,400 yards closing. It was a good beam shot.

"After firing, I went inside the pilot house, called the Admiral on the TBS, and told him my exercise was completed. I don't know quite why I used these words. I remember having an idea in my head that the Japs might be listening on the circuit and I didn't want them to know that I didn't have any more torpedoes."

The *Hoel* did not return after her torpedo attacks. Two minutes before launching her first half salvo of torpedoes at the leading Jap battleship, the *Kongo*, she was hit for the first time—on the director platform. Nevertheless torpedoes were launched at a range of 9,000 yards. Immediately afterwards a 14-inch shell dug its way into the after turbine, causing the loss of the port engine. Another hit from a battleship shell knocked out the after guns and the electrical steering gear.

In the melee it was hard to see if the torpedoes hit or not. The smoke screen, the rain squalls, and all the ships dashing in and out made it difficult to get a smooth idea of which ships were which.

The commanding officer of the *Hoel* felt that it was necessary to stop both columns of enemy ships—the battleships and the cruisers—if the escort carriers were to be saved. So he selected the leading heavy cruiser as a target for his second half salvo of torpedoes. Using one engine, hand steering, and training the torpedo mount manually (all electric power was by now disrupted), the *Hoel* loosed her second load of torpedoes at 7:35. Geysers of water were seen to shoot up from the Japanese cruiser (probably the *Kumano*), at about the time the torpedoes should have hit.

"With our fish fired," said one of the officers of the *Hoel*, "we decided that it was time to get the hell out of there. We attempted a retirement to the southwest, but this was impossible for we were boxed in on all sides by enemy capital ships—battleships 8,000 yards on the port beam and heavy cruisers 7,000 yards on the starboard quarter. By fishtailing and chasing salvoes and making all possible speed, we were able to remain afloat for more than an hour in this precarious position. We had only two guns left to fire. They were forward, which made it difficult to continue firing while attempting a retirement. The gun crews did almost a miraculous job. Each gun expended close to full allowance.

"Before the ship sank we had to send people up to those two guns to chase the men out of there and make them cease firing and get off the ship. They did not leave the gun mounts until there was a good list on the ship and she was settling by the stern."

At 8:55, after having received over 40 hits from 5-inch, 8-inch, and 14-inch shells, the *Hoel* sank.

Under cover of the rain squall the escort carriers had gradually changed course to the southward, feeling their way toward Leyte Gulf and the protection of Admiral Oldendorf's heavy ships. By this time the escort carriers, too, were laying a thick carpet of black smoke.

(In the northern transport area in Leyte Gulf, Admiral Wilkinson, aboard his flagship *Mount Olympus*, lying to alongside Admiral Kinkaid's *Wasatch*, anxiously followed reports of the battle. Admiral Barbey had gone south with his group, but most of Wilkinson's group was still in Leyte Gulf unloading cargoes sorely needed by the troops ashore.

"I felt," remarked Wilkinson, "much like the heroine watching the hero and the villain struggle for her favors.")

When the baby flat-tops came out of the squall at 0730, they were still in good formation—a large circle with the *St. Lo* to the north, and in clockwise rotation the *Kalinin Bay*, *Gambier Bay*, *Kitkun Bay*, *White Plains*, and *Fanshaw Bay* (Admiral Cliff Sprague's flagship).

"The enemy's main body, that is, the battleships," related the commanding officer of the *Gambier Bay*, "were about ten miles to the north of us. A division of four Japanese cruisers (the *Haguro*, *Chokai*, *Tone*, *Chikuma*) had gained station about 15 or 16,000 yards to the northeast of the formation. The wind was generally from the northeast. As a result the *Gambier Bay* and the *Kalinin Bay* were on the exposed windward flank of the formation where our own smoke provided very little coverage between us and these cruisers to the northeast. It did offer more protection to the other ships of the formation. And the destroyers' smoke and their attacks, momentarily at least, suppressed the fire from the main enemy battleship body to the north.

"These cruisers, to the northeast and closing our port flank, were unopposed and in an excellent position to pour in a rather heavy fire upon the *Gambier Bay* and *Kalinin Bay*, which they proceeded to do without delay. However, their fire was somewhat inaccurate, not very fast—salvoes were about a minute or a minute and a half apart, and not particularly large. Their spotting was rather methodical and enabled us to dodge.

"I maneuvered the ship alternately from one side of the base course to another as I saw that a salvo was about due to hit. One could observe that the salvoes would hit some distance away and gradually creep up closer, and from the spacing on the water we could tell that the next one would be on if we did nothing. We would invariably turn into the direction from which the salvoes were creeping, and sure enough the next salvo would land right in the water where we would have been if we hadn't turned. The next few salvoes would creep across to the other side and gradually creep back and would repeat the operation. The process lasted for, believe it or not, a half hour during which the enemy was closing constantly.

"When the range was finally reduced to about 10,000 yards, we weren't quite so lucky and we took a hit through the flight deck, followed almost immediately by a most unfortunate piece of damage which I believe was caused by a salvo which fell just short of the port side of the ship. The shell exploded very near the plates outside of the forward engine room, flooding it rapidly. With the loss of this one engine my speed dropped from full to about 11 knots. Of course I dropped astern of the formation quite rapidly, and the range closed at an alarming speed.

"The Japs really poured it on then, hitting us with practically every salvo. During the period from this first hit, which was around 8:10, until we sank, which was about 9:10, we were being hit probably every minute."

The three U.S. destroyers by this time had made their torpedo attacks. Now it was time for the slower, thin-skinned destroyer-escorts to get rid of their "fish" in a follow-up attack.

"Small boys form our second attack!" came the orders from Admiral Sprague over the voice radio.

The DE's had become scattered in the rain and smoke, so each attack was an individual affair. The *Samuel B. Roberts*, under smoke cover, approached to within 4,000 yards of a heavy cruiser before launching her torpedoes about 8 a.m. The *Dennis* and *Raymond* also launched theirs about the same time, but from greater range.

Their torpedoes expended, except for the *John C. Butler*, which had not been in a firing position, the scrappy DE's began to slug it out with the Japanese cruisers. It was as if a bantamweight were put in the ring with a ham-fisted heavy. For destroyers with their five 5-inch guns to take on the Japanese heavies was plucky enough, but for DE's with only two 5-inchers—well, it was unbelievable.

An officer on the *Samuel B. Roberts* graphically describes the action on that ship:

"The rapid and continuous fire from Gun 2 was an inspiration to every man on the ship. We had to maneuver radically in order to avoid the oncoming salvoes, and although we operated with very little fire control equipment, we were able to obtain a great many hits on a Jap heavy cruiser. We positively knocked out their number three 8-inch gun turret, demolished their bridge, and started fires aft under their secondary control tower.

"After we had been in action perhaps 50 minutes, we received our first hits. At that time No. 2 gun's ammunition hoist went out of commission. That did not delay his rate of fire in the least. The Japanese had our range by this time and we were being hit continuously by salvoes of 8-inch and 14-inch shells, which finally disrupted all power and communication to the gun mount.

"Our action report tells the story: 'After all power, air, and communications had been lost and before the word to abandon ship was passed, the crew of Number 2 gun, who as a crew distinguished themselves throughout the entire action, loaded, rammed, and fired six charges entirely by hand and with a certain knowledge of the hazards involved due to the failure of the gas-ejection system caused by the air supply having been entirely lost.

"'While attempting to fire the seventh round, the powder charge cooked off before the breach closed, wrecking the gun and killing or wounding all but three crew members, who were critically injured and two of whom were blown clear of the mount and the ship as a result of the explosion.

"'The first man to enter the mount after the explosion found the gun captain on the deck of the mount, holding in his hands the last projectile (weight 54 pounds) available to his gun, even though he was severely wounded from his neck down to the middle of his thighs. He was completely torn open and his intestines were splattered throughout the inside of the mount. Nevertheless, he held in his hand the 54-pound projectile—held it up above his head and begged the petty officer who had entered the mount to help him get that last round out. You must appreciate that the breach of the gun had been blown into an unrecognizable mass of steel. The mount, itself, was torn to pieces. He was the only man capable of physical movement within the mount, and yet his only idea was to get out that last round.

"'The petty officer, who entered the mount, took the projectile from the wounded gunner and removed one of the other men who was wounded and unconscious to the main deck in order to render him first aid. When he returned to the mount, there was the Gunner's Mate again with the projectile in his hand, still attempting, although horribly wounded, to place the projectile on the loading tray and thereby utilize his last chance to do damage to the Japanese.'"

He was immediately removed from the mount but died within five minutes.

Although the jeep carriers were making smoke and taking violent evasive turns at full speed, the dye-colored shells from Kurita's battleships and cruisers continued to fall near. As the four fast cruisers continued to close in on the port quarter of the fleeing ships, the four destroyers and one light cruiser of Kurita's Destroyer Squadron 10 pressed in on the right flank in a flying pincer movement. When the men aboard the *Kalinin Bay*—"Tail-End Charlie" of the carrier formation—first saw these destroyers approaching head-on, they thought them to be friendly; but when the destroyers opened fire, they changed their minds and immediately began firing back with the only thing at their disposal—a single five-inch gun on the stern.

As they ran, all the carriers fired steadily with their stern "peashooters."

"Being able to fire that one five-inch gun," commented the commanding officer of the *Kitkun Bay*, "contributed greatly to the morale of the crew because they felt that at least we were throwing something at the enemy. It was pretty tough for the men because all the 40 mm and 20 mm. gun crews, all the flight deck personnel, and other topside personnel had nothing to do except watch the progress of the battle."

A 40 mm battery officer tried to lift the spirits of his gun crew. "It won't be long now, boys!" he said. "We're sucking them into 40 mm range!"

The great danger to the escort carriers came from the heavy enemy cruisers on their port quarter. In spite of air and torpedo attacks and heavy shelling, these cruisers continued to draw nearer and nearer the egg-shelled carriers, and their salvoes were connecting: the *Fanshaw Bay*, *Kalinin Bay*, and *Gambier Bay* had all been hit before 8:30. Many of the Jap shells were armor-piercing and passed entirely through the ships without exploding.

Over the noise of battle the voice radio barked out an urgent order from Admiral Sprague: "Small boys (DDs and DEs) on my starboard quarter intercept enemy cruiser coming in on my port quarter!"

Forty seconds later the order was repeated in short, quick tones: "Intercept enemy heavy cruiser coming in on port quarter! Expedite!"

The 8-inch guns of the *Haguro* were finding their range.

"Intercept" the order had been, but there was not much left to intercept with. The *Hoel* was sinking under heavy fire. The *Johnston*, mortally wounded, could only make fifteen knots. Only two of her guns were in full operation. Killed and wounded littered her decks. But her captain, holed by numerous shrapnel wounds and with two fingers blown off, continued to fight his ship. The *Heermann* alone was still in good shape.

But in the entire force there was not a single torpedo left.

"Smoke hung heavy on the sea," said the *Heermann*'s skipper, "as we started to cross the formation to the port quarter. Immediately it was obvious that the *Johnston* was badly damaged and couldn't make the speed we could. The radar was hanging down on her yardarm, and her skipper sent me a signal, 'only one engine, no radar, and no gyros.' We left him and started to the port quarter of the carrier formation by ourselves.

"Actually I guess the *Johnston* made a better trip across than we did, because our haste only slowed us up. I had the ship trying to make full speed, when suddenly the *Fanshaw Bay* was very close ahead of me. I gave an emergency crash back. We avoided the *Fanshaw Bay* and went crash ahead again. No more had we started forward than here was the *Johnston* coming out of the smoke on the port bow. I crash backed again. This time it was too close for comfort. We missed the *Johnston* by a mere matter of three inches—people could have touched as our bows missed each other. Everyone thought we would hit. As we cleared, a spontaneous cheer arose from each ship.

"As we passed under the *Johnston*'s stern, we came out of the smoke and saw the *Gambier Bay* lying to in the water. She had about a 20-degree list to starboard, and an enemy cruiser of the *Tone* class had her under fire. There were other enemy cruisers firing at her, too.

"When we started to fire at the *Tone*-class cruiser, she shifted fire from the *Gambier Bay* and engaged us. Actually this didn't do the *Gambier Bay* very much good, because there were so many Jap ships there firing at her that I don't believe one less made much difference. We paralleled the *Tone* at about 12,000 yards and started to slug it out. As she shifted her fire to us, we noticed three more heavy cruisers astern of her.

"Four minutes later, at 8:45, we received a shrapnel hit on the bridge which killed three men and mortally wounded the steersman. Our Chief Quartermaster, thrown to the deck, rose to his knees, reached over the mortally wounded steersman, took the wheel, and carried out an unexecuted order I had given.

"I conned the ship from the top of the pilot house, where I could see better, and we continued to chase salvoes while engaging the enemy cruisers—we were under fire from four of them now. I realized that it was four ships by the fact that there were several colors of splashes. There were red, yellow, green, and no-color splashes all around us. It looked like a rainbow. There was more red than anything else. In fact it looked kind of rosy, looking through it, although I guess it was probably rosier for the Japs than it was for us at that particular moment.

"One shell hit tore a jagged hole in our hull and flooded the forward magazines. One hit a stowage locker full of dried Navy beans and reduced the beans to paste. Another hit the uptake from our forward boiler. The bean paste was sucked up by the hot blast of the uptake and thrown in the air. One officer was nearly buried in the stuff.

"The *Heermann* plunged down by the bow until her anchors were dragging in the bow wave. It seemed as if the ship would dive headfirst beneath the surface. Racing at flank speed as we were, torrents of water were coming up over our deck. But only one gun had been knocked out, and we continued firing."

The four enemy cruisers, the *Chokai*, *Haguro*, *Tone*, and *Chikuma*—(the Suzuya having dropped out to aid the injured *Kumano*)—continued to close, forcing Admiral Sprague's carriers more and more toward Samar, only 15 miles away. The Japanese battleships pressed the attack from astern, gaining ground each minute.

The smoke screen was getting thinner and the salvoes were creeping closer.

"Small boys on my starboard quarter interpose with smoke between men (CVEs) and enemy cruisers!" crackled Sprague's order over the TBS at 8:30.

For the next forty minutes the "small boys" did the work of giants—zig-zagging back and forth at their best speeds, laying great rolling clouds of smoke, shooting at any Jap within range: the four heavy cruisers to port or the destroyers to starboard. It was during this phase of the battle that the limping *Johnston* was fatally hit.

In spite of these heroic efforts the Japanese cruisers continued to close. By this time the torpedo planes of the task group had expended all their bombs and torpedoes and were forced to make dummy torpedo runs on the enemy ships. The fighters strafed, but it was like rain falling on a tin roof. The jeep carriers' 5-inch guns were low on ammunition, having been firing since 7:40.

By 9:10 a.m. the carrier formation had been forced around to a southwesterly course and was heading straight for Leyte Gulf.

Ten minutes later the four Japanese destroyers on the starboard flank, led by the light cruiser *Yahagi*, made a last torpedo attack from 10,000 yards. The first indication that the *Kalinin Bay* had of the attack was when a torpedo plane from the *St. Lo*, which had been circling the formation, went into a steep glide and strafed the wake of the *Kalinin Bay*, about 100 yards astern. Two enemy torpedoes exploded. Immediately after this another torpedo was sighted broaching directly astern in the wake. The five-inch gun on the *Kalinin Bay*'s fantail opened fire. An exploding shell near the approaching torpedo caused it to veer to port.

All of the Japanese torpedoes fired in this attack paralleled the course of the fleeing jeep carriers, and no damage was done.

Then the Japanese did a strange and puzzling thing. By 9:20 two flanking cruisers to port had closed to 10,000 yards—point blank range for their eight-inch guns—forcing the jeep carriers more and more to the right, and threatening to cut off the escape route to Leyte Gulf. The *Gambier Bay* had been sunk. The *Hoel*, *Johnston*, and *Samuel B. Roberts* were either sunk or sinking. The *Fanshaw Bay*, *Kalinin Bay*, *Dennis*, and *Heermann* were badly hit. But just when the situation seemed most desperate, the Japanese quit!

The Jap's last gesture were two salvoes, which fell short, and a minor torpedo attack from the cruisers. With that they broke off the engagement, turned about, and headed north.

That part of the battle was over. A strange quietness settled over the escort carriers. There was no more gunfire, and no more shells fell near the ships. On the bridge of one carrier the silence was broken by a signalman:

"Damn it!" he said. "They got away!"

*From Volume IV of the Battle Report series, to be published in book form by Rinehart and Company, Incorporated. This excerpt is printed in advance in the *Proceedings* by special arrangement with the book publishers.

About the Authors

After a successful career as a Washington and foreign correspondent for magazines and newspapers, **Captain Karig** joined the Naval Reserve in 1942. The author of numerous novels in addition to the previous volumes of the Battle Report series, he is at present on duty in the Executive Office of the Secretary of the Navy, Navy Department, Washington, D.C.

A native of Arkansas, **Lieutenant Commander Harris** graduated from the University of Notre Dame in June, 1941, and two weeks later plunged into naval life at the Reserve Midshipman's School, Northwestern University. Then followed Panama, sea duty, Stateside assignments, and more sea duty in the order named. In Washington after the war he collaborated on the fourth and fifth volumes of Battle Reports.

Lieutenant Commander Manson graduated from Northeastern State College, Oklahoma, in 1941, and taught in high school prior to reporting to Cornell University for Naval training. He served on the staff of ComDesLant and later was Communications Officer of the kamikazed destroyer *Laffey* in the Pacific. He, too, is collaborating on both volumes four and five of Battle Reports.

20

SEVEN DECADES OF DEBATE

Alan Rems

Naval History, October 2017

"It's your fault!" During a cocktail hour at Pearl Harbor attended by senior officers the evening after the guns fell silent at Leyte Gulf, Lieutenant Commander Chester W. Nimitz Jr. fired that shot across his father's bow. The younger Nimitz had just learned that Admiral Chester W. Nimitz, Commander-in-Chief of the Pacific Fleet, waited hours before trying to determine what the U.S. Third Fleet's battleships were doing. Even more stunning was hearing that Admiral William F. "Bull" Halsey, the fleet's commander, had been given carte blanche to engage the Japanese Navy at the cost of protecting the Leyte invasion forces. Admiral Nimitz abruptly ended the discussion, grumbling, "That's your opinion."[1]

By Heavenly Dispensation

Well aware of the questions his actions must have raised, Halsey tried to get in front of the story. Dashing off a message to Nimitz, he wrote: "As it seemed childish to me to guard statically San Bernardino Strait, I concentrated Task Force 38 [the Third Fleet's fast carrier force] during the night and steamed north to attack the Northern Force at dawn. I believed that the Center Force had been so heavily damaged in the Sibuyan Sea that it could no longer be considered a serious menace to Seventh Fleet."[2]

Nimitz was not ready to accept that explanation, but he also needed to do some explaining. Whatever else happened, Halsey had not violated orders. In his message to Admiral Ernest J. King, Commander-in-Chief of the U.S. Fleet, Nimitz wrote: "[My] regret is that the fast battleships were not left in the vicinity of Samar when Task Force 38 started after the

— 304 —

striking force reported to be in the north.... It never occurred to me that Halsey, knowing the composition of the ships in the Sibuyan Sea, would leave San Bernardino Strait unguarded, even though the Jap detachments in the Sibuyan Sea had been reported seriously damaged. That Halsey feels that he is in a defensive position is indicated in his dispatch." Recognizing how much worse things might have gone, Nimitz added, "That the San Bernardino detachment of the Japanese Fleet ... did not completely destroy all of [the] escort carriers and their accompanying screen is nothing short of special dispensation from the Lord Almighty."[3]

Thanks to Halsey's splendid performance until then, and well aware that he gave Halsey much leeway, Nimitz chose to suppress criticism. Refusing to sign a draft copy of the official report on the battle, Nimitz lashed back at the chief of his analytical section, snapping: "What are you trying to do . . . start another Sampson-Schley controversy? Tone this down."[4] But the facts were too significant to be permanently suppressed, and the controversy that finally erupted would resonate as loudly as the Spanish-American War imbroglio that Nimitz did not want repeated.

Benefiting further from the considerable goodwill he had accumulated, Halsey avoided criticism from the topmost level. Rejecting complaints expressed by his staff, General Douglas MacArthur voiced his full confidence in Halsey. Even volcanic King suppressed his anger. When Halsey said he was wrong in turning his battleships around with the enemy virtually under his guns, King responded, "You've got a green light on everything you did."[5]

But fortune soon turned against the Third Fleet commander in the form of two typhoons. Most destructive was the first, in December 1944, which claimed three destroyers and hundreds of men and aircraft. A court of inquiry judged that Halsey was primarily to blame, but both Nimitz and King added endorsements that largely nullified the verdict. When his fleet was caught once more by a typhoon in May 1945, Halsey again was found responsible. Nimitz decided that Halsey was guilty of gross stupidity in both typhoons, and only King's appreciation of his past service and the expected effect on national morale saved Halsey from retirement.

With the coming of peace, the other side of the story of Leyte Gulf became known. Interrogations of the major Japanese commanders included the leader of the Northern Force, Vice Admiral Jisaburo Ozawa, who asserted that his sole mission was to act as a decoy while expecting the complete destruction of his fleet.

War of Words

Awareness that Halsey was duped affected how his actions were subsequently viewed. During 1947, books and book reviews seriously questioned his judgment. In response, Halsey sought vindication through his memoirs, serialized in the *Saturday Evening Post* before book publication.[6]

Halsey explained his thinking in pursuing the enemy carriers: "The crippled Central Force's dogged second approach to San Bernardino, and the weak Southern Force's simultaneous approach to Surigao against overwhelming strength, were comprehensible only if they were under adamant orders to rendezvous with the carriers ... for a combined attack on the transports at Leyte." But the Central Force was far from "crippled," and Ozawa's intent was very different. In explaining the grossly incorrect damage estimate for the Center Force, Halsey noted, "The pilots' reports proved dangerously optimistic, but we had no reason to discredit them at the time." Surely, Halsey knew how seriously aviators could overestimate results in the heat of battle.

Particularly striking was Halsey's limited concern about the harm the Center Force might inflict. He wrote: "Even if the Central Force meanwhile penetrated San Bernardino and headed for Leyte Gulf, it could hope only to harry the landing operation. It could not consolidate any advantage, because no transports or supply ships accompanied it. It could merely hit and run." This is surprising from someone who could recall the devastating Japanese battleship bombardments of U.S. Marines on Guadalcanal and the heavy cruiser threat against the Bougainville beachhead that impelled him to run great risks with his carriers to avert it.

Halsey then unloaded on Seventh Fleet Commander-in-Chief Vice Admiral Thomas C. Kinkaid. Describing how that fleet's escort carriers were surprised off Samar, he wrote: "I wondered how Kinkaid had let [Rear Admiral Clifton] 'Ziggy' Sprague get caught like this, and why Ziggy's search planes had not given him warning.... I figured that the eighteen little carriers had enough planes to protect themselves until [Kinkaid's battleship commander] could bring up his heavy ships."

Describing his reaction on receiving Kinkaid's calls for help, Halsey wrote: "That surprised me. It was not my job to protect the Seventh Fleet. My job was offensive ... and we were even then rushing to intercept a force which gravely threatened not only Kinkaid and myself, but the whole Pacific strategy." To Halsey, what happened to the Seventh Fleet was entirely Kinkaid's fault.

In conclusion, Halsey declared clumsily, "[T]he fact [that the battle] was not coordinated under any authority was an invitation which disaster nearly accepted." Stated plainly, Halsey believed if he had been given total control, he could have prevented Kinkaid's and his own problems.

Reading the article, King grasped the dissension it would inevitably create and urged a rewrite of the still-unpublished book. Halsey refused to make any changes.

Provoked into ending his long silence, Kinkaid arranged with a *Life* magazine writer to tell his side of the story. The article began by asking, rhetorically, "Was . . . Halsey right in dashing off to destroy the Japanese aircraft carriers instead of the battleships—or did he leave a fellow American admiral in the lurch?"[7] Vividly, that question was answered in describing Halsey's attitude on receiving Kinkaid's plea for help: "There was apparently no thought . . . that Papa Nimitz had told him to protect the kid brother from neighborhood bullies." And, criticizing Halsey's inept employment of his own battleships, the article noted, "The American fast battleships spent about half a day steaming north to engage the Japanese force, and half a day steaming south to engage another, but in the end did not fire a shot at either."[8]

In May 1952, the U.S. Naval Institute's *Proceedings* published an article written by Halsey titled "The Battle for Leyte Gulf," much of it word-for-word from his book. Gone were many of the criticisms of Kinkaid, replaced by Halsey's military philosophy that he invoked to justify his decision to keep the fleet intact: "In modern naval warfare there is no greater threat than that offered by an enemy carrier force. To have such a force untouched and to attack it with anything less than overwhelming destructive force would not only violate this proven principle but in this instance would have been foolhardy in the extreme."[9] This ignores the fact that Japanese surface forces posed a greater threat than carrier forces at Leyte Gulf, with enemy carrier power so depleted it could have been overcome with much less than "overwhelming destructive force."

Morison and Reynolds Weigh In

A year earlier, historian Samuel Eliot Morison had delivered a lecture characterizing the pursuit of the Japanese carriers as "Halsey's Blunder." Insisting on conditions that no responsible historian could accept, Halsey wrote to Morison, "To correctly evaluate any decisions . . . it is necessary to consider only the information available . . . at the time such a decision was made."¹⁰ Halsey had good reason for concern, as Morison's multivolume history of U.S. naval operations in World War II was nearing Leyte Gulf.

When that volume appeared in 1958, Halsey's fears were fully realized. The book was dedicated to Ziggy Sprague, whose carriers had been imperiled by Halsey's actions. Paradoxically, since the Japanese were soundly defeated, Morison reserved his highest praise for Ozawa, writing, "He performed his mission of drawing off the major portion of the Pacific Fleet ... and saved Kurita, as well as his own force, from annihilation."¹¹

Both Kinkaid and Halsey were faulted for enabling Vice Admiral Takeo Kurita's descent on the Seventh Fleet. While Kinkaid placed too much confidence in Halsey, Halsey overrelied on his aviator reports, leaving San Bernardino Strait uncovered. A single destroyer posted there could have alerted the escort carriers in time to get beyond Kurita's gunfire range and prepare for battle.¹²

Though Kinkaid was roundly criticized, it was Halsey who drew Morison's heaviest fire. Regarding the decision to concentrate against Ozawa, he wrote, "Halsey ignored the stronger [force] ... because he mistakenly assumed that it was the weaker, and 'no serious menace.'" Attacking the validity of Halsey's assertion that it was essential to keep his forces concentrated, Morison observed: "It was not a case of either-or. Halsey had enough gun and air power to handle both Japanese forces."¹³

Morison addressed Halsey's lost opportunity as follows: "If [the battleships] had been detached a few hours earlier, after Kinkaid's first urgent request for help, and had left the destroyers [that needed refueling] behind, a powerful battle line of six modern battleships ... would have arrived off San Bernardino Strait in time to have clashed with Kurita. ... There is every reason to believe that [Task Force 34 commander Vice Admiral Willis] Lee would have crossed Kurita's T and completed the destruction of Center Force."¹⁴

Infuriated by Morison's criticisms, Halsey suggested his former staff members uncover deficiencies in Morison's writings, "to poke fun at him as a very poor historian and cite some instances to prove our point. In other words, make a laughing stock of him."¹⁵ Halsey wrote to one supporter, "My idea is to get the son-of-a-bitches [sic] cajones in a vise and set up on them."¹⁶ However, Halsey's former chief of staff, Admiral Robert B. Carney, convinced him to back off, observing that Morison "is firmly established in public opinion as a professional and competent historian.

No blast of yours, however justifiable, will destroy that structure; it would far more likely boomerang."[17]

Halsey died on 16 August 1959, caught up in controversy over Leyte Gulf during the last dozen years of his life. Thereafter, opinion about his performance in the battle, and indeed his entire legacy, has been left to others who remain fascinated with what may stand as the world's last great fleet action.

With the appearance in 1968 of Clark G. Reynolds' forthright study, *The Fast Carriers: The Forging of an Air Navy*, Halsey's reputation suffered a devastating blow. Reynolds' assessment of Halsey's performance late in the war would fundamentally influence opinion ever after. He wrote, "When Halsey took command [after leaving the South Pacific], he looked upon himself as the fast carrier commander, having little real use for [Vice Admiral Marc A.] Mitscher.... This attitude was dangerous, for Halsey lacked the experience of Mitscher."[18]

Reynolds observed, "Tactically, Halsey was a meleeist in the tradition of [Vice Admiral Horatio] Nelson.... He had daring and was unafraid to take risks, but he was also sloppy in his procedures."[19] The indictment concluded: "Admiral Halsey proved to be an embarrassment to the Pacific Fleet after his arrival in the Central Pacific in mid-1944.... Halsey managed to leave the Leyte beachhead uncovered to a Japanese fleet bombardment and then took the carriers into two typhoons.... The war simply became too complicated for Halsey."[20]

The following year, in *Proceedings*, U.S. Naval Academy professor E. B. Potter compared the command personalities of Halsey and Fifth Fleet Commander-in-Chief Admiral Raymond A. Spruance. Potter characterized Spruance as a "capabilities man," whose actions were governed by what the enemy could do. In contrast, Halsey was deemed a "probabilities man," who acted by considering what the enemy would probably do. Potter also likened Halsey to Nelson, whose unsystematic style led to wild-goose chases but who nevertheless succeeded by being pitted against an incompetent and demoralized enemy. Potter wrote, "It was Halsey's misfortune to be dealing with a highly motivated, alert enemy."[21]

Halsey to Posterity

In the next half century, much has been written about Leyte Gulf, with Thomas J. Cutler's *The Battle of Leyte Gulf* particularly useful. Regarding Halsey's perceived need to keep his fleet intact, Cutler noted how thoroughly Halsey had absorbed Alfred Thayer Mahan's insistence on concentration of forces as a "first principle." In Cutler's view: "There is a tendency for students of warfare to seek ironclad principles and axiomatic rules devised by others.... It appears that Halsey was just such a student...he appears to have been unable to divest himself of some of the dogmatic baggage that had been part of the Mahanian battleship era."[22]

Not only was Halsey's embrace of Mahan important, Cutler considered it all-important. "Had Halsey divided his forces before going north, had he left part of his tremendous combat capability behind at San Bernardino Strait, instead of taking the entire Third Fleet with him, all of the other errors would be cancelled out."[23] Halsey's interpretation of his mission, the unclear and misunderstood messages, and all the other problems hardly would have mattered.

Halsey's legacy, heavily weighted down by Leyte Gulf and the typhoons, remains a subject of debate among historians. Writing at length about those blunders, with minimal consideration of Halsey's service as South Pacific area commander, Walter R. Borneman ascribes Halsey's enduring stature as merely reflecting the public's need for heroes.[24] Feeling far differently about the significance of the South Pacific campaign, Eric M. Bergerud considers Halsey's leadership there sufficient to "rank him among the great admirals of history."[25] Also at the opposite pole from Borneman stands John Wukovits, who rates Halsey as at least the equal of Nimitz as the United States' top World War II naval commander. Explaining away Leyte Gulf, Wukovits argues, "The mistakes were made by a desire to strike the enemy and were executed with the blessing of Admiral Nimitz, upon whose shoulders much of the blame must rest." As though such errors might simply cancel each other out, Wukovits wipes Halsey's slate nearly clean, maintaining, "only with the typhoons can Halsey be charged."[26]

Most recently, in his 2016 biography of Halsey, Thomas A. Hughes recognizes Halsey's "inexplicable mistakes and grand blunders" but appreciates as well his inspired leadership in the South Pacific. Thus, Hughes is in full agreement with Richard B. Frank, who rated Halsey's performance "outstanding" up to 1944 and "poor" thereafter.[27] In line with Cutler's observations about the influence of Halsey's early training, Hughes writes, "By 1944, the war had become too large, too modern, and too bureaucratized for his deeply etched patterns of thought and habits of command, learned three decades earlier." In sum, "[Halsey] was a little bit more, and a little bit less, than a silhouette of his outsized legend."[28]

Though the debate will surely continue, almost all can at least agree that if Halsey was not a man for all campaign seasons, he excelled when he was most needed by the nation.

About the Author

Mr. Rems is the author of *South Pacific Cauldron: World War II's Great Forgotten Battlegrounds* (Naval Institute Press, 2014). He has been a regular contributor to *Naval History* since his article titled "Halsey Knows the Straight Story" appeared in the August 2008 issue and earned him selection as the magazine's Author of the Year.

Notes

1. E. B. Potter, *Nimitz* (Annapolis, MD: Naval Institute Press, 1976), 342–43.
2. Ibid., 344.
3. Ibid.
4. Ibid.
5. E. B. Potter, *Bull Halsey* (Annapolis, MD: Naval Institute Press, 1985), 307.
6. FADM William F. Halsey, USN, wt. LCDR J. Bryan III, USNR, "Admiral Halsey Tells His Story," (seventh of nine articles) *Saturday Evening Post*, 26 July 1947, pp. 26, 63–71. The same content appeared in Halsey and Bryan, *Admiral Halsey's Story* (New York: McGraw-Hill, 1947), 216–27.
7. Gilbert Cant, "Bull's Run: Was Halsey Right at Leyte Gulf?" *Life*, 24 November 1947, 75–90.
8. Ibid., 90.
9. FADM William F. Halsey Jr., USN (Ret), "The Battle for Leyte Gulf," U.S. Naval Institute *Proceedings* 78, no. 5 (May 1952): 494–95.
10. Potter, *Halsey*, 378.
11. Samuel Eliot Morison, *History of United States Naval Operations in World War II*, vol. 12, *Leyte: June 1944–January 1945* (Boston: Little, Brown, 1958), 336.
12. Ibid., 293.
13. Ibid., 193–94.
14. Ibid., 330.

15. Potter, *Halsey*, 379.
16. John Wukovits, *Admiral 'Bull' Halsey: The Life and Wars of the Navy's Most Controversial Commander* (New York: Palgrave MacMillan, 2010), 242.
17. Potter, *Halsey*, 379.
18. Clark G. Reynolds, *The Fast Carriers: The Forging of an Air Navy* (Annapolis, MD: Naval Institute Press, 1968), 257.
19. Ibid., 258.
20. Ibid., 387.
21. E. B. Potter, "The Command Personality," U.S. Naval Institute *Proceedings* 95, no. 1 (January 1969): 18–25.
22. Thomas J. Cutler, *The Battle of Leyte Gulf: 23–26 October, 1944* (New York: HarperCollins, 1994), 137–38.
23. Ibid., 293.
24. Walter R. Borneman, *The Admirals* (New York: Little, Brown, 2012), 415.
25. Eric M. Bergerud, *Fire in the Sky: The Air War in the South Pacific* (Boulder, CO: Westview Press, 2000), 635.
26. Wukovits, *Halsey*, 246.
27. Richard B. Frank, "Picking Winners?" *Naval History*, June 2011, 26, 30.
28. Thomas Alexander Hughes, *Admiral Bull Halsey: A Naval Life* (Cambridge, MA: Harvard University Press, 2016), 418.

21

"WHERE IS TASK FORCE THIRTY-FOUR?"

Capt. Andrew Hamilton, USNR

Proceedings, October 1960

One of the best known messages of World War II—and perhaps the most hotly argued—was a dispatch sent on Wednesday 25 October 1944 from the CinCPac headquarters of Admiral Chester W. Nimitz at Pearl Harbor to the flagship of Admiral William F. Halsey, Jr., Commander Third Fleet. As delivered to Admiral Halsey on the bridge of USS *New Jersey*, a part of Task Force 34, it was a gem of sarcasm: "WHERE IS TASK FORCE THIRTY-FOUR THE WORLD WONDERS?"

In his book, *Admiral Halsey's Story*, the latter described the circumstances under which it was received. The mighty U.S. Third and Seventh Fleets were locked with the Japanese Navy in the Battle for Leyte Gulf—one of the greatest naval engagements of all times. Greatest in number of men, number of ships and area of conflict.

It was at this crisis of human emotions and smoking battle that Admiral Halsey received what he called an "infernally plausible" message, "WHERE IS TASK FORCE THIRTY-FOUR THE WORLD WONDERS?"

"I was as stunned as if I had been struck in the face," he wrote. "The paper rattled in my hands. I snatched off my cap, threw it on the deck and shouted something I am ashamed to remember.

"Mick Carney rushed over and grabbed my arm, 'Stop it! What the hell's the matter with you? Pull yourself together.'

"I gave him back the dispatch and turned my back. I was so mad I couldn't talk. It was utterly impossible for me to believe that Chester Nimitz had sent me such an insult. He hadn't, of course, but I didn't know the truth for several weeks."

As demonstrated later, the message was a communicator's garble—or, what is more incredible, two communicators' garbles. Because of communications security, the full story of those errors has never been told.

Recently, however, I was privileged to read a report to Admiral Nimitz from Rear Admiral John R. Redman (who was CinCPac communications officer at the time) which describes in detail the amazing double garble. I also discussed the dispatch at length with Admiral Nimitz and corresponded with the late Admiral Halsey about it before his death. But first, let's set the stage and recall exactly what Admiral Halsey and Admiral Nimitz were doing on the morning of 25 October 1944 and what the circumstances were.

While other American naval forces were engaged elsewhere in Philippine waters, Admiral Halsey in New Jersey was northeast of Luzon, steering north at high speed with 65 ships in four task groups. He hoped to obliterate Admiral Jisaburo Ozawa's Northern Force of seventeen ships—one large carrier, three small carriers, two battleships (with flight decks aft), three light cruisers, and eight destroyers. Planes from Admiral Halsey's carriers had already hit the Japanese carriers. Now he was closing in for the kill with his 16-inch battleship guns.

Admiral Halsey's mission had been to guard General MacArthur's landing at Leyte Gulf, but he was to miss no opportunity to engage the Japanese fleet in action. The battle plan was this: if the Japanese fleet sent its Center Force through the San Bernardino Strait, the Third Fleet's fast battleships would be detached and formed as Task Force 34 to oppose it. The previous day, the Center Force had reversed course in the Sibuyan Sea. Reversing course again, it passed through the Strait around midnight. Admiral Halsey then sighted the Japanese Northern Force and went after it with his fast battleships and carriers.

As Samuel Eliot Morison says in *Leyte*, Volume XII of *History of the United States Naval Operations in World War II*, "Admiral Halsey was no man to watch a rathole from which the rat might never emerge."

Under cover of darkness, however, the Japanese Center Force returned and brought under heavy fire the force of small jeep carriers and destroyers commanded by Rear Admiral C. A. F. Sprague. Admiral Thomas Kinkaid, Commander Seventh Fleet, thinking that Task Force 34 was guarding San Bernardino Strait, sent several urgent dispatches to Admiral Halsey asking for help. Admiral Kinkaid had under his command the old pre-Pearl Harbor battleships, but after the battle of Surigao Strait they were low on ammunition.

With the Japanese Northern Force practically under his guns, Admiral Halsey was faced with a difficult decision. Should he press on or should he turn back and help the force of jeep carriers and destroyers? He was like a man fighting a bully he had wanted to settle scores with for a long time, then getting a frantic call for help from his younger brother who was taking a beating from the bully's brother.

Meanwhile, 3,000 miles to the east in the big, gray concrete building on [the] extinct Makalapa crater that served as CinCPac Headquarters, Admiral Nimitz and staff officers anxiously scanned dispatches from the Third and Seventh Fleets. Their only contact was through the magic of electronics and each message was read with keenest interest. As Admiral Kinkaid's anxiety grew over the pounding being taken by Admiral Sprague's jeep carriers, so did Admiral Nimitz's.

Admiral Nimitz also was under the impression that Task Force 34 had been formed to guard the San Bernardino Strait. To clarify the situation in his own mind, he instructed his Chief of Staff, the late Admiral Forrest Sherman, to find out what had happened to Admiral Halsey's fast battleships. Admiral Sherman scribbled on a pad and sent the dispatch to the communications department in the basement of CinCPac headquarters building: "WHERE IS RPT WHERE IS TASK FORCE THIRTY-FOUR?"

During World War II, Pacific Fleet communications instructions required the use of "padding" at both the beginning and end of short messages to protect them from crypto-analytical attack by the enemy. This padding was not to contain any connection with the text of the message in form, thought or wording. It was not to consist of such common phraseology as "Here we go again," "Happy days," "This is a long one," "That's all," or similar stereotyped wordage. Furthermore, for the sake of clarity, it was specified that padding must be separated from the text of the message by double letters—LL, FF, MM or some such combination. These rules had been in force for some time and were commonly observed throughout the Fleet.

In the communications room, Admiral Nimitz's message was routed through the usual channels. A young ensign added padding at the beginning and end, separating the text with double letters to make it read as follows: "TURKEY TROTS TO WATER GG (ADDRESS) X WHERE IS RPT WHERE IS TASK FORCE THIRTY-FOUR RR THE WORLD WONDERS"

Here the first mistake occurred. The phrase at the end, "THE WORLD WONDERS" plainly violated communications procedure which stated that "padding must have no connection with the text in thought, form, and wording."

Admiral Halsey himself had directed that when messages were sent to him on the bridge, they were to contain no padding. "Padding was confusing when you had to read a message in a hurry," he wrote to me. In any event, the padding should have been entirely different from the text—as was the padding preceding the text. The fact that Admiral Halsey, in the heat of battle, considered the padding a part of the message indicates how closely connected in thought the two phrases really were. "It was so plausibly a part of the message that I thought it was the message," he declared.

But if the communications officer at CinCPac headquarters who handled the fateful dispatch was wool-gathering, the violation aboard Admiral Halsey's flagship was perhaps even worse.

The separator letters GG and RR were properly used and it should have been quite obvious to any decoding officer that the phrase "THE WORLD WONDERS" was nothing but padding. Its transfer to the final write-up copy and delivery to Admiral Halsey—either as part of the basic text or in any form—was in gross violation of Pacific Fleet communications rules. What happened, for example, to the padding at the beginning, "TURKEY TROTS TO WATER"?

But whether or not the deciphering aboard USS *New Jersey* allowed only the final padding, inadvertently or otherwise, to remain in the message, the non-military nature of the language should have provoked curiosity. Furthermore, Admiral Halsey's decoding officer surely was well aware of the regulations on the use of double letters. Why, then, did he leave the padding at the end to confuse and distress our highest-ranking seagoing commander at the height of a crucial battle?

The young ensign who enciphered the message was later called on the carpet by Rear Admiral (then Captain) Redman. He swore that he meant nothing by the phrase. "It just popped into my head," he said. (A popular magazine article stated that the phrase came from Tennyson's Charge of the Light Brigade, but this does not seem to be substantiated.) Although the anonymous ensign's reputation among his associates was excellent and he had possessed a good record up to this point, by order of Admiral Nimitz he was transferred to other duties "to prevent him from further possible temptation of expressing personal thoughts in padding." In his autobiography, Admiral Halsey is blunter about it. He wrote: "Chester blew up when I told him about it; he tracked down the little squirt and chewed him to bits, but it was too late then, the damage had been done."

No information is available as to the fate of Admiral Halsey's communicator, but it is to be presumed that he also was chewed out and removed from "temptation."

What was the final effect of the garbled message?

Up to this point, Admiral Halsey had received four urgent messages from Admiral Kinkaid—some of them in plain language—asking for help from Task Force 34. Admiral Nimitz's message, "WHERE IS TASK FORCE THIRTY-FOUR THE WORLD WONDERS," came through at 1000. It tipped the scales. Reluctantly Admiral Halsey decided to turn back and help defend Admiral Sprague's jeep carriers and destroyers, knowing full well that he was missing a chance to slaughter the Japanese Northern Force in a surface fight.

He tells his reactions in *Admiral Halsey's Story*: "The orders I now gave, I gave in rage, and although Admiral Ernie King assured me they were the right ones, I'm convinced that they were not. My flag log for the forenoon watch that day, the twenty-fifth, gives the bare bones of the story: 'At 0835 c/s (changed speed) to 25K to close enemy. At 0919 c/c (changed course) to 000. At 1115 c/c to 180—or from due north to due south.'

"At that moment the Northern Force (Japanese), with its two remaining carriers crippled and dead in the water, was exactly forty-two miles from the muzzles of my 16-inch guns, yet I turned back on the opportunity I had dreamed of since my day as a cadet. For me, one of the biggest battles of the war was off and what has been called the Battle of Bull's Run was on. I notified Kinkaid: 'TG 38.2 6 FAST BATTLESHIPS PROCEEDING LEYTE BUT UNABLE ARRIVE BEFORE 0800 TOMORROW.'"

Thus a double communications error may have prevented one of the heaviest slugging matches of World War II—an action on which Admiral Halsey had set his heart. Actually, Admiral Halsey missed a second opportunity to fight the Japanese at Leyte Gulf. Task Force 34 arrived three hours too late to catch the Japanese Center Force outside the Strait. The Center Force, which suffered its communications problems too, had broken off the action and fled.

It has since been revealed by Rear Admiral Tomiji Koyanagi, former chief of staff to Vice Admiral Takeo Kurita, Commander in Chief of the Second Fleet of the Japanese Navy, that Admiral Ozawa's Northern Force was a diversionary force—designed to lure Admiral Halsey and his fast carrier taskforces out of the vicinity of Leyte Gulf. And had the Center Force under Admiral Kurita not run away from Admiral Kinkaid's destroyers and tinplate jeep carriers (Kurita thought they were battleships), Admiral Halsey's powerful 16-inch guns would certainly have been needed.

On the other hand, Admiral Halsey wrote to me, "This all happened on the morning of October 25, 1944. As early as October 20—five days previously—Admiral Ozawa had apparently accepted the view that the greater part of the U.S. Third Fleet had been destroyed off Formosa. That view was being broadcast exultantly by Tokyo Rose in plain English. Yet on the 25th Ozawa was using his force as a feint—according to him—to draw me away from Leyte Gulf. I am sure his hindsight is better than his foresight."

But these are some of the imponderables of battle that naval officers will be arguing about for many years to come. And if nothing else, the fateful double-blooper message from Admiral Nimitz to Admiral Halsey proves that in the most technological of all worlds, the human link in the chain of battle is sometimes the weakest.

About the Author

A graduate of the University of California at Los Angeles, **Captain Hamilton** served as a public information officer on the staff of Admiral Nimitz in the Pacific during World War II. He is at present Director of Information at the University of California. Since 1946 he has also been a freelance writer and has had material published in the *Reader's Digest*, *Saturday Evening Post*, *Coronet*, *Think* and other national magazines.

22

SECOND SALVO AT SURIGAO STRAIT

Adm. James L. Holloway III, U.S. Navy (Ret.)

Naval History, October 2010

Shortly after 0300, the USS *Bennion* (DD-662) made first visual contact with the Japanese battleships. It was 25 October 1944 and I was standing up through the hatch in the ship's Mark 37 director, scanning the horizon with 7x50 binoculars. The rumble of heavy gunfire had become continuous, and the lower quadrant of the southern sky was now a pulsing glow from muzzle flashes. The PT boats had sprung their ambush on the Japanese column and triggered a fierce firefight. The Battle of Surigao Strait in Leyte Gulf was under way.

There was a tug on my trouser leg and the Sailor at the pointer's station next to me motioned to my eyepiece. Looking through the magnification of the director's optics, the scene to the south became clearer. The crosshairs of the lens were fixed at the base of the jumbo pagoda superstructure of a Japanese battleship. The flashes from her main turret salvos and the rapid fire of the secondary battery were lighting up the entire ship. From her clearly visible bow wave she was making at least 25 knots.

The radar operator sitting behind me tersely reported that he had picked up the target and was getting good ranges. I pushed down the bridge switch on the 21MC intercom and reported that we were tracking a battleship and locked on with the fire-control radar. The captain replied that the "Martinis"—the radio call for the PT boats—were reporting that two battleships, a cruiser, and at least three destroyers had passed through the narrows. Our target was to be the second battleship. "Let me know when you have a fire-control solution on the Big Boy. Have the gun battery ready but don't shoot unless I specifically tell you to. We have been directed to make a torpedo attack with five fish." His voice was clear and businesslike. In the background over the intercom I could hear the excited chatter of the Martinis on the TBS tactical voice radio as they maneuvered to launch their torpedoes. Going back to the optics I could now see the two battleships in column. I moved the crosshairs to the second one, got a confirmation from the radar operator that he was locked on, and called the plotting room to tell them to let me know when they had a firing solution on the new target.

Now that the battleship had emerged from the strait, the image on the radarscope was clear of ground clutter and the fire-control radar was ranging consistently. In minutes, the plotting-room talker reported "tracking in automatic." I passed this to the bridge and the captain acknowledged: "Very well. Train out the tubes but don't launch or shoot until I give the order." I switched the five-inch guns and both quintuple torpedo mounts to director control, and again standing up in the hatch, looked aft to see the torpedo mounts trained out on the beam.

Our ship was running in and out of rainsqualls and it was very dark. I could barely make out the other two destroyers in our division. Like the *Bennion*, both were *Fletcher*-class destroyers. We were keeping a 300-foot interval in a loose column. The division was loitering at five knots, close to the western coastline of Leyte Gulf, using land clutter to hide from enemy radars. It was quiet in the director. Each member of the crew was absorbed in his particular duties. Our small talk had been used up long ago.

For the past seven months the five of us had been together eight hours a day in this hot, cramped steel box, standing watches or at general quarters (GQ), shooting at the Japanese. At Peleliu, the *Bennion* had emptied her magazines three times in a single week. We considered ourselves experienced veterans. We had fought at Saipan, Tinian, Guam, and Peleliu. There was one new member of the director crew this night in Surigao Strait. The third-class fire controlman who normally manned the pointer's station in the director was in sick bay. Both he and my assistant gunnery officer had been wounded two days earlier when a shell from a Japanese shore battery on Leyte had struck close aboard the *Bennion*, unleashing a shower of shrapnel. Although I was standing just inches from them, I had not been hit. The assistant gunnery officer, Lieutenant (junior grade) "Robbie" Robertson, had been terribly torn up and was wrapped in a blanket, strapped to the dining table in the officers' wardroom—now the ship's main battle-dressing station. The war was over for Robbie, but he didn't know it yet. He was full of morphine. He survived but lost his right arm at the shoulder. A young ensign from the gunnery department was filling in at his GQ station.

I was a 22-year-old lieutenant, the *Bennion*'s gunnery officer. This was my second destroyer assignment since graduation from the U.S. Naval Academy in June 1942. After General Douglas MacArthur's landing at Leyte on 20 October 1944 it was fully expected that the Imperial Japanese Navy would attack Allied forces in the Leyte Gulf area. There were reports from our submarines and Navy patrol aircraft indicating that two separate Japanese task forces were headed in the direction of Leyte Gulf. The hundreds of Allied transports, supply ships, amphibious craft, and support vessels anchored off Tacloban, providing support and resupply for the Army ashore, were a prime target for the Japanese fleet.

On the morning of 24 October, the *Bennion* was on picket station in the eastern approaches to Leyte Gulf when her captain, Commander Joshua Cooper, called me down from the gun director during morning GQ to show me a message: The southern group of Japanese ships was moving in a direction that suggested an attack through Surigao Strait, the southern entrance to Leyte Gulf. He thought we probably would be involved in a night action within 24 hours. When I returned to the director, I used the sound-powered phone circuit to inventory the distribution of our five-inch ammunition among the magazines and the five upper handling rooms. I also directed the torpedo officer to make sure that the torpedoes, which had not been exercised since our training evolutions while undergoing shakedown, were ready in all respects for a war shot. With the 12-to-4 watch as officer of the deck on the bridge that afternoon, I was able to read the incoming voice radio and flashing-light traffic that laid out the disposition of our forces. Rear Admiral Jesse B. Oldendorf had six old battleships, eight cruisers, and 26 destroyers to stop the Japanese force that was expected to come through Surigao Strait.

Thirty-nine PT boats also were assigned to the Leyte Gulf force. I had been on the wing of the *Bennion*'s bridge on 23 October when their formation passed us on the way to set up an ambush in Surigao Strait. I had never heard such a racket. We could hear the PT engines five miles away and see them at even greater distances, because they were engulfed in a cloud of their own exhaust fumes. It was my first encounter with PT boats; I was not impressed.

During the afternoon watch, Oldendorf's detailed plan for the disposition of his forces came through by message and the next several hours were spent deploying to assigned positions. The *Bennion*'s tactical assignment was the same as its administrative organization: The nine *Fletcher*-class destroyers of Destroyer Squadron 56 (DESRON 56), under the command of Captain Roland Smoot, were organized into three divisions of three ships each. DESRON 56 was assigned to attack the column of Japanese battleships and cruisers after it had emerged from Surigao Strait. In his battle plan, Oldendorf had specified that the destroyers were each to expend only five of their total of ten onboard torpedoes during the attack and hold five in reserve. Torpedo reloads for destroyers were hard to come by in the western Pacific.

Smoot planned for coordinated torpedo attacks, conducted separately by each of the three divisions: one against the eastern flank; the second, head-on; and the third (of which the *Bennion* would be part) against the western flank. Each division would approach in a three-ship column, and each destroyer would successively launch a salvo of five torpedoes as the column turned, and then retire. Because the *Bennion* was the last ship in the third division, it would be among the last destroyers to launch their fish. That meant the range from the enemy would continue to close for us as the column executed the corpen maneuver. Smoot further instructed that we should not fire our five-inch guns during the attack lest they provide Japanese gunners with convenient aim points.

As the ships of DESRON 56 converged at the designated rendezvous points in northern Leyte Gulf to form their disposition for the anticipated night action, we remained at GQ. The *Bennion* had been on picket station at the gulf's eastern entrance, and we had been under sporadic Japanese air attacks, which continued as we were steaming to the rendezvous point. The cloud cover was about 60 percent, and the enemy aircraft were popping in and out of the cumulus clouds. The *Bennion*'s five-inch battery brought down a "Val" bomber, and the 40-mm and 20-mm guns combined to destroy a "Zeke" fighter close aboard.

We were deployed in our attack disposition by 1800. The crew was being fed in relays, a few men from each battle station going down to the mess line to pick up battle rations—inch-thick bologna sandwiches. With the number of pickets deployed, both PT boats and destroyers, we would not be taken by surprise.

Shortly after 0300, the soft purr of the idling fireroom blowers suddenly rose to a high-pitched whine. The bridge had rung up full power.

The director began to tremble and the deck plates vibrated from the propellers' cavitation as the ship accelerated. Almost simultaneously, the ship's general announcing system and a sound-powered phone talker announced, "Starting run-in for the attack." I had been momentarily diverted and looking through the optics again, I was startled to see how much larger the image of the Japanese battleship had grown. The enemy column was headed in our direction at 25 knots and closing fast.

With the signal to commence the run-in to the attack, the three destroyers in our section turned in column to a southerly course to intercept the enemy, maintaining the 300-foot interval between ships. As we increased to 25 knots, the engine rooms were ordered to make black smoke to screen our division. At "darken ship" there was only the dim blue light from the battle lanterns for illumination. Standing in the open hatch of the director, I could watch the entire panorama of the two converging fleets, and through the high-powered lenses of the director, the enemy ships could be seen in stark detail. As our destroyers broke out of the shadow of the shoreline, we were immediately taken under fire by the Japanese battleships and cruisers. It was strange to be rushing through the dark, closing with the enemy at a relative speed of more than 50 knots, not firing our own guns but seeing the steady gunfire of the Japanese ships and running through the explosions of their shots falling around us. The towering splashes of the 14-inch and 8-inch shells were close enough to wet our weather decks. Both sides also were firing star shells, their illumination adding to the eerie aspect of the scene.

As the Japanese came into range, Oldendorf's battleships and cruisers, deployed in an east-west line to cross the "T" at the top of the Japanese column, opened up with their main batteries. All along the northern horizon, enormous billows of flame from their 16- and 14-inch main battery guns lit up the battle line. Directly over our heads stretched a procession of tracers as the battleships' shells converged on the Japanese column. The apparent slowness of the projectiles was surprising. Taking 15 to 20 seconds in their trajectory before reaching the target, they seemed to hang in the sky. Through the director optics, I could clearly see the explosions of the shells bursting on the Japanese ships, sending up cascades of flame as they ripped away topside gun mounts and erupted in fiery sheets of molten steel tearing into the heavy armor plate.

When the first destroyer in our division reached the firing point, the enemy was just 6,000 yards away. Each of the three destroyers in the column in succession executed a hard turn to starboard, launching five torpedoes when the enemy bearing was on the port beam. When it was the *Bennion*'s turn, the bridge called out: "Launch torpedoes!" The battleship *Yamashiro* completely filled the viewing glass of my optics. The crosshairs were stabilized on the waterline just below the foremast. Plot was repeating, "We have a good solution." Glowing dials showed the torpedo tubes were trained clear and the torpedo gyros set. I pushed the "fire" button on the console and stood up to see our five fish shoot out of their tubes. I heard them slap the water. All were running hot and straight.

As each destroyer adjusted its turn at the launch point to have the target on the beam at the moment of firing, the formation became ragged, and the ships began maneuvering independently to avoid enemy gunfire. As the *Bennion* began to retire at 30 knots, still making black smoke, the scene of action was one of growing confusion. The Japanese formation had disintegrated. Some ships circled out of control, some were dead in the water. Many were on fire, and they shuddered from massive explosions. Others were unrecognizable, with bows gone, sterns blown away, and topsides mangled.

Standing up through the gunnery officer's hatch in the main gun director, I had an almost unobstructed 360-degree view of the entire scene of action. Suddenly, a large warship loomed on our port bow. Using the slewing sight, I swung the director to point directly at this new target, instructing the rangefinder operator to track and identify this contact. If hostile, the fire-control radar would be locked on and the plotting-room computer would then generate a target course and speed. I called down to the captain—no phone or intercom was needed as he was on the port wing of the bridge, one level below me—to report the strange contact. It was at that juncture that the unidentified warship commenced firing what appeared to be its secondary battery. From the clearly visible tracers, I could see that the rounds were being directed at the USS *Albert W. Grant* (DD-649), a destroyer in our squadron that earlier had been hit and damaged by gunfire—some of it friendly fire from our cruisers—during the retirement from the torpedo attack. The *Grant* had lost all power and was adrift in the middle of the strait.

When the unidentified large ship opened fire she had immediately established her identity as enemy, because her salvos were ripple fire. That was a characteristic of Japanese naval gunfire, in contrast to the simultaneous salvoes of U.S. warships. I shouted to the captain that the ship was Japanese. No sooner had he acknowledged that intelligence than the fire controlman on the director rangefinder reported that we were locked on with fire-control radar, and that the plotting room already had a good solution for a torpedo attack.

I shouted this information to the captain and recommended we fire our five remaining torpedoes, because the ship was obviously a cruiser or battleship, too lucrative a target to ignore. Without hesitation he gave an affirmative reply, even though he must have had in mind, just as I did, Oldendorf's instructions to expend only five torpedoes in the squadron attack. Clearly this was not the time for equivocation, and the captain repeated his instructions to fire all five of our remaining fish at this close-in target.

I passed the instructions by sound-powered phone to Lieutenant (junior grade) Tom Bayliss, the torpedo officer. He was manning the Mark 27 torpedo director back at the tubes, wearing the sound-powered phones himself and personally making the target data inputs and torpedo settings. I told him to set the torpedoes "deep"—the recommended depth setting for a battleship or cruiser target, so that the torpedo would hit the vessel below its torpedo-defense blisters. Bayliss had been monitoring my conversation with the captain and was aware that the target was a large man-of-war; he already had set the "deep" option. I looked aft and saw the quintuple torpedo mount training out to port, with the plotting room repeating the messages on the intercom, "We have a solution." I stood up, reached out, and pressed the red torpedo-firing buttons on the interior bulkhead of the director, launching five torpedoes in a salvo. Still standing in the hatch, I could see the torpedoes come out of their tubes in quick succession with their motors already running, slap the water, submerge, and head for that Japanese heavy, now only 3,000 yards away. I felt sure we would get a hit with our spread of five torpedoes. We were too close to have missed.

The *Bennion* heeled sharply as the captain ordered "Full right rudder, all ahead flank," and we swung to a northerly course in the direction of the postattack rendezvous point. Captain Cooper did not wish to linger in no-man's-land, especially considering the fate of the hapless *Grant*.

By 0430 DESRON 56 had reformed north of Surigao Strait and, as first evidence of the morning twilight appeared, the destroyers were ordered to proceed south at high speed to engage and destroy the remnants of the Japanese force. In the pale predawn light, the scene in the lower gulf was appalling. I counted six distinct fires, and debris littered the oily surfaces of the gulf. Groups of Japanese sailors were clinging to pieces of floating wreckage, calling out to us as we raced by. There was no time to pause to deal with survivors. In the smoke of the early morning gloom the Japanese destroyer *Asagumo* was limping south, badly damaged and afire. If the *Asagumo* still had torpedoes on board, she remained a deadly threat. The *Bennion* was ordered to deliver the coup de grâce. Changing course to intercept her, the *Bennion* opened fire with the five-inch battery at 10,000 yards and began to hit on the third salvo. I shifted to rapid continuous fire at 6,000 yards, and as our rounds penetrated the *Asagumo*'s hull and exploded, flames burst from her hatches. When we had closed to about 2,000 yards, the Japanese destroyer slid beneath the gray, choppy waters, bow first, her screws still slowly rotating as we passed close aboard.

As the *Bennion* turned to rejoin the formation, a Zero broke out of the low clouds on our port beam heading directly toward us. Again using the slewing sight at the director officer's hatch, I swung the *Bennion*'s five-inch battery to the incoming plane and commenced firing. In a no-deflection head-on shot, a five-inch round scored a direct hit on the plane's nose. The Zero vanished in a fiery explosion. Flaming debris fell into the sea around us.

At daylight on 25 October 1944, the *Bennion*'s crew was tired. We had been up more than 24 hours—since 0400 the day before, when we loaded five-inch ammunition from a Liberty Ship anchored off Tacloban as Navy Wildcats tangled with Zeros overhead. We had been at GQ for more than 12 hours. Now, as we listened to the reports come in over the TBS and saw yet more survivors clinging to the smoking wreckage of a Japanese fleet, we sensed that a great victory had been won. A major Japanese force of battleships and cruisers had been virtually immolated with serious damage to just one of our ships, the destroyer *Grant*. The showdown in Surigao Strait, along with close-by naval engagements of 24–25 October, collectively came to be called the Battle of Leyte Gulf. Samuel Eliot Morison, the distinguished naval historian, later would call Leyte the greatest naval battle in history.

A few days passed before we in the *Bennion* had the time to analyze the engagement and submit our action report to commander DESRON 56 for consolidation with the reports of the other eight destroyers, and to assess the performance of our ship during the engagement. Torpedoman First Class Tom Bowen had been assigned to time the run of each torpedo salvo with a stopwatch to note if an explosion (or explosions) occurred at the moment of expected impact on the target. Bowen reported seeing an explosion at the expected impact time of one of our torpedoes. He also said in his report that the *Bennion*'s sonar had detected an underwater explosion at the same time as his visual sighting. But it was not identified whether that presumed hit occurred as a result of our first salvo or second salvo.

A week after the battle I transferred off the *Bennion*. As I said goodbye to my skipper, Commander Cooper, a splendid gentleman and captain, he said he was sorry to see me leave the destroyer Navy. I thought for a moment before I replied: "Captain, in the past 48 hours we silenced four shore batteries, shot down three planes, sank a destroyer by gunfire, and made a close-in torpedo hit that helped sink a Japanese battleship. I think I'd now like to try something new."

Thus did the *Bennion* and I go our separate ways. I had orders to report for flight training. During a Japanese air raid I was transported via whaleboat to a departing cargo ship, beginning a long, slow hitchhike across the Pacific that marked the start of a career as a carrier pilot. The *Bennion* went on to the Mindoro and Lingayen Gulf landings, the assault on Iwo Jima, and received a Presidential Unit Citation at Okinawa, all without me. Not quite a year later, the war was over.

And there, but for a turn of fate decades later, the story might have ended, the *Bennion*'s place in the history of Surigao Strait never fully secured. Save for Torpedoman Bowen's ambiguous report and the "too-close-to-have-missed" hunch that I and others had felt at the time, we had no documentation, official or otherwise, that the *Bennion* may have helped sink the *Yamashiro*.

In 1958 Morison published Volume XII of his seminal *History of United States Naval Operations in World War II*. Volume XII is titled simply *Leyte*, and like the other volumes it is based on official U.S. Navy after-action reports available to him at the time. In *Leyte* he states that because the Japanese column conducted a course reversal at the time DESRON 56 made its coordinated attack, just one torpedo from the squadron—from the *Newcomb* (DD-586)—is believed to have hit its target. The author makes no mention whatsoever of the *Bennion*'s second five-torpedo salvo.

Morison offers a tacit explanation for any missing details—while at the same time establishing ultimate authority for the battle—in his preface to *Leyte*. There, he acknowledges the assistance of Rear Admiral Richard W. Bates and his staff at the U.S. Naval War College, who "have been working on an exhaustive and detailed study of the battle for Leyte Gulf" and granted Morison access to their research.

That "exhaustive and detailed study"—which was not yet published when Morison's volume went to press—became the Naval War College's *The Battle for Leyte Gulf, October 1944: Strategical and Tactical Analysis. Volume V. Battle of Surigao Strait, October 24th–25th*. The study was published in 1958 and classified "confidential"—which severely limited its distribution.

Nearly half a century later, in 2004, Naval Historical Foundation researcher John Reilly by chance encountered the study, by then declassified. He provided me a copy, but because I was deeply involved in a large project of my own at the time, I gave it just a perfunctory scan, then put it in my desk. There it stayed until 2008, when I picked it up again to research another aspect of the Battle of Surigao Strait. And that is when I discovered two references to the *Bennion*'s role in the sinking of the *Yamashiro*. Said the report:

> The YAMASHIRO ... continued to close the enemy as she advanced. Shortly after being taken under fire she started to burn. At 0356 she turned to the west and at 0405 *she was hit by a torpedo fired by the BENNION.... At 0359 the BENNION had fired a second salvo of five intermediate speed torpedoes at what she thought was a second battleship, and [hit] the YAMASHIRO....* At 0419, she [YAMASHIRO] suddenly sank. (Emphasis added.)

The *Bennion*'s torpedo hit on the *Yamashiro* is confirmed in the appendices of the Naval War College battle report, as well. The analysis had made extensive use of the interrogations of Japanese survivors, including a warrant officer from the battleship.

Sadly, most of the *Bennion* crew are gone, but it's never too late to set the historical record straight. Thus, on the basis of the critical review of all official and authoritative information available, the *Bennion* today at long last can properly be credited with her torpedo hit on the *Yamashiro*, which directly contributed to the Japanese battleship's sinking at the Battle of Surigao Strait in Leyte Gulf.

About the Author

Admiral James L. Holloway III, a U.S. Naval Academy graduate and veteran of World War II, Korea, and Vietnam, was the 20th Chief of Naval Operations. He retired in 1978 after 39 years of active duty.

23

IOWA VS. YAMATO
The Ultimate Gunnery Duel [Professional Notes]
Thomas Hone and Norman Friedman

Proceedings, July 1983

When considering the outcome of a hypothetical clash between one or more of the *Iowa*-class battleships and the *Yamato* of the Imperial Japanese Navy, we must find sensible answers to at least four questions. First, were there any circumstances under which the great ships actually could have engaged in battle? Second, what were the comparative ranges, rates of fire, and penetrating potentials of the respective vessels' main battery guns? Third, which ship would have been capable of more accurate shooting? Finally, how well could the armor built into each type of ship have resisted the shells of the other? To answer these questions, we combined historical research with calculation and discussions with gunnery specialists.

After reviewing the October 1944 Battle of Leyte Gulf, we decided that U.S. and Japanese battleships might have clashed on two occasions. The first was on the morning of 25 October, when four Japanese battleships (the *Yamato, Nagato, Kongo,* and *Haruna*) with cruisers and destroyers sailed through San Bernardino Strait on their way to an epic engagement with U.S. destroyers and escort carriers off the island of Samar. No U.S. battleships blocked the strait because Admiral William F. Halsey had taken all six—the *Iowa* (BB-61), *Washington* (BB-56), *South Dakota* (BB-57), *Massachusetts* (BB-59), *Indiana* (BB-58), and the fleet flagship *New Jersey* (BB-62)—with him in his pursuit of what he thought was the Japanese main body. Admiral Willis A. Lee, commander of the battle line, had asked Halsey to leave several battleships behind to guard the strait; if Halsey had done so, there would have been a daylight battleship engagement. Later that same day, Halsey sent the *Iowa* and *New Jersey*, plus three light cruisers and eight destroyers, south at high speed to catch what was left of the Japanese surface squadron as it retreated back through the strait. They missed the Japanese battleships, but not by much. If Halsey had responded faster to the calls for help from the units off Samar, the *Iowa* and the *New Jersey* might have tangled with the *Yamato* in the dark in the waters of San Bernardino Strait.

Table 1 gives pertinent ballistics data for the *Yamato*'s 46-cm. guns and for the *Iowa*'s 16-in./50-cal. weapons. Table 2 compares the penetrating power of the two guns; also included are figures for the 16-in./45-cal. pieces carried by the other U.S. battleships. Table 3 lists the horizontal and vertical armor protection given the *Yamato* and the *Iowa*.

These tables show that, at the maximum ranges of their guns, neither battleship was immune to the other's gunfire. Both the 46-cm. and the 16-in./50-cal. guns could penetrate ten inches of deck armor at about 38,000 yards. When the *Yamato* and the *Iowa* were designed, however, accurate shooting at such a range was extremely difficult. The *Yamato*, in consequence, was designed to fight at closer ranges, and at those ranges she had an advantage in protection over the *Iowa*. The latter was designed to a treaty limit of 45,000 tons; on that displacement, she could not be given high speed and heavier protection than that already planned for the *South Dakota*s. But the *Iowa* was given a better gun than previous classes; as Table 2 shows, the 16-in./50-cal. was clearly superior to the 16-in./45-cal. when matched against armor protection on the scale of the *Yamato*s.

More to the point, the tables illustrate the Navy's development of radar fire control, and a firing doctrine which stressed getting in the first hits at very long range. The *Yamato*'s armor advantage did her very little good at ranges beyond 35,000 yards. Her deck armor was vulnerable to even the 16-in./45-cal. at extremely long range. The issue, then, is whether the *Iowa*'s gunners could have hit the *Yamato* while the latter was still over the horizon and before she could return fire. All the U.S. battleships with the Third Fleet carried Mk-8 fire control radars. During the night engagement at Surigao, the three old battleships equipped with the Mk-8 were able to compute firing solutions on their Japanese targets at ranges of nearly 40,000 yards. It is not certain that, even with similar solutions, gunners on the *Iowa* and *New Jersey* could have hit the *Yamato* at such great range. The problem was the resolution of the Mk-8's radar. Its beam width was 2°. At 40,000 yards, a radar with that beam width could not distinguish between two adjacent targets with a combined length (including the space between them) of less than about 1,400 yards. The *Yamato* was 288 yards long; at Leyte, she was accompanied by *Nagato*, 240 yards in length. With 600 yards dividing them, the two ships would have covered a total of about 1,200 yards, and they would not have appeared as two distinct points on the *Iowa*'s Mk-8 radar.

For the *Yamato*, matters were much worse. She had no radar fire control at all. Her surface search set could have been used only to guide her gunners, and even then it could not have been of much help at 40,000 yards. The reason was resolution, which at that range was about ten times less precise than the U.S. Navy's Mk-8. In short, the Japanese radar could not have resolved the combined image of the whole U.S. battle line into its separate parts at 40,000 yards.

Both sides were unable to distinguish separate targets at 40,000 yards; in addition, the salvo patterns of the *Iowa* and *Yamato* were very tight. Tight patterns were easier to spot and correct in a daylight engagement, or when radar resolution was precise; resolution improved as the range closed. For example, at 31,000 yards the resolution of the Mk-8 was 1,080 yards; at 20,000 yards, the resolution was less than 700 yards. As a result, the *Iowa* could target better at extreme range during the day. At night, to achieve the same degree of accuracy, she would have to reduce the range. Yet accurate fire at long range was the preferred doctrine; it was also the best way to deal with the massive armor protection given to the *Yamato*.

The key factor in any engagement at long range between the *Iowa* and *Yamato* would have been fire control. At very long range, 35–40,000 yards, the *Iowa* would have the advantage, because her radar fire control fit the ranging capability of the 16-in./40-cal. gun. The advantage would have held as long as the *Iowa* stayed outside the *Yamato*'s immune zone, between 28,200 and 33,600 yards (see Table 2). At longer ranges, however, the percentage of hits, even with radar fire control would not be great; a few hits might disable the *Yamato*'s fire control, but the chances are not high that they would have destroyed her ability to steam and fight at close range.

The task facing the *Iowa* would have been to hurt the *Yamato* without reducing her own ammunition supply so severely that her gunners could not inflict more damage on the Japanese giant later. The *Yamato*'s reliance upon optical fire control was her weak point, especially at night; she was also vulnerable during the day. Had the U.S. battleships covered themselves with a smokescreen, they still could have ranged on the *Yamato*, but she could not have returned accurate fire.

The *Yamato* had superior armor, slightly superior range, and somewhat greater striking power. But these strengths would have been offset by the more accurate fire control of the U.S. Navy's battle line (*Iowas*, *South Dakotas*, and *Washington*). This difference would have applied no matter who commanded the ships. But—given his handling of the Japanese battleships at Samar—we believe that Admiral Takeo Kurita would not have performed well against the likely U.S. commander, Admiral Lee. Lee was an ordnance specialist; he well understood the need to strike quickly in a surface battle, and at the greatest possible range. He knew that the 16-in./50-cal. gun, linked with radar fire control, gave his ships the chance to do so. Having looked closely at the available evidence, we believe that he would have maneuvered them so they could have done precisely that.

Author's Note

The following persons were generous with their assistance, but do not necessarily agree with our conclusions: VADM L. M. Mustin, USN (Ret.); VADM E. B. Hooper, USN (Ret.); RADM John Chase, USN (Ret.); CAPT Charles Allen, USN (Ret.); and CDR L. A. Short, USN. Dr. Dean Allard, head of the Navy's Operational Archives, suggested we consult the Naval Technical Mission to Japan reports and Paul Stillwell of the Naval Institute gave us our initial start.

Sources

1. Morison, Samuel E., *History of U. S. Naval Operations in World War II*, Vol. XII, Little, Brown & Co., Boston, 1958.
2. *Armor Penetration Curves* (Revised), U.S. Navy, Bureau of Ordnance, ORD #653, Washington, D.C., January 1942.
3. "Japanese 18" Gun Mounts" (0–45N), "Japanese Surface and General Fire Control" (0–31), and "Japanese Fire Control" (0–29), U.S. Naval Technical Mission to Japan, in the Classified Operational Archives of the U.S. Navy, 1946.
4. Dulin, R. O. and W. H. Garzke, *Battleships: United States Battleships in World War II*, Naval Institute Press, Annapolis, Maryland, 1976.

Table 1: *Comparative Ballistic Data*

	Yamato	Iowa
Gun Size/Caliber	46 cm (18.1")/45	40.6 cm (16")/50
AP Projectile Weight	3,200 lbs.	2,700 lbs.
Maximum Range	45,000 yds.	42,000 yds.
Rate of Fire	1.5 rounds/min.	2 rounds/min.

Table 2: *Armor Penetration Ranges (in yards)*

	Yamato	Iowa	Other BBs
12" (side)	38,300	38,000	31,600
16" (side)	28,700	28,200	23,000
8" (deck)	35,100	33,600	31,000
10" (deck)	38,300	38,000	34,400

Table 3: *Armor Protection*

	Yamato	Iowa
Main Side Belt (Maximum)	16.1" (410 mm.)	12.1" (307 mm.)
Armor & Splinter Decks	7.8" (200 mm.)	6.6" (169 mm.)

About the Authors

Mr. Hone is employed by Delex Systems, Inc., in Arlington, Virginia, and holds a PhD from the University of Wisconsin at Madison.

Dr. Friedman is an analyst at the Hudson Institute in Croton-on-Hudson, New York, and author of *U.S. Destroyers: An Illustrated Design History* (Naval Institute Press, 1982).

24

"*IOWA* VS. *YAMATO* THE ULTIMATE GUNNERY DUEL" [COMMENT AND DISCUSSION]

(See T. Hone, N. Friedman, pp. 122–123, July 1983 *Proceedings*; L. E. Hoskins, pp. 102–103, September 1983 *Proceedings*)

─────── Vice Adm. Lloyd M. Mustin, U.S. Navy (Ret.) ───────

Proceedings, November 1983

The authors' note includes my name among those "generous with their assistance," but I'm having trouble finding signs of my assistance.

I don't intend to go into some minor irrelevancies and debatable conclusions in the article, at least some of which had been pointed out in the extended discussion I had with Dr. Hone.

But one point has significance to the way the authors develop their conclusion: the treatment of U.S. Navy radar-controlled surface gunnery of that era. They postulate that it was significantly limited by the resolution capability of the Mk-8 fire control radar. That analysis is flawed.

The authors mention the Mk-8's angular beam width, then go through the exercise familiar in the early radar days—distinguishing between two "adjacent" targets both lying within the radar beam. They conclude that the *Iowa*'s Mk-8 could not distinguish separate aiming points in an engagement with two such targets, in their case, the *Yamato* and *Nagato*.

They don't mention that for two targets within the beam width to be indistinguishable, both must also be at the same range from the radar, to within the limits of the radar's range resolution capability.

Radar range resolution is a function of pulse length, which for the Mk-8 was quite short for its day. My recollection is that it may have been one-tenth microsecond, which would give range resolution on the order of 30 yards. Something just about like that was what we were looking at every day in the fleet, and we knew how to use it.

In other words, for the *Yamato* and *Nagato* to be indistinguishable as separate targets to a U.S. Mk-8 radar, they would have had to remain not only within its angular beam width, but also within about 30 yards of identical ranges from the Mk-8. This would be extremely difficult for battleships of dissimilar classes in high-speed combat maneuvers. It would be impossible if there were more than one Mk-8-equipped U.S. ship to contend with, as in the situation proposed, especially when the U.S. tactical commander has the speed advantage, knows the potential problem, and doesn't want it to happen.

The authors apply the same flawed analysis to the question of correcting the fall of salvoes by radar spotting. Because of its short pulse length, the Mk-8 gave a superb map picture of the fall of shot around the target. It was a superior tool for spotting. One black night it helped me put about 80 salvoes onto a Japanese ship, all by radar until we had her burning brightly.

So the authors seem to have used incomplete radar premises to develop their conclusion that it was not certain an *Iowa* could hit the *Yamato* at 40,000 yards. Having spent World War II at sea in gunnery, and having been Vice Admiral Willis A. Lee's staff gunnery, radar, and combat information center officer from 1944 on, I can assure the authors that it was as certain as anything can be in war.

The 16-inch guns in the fast battleships were beautifully accurate. Admiral Lee demanded that the gun batteries be kept meticulously aligned and calibrated; he conducted frequent firings to confirm it; and he was there personally to observe the results. Those of us who have seen the first salvo come down at 40,000 yards in a nine-gun, 300-yard straddle pattern have few doubts.

It's unlikely the engagement would have remotely resembled the set piece the authors visualize, the results of which could be measured numerically from tables of projectile penetrations and main armor thicknesses.

After our first few salvoes, the *Yamato* would have had to resort to evasive steering, if she was still under control. The authors' source on Japanese fire control is not cited as to what degradation this might impose on the *Yamato*'s ability to hit; my incomplete recollection is that it might have been insignificant. As to our continuing to hit her despite her evasion, we had doctrines for the situation, and the Mk-8 assisted their application by almost instant detection of target maneuver.

On the U.S. side, the tactical commander should be assumed not to give the *Yamato* a steady-course target. Because typical evasive maneuver would not seriously disturb our fire control, and with the speed advantages it would not be a problem.

Of course, further variables enter from the effects of projectile hits which—though they might not penetrate main armor—cause fires, explosions, and secondary missile damage in the lighter gun batteries and the extensive superstructures, destroy or blind ship control and fire control stations, rupture and ignite fuel bunkers, and degrade main propulsion. These can lead to helpless disaster.

The authors seem to take no account of these and other incidents of combat; it is not possible to do so by their method of analysis. One might just as well rely on the victory going to the side which could hit first, hard, and often. On that basis, those of us who were there would expect the outcome to be just as Drs. Hone and Friedman conclude, even though we arrived at the conclusion by a different route.

About the Author

Admiral Mustin helped develop the Navy's first lead-computing anti-aircraft gun sight, used extensively and effectively during World War II. During that conflict, he served in the cruiser USS *Atlanta* during the Naval Battle of Guadalcanal. His postwar service included commands at sea and the development of advanced weapon systems.

Epitaph

In the hallowed passageways of Pringle Hall at the Naval War College is a map display commemorating the Battle of Leyte Gulf. Included in that display are the following words:

> In October 1944, the greatest seafight in history—perhaps the world's last great fleet action—broke the naval power of Japan and spelled the beginning of the end of the war in the Pacific. The Battle for Leyte Gulf, fought off the Philippine Archipelago, sprawled across an area of almost 500,000 square miles, about twice the size of Texas. Unlike most of the action in World War II, it included every element of naval power from submarines to planes. It was as decisive as Salamis. It dwarfed the battle of Jutland in distances, tonnages, casualties. But unlike Jutland, there was no dispute about the outcome. After Leyte Gulf, the Japanese fleet was finished. Yet it was a battle of controversy.
> —Hanson W. Baldwin
> *Sea Fights and Shipwrecks*, 1955

> The climax of the Pacific War occurred in late October 1944 at Leyte Gulf, when the two axes of our advance (Nimitz in the center, MacArthur from the southwest), met together in the Philippines, two U.S. fleets (Nimitz's Third under Halsey, MacArthur's Seventh under Vice Admiral Thomas C. Kinkaid) fought the greatest sea battle of all time, and the final curtain call for the Imperial Japanese Navy. Leyte Gulf was an engagement unlike any other, not only in size but in variousness, in confusion, and in closeness of decision. Even at this late date the Japanese Fleet was a formidable force; for this occasion, it emerged in full strength, and it came within a cat's whisker of winning a major victory. What prevented our defeat was the fighting quality that the U.S. Navy in the Pacific had by this time achieved, a combination of numbers, skill, and bravery that compels not only admiration but awe.
> —Eric Larrabee
> *Commander in Chief*, 1987

War is probably mankind's greatest folly. It is wasteful, tragic, and frequently unnecessary. But when it does occur, in an ironic twist, it brings out what is in some ways best about mankind. Many brave men, American and Japanese, fought at Leyte Gulf. Too many died there, while others live even today as flesh-and-blood monuments to those virtues that shine forth from the wreckage and tragedy of war. Admirals Halsey, Kinkaid, and Sprague, General MacArthur, Captain Adair, Commanders Evans and McCampbell, Lieutenant Digardi, Petty Officer Roy West, Seaman Billy, and the thousands of others like them are to be honored just for being there at Leyte Gulf—for doing their jobs under arduous circumstances, for serving and sacrificing for their country. The causes for which these men fought and sacrificed have faded with time; the machines they used to carry out their deadly business are now rusted relics of another era; the sands have swallowed their footprints and the waters show no trace of their wakes. But the glory of their deeds will never be tarnished by time.

—Thomas J. Cutler
The Battle of Leyte Gulf, 1994

The Naval Institute Press is the book-publishing arm of the U.S. Naval Institute, a private, nonprofit, membership society for sea service professionals and others who share an interest in naval and maritime affairs. Established in 1873 at the U.S. Naval Academy in Annapolis, Maryland, where its offices remain today, the Naval Institute has members worldwide.

Members of the Naval Institute support the education programs of the society and receive the influential monthly magazine *Proceedings* or the colorful bimonthly magazine *Naval History* and discounts on fine nautical prints and on ship and aircraft photos. They also have access to the transcripts of the Institute's Oral History Program and get discounted admission to any of the Institute-sponsored seminars offered around the country.

The Naval Institute's book-publishing program, begun in 1898 with basic guides to naval practices, has broadened its scope to include books of more general interest. Now the Naval Institute Press publishes about seventy titles each year, ranging from how-to books on boating and navigation to battle histories, biographies, ship and aircraft guides, and novels. Institute members receive significant discounts on the Press' more than eight hundred books in print.

Full-time students are eligible for special half-price membership rates. Life memberships are also available.

For a free catalog describing Naval Institute Press books currently available, and for further information about joining the U.S. Naval Institute, please write to:

Member Services
U.S. Naval Institute
291 Wood Road
Annapolis, MD 21402-5034
Telephone: (800) 233-8764
Fax: (410) 571-1703
Web address: www.usni.org